*SPECIAL NOTE: These *diamonds* are from a collection of material that the author gathered and formatted for the radio, which was heard daily, Monday through Friday, for many years on the inspirational radio program called *Diamonds for Dusty Roads* aired on KYCC. Joy Haney has worked countless hours compiling these diamonds; plus, she has added new diamonds to make it a full year.

The title for this program, and now a book, actually came to her in a dream. In the dream, instructions were given to her for the radio program. She was to use the three w's in her format: wit, wisdom and the Word. When the dream came, there was nothing but a dream, but God opened the door for this to come to pass. The instructions given in the dream are what she based her program on, working long hours to produce one program. This work reflects the many years of her labor.

In the compilation of this book, she has done her best to give proper credit to any material used by other authors. With great appreciation, she wishes to honor authors and poets from other eras, as well as those living in more recent times, and is thankful to them for the influence they have had in this book.

JOY HANEY

WORD AFLAME PRESS

Diamonds for Dusty Roads

by Joy Haney

©Copyright 2006 Word Aflame Press
Hazelwood, MO 63042-2299

Cover design by Ben Meydam

All Scripture quotations in this book are from the King James Version of the Bible unless otherwise identified.

All rights reserved. No portion of this publication may be reproduced, stored in an electronic system, or transmitted in any form or by any means, electronic, mechanical, photocopy, recording, or otherwise, without the prior permission of Word Aflame Press. Brief quotations may be used in literary reviews.

Printed in United States of America

Printed by

WORD AFLAME PRESS
8855 Dunn Road, Hazelwood, MO 63042
www.pentecostalpublishing.com

Library of Congress Cataloging-in-Publication Data

Haney, Joy, 1942-
   Diamonds for dusty roads : 365 daily inspirations / by Joy Haney.
     p. cm.
   ISBN 1-56722-686-8
   1. Devotional calendars. I. Title.
   BV4811.H25 2006
   242'.2—dc22

                                                                  2006007385

Acknowledgements

To those authors, representatives, and publishers who have allowed us to use their work without charge; to those who allowed us special arrangement—and to those whose work is now in the public domain, we are deeply grateful.

Some, after diligent search, we were unable to contact. Should there be such—whose work appears here without proper arrangement or acknowledgment—please allow us to make such in the next printing. It is not our desire or intention to use anyone's material without permission or proper credit. Indulgence is begged in case of failure to reach any other author of copyrighted portions.

The author has also made every effort to trace the authorship of all selections. When no name appears the authorship is unknown.

Acknowledgment is made to the following who have granted permission to use copyrighted material:

"Search for the Black Box" by Felix Jimenez is reprinted with permission from *Guideposts* magazine. Copyright © 1997 by *Guideposts*, Carmel, New York 10512. All rights reserved.

"The Power of Hope" is reprinted with permission from *Guideposts* Magazine. Copyright © 1999 by *Guideposts*, Carmel, New York 10512. All rights reserved.

All material used in the form of stories, quotes, poems and readings from the book *Encyclopedia of 7700 Illustrations*, by Paul Lee Tan, originally published by Assurance Publishers in 1979, is used with permission from Bible Communications, Dallas, Texas 75379. All rights reserved.

Material taken from the book, *A Field of Diamonds*, © 1999 by Joseph S. Johnson, Jr., is used with permission. All rights reserved.

All quotes, stories, and illustrations from, Walter B. Knight, *Knight's Teasury of Illustrations*, © 1963 Wm. B. Eerdmans Publishing Company, Grand Rapids, Michigan. Reprinted by permission of the publisher; all rights reserved.

Special Thanks

Thank you, Daddy, for being such a great Christian and inspiration to me and for your sense of humor.

Special honor is given to my mother, Margaret McDonald, who went to be with the Lord in 1974. Her heart was pure gold, and what a great Christian she was! I'm thankful for her example.

Thanks to my husband for being the best husband in the world and for "pushing" me to write.

Thanks to Margie McNall for her professional help and encouragement and for her hard work in getting this book to press.

Special thanks to Bethany Sledge for her proofreading.

Thanks to Ben Meydam for doing such an excellent job on the cover.

Thanks to Jina Crain for her skills as production manager.

Thanks to all the unnamed people in the publishing department who helped produce this book.

A special thank you to all those whose stories appear within these pages. Without their contributions, this book would not be.

Last of all, I want to give thanks to my dear Lord Jesus. He is the breath of my life, and without Him there would be nothing.

Dedication

I dedicate this book to my wonderful family. They have been an important and integral part of my life for many years.

Reverend Kenneth Haney, my awesome and beloved husband.
My dear father and stepmother: Travis Roy and Lois McDonald.
My precious children—listed by birth: Sherre and Glen Woodward, Reverend Nathaniel and Kim Haney, Stephenie Haney, Elizabeth and Reverend John Shivers, and Angela Haney.
My darling grandchildren—listed by birth: Mychail Haney, Jonathan Shivers, Kailah Haney, Brittany Shivers, Joshua Haney, Dylan Woodward, Giahna Haney, and Aunalee Haney.
My sweet sisters and brothers-in-law: Janet and James Jones, Beverly and Lewie Davies, Mary and Reverend Nathaniel Wilson, Priscilla and Reverend Carroll McGruder, Julie and Ron Short.
My wonderful brother and his dear wife: Reverend John McDonald and Marilyn.
All my nephews and nieces on the McDonald side:
Mark Morton and his wife, Farah
Reverend Nathan Morton and his wife, Kristi
Rachelle and her husband, Steven Gillespie
Andrew Davies and his wife, Shaunie
Barak Davies
Reverend Jonathan McDonald and his wife, Stephenie
Andrea and her husband, Reverend Johnny Arcovia
Debbie and her husband, Reverend Robert Tisdale
Rebecca and her husband, Doug Salters
Sheila and her husband, Reverend Myles Young
Eric McGruder and his wife, Michelle
Shawnee and her husband, Tim Trowbridge
Holly McGruder
Charity and her husband, Jared Sweetin
Heather, Sarah, and Jenna Short
My sweet sisters-in-law and brothers-in-law: Shirley Garner, Evangeline and Ben Britt, Joni and Reverend James Larson.
My nieces and nephews on the Haney side:
Reverend Jeff Garner and his wife, Julie
Kimberly and her husband, Mike Sarale
Vince Larson and his wife, Nancy.

January 1

"To every thing there is a season, and a time to every purpose under the heaven" (Ecclesiastes 3:1).

Now is the time to live, to dream, and to accomplish! It is a new year, a new day and a new opportunity. There is no day like today, so live it well.

THE NEW LEAF
He came to my desk with a quivering lip;
The lesson was done:
"Dear Teacher, I want a new leaf," he said,
"I have spoiled this one."
I took the old leaf, torn and blotted,
And gave him a new one, all unspotted,
And into his sad eyes smiled:
"Do better now, my child!"

I came to the Throne with a trembling heart;
The year's work was done;
"Dear Father, I want a new year," I said,
"I have spoiled this one."
He took the old year, torn and blotted,
And gave me a new one, all unspotted,
And into my sad heart smiled:
"Do better now, my child!"
—Helen Field Fischer[1]

There is no better day than today to begin over again. It is the greatest day of your life with new opportunities awaiting you. Do not allow past failures to blemish this year, but go forward and win!

This is your hour—creep upon it!
Summon your power, leap upon it!
Grasp it, clasp it, hold it tight!
Strike it, spike it, with full might!
If you take too long to ponder,

Opportunity may wander.
Yesterday's a bag of sorrow;
No man ever finds Tomorrow.
Hesitation is a mire—
Climb out, climb up, climb on higher!
Fumble, stumble, risk a tumble,
Make a start, however humble!
Do your best and do it now!
Pluck and grit will find out how.
—HERBERT KAUFMAN[2]

Today is the day that is important. Only you can take charge and move forward: you and God together can do it. Let this be the best year of your life!

January 2

"*Behold, I will do a new thing*" (Isaiah 43:19).

God will do a new thing if we allow Him to do so. It is a new year and a new day, and old things are gone, only the present remains. This year is a fresh beginning and can be well lived by starting out with praying the following prayer:

Just one thing, O Master, I ask today,
Now that the old year has passed away,
And a promising New Year, through grace of Thine,
With all the dreams of youth is mine—
Just one thing I ask, and nothing more,
Not to linger behind, nor run before,
O Master! This is my only plea—
Take hold of my life and pilot me.
—AUTHOR UNKNOWN[3]

When we are guided by God's hand, we will walk the right pathways and do the right things, but often the way that He leads is the way of the cross. Wherever He leads, let us resolve to follow Him.

RESOLVED:
I will make it a year of faith and prayer,
A year of high endeavor;
I will crowd it with deeds both brave and fair,
I will act the hero ever.
I will travel God's path at God's own rate;
I will welcome both gain and loss:
Nor will I rebel when heaven's gate
Looks tragically like a cross.
—Author Unknown[4]

His ways are beyond understanding, but they work. May this year be the best year of your life, as you learn to follow the author and finisher of your faith, the One who will lead you to victory!

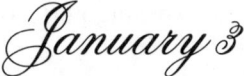

"Give us this day our daily bread" (Matthew 6:11).

*H*ow much does a prayer weigh? There was once a man who owned a little grocery store on the west side of town. It was the week before Christmas after World War II. A tired-looking woman came into the store and asked him for enough food to make a Christmas dinner for her children. He asked her how much she could afford to spend. She answered, "My husband was killed in the war. I have nothing to offer but a little prayer."

The man was not very sentimental towards her and told her the grocery store could not be run like a bread line. Then he roughly told her, "Write it on paper," and turned to go about his business. Then to his surprise, the woman plucked a piece of paper out of her pocket and handed it to him over the counter and said, "I did that during the night watching over my sick baby."

The grocer took the paper and without even reading it placed it on the weight side of his old-fashioned scales and said, "We shall see how much food this is worth."

To his astonishment, the scale would not go down when he put a loaf of bread on the other side. To his confusion and

embarrassment, it would not go down though he kept adding food, anything he could lay his hands on quickly because the people were watching him. He tried to be gruff and finally said, "Well, that's all the scales will hold anyway. Here's a bag. You'll have to put it in yourself. I'm busy."

The little woman started packing in the food, wiping her eyes on her sleeves every time her arm was free to do so. She thanked him and gave him a smile of gratitude, and when she had left, the grocer went to look at the scales. To his astonishment, his perfectly good scales were broken.

The grocer to this day says he remembers that woman more than any other woman he ever met and for many years kept the piece of paper the little woman laid on the counter. It simply was her prayer, "Please, Lord, give us this day our daily bread."

That mother prayed during the night in her desperation and wrote out her need by faith. That faith overcame her shyness and caused the scale that was working perfectly to break so that her prayer of faith could be answered.

This is the day to pray and believe. He said in Psalm 50:15: "Call upon me in the day of trouble: I will deliver thee, and thou shalt glorify me." Prayers carry a lot of weight; invest in them today and watch God do a miracle.

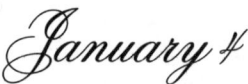

"In the morning will I direct my prayer unto thee" (Psalm 5:3).

This is the day to call upon the Lord. The psalmist said in Psalm 5:3, "My voice shalt thou hear in the morning, O Lord; in the morning will I direct my prayer unto thee, and will look up." Look up! God is still on the throne.

"If we felt more the majesty of life we should be more careful of its mornings. He who rushes from his bed to his business and waiteth not to worship is foolish as though he had not put on his clothes or cleansed his face, and as unwise as though he dashed into battle without arms or armor. Be it ours to bathe in the softly flowing river of communion with God

before the heat of the wilderness and the burden of the way begin to oppress us." —C. H. SPURGEON[5]

Sometimes in life the lack of heavenly water causes emotional thirst and then depression and oppression. The story is told of how once there was an eastern caravan who was overtaken in the desert with a failure of the water supply. The accustomed fountains were all dried; the oasis was a desert. They stopped an hour before sunset to find, after a day of scorching heat, that they were perishing for want of water. Dismay was upon all faces; despair was in all hearts. Suddenly an old man approached the sheik and advised him to unloose the two beautiful deer that he was taking home as a present to his bride. Surely the sensitive nostrils of the deer would detect the presence of water if any was to be found. Their tongues were protruding with thirst; their bosoms heaved with distress, but as they were led out to the borders of the camp, they lifted their heads and sniffed the air. Then, with unerring instinct, with a course as straight as an arrow and speed as swift as the wind, they darted off across the desert. Swift horsemen followed close behind, and an hour or two later hastened back with the good news that water had been found. The camp moved with shouts of rejoicing to the newly discovered fountains.

Isaiah 41:17-18 says, "When the poor and needy seek water, and there is none, and their tongue faileth for thirst, I the LORD will hear them. . . . I will open rivers in high places, and fountains in the midst of the valleys: I will make the . . . dry land springs of water."

When things go wrong, look for water; do not give in and die. Jesus said in John 7:37-38, "If any man thirst, let him come unto me, and drink. He that believeth on me, as the scripture hath said, out of his belly shall flow rivers of living water."

Your thirst will not be satisfied by anything else. It will only be satisfied by the true living water, which is the Spirit of the Lord.

Psalm 42:1-2 states, "As the hart panteth after the water brooks, so panteth my soul after thee, O God. My soul thirsteth for God, for the living God."

Make sure your soul pants after the right things. Pant or seek vigorously after God, His Word, His Spirit, and He will give you those things that will enrich your life. He will lift you out of depression and fill you with new inspiration and power.

January 5

"*For in him we live, and move, and have our being*" (Acts 17:28).

The rest of this scripture is, "For we are also his offspring." That means He is our Father and we are His children. If we belong to Him, then we should live more aware and alive to the things He has created. Life should not become mundane, full of complaining and regrets, but every day should be lived with zest and fulfillment.

"*If we are ever to enjoy life, now is the time—not tomorrow, nor next year. . . . The best preparation for a better life next year is a full, complete, harmonious, joyous life this year. Our beliefs in a rich future life are of little importance unless we coin them into a rich present life. Today should always be our most wonderful day.*" —THOMAS DREIER[6]

The best way to live as He would want us to live is to walk with Him, learn of Him and follow His example. This is the year to begin correctly, and that is to stand in awe of His presence and let Him be a part of our life as the following poem paints the picture:

HIS UNFAILING PRESENCE
Another year I enter
Its history unknown;
Oh, how my feet would tremble
To tread its paths alone!
But I have heard a whisper;
I know I shall be blest;
"My presence shall go with thee,
And I will give thee rest."

What will the New Year bring me?
I may not, must not know;
Will it be love and rapture,
Or loneliness and woe?
Hush! Hush! I hear His whisper;
I surely shall be blest:
"My presence shall go with thee,

And I will give thee rest."
—Author Unknown[7]

This is the day to believe in Him, who is leading, and not in your own feelings and experiences. He is the rock of your salvation. "It is not the rock that ebbs and flows but the sea." He is the best foundation on which you can stand, so keep your feet firm on that rock and this will be a good day!

January 6

"A word spoken in due season, how good is it!" (Proverbs 15:23).

Today is the day to believe in people, to encourage them and give them hope. Belief is like an injection of hope.

There was once a boy, who worked long hours in a factory in Naples. He yearned to be a singer. When he was ten years old, he took his first lesson in voice. "You can't sing. You haven't any voice at all. Your voice sounds like the wind in the shutters," said his teacher. The boy's mother, however, had visions of greatness for her son. She believed that he had a talent to sing. She was very poor. Putting her arms around him, she encouragingly said, "My boy, I'm going to make every sacrifice to pay for your voice lessons." Her confidence in him and constant encouragement paid off. That boy became one of the world's greatest singers: Enrico Caruso![8]

Then there was a red-haired, talented Polish young boy who wanted to be a pianist. However, teachers at the conservatory gave no encouragement. He was told that his fingers were too short and thick for the piano. Later he bought a cornet. The same answer was given to him with the statement that he should try another instrument. Embittered, discouraged, he chanced to meet the famous composer and pianist, Anton Rubinstein, who asked him to play for him. Rubinstein praised and encouraged him. He then promised to practice seven hours a day. Words of praise changed the entire world for Jan Paderewski, who became a great pianist. —Loy C. Laney[9]

When Thomas Edison was sent home from school saying that his brain was addled, his mother marched back down to the school and said, "My son has more intelligence than you have in your little finger. I will teach him and he will learn." Learn he did. She started teaching him when he was in the third grade. The world does not know the name of his negative, opinionated teacher, but the world knows Thomas Edison.

A kind, cheerful word, encouraging word, spoken by an English naval officer, saved a youthful sailor from disgrace and dishonorable discharge. The sailor was only fourteen years old. During a fierce engagement with an enemy ship, the volleys from a number of firearms so frightened the sailor that he trembled and almost fainted. The officer, seeing him, came close beside him and said, "Courage, my boy! You will recover in a minute or two. I was just like you when I went into my first battle!" Afterward the young man said, "It was as if an angel had come to me and given me new strength."

Only a word of kindness,
But it lightened one heart of its grief;
Only a word of sympathy,
But it brought one soul relief.
Only a word of gentle cheer,
But it flooded with radiant light
The pathway that seemed so dark before,
And it made the day more bright.
—Author unknown

January 7

"Ye thought evil against me; but God meant it unto good" (Genesis 50:20).

This is the day to be big inside. When Abraham Lincoln was a young, struggling lawyer, he was employed on an important case. The fee was large. He journeyed to a distant city for consultation with other lawyers on the case. One of the lawyers got a glimpse of Lincoln as he sat in the reception room. "What's he doing here? Get rid of him. I will not be associated with such a

gawky ape as that!" Lincoln pretended that he did not hear him, though he knew that the insult was deliberate. In spite of his mortification, he went downstairs where he met with the group of lawyers. Then all went into the courthouse. As the trial got under way, Lincoln was ignored. He did not sit with the other lawyers. The lawyer who had so cruelly insulted him brilliantly defended his client. His logic was masterful. His handling of the case held Lincoln spellbound. He won the case. That night Lincoln said, "His argument was a revelation to me. I have never heard anything so finished and so carefully prepared. I can't hold a candle to him. I'm going home to study law all over again."

Time passed. Lincoln became President of the United States. Among his most outspoken critics was the lawyer who had insulted him and so sorely wounded him. But Lincoln never forgot that the lawyer of the brutal words was also the lawyer of the brilliant mind. When he selected a man for the vital post of Secretary of War, he chose Edwin M. Stanton, the one who had wounded and insulted him. Only a man of Lincoln's character and forgiving spirit could have risen above Stanton's insult.

Later, Lincoln lay dying, the victim of an assassin's bullet. When Lincoln's eyes finally closed in death, Stanton, filled with inconsolable grief, said, "Now he belongs to the ages." Lincoln won Stanton over and became friends because he was too big to be little. Lincoln rose above personal insult so the best minds could govern the United States of America. —TOLD BY WALTER B. KNIGHT[10]

Joseph of the Old Testament was a big man. He rose above the insults, false accusations, and hatred directed toward him from his own brothers. He did not let their taunts crush his dreams or soil his integrity. He rose to the top and then surrounded himself with his brothers and did not seek to get even with them, but instead forgave and blessed them.

This is the day to be big inside. There is no room for grudges, resentments, and vengeance on the road to greatness. Great souls learn to forgive and understand, instead of shriveling in bitterness.

Jesus said in Matthew 5:44: "Love your enemies . . . do good to them that hate you, and pray for them which despitefully use you."

To forgive has always been the way to greatness; this has not changed.

January 8

"By this shall all men know that ye are my disciples, if ye have love one to another" (John 13:35).

*R*ev. T. W. Callaway told the story of how in one of his churches in Macon, Georgia, two women became estranged from each other. With the passing of time, the ill will hardened into hatred of the bitterest kind. He said he visited one day in the home of one of the embittered women. She began to talk severely against the other woman. Dr. Callaway listened silently; then he asked, "Did she press cruel thorns onto your brow? Did she spit in your face?"

"Why, indeed, she didn't," replied the wrathful woman.

Dr. Callaway then asked, "Did she drive cruel spikes through your hands and feet?" Then there was silence. Eyes which formerly flashed hatred became filled with tears. "Oh," she exclaimed, "I see what you are driving at! How wicked I have been in allowing a root of bitterness to rankle in my heart. How could I have been so unlike my Master?"

In a short while, the two women confessed their sins, asked each other's forgiveness and God's forgiveness.[11]

The question today is, "Are we really like the Master?"

Before the turn of the century, an ardent and dedicated Christian wrote a tract entitled "Come to Jesus." It became famous and influenced many for Christ. Later he became engaged in theological dispute. In reply to a publication by an opponent, he wrote an article bristling with criticism, sharp and cutting as a razor. Looking for a title, he asked his friend. His friend wisely suggested: "Call it 'Go to the Devil' by the author of 'Come to Jesus.'" He destroyed the article.

God's children are to reflect Christ, not to argue, hate and tell people off. Gentleness, kindness, and love are to be the trademark of the redeemed.

King Henry VI of England had it said of him: "He never forgot anything but injuries." Of Cranmer it was said: "If you want to get a favor from him, do him a wrong." Emerson said of Lincoln: "His heart was as great as the world, but there was no room in it for the memory of a wrong." —Rev. David L. Currens[12]

Spurgeon gave this advice: "Cultivate forbearance till your

heart yields a fine crop of it. Pray for a short memory as to unkindness."

Remember the trademark that Jesus said would identify His followers. He said in John 13:35, "By this shall all men know that ye are my disciples, if ye have love one to another." *If ye have love* is the trademark.

January 9

"Be not afraid, only believe" (Mark 5:36).

*D*r. V. Raymond Edman wrote the following: *"Believe your beliefs that are founded on the Word of God, and doubt your doubts that come from disease, despair, disappointment, or disobedience. Doubt paralyzes—faith vitalizes. Faith is dead to doubts, dumb to discouragements, blind to impossibilities, knows nothing but success. Faith lifts its hands up through the threatening clouds, lays hold of Him who has all power in heaven and on earth. Faith makes the uplook good, the outlook bright, the inlook favorable, and the future glorious."*[13]

Life must be lived with faith whether in everyday happenings, in times of trouble or even in war.

"At a meeting in London, Winston Churchill gave the story of his escape from a South African military prison in Pretoria. Churchill told how, after wandering in the region round Pretoria for two or three days, and feeling at the end of his tether, he made up his mind to present himself at the door of one of the houses whose lights were twinkling in the valley below. Although a price had been set upon his head, he thought there was a chance of some friendly soul in the heart of that enemy country, and he prayed earnestly that he might be guided to the right house. Then he went up to the door of one of the houses and knocked. A man opened the door and asked him what he wanted. 'I am Winston Churchill,' he replied. 'Come in,' said a friendly voice. 'This is the only house for miles in which you would be safe.'" —BERNARD M. ALLEN[14]

Only God could arrange that. This was in answer to a desperate prayer and an act of faith. What is it you are facing today? Nothing is too big for God to do.

When God told Joshua to march around the walls of Jericho for seven days, it was simply an act of faith that defied the laws of nature and man's wisdom. God said the walls would fall down, but it took obedience to God's Word for it to happen. If the people would not have marched, the walls would have not fallen.

Jesus said in John 14:13, "Whatsoever ye shall ask in my name, that will I do." Faith is the activator of this scripture. Remember to believe your beliefs founded on God's Word and doubt your doubts founded on disease, discouragement and despair. God is still bigger than your problems. Trust Him today.

January 10

"Forasmuch as ye are manifestly declared to be the epistle of Christ" (II Corinthians 3:3).

What the hand is to the lute,
What the breath is to the flute,
What the fragrance is to the smell,
What the spring is to the well,
What the flower is to the bee—
That is Jesus Christ for me.

What's the mother to the child,
What's the guide to pathless wild,
What is oil to troubled wave,
What is ransom to the slave,
What is water to the sea—
That is Jesus Christ to me.
—SPURGEON[15]

As Jesus is to you, so you should express your love for Him to others by showing forth His characteristics as penned in the following poem:

Not merely in the words you say,
Not only in your deeds confessed,

> *But in the most unconscious way*
> *Is Christ expressed.*
>
> *For me 'twas not the truth you taught,*
> *To you so clear, to me so dim;*
> *But when you came to me you brought a sense of Him.*
> *And from your eyes He beckons me,*
> *And from your heart His love is shed,*
> *Till I lost sight of you and see*
> *The Christ instead.*
>
> —AUTHOR UNKNOWN[16]

Walter B. Knight tells the story of an earthen vessel of no particular beauty. But all who came near it were charmed by the exquisite, delicate odor emanating from it. Someone asked the potter, "What did you put into the clay you used to mould this vessel to make it so appealing to all who enter your shop?"

"Nothing, nothing at all. I, too, noticed the flowerlike fragrance of the clay from which I wrought the vessel. So I went to the place from where the clay came and there I found a wild rosebush growing. Its petals covered the ground and filled the atmosphere with fragrance. The petals it shed year after year must have given the clay its odor."[17]

God's children need to stay so close to Christ that their daily lives will radiate His grace, goodness and sweetness.

On a bronze tablet at one of the churches in Philadelphia are these words: "In loving memory of John Wanamaker—founder—By reason of him many went away and believed on Jesus."

What does your life say about Jesus today?

January 11

"Though an host should encamp against me, my heart shall not fear" (Psalm 27:3).

Psalm 18:2-3, 48 declares: "The LORD is my rock, and my fortress, and my deliverer; my God, my strength, in whom I will trust; my buckler, and the horn of my salvation, and my high

tower. I will call upon the LORD, who is worthy to be praised: so shall I be saved from mine enemies. . . . He delivereth me from mine enemies: yea, thou liftest me up above those that rise up against me: thou hast delivered me from the violent man."

The following story proves that God can protect anytime or anywhere, even from bullets: Out of the Cold Harbor slaughter emerged Carter E. Prince of the 4th Maine Volunteers. A bullet hit his suspender buckle and carried it through to the New Testament in the pocket of his shirt. Pushed by the bullet, the buckle went through all the chapters between Revelation and St. Mark and came to rest at Mark 12:36, where is recorded the saying of the Lord: "Sit thou on my right hand, till I make thine enemies thy footstool."

God's ways are unique and unparalleled. His Word can even stop a bullet intended to destroy, and then let it stop at a passage that is relevant to the moment. God has promised to be with His children no matter where they might be.

"No weapon that is formed against thee shall prosper. . . . This is the heritage of the servants of the LORD" (Isaiah 54:17).

Many are the miraculous interventions down through history. *"A tide was kept back strangely for twelve hours once, and so a host of Christians in Holland were saved from slaughter by the Duke of Alva. A tremendous wind once scattered the Armada of Spain over the wastes of the North Sea, and so Protestant England was spared to the world. John Knox moved his usual seat away from above before the window one night, pressed by a feeling he could neither understand nor resist; an hour later there came a musket-ball crashing through the glass and burying itself harmlessly in the opposite wall."* —C. S. ROBINSON[18]

Elisha was surrounded by the enemy at Dothan, and God sent chariots of fire and horses that stood on top of the mountains. Not only did God send heavenly help, but He allowed Elisha to see them with his natural eyes. When his servant full of fear reported the enemy's intention, Elisha said, "Fear not: for they that be with us are more than they that be with them." Then the Lord opened the servant's eyes, and lo and behold, he saw what Elisha had already seen.

Have no fear today, for the Lord is with you and will protect you and keep you. You are in His hands.

January 12

"Provide things honest in the sight of all men" (Romans 12:17).

A baker living in a village not far from Quebec bought his butter from a neighboring farmer. One day he became suspicious that the butter was not the same weight, so for several days he weighed the butter and then found that the rolls of butter that the farmer brought were diminishing in weight. This so angered him that he had the farmer arrested. "I assume you have weights," said the judge. "No, sir," replied the farmer.

"How then do you manage to weigh the butter that you sell?" asked the judge.

"That's easily explained, Your Honor," said the farmer. "When the baker began buying his butter from me, I thought I'd get my bread from him, and it's the one-pound loaf I've been using as a weight for the butter I sell. If the weight of the butter is wrong, he has himself to blame." —SUNDAY SCHOOL CHRONICLE[19]

Anytime the Word of God is violated, there is always trouble. Honesty and integrity are the pillars of character. Without them a building will fall. They speak loud and clear.

King Edward III of England wanted a governess for his children. A Scottish lady of integrity and character was recommended to him. The king offered her the position. She modestly declined his offer. "Royal children need a much more learned person than I am," she said. The king, however, refused her declination, saying, "Madam, I wish you to accept the position because you are an honest, good woman. I can employ others who are possibly better prepared scholastically than you, but I cannot buy integrity and honesty." —SOUTHPORT METHODIST[20]

This is the day to live our lives in such a way that the influence of integrity will be handed down from generation to generation. An aged Christian man who mended umbrellas knocked at the back door of Dr. Harry A. Ironside's house many years ago and asked if he had any umbrellas which needed fixing. Dr. Ironside said yes and went to get his umbrella whose cover was torn and whose ribs were broken. The old man sat on the steps and carefully removed the torn cloth. With equal care he measured the new

cloth and repaired the broken ribs. Dr. Ironside noticed how he put his best into what he was doing and said, "You seem most careful in your work." The man answered, "I try to do the best possible work."

"But your customers would not know the difference until you were gone. Perhaps you expect to come back this way again someday," Dr. Ironside suggested.

"No," said the old man, "I will probably never come this way again." When asked why he was so particular to do the best work, he replied, "So it will be easier for the man who follows me. If I do shoddy, bad work, my customers will soon find it out, and the next mender of umbrellas who comes along will get the cold shoulder."[21]

One life touches another life and greatness of soul can influence each generation if the present one cares enough to have honesty and integrity. So remember today to follow the instructions of Paul to *provide things honest in the sight of all men.* That is the hallmark of great people and the criteria of heaven. It is worth it.

January 13

"Keep thy tongue from evil" (Psalm 34:13).

Psalm 34:12-13 says, "What man is he that desireth life, and loveth many days, that he may see good? Keep thy tongue from evil, and thy lips from speaking guile."

I Peter 3:10 reiterates this truth: "For he that will love life, and see good days, let him refrain his tongue from evil, and his lips that they speak no guile."

The way to life is through the tongue. Jesus said in Matthew 12:37, "For by thy words thou shalt be justified, and by thy words thou shalt be condemned." Be careful what you say.

Some people have to find fault no matter what, and most of the time they do not know what they are talking about. They only have half the picture.

Scrutinizing an owl, a man said: "That owl is not stuffed right. Its head is not on right. The body is not poised right. The feathers are not fixed right. If I could not stuff an owl better than that, I would go out of the taxidermy business." Just then the owl moved. The man had criticized a live owl. —THE SUNDAY SCHOOL TIMES

A grouchy father attended church with his little boy. There was nothing in the service which the faultfinding father liked. As he walked home with his boy, he criticized the minister and his sermon. He found fault with the choir and with everything in general. The boy had noticed that when the offering was taken, his father had put a dime into the collection plate. So he asked his father, "Well, Dad, what can you expect for a dime?" —WALTER B. KNIGHT

A dime or a dollar—it makes no difference—there is nothing in the Word of God that gives anyone a right to criticize and pull people down.

Evil is that which is injurious; that which produces sorrow or distress; or anything impairing the happiness or welfare of another.

There is a legend that illustrates what gossip and malicious slander do. There was a man who enchanted an arrow which flew around killing people. But after it had killed everyone, leaving no new victims, it came back to destroy the man. The man then spent the rest of his life running from the arrow he had sent against others.

You choose today to continually criticize or to uplift. What you do with your tongue will determine your destiny.

January 14

"Glorify God in your body, and in your spirit, which are God's" (I Corinthians 6:20).

"*I* lived in an old house in the country once, where the wind would sometimes whistle around so that I thought I would have some music if it must blow like that. So I made a rude Aeolian harp of mere sewing-silk strung across a board, and placed it under the slightly lifted sash of a north window, and the music was so sweet through all the house when the wild storms came. Is there any north window in your life? Could you not so arrange the three wires of faith, hope, and love that the storms of life should only bring more music into this sad world?" —CRUMBS

The Lord lets the winds blow, not to destroy you, but to strengthen you. Not only does He desire the winds of adversity to

bring strength to your soul, but He also desires to have your life, so that He can play beautiful music through it. It is difficult at times to release self to Him when we want to be in control, but releasing always brings the greater dimension of life.

It is said that once Mendelssohn, the great composer, came to see the great Freiburg organ. The old custodian refused him permission to play upon the instrument, not knowing who he was. At length, however, he reluctantly granted him leave to play a few notes. Mendelssohn took his seat, and soon the most wonderful music was breaking forth from the organ. The custodian was spellbound. He came up beside the great musician and asked his name. Learning it, he stood humiliated, self-condemned, saying, "And I refused you permission to play upon my organ!"

Notice how he called it his organ, just the way we do with our lives. We are custodians of our life, but we get to feeling that we are not only in charge of it, but that we own it and have the final say over it, when we are here only because life has been given us by God.

Choices are being made today. When the storms of life come your way, you choose to arrange the three wires of faith, hope, and love in such a position that music can be made. You also choose whether to let the Master have charge of the heartstrings of your life. He can only make beautiful music if He is allowed to have full control of the instruments of your life.

Jesus said, "Release your life to me and you will find life." Luke 9:24 says, "For whosoever will save his life shall lose it: but whosoever will lose his life for my sake, the same shall save it." Will you let Him make beautiful music in your life today?

"He shall baptize you with the Holy Ghost, and with fire" (Matthew 3:11).

"Once upon a time in the wilderness there was a thorn bush. It looked at its surroundings and sighed. Could anything be more unfortunate? Above was a heaven of brass whence the sun shot out its fiery darts; about it danced the quivering air like the heat of a furnace. And below was the wilderness; here

the barren rock cropped up from the ground; here the sand of the desert lay without a grass blade; there some stunted shrub struggled for existence; and yonder there was a patch of scanty herbage. 'Ah, if I were only in the king's garden,' it sighed, 'such as I have heard the travelers tell of, cared for and tended, there might be some hope for me. Or if, indeed, I were worth anything—hung with luscious fruit like the fig tree, or the vines which grow about the cottages of the people, and make glad the sons of men. Or if I were like the stately cedar of Lebanon, or the oak or ash. Or if I could distill some balm for the healing of the nations; or could crown the year with gladness like the golden corn. But a thorn bush; where there is never so much as a bird to build its nest in my branches.'

"*So the thorn bush whispered to the night winds, and told its sorrow to the stars when the nights were very still.*

"*But lo! it chanced one day that Moses led his sheep to the back of the desert, and the thorn bush burned with fire, yet was unconsumed. And God dwelt in the bush. And forth from it there went the great commission for the deliverance of Israel; and all the ages have been lit up and blessed by the vision and by the message that came from the bush on fire.*"
—MARK GUY PEARSE

You may feel like you are unimportant in the kingdom of God, but everyone is important in the great plan of God. God has plans for your life, but first He wants you to be on fire. He did say in Revelation 3:15 that He wanted His church to be "hot."

Coldness is reserved for the lifeless and the mummies. John said of Christ in Luke 3:16, "He shall baptize you with the Holy Ghost and with fire."

If you are on fire, God will shine through you and you will become a message to the world of the glory of God. This is not the time to retreat or feel sorry for self, but it is the time to become hot flaming torches for God. He has great things planned for you.

January 16

"This one thing I do" (Philippians 3:13).

God does not ask you to live yesterday over again; He just asks that you live today well. Deuteronomy 30:15 states that He gives us each day: "See, I have set before thee this day life and good." The choice is ours what we do with the day. We can face it with trepidation and feel like life is too hard, or we can live one day at a time and make it, as illustrated in the following story:

There was once a pendulum waiting to be fixed on a new clock. It began to calculate how long it would be before the big wheels were worn out and its work was done. It would be expected to tick night and day, so many times a minute, sixty times that every hour, and twenty-four times that every day. It was awful! Quite a row of figures, enough to stagger you! Millions of ticks! "I can never do it," said the poor pendulum. But the clockmaster encouraged it; "You can do one tick at a time?" he said. "Oh, yes," the pendulum could do that. "Well," he said, "that is all that will be required of you." So the pendulum went to work, steadily ticking, one tick at a time, and it is ticking yet, quite cheerfully. —DWIGHT LYMAN MOODY[22]

Paul said "I do one thing" and that is to press forward. This is the year to press forward and accept what is before us. It is unknown and never lived before, but it is there to those who will accept its challenge.

THE NEW YEAR
A flower unblown; a book unread;
A tree with fruit unharvested;
A path untrod; a house whose rooms
Lack yet the heart's divine perfumes;
A landscape whose wide border lies
In silent shade, 'neath silent skies;
A treasure with its gifts concealed—
This is the year that for you waits
Beyond tomorrow's mystic gates.
—HORATIO NELSON POWERS[23]

Make up your mind that this day you will go forward with courage in your heart, knowing that God is with you and that He will help you live successfully the days and hours that He has given you on earth. You can do all things through Christ so live it well!

January 17

"For with God nothing shall be impossible" (Luke 1:37).

Charles Kettering, the famous research scientist, was known to be impatient with people who spoke of insurmountable obstacles. "It is like the doctors with their incurable diseases," he said. "Did you ever stop to think what an incurable disease is? It is one the doctor doesn't know how to cure." —Dutton[24]

There are no insurmountable obstacles with God. He took several million Israelites to a Red Sea and there was no way to cross it, but He being God told Moses to stretch forth his rod over the sea. When Moses obeyed, the Lord rolled the sea back and held it in a standing position until several million people walked across on dry land.

When Elijah was on Mount Carmel in a contest with the prophets of Baal, they tried to get fire to come down out of heaven, but they were unable to do so, because their god was false. But Elijah prayed a simple prayer of faith, and God rained fire down out of heaven and it burned up the sacrifice, licked up the water, and burned up the stones and dust. His God did the impossible.

When Lazarus had died and was buried four days, Jesus came and called him forth out of the grave and he walked out bound in grave clothes. Jesus said to the people, "Loose him, and let him go!" They unwrapped him, and he lived many years after this notable miracle.

Once when King Hezekiah was surrounded by the enemy and Sennacherib had mocked him by sending a letter saying that Hezekiah's God was unable to save the people from out of his hand, he bragged too soon. Sennacherib boasted in the letter, "Let not thy God in whom thou trustest deceive thee, saying, Jerusalem shall not be delivered into the hand of the king of Assyria."

Hezekiah went to the Lord God and prayed in II Kings 19:15-16, 19 the following prayer. "O LORD God of Israel, which dwellest between the cherubims, thou art the God, even thou alone, of all the kingdoms of the earth; thou hast made heaven and earth. LORD, bow down thine ear, and hear: open, LORD, thine eyes, and see: and hear the words of Sennacherib, which hath sent him to reproach the living God. . . . O LORD our God, I beseech thee, save thou us out of his hand, that all the kingdoms of the earth may

know that thou art the LORD God, even thou only."

The Lord, for whom there is nothing impossible to do, solved King Hezekiah's problem. II Kings 19:35-37 says, "And it came to pass that night, that the angel of the LORD went out, and smote in the camp of the Assyrians an hundred fourscore and five thousand: and when they arose early in the morning, behold, they were all dead corpses. So Sennacherib king of Assyria departed, and went and returned, and dwelt at Nineveh. And it came to pass, as he was worshipping in the house of Nisroch his god, that Adrammelech and Sharezer his sons smote him with the sword." No one speaks against God and gets by with it.

With God all things are possible. Think not today on that which is impossible, but think of Jeremiah 32:17, "Ah Lord God! behold, thou hast made the heaven and the earth by thy great power and stretched out arm, and there is nothing too hard for thee."

What is it that is impossible, or incurable, or that particular thing in which you have given up hope? This is the day to gain new hope, keep believing for a miracle, for the people who received their miracle believed more than they doubted.

"For what shall it profit a man, if he shall gain the whole world, and lose his own soul?" (Mark 8:36).

A brilliant Chinese student was offered a fine position some years ago with the American government. When Bishop Wilson S. Lewis asked the young man why he refused the splendid offer and volunteered to preach the gospel for a mere pittance, he said: "During the Boxer Uprising I lived in an inland village where there was a temple for devil worship. The Christians were led by the soldiers to that temple and ordered to renounce their religion and bow before the devil image or they would be executed. I saw one hundred and sixty-three of my townsmen walk by the devil god with heads erect, when a little bow would have saved their lives—then out to a great beam over which they placed their heads for the swift stroke of the executioner's sword that sent their heads rolling in the dust. My father was one of that number. It was the unshaken

integrity of their faith that thrilled me and gave me a longing for the new life. I must go back and tell my fellow townsmen of Christ who loves them, and of His power to save." —*The Upper Room*[25]

The way of the cross is not always an easy way, but it is a blessed way. Many great works were founded because of sacrifice, just as the early church was. It has been said, "The blood of the martyrs became the seed of the church." There have been and always will be those who will die for their belief if need be, just as the Chinese father was willing to die for his belief in Jesus Christ. Christianity is not a dream; it is a battle. It requires strong hearts that are willing to buck the modern tide of ease, laziness and cream puff religion.

Once a missionary society, deeply impressed by the courageous devotion of David Livingstone who worked alone in Africa, wrote to Livingstone, asking: "Have you found a good road to where you are? If so, we want to send other men to join you." Livingstone replied: "If you have men who will come only if there is a good road, I don't want them. I want men who will come if there is no road at all."

Do not pray for easy lives.
Pray to be stronger men and women.
Do not pray for tasks equal to your powers.
Pray for powers equal to your tasks.
—Phillips Brooks

This is the day to not faint but to be strong and resolute in your determination to follow the Lord Jesus. He is looking for workers who are not ashamed and who will stand up in the face of the enemy or hardship and forge ahead with victory. This is no time to let up, ease up, or give up, but it is the time to regroup, rededicate, and regain any territory lost. The call is sent forth today to follow Christ at any cost.

January 19

"Choose you this day whom ye will serve" (Joshua 24:15).

*J*oshua of old sent forth the challenge, "Make a choice of whom you will serve!" Jesus said in Luke 16:13, "No [one] can serve two masters: for either he will hate the one, and love the other; or else he will hold to the one, and despise the other."

Who or what is controlling you? What have you resolved to do today? Where are you going and in what direction are you heading?

Today is the day to resolve to do the following things:

Forget past mistakes and press on to greater achievements.

To put first things first.

To make your work a joy.

To allow nothing to disturb your peace of mind.

To never lose self-control.

To spend so much time improving yourself that you have no time for criticism of others.

To think the best, work for it, and expect it.

To be a true friend.

To stand for the right.

To be kind.

To take every disappointment as a stimulant.

To live on the sunny side of every cloud.

To smile.

To look ahead and keep moving forward. —AUTHOR UNKNOWN

Benjamin Franklin said, "Resolve to perform what you ought; perform without fail what you resolve."

This is the day to resolve or make up your mind to do that which is noble, good and right; then do it. This is not a day for cowards, but there is a call going forth to stand tall and true; to step away from that which destroys and debilitates the soul, and to move ahead to victory.

The story is told of how Bishop Latimer once preached a sermon before King Henry VIII which greatly offended him. The king ordered him to preach again next Sabbath and to make public apology for his offense. The bishop ascended the pulpit and read his text, and thus began his sermon: "Hugh Latimer, dost thou know before whom that art this day to speak? To the high and mighty monarch, the king's most excellent majesty, who can take away thy life if thou offendest; therefore take heed that thou speakest not a word that may displease. But then, Hugh, consider well. Dost thou not know from whom thou comest—upon

whose message thou art sent? Even the great and mighty God, who is all present and able to cast thy soul into hell. Therefore take care that thou deliverest thy message faithfully." And with increased energy, he preached the selfsame sermon as the week before. The fear of God delivered him from the fear of man. —*THE WATCHMAN-EXAMINER*[26]

Just as Bishop Latimer made a choice to follow the higher set of laws, those which are set forth in the Holy Bible, so must our resolves and choices be founded upon the higher laws of God! This is not the day to be destroyed by weak resolves or no resolves at all, but it is the day to be strong in the Lord and stand forth for that which is noble, true and right.

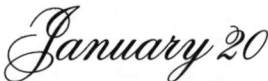

"I can do all things through Christ" (Philippians 4:13).

*I*s your dream still inside you or has it died within you? Have you become a person who is going through the motions of life? Have you lost the glow and wonder of your youthful dreams? Is life just a drudge, another day to live and to get through as quickly as possible? Is it just a time to get up in the morning, endure the day and then go to bed to try to sleep away the disappointment and raw deal that life has handed you?

Life does not have to be that way. You can recapture the glow, the zeal and the passion you once had. The secret is to not give up when the going gets tough even when life knocks you down time after time. Just answer the falling-down times with the scripture in Micah 7:7-8, "Therefore I will look unto the LORD; I will wait for the God of my salvation: my God will hear me. Rejoice not against me, O mine enemy: when I fall, I shall arise; when I sit in darkness, the LORD shall be a light unto me."

You must have tenacity even when others do not believe in you or your dream.

Ski instructor Pete Seibert was considered crazy when he first disclosed his dream to start a ski resort. Standing on the summit of a mountain in the Gore Range in Colorado, Seibert described a

dream he had carried with him since age twelve, and began the challenge of convincing others that it was possible. Seibert's dream is now a reality called Vail.

During its first year of business, the Coca-Cola Company sold only four hundred Cokes.

Richard Bach completed only one year of college, then trained to become an Air Force jet-fighter pilot. Twenty months after earning his wings, he resigned. Then he became an editor of an aviation magazine that went bankrupt. Life became one failure after another. Even when he wrote *Jonathan Livingston Seagull*, he couldn't think of an ending. The manuscript lay dormant for eight years before he decided how to finish it—only to have eighteen publishers reject it. However, once it was published, the book went on to sell seven million copies in numerous languages and made Richard Bach an internationally known and respected author.

In 1902, the poetry editor of the *Atlantic Monthly* returned the poems of a twenty-eight-year-old poet with the following note: "Our magazine has no room for your vigorous verse." The poet was Robert Frost.

John Bunyan wrote *Pilgrim's Progress* while confined to a Bedford prison cell for his views on religion; Martin Luther translated the Bible while confined in the Castle of Wartburg.

Someone once said, "One of the secrets of success is to refuse to let temporary setbacks defeat us."

This is the day to let the Lord be your light and to let His inspiration flow through you and help bring your dreams to pass. Dreams and goals are not to die and be buried, but they are to be nurtured and released into being. You can do all things through Christ which strengthens you!

"If thou canst believe, all things are possible to him that believeth" (Mark 9:23).

The Brooklyn Bridge that spans the river between Manhattan and Brooklyn is simply an engineering miracle. In 1883, a creative

engineer, John Roebling, was inspired by an idea for this spectacular bridge project. However, bridge-building experts told him to forget it, it just was not possible. Roebling convinced his son, Washington, an up-and-coming engineer, that the bridge could be built. The two of them conceived the concept of how it could be accomplished and how to overcome the obstacles. Somehow they convinced bankers to finance the project. Then, with excitement and energy, they hired their crew and began to build the bridge. The project was only a few months under way when a tragic on-site accident killed John Roebling and severely injured his son. Part of Washington's brain was damaged and he could neither walk nor talk. Everyone thought the project would have to be scrapped, since the Roeblings were the only ones who understood how the bridge could be built.

Though Washington Roebling was unable to move or talk, his mind was as sharp as ever. One day as he lay in his hospital bed, an idea flashed in his mind as to how to develop a communication code. All he could move was one finger, so he touched the arm of his wife with that finger. He tapped out the code to communicate to her what she was to tell the engineers who continued to build the bridge. For thirteen years, Washington tapped out his instructions with one finger until the spectacular Brooklyn Bridge was finally completed.

The question is, "What are you doing with your one finger? And if you have a whole body and mind, what are you doing with it?"

This day demands excellence even in the face of decadence. Do not lie down and die, but keep believing and pressing on and you will build that bridge in your life for the next generation to walk over it. Whatever the Lord has called you to do, even if you have had setbacks, disappointments and hardships enter into the picture, you can at least communicate something positive in the face of disaster if you *will* to do so, just as Washington Roebling determined to do.

When Paul the apostle was locked up in prison and his voice was stilled in the marketplaces and his missionary journeys were over, he did not lie down and die. Instead he kept tapping out letters and messages of faith, even from a dark, damp, smelly dungeon.

Where are you today, what is your position and how are you handling your misfortune? Have you succumbed to the disasters of life and are half-dead in your spirit or are you still tapping out faith, if need be with only one finger?

January 22

"In all labour there is profit" (Proverbs 14:23).

Although Henri Matisse was nearly twenty-eight years younger than Auguste Renoir, the two great artists were dear friends and frequent companions. When Renoir was confined to his home during the last decade of his life, Matisse visited him daily. Renoir, almost paralyzed by arthritis, continued to paint in spite of his infirmities. One day as Matisse watched the elder painter working in his studio, fighting torturous pain with each brush stroke, he blurted out: "Auguste, why do you continue to paint when you are in such agony?"

Renoir answered simply: "The beauty remains; the pain passes."

Life isn't always easy, but one must focus not on the pain of it, but on the beauty of it.

Someone once said about all of life's painful experiences, "This too shall pass." Nothing lasts forever, except God, heaven and the Word. The bodies we now live in will not last forever, but they shall be changed as stated in I Corinthians 15:51-53, 57: "Behold, I shew you a mystery; We shall not all sleep, but we shall all be changed, In a moment, in the twinkling of an eye, at the last trump: for the trumpet shall sound, and the dead shall be raised incorruptible, and we shall be changed. For this corruptible must put on incorruption, and this mortal must put on immortality. . . . But thanks be to God, which giveth us the victory through our Lord Jesus Christ." Verse 58 says, "Therefore, my beloved brethren, be ye stedfast, unmoveable, always abounding in the work of the Lord, forasmuch as ye know that your labour is not in vain in the Lord."

No matter what you are going through, just keep being faithful, remembering that the beauty or good that you can paint into another person's life is what will count in eternity. Underline the last phrase of verse 58: *Know that your labor is not in vain in the Lord.*

This world that houses humanity now will someday pass away, but what you do in this world for the Lord Jesus Christ, even if there are pain and hardship involved, will forever be remembered as some-

thing beautiful. The pain will pass but the beauty will remain forever.

The day will come when the books will be opened and your labor will be acknowledged. Revelation 20:12 states: "And I saw the dead, small and great, stand before God; and the books were opened: and another book was opened, which is the book of life: and the dead were judged out of those things which were written in the books, according to their works."

Your labor for the Lord, that which benefits another or His kingdom, is being written down and it will be rewarded. The pain will pass, but the beauty will remain. So keep being faithful, in helping to bring life and joy into the lives of others and spreading the gospel of Jesus Christ, even though it is not always easy to be faithful. Someday you will forget the hardship and the pain and only the beauty will remain. Your labor is never in vain!

"Yet shew I unto you a more excellent way" (I Corinthians 12:31).

"We are challenged on every hand to work untiringly to achieve excellence in our lifework. Not all men are called to specialized or professional jobs; even fewer rise to the heights of genius in the arts and sciences; many are called to be laborers in factories, fields and streets. But no work is insignificant. All labor that uplifts humanity has dignity and importance and should be undertaken with painstaking excellence. If a man is called to be a street sweeper, he should sweep even as Michelangelo painted, or Beethoven composed music, or Shakespeare wrote poetry. He should sweep streets so well that all the host of heaven and earth will pause to say, 'Here lived a great street sweeper who did his job well.'" —MARTIN LUTHER KING JR.

John Eliot on the day of his death, in his eightieth year, was found teaching the alphabet to an Indian child at his bedside. "Why not rest from your labors?" asked a friend. "Because," said he, "I have prayed to God to make me useful in my sphere, and He has heard my prayer, for now that I can no longer preach, He leaves me strength enough to teach this poor child his alphabet."

Eighty years of age and bedridden, yet still at work for others.
—GRACE AND HOPE EVANGEL[27]

This is the spirit of excellence. He did his job well.

Years ago an explorer was going through the wilds of Alaska. It was bitterly cold. He came to a little church and mission school where a lone missionary preached and taught. "What are you doing here in this cold, dreary, out-of-the-way place? How can you waste your life in a place like this?" asked the explorer. The missionary smiled and answered, "God sent me here. Here I shall remain until I die, or until God gives me further orders." The explorer said, "But the task here is hopeless. You have made so few converts in all these years; the results have been so small." The missionary answered, "Results are not my business. I leave the results with God. I must be faithful and do my best for God. Some day results will come."

Remember no work is insignificant. All labor that uplifts humanity has dignity and importance and should be undertaken with painstaking excellence. The excellent way is a way of love that involves God. It is not that man would shine, but that God would shine through the man or woman; that a spirit of excellence would grip the soul, so that all jobs and responsibilities would be performed with a spirit of greatness, knowing that one act is connected to another act and nothing stands alone, but that all your life is connected. So live it well and give God your best, for He is a good bookkeeper. Nothing done for Him or others is ever wasted.

"For I know that my redeemer liveth" (Job 19:25).

Where God is, there is majesty. Where God is, there are hope, life, and power. He creates within the heart of mankind a desire for better things. He always makes better. His magnificence is shown in all He created.

When Jenny Lind was coming to this country for her first concert tour she expressed to the captain of the vessel a desire to behold a sunrise at sea. Accordingly, one cloudless morning, he had her called at early dawn. Silent and motionless she stood by his side upon the deck watching every change of shade and tint in

the sky and their reflection upon the waking waters until the first golden rays shot up from the horizon. As the sun leaped up from the waves she burst into rapturous song.

She was unconscious of the presence of the captain and a few sailors who stood near. In the ecstasy of her emotion she lifted her voice to an unseen Hearer, to whose majesty and glory she paid her tribute. Little wonder that Captain West in describing the scene exclaimed: "No one will ever hear the song: *I know that My Redeemer Liveth*, sung as I heard it that morning."[28]

Yes, He does live. He lives so that His children can know the abundant life in Him. His majesty is all around us, but most importantly it is in our hearts.

Acts 17:28 says, "For in him we live, and move, and have our being; as certain also of your own poets have said, For we are also his offspring."

Remember who you are. You are God's child. His Spirit dwells within you. It guides you, empowers you, and lifts you to a higher realm that cannot be attained except through the Lord Jesus Christ.

It was Martin Luther who wrote to the prime minister in Germany these words: "I have lately seen a miracle. I looked out of the window at the stars in God's whole heavenly dome. I saw no pillars where the Master had placed them, yet such a dome still stands fast. There are some who seek such pillars and would like very much to feel and grasp them; because they cannot do it, they tremble and write as if the heavens would certainly fall for no other reason than that they cannot seize pillars. I would sooner expect to see the heavens fall than to see one jot or tittle of all the Word of God fail." —*THE BIBLE FRIEND*[29]

This kind of faith will shake kingdoms, subdue lions, and cause the enemy to run. The world does not need more doubt; it needs more faith. Pray the Lord will give you a good dose today, for it is the thing that will take you to victory!

January 25

"God is our refuge and strength, a very present help in trouble" (Psalm 46:1).

I sought a shelter from the storms
Of life, and as they beat
Upon my craft's frail, trembling sides,
God whispered, "No retreat,
But rather strength to face the task,
To make your work complete."

"But Lord," I cried, "it is too great
A job for me to do."
And He agreed it was too much
For one, but not for two.
"Have faith," He cried, "Have I not said
That I will see you through?"
—JOHN W. LITTLE

Sometimes life gets to be too much for you and you want to get away from the pressure of it all. The story is told about how some six miles above the panhandle of Texas, a jet bomber on S.A.S. patrol was fatally disabled when No. 6 engine exploded and the wing was enveloped in flames. The chief pilot gave the word to abandon ship and the necessary apparatus went into effect blowing off the canopy and ejecting the seats.

Lieutenant J. E. Obenauf, however, had trouble bailing out. His ejection seat failed. As he went stumbling through the ship trying to find an escape hatch, he stumbled over the body of Major Joseph Maxwell. What would he do? To hesitate would mean certain death. Why not jump and leave the unconscious body where it lay? Without hesitation, Obenauf deliberately turned around and got into the pilot's seat. In spite of intense heat and imminent danger, he performed a superhuman task. Alone he took the ship down through a storm and fog and landed in safety. It was a miracle but Maxwell, the man who lay unconscious in the belly of that cabin, was saved and given a second chance in life.

What if the pilot's ejection seat had not failed, which caused him to stumble over the body of the unconscious man? What if he would have bailed out? For sure one man would have died, possibly two. Because he chose to land a disabled plane, God intervened and helped bring him to safety.

You may feel disabled and it looks like total disaster ahead, but hang on, don't bail out, the Lord and His angels are with you and you will land safely. The Lord will give you strength when you

feel like it is all over—but remember, it is not over with God.

David said it well in Psalm 27, "The LORD is my light and my salvation; whom shall I fear? the LORD is the strength of my life; of whom shall I be afraid? For in the time of trouble he shall hide me in his pavilion: in the secret of his tabernacle shall he hide me; he shall set me up upon a rock."

The Lord is with you, He will give you strength so you will not fail as stated in Psalm 18:36: "Thou hast enlarged my steps under me, that my feet did not slip." The Lord will help you in the time of crisis. He will be with you when it looks like total disaster. He is the God who specializes in doing the impossible. Don't bail out, but lean on the Lord. He is able to take you through to victory. A miracle is waiting for you today; just trust in the Lord when it looks like you can't go any further, and He will give you strength and take you to safety.

"*He . . . shall neither slumber nor sleep*" (Psalm 121:4).

Victor Hugo wrote, "*Have courage for the great sorrows of life and patience for the small ones, and when you have accomplished your daily task, go to sleep in peace. God is awake.*"

"God is awake!" Psalm 121:1-5, 8 says, "I will lift up mine eyes unto the hills, from whence cometh my help. My help cometh from the LORD, which made heaven and earth. He will not suffer thy foot to be moved: he that keepeth thee will not slumber. . . . He . . . shall neither slumber nor sleep. . . . The LORD is thy keeper: the LORD is thy shade upon thy right hand. The LORD shall preserve thy going out and thy coming in from this time forth, and even for evermore."

The story is told of Gene Tipps: one day he woke up and discovered the Vietnam War was over. His old girlfriends had long since married and had children. "Last thing I remember is that we were all kids and single. I know I'm twenty-eight, but to me I'm still twenty." He had eight years of almost constant sleeping.

Tipps was critically injured in an automobile accident May 21, 1967. He suffered shock and acute swelling of the brain associated with trauma, and doctors held little hope of recovery. He was comatose for three weeks following the accident, but after he came out of the coma he suffered from complete amnesia. "We would get him up and feed him and no matter what we did, he would go lie down and go to sleep. He had no desire to do anything," says his mother. When he finally came out of his eight-year daze Tipps thought he had been asleep only two weeks. He doesn't remember when he used to sit in a chair, staring, or his parents' efforts in the past five years to exercise him on a stationary bicycle to maintain his muscle tone. He did not remember anything.

This story makes the statement in Psalm 121 even more powerful. The Lord never sleeps nor slumbers. He does not even doze or take catnaps. He is always watchful of His children. II Chronicles 16:9 says, "For the eyes of the LORD run to and fro throughout the whole earth, to shew himself strong in the behalf of them whose heart is perfect toward him."

You can relax today, for God is awake. He is in control and will have the last word concerning all things. So do everything you can do: pray, follow the Lord, work hard, give everything your best shot, then relax. Don't worry, for those who are on the Lord's side will always win.

Philippians 4:6-7 states: "Be careful for nothing; but in every thing by prayer and supplication with thanksgiving let your requests be made known unto God. And the peace of God, which passeth all understanding, shall keep your hearts and minds through Christ Jesus."

In other words, God is awake and will keep your heart and mind in peace, so do not worry or fret. God is going to work all things out according to His will. This is the day to trust in Him.

January 27

"Looking unto Jesus the author and finisher of our faith" (Hebrews 12:2).

    Someone once wrote: "*If you want to be distressed, look to yourself. If you want to be perplexed, look to others. If you want to be radiant, look to Jesus.*" Only the Sun of righteousness can shine grace into your soul during a crisis and bring peace.

    Humboldt in his *Travels* describes his experiences during a mighty earthquake and accompanying tornado. He was filled with fear when he saw the churning waves receding from the bay. His vessel toppled over on the beach. Huge trees were uprooted. Ominous, black clouds darkened the sky. The scene was terrifying. He chanced to look up through a rift in the dark cloud and there he saw the sun shining in its glory. Soon the earth ceased to throb. The wind subsided. The sky cleared, and the sun brought warmth and cheer. —TOLD BY WALTER B. KNIGHT[30]

    We must look towards the Lord who is high and lifted up as is recorded in Isaiah 6. During times of dismay, crumbling situations, and midst upheavals, God remains unchanged. He is the same yesterday, today and forever. So remember to look up to God during these times. He alone can help you and bring you radiant happiness.

    A farmer once caught a young eagle and placed it with his chickens. The eaglet ate with them and soon adapted itself to their ways. One day a naturalist visited the farmer. Seeing the eagle, he said, "That's not a chicken. That's an eagle." "That's right," said the farmer, "but he's no longer an eagle in his nature. He's a chicken now, for he eats chicken feed and does everything chickens do. He'll never fly again." "You're wrong," said the naturalist. "He's an eagle still, because he has the heart of an eagle." After making several unsuccessful efforts to get the eagle to fly, the naturalist carried the eagle to the foot of a high mountain just as the sun was rising. The instant the eagle got a vision of the rising sun, he uttered a wild scream of joy, stretched his wings, and mounted higher and higher into the sky—never to return to the farmyard. —TOLD BY WALTER B. KNIGHT[31]

    This is the day to get a glimpse of the Sun of righteousness who the Scriptures say shall rise with healing in His wings.

    You are an eagle today. Do not let anyone tell you that you are a chicken. The Bible likens you to an eagle. You may be weary, pecking around in the chicken pen, but it is time for you to fly. Isaiah 40:31 underlines this: "But they that wait upon the LORD shall renew their strength; they shall mount up with wings as

eagles; they shall run, and not be weary; and they shall walk, and not faint."

Wait on the Lord, look to Him, and fly!

January 28

"Give, and it shall be given unto you" (Luke 6:38).

When one is in financial trouble, the way to get out is to start giving God what is due Him. If you pay Him ten percent of all your income, He will teach you to profit and how to get out of debt.

A. A. Hyde, a millionaire and manufacturer, said he began tithing when he was one hundred thousand dollars in debt. Many men have said they considered it dishonest to give God a tenth of their incomes while they were in debt. Mr. Hyde said he agreed with the thought until one day it flashed upon him that God was his first creditor. Then he began paying God first, and all the other creditors were eventually paid in full. —THE SUNDAY SCHOOL TIMES[32]

It was W. L. Douglas, a shoe manufacturer, who became nationally known. From his early, struggling years comes this story. He had been unemployed so long that he was down to his last dollar. Nevertheless, he put half of it [fifty cents] in the collection plate at his church. Next morning he heard of a job in a neighboring town. The railroad fare to that town was one dollar. To all appearances it would have been wiser if he had kept the fifty cents. However, with the half dollar remaining he bought a ticket and rode halfway to the desired place. He stepped from the train and began to walk to the town. Before he had gone one block he heard of a factory right in that town where they were employing men. Within thirty minutes he had a job at a salary five dollars more a week than he would have received had he gone on to the other town. —ARTHUR TONNE[33]

When W. L. Douglas gave money to the Lord, he invested in the best bank that keeps good records.

"Charlie Page was a young man, broke, penniless and jobless. One day he stopped on the street to listen to a Salvation Army service. When the tambourine was passed around for the collection, he told the girl who held it out before him that he would like to give something but had nothing himself, even for his food. She gave him a dollar saying, 'Take this: put ten cents in the offering, and hereafter give a tenth of all you get to God. Keep this up all your life, and you'll never be penniless again.' He did so, got a job, and began giving his tenth regularly. By and by he became a millionaire and gave much more than a tenth, building hospitals and helping in many ways to carry on the work of the Lord." —A. NAISMITH[34]

Consider the Lord today, do it His way and He will prosper and bless you and pour out His blessings upon you.

January 29

"And the LORD shall guide thee continually" (Isaiah 58:11).

*S*omeone once said, *"God does not promise help before help is needed. He does not remove obstacles out of our way before we reach them. Yet when we are on the edge of our need, God's hand is stretched out."*

This is proven in the story told in Joshua 3:13 about the crossing of the river: "As soon as the soles of the feet of the priests shall rest in the waters the water shall be cut off."

The reason people become frustrated and fearful of difficulties and things that stand in their way is because they expect to see them removed before they pass through them. The answer is to move straight ahead by faith, in the way the Lord leads. He will make a way where there seems to be no way.

It was Dr. George Washington Carver who wrote the following: *"There is no need for anyone to be without direction in the midst of the perplexities of this life. Are we not plainly told, 'In all thy ways acknowledge him, and he shall direct thy path'?"* Dr. Carver's custom was to arise every day at four A.M. and seek God's guidance for his life. In speaking of the blessings of those early morning hours, he said, "At no other time have I so sharp an understanding of what God means to do with me as in those hours when other folks are still asleep. Then I hear God best and learn His plan!" —WALTER B. KNIGHT[35]

That is the best way to find God's plan. Early in the morning when the day is fresh, just talk to Him and listen for His voice. When God speaks, it is time to move even if the waters are not parted. Walk anyway, and as you walk, the waters will part.

F. B. Meyer tells of being on a ship crossing the Irish Channel one starless night, standing on the deck by the captain, asking him, "How do you know Holyhead Harbor on so dark a night as this?" He said, "You see those three lights? All of them must line up together as one, and when we see them so united, we know the exact position of the harbor's mouth." Dr. Meyer continued to say, "When we want to know God's will there are three things which always concur: the inward impulse, the Word of God, and the trend of circumstances—God in the heart and God in circumstances, indicating His will. These three things will agree."[36]

God will guide and instruct you, and when He speaks, go forward and faint not. He will be with you and lead you safely even in the darkest night, for He is the Captain of your life.

January 30

"Now thanks be unto God, which always causeth us to triumph in Christ" (II Corinthians 2:14).

God gets His greatest victories out of apparent defeats. The enemy may seem to triumph for a short while, but God comes in with great victory and defeats the work of the enemy.

"Years ago, in a certain city of Texas visited by crusader Frances E. Willard, there was also the leader of the saloon interests who boasted in a public speech: 'We are bound to win. We have the drinking men on our side; we have the foreigners on our side; we have money on our side—and money is a power, and don't you forget it.'

"The following evening in the same city Frances Willard closed an eloquent public appeal for the home with these words: 'We are bound to win. We have the sober men on our side; we have the women on our side; we have God on our side—and God is a power, and don't you forget it.'" —*LIVING CHURCH*[37]

The truth of the matter is that God has all power in heaven and earth and He will defeat all the enemies in time. With God on your side you will triumph. The gates of hell shall not triumph or

prevail against the church and you are the church if you house His Spirit within you.

Stand up and march forward! Be not afraid, no matter what you face, for God is with you.

You'll find the road is long and rough,
with soft spots far apart,
Where only those can make the grade
that have the Uphill Heart.
And when things stop you with a thud or jolt,
Let Courage call the signals as you keep on coming back.
For when the One Great Scorer comes,
He will write about how you played the game.
—GRANTLAND RICE

How are you playing the game of life? How are you taking the blows of the enemy? Has he got you backed into a corner, afraid, and cowered down? If so, break out of that corner, saying as little David said to Goliath, "I come to you in the name of the Lord."

Remember it is "Not by might, nor by power, but by my spirit, saith the LORD" (Zechariah 4:6). With God on your side, you will win, for God never loses, so play the game well—with all your heart, soul, mind and strength. Let courage and faith be your partners as you climb the hill of difficulty.

This is the day to never give up, but keep forging ahead in spite of the temporary setbacks. Victory is ahead!

January 31

"But rejoice, inasmuch as ye are partakers of Christ's sufferings; that, when his glory shall be revealed, ye may be glad also with exceeding joy" (I Peter 4:13).

"Obstacles ought to set us singing. The wind finds voice, not when rushing across the open sea, but when hindered by the outstretched arms of the pine trees." —MRS. CHARLES COWMAN[38]

It was an obstacle that set Paul's pen in motion and became a

place of inspiration. The obstacle of prison became a prism of light to a darkened world.

It was an obstacle that thrust Joseph to the throne. The dark prison was where he met the baker and the butler of the king. It was the butler who remembered Joseph two years later when the king had a dream which he could not interpret. Because of the prison he was able to go to the palace.

Obstacles were what caused many beautiful songs to be written through the ages. The story of just such one is that of Charles Wesley, who was conducting one of his many open-air meetings in Ireland. During the course of his preaching, a number of men who took exception to his views assaulted him. Unable to withstand the mob, Wesley fled for his life. He took refuge in a farmhouse nearby. Jane Moore, a kindhearted wife of a farmer, hid the panting evangelist in the milk house. She was barely in time, because at that moment some of Wesley's assailants rushed up.

Mrs. Moore tried to divert their attention by preparing refreshments. Fearful that they might search the premises and discover the evangelist, she went to the milk house on the pretext of getting a cold drink for her visitors.

"Quickly," she bade him, "get through the rear window, and hide under the hedge." He clambered through the window and found a little brook flowing beside the hedge, forming a pool with overhanging branches that afforded a pleasant and safe retreat.

While waiting for the angry Irishmen to leave, Wesley pulled a pencil and paper from his pocket and wrote the words to "Jesus, Lover of My Soul." —E. H. JORDAN[39]

When obstacles come, remember that is the time to sing, to write, to glorify the Lord, to make music unto Him, for a song unto the Lord is precious to Him.

There was once a preacher who said to an aged brother who never had much of this world's goods, "You gave the Lord two hundred dollars this morning." The brother answered, "I don't have it to give."

"I heard you singing," replied the preacher. "I counted five hymns of praise to the Lord. The psalmist said in Psalm 69:30-31 that a song of praise would please the Lord more than an ox. A cow would be worth at least forty dollars. So you have given the Lord two hundred dollars."[40]

This is the day to give of yourself in praise and thanksgiving even when obstacles surround you. For remember the wind finds voice, not when rushing across the open sea, but when hindered by the outstretched arms of the pine trees. As hindering forces stretch across your pathway, let your life sing unto the Lord His great and mighty praises, for He does all things well.

February 1

"And all things, whatsoever ye shall ask in prayer, believing, ye shall receive" (Matthew 21:22).

Matthew 15:23 gives an eloquent statement: "He answered her not a word." *"The silences of Jesus are as eloquent as His speech and may be a sign, not of His disapproval, but of His approval and of a deep purpose of blessing for you."* —Mrs. Charles Cowman

The story surrounding this verse is about a woman coming to Jesus for the healing and deliverance of her daughter. Maybe Jesus was so stunned by her great faith that He just did not say anything.

What is the Lord hearing you say today? Does He see your faith as He did with the little woman who was so desperate: a woman who would not take "no" for an answer, neither would she be ignored; she just would not let go, but kept following Jesus and talking to Him, knowing in her heart, that she would receive her answer? Jesus said about this persistent faith, "O woman, great is thy faith: be it unto thee even as thou wilt."

It is like the story of John W. Knight, an old circuit rider many years ago. A destroying drought had cast its shadow across the countryside. Crops were withering and lying in the parched fields. John Knight along with others made their way to the little Crawford Church in Putnam County, Georgia, to pray for rain, but John Knight was the only who took an umbrella with him to the prayer meeting. On bended knees the old man began to pray, "O Lord, we need rain. O Lord, we need much rain. O Lord we don't want any drizzly-drazzly rain, we want a gully-washer!" God honored the simple faith of the old circuit rider with the umbrella and sent a gully-washer just as he had requested.

The following poem speaks the heartthrob of desire for such faith:

O for a faith that will not shrink,
Tho' pressed by every foe.
That will not tremble on the brink
Of any earthly woe!
That will not murmur nor complain
Beneath the chastening rod
But in the hour of grief and pain
Will lean upon its God;
A faith that shines more bright and clear
When tempests rage without,
That when in danger knows no fear,
In darkness feels no doubt.
—William Bathurst[41]

God hears and listens not only to words spoken, but He sees the faith and belief of the heart. This is the day to pray for and seek to acquire the faith that will not let go: a faith that will bring it to pass through the power of Christ.

February 2

"My God hath sent his angel, and hath shut the lions' mouths, that they have not hurt me" (Daniel 6:22).

*T*rue faith leans on God and believes before it sees. When we walk by faith we need no other evidence than God's Word. It has been written, "Never put a question mark where God has put a period."

Elton Trueblood said, "*Faith is not belief without proof, but it is trust without reservations.*" This is the day to have no reservations about God, but to believe in Him and His Word, for it is without question the inspired Word of God.

There is a sermon that is preached every October 16th at a church in London. It is called the "Lion Sermon." The story is told how once a very pious man called Sir John Gayer, who served as Lord Mayor of London, happened to be in Asia at one period of his life. He was traveling through a desert place and found himself

alone face to face with a lion. Everybody of his company who could have helped him had gone on ahead. Sir John knew that only God could help deliver him. He thought of Daniel in the den of lions, and fell on his knees there before the beast and shut his eyes and cried to God to shut the mouth of the lion. When he had finished his prayer and opened his eyes, the lion was nowhere to be seen. So when he came back to London he set aside a sum of money to be given away in gifts to poor people every October 16th and secure that a sermon should be preached to tell the generations to come how God had heard his prayer and delivered him from the mouth of the lion.[42]

You can stake your life on the promises of God. They are true and will help you in the time of need. Just as the Lord Mayor of London exercised his faith, it is needful for us to exercise our faith when the lions of discouragement, defeat, despair, and trouble look us in the eye.

God can make them leave and go away. He can uplift, He can bring victory; He not only can, but He will be a present help in the time of trouble.

David wrote in Psalm 138:7, "Though I walk in the midst of trouble, thou wilt revive me: thou shalt stretch forth thine hand . . . and thy right hand shall save me."

You *can* trust God and His Word. He will save you and help you in the time of desperate need. It is in the Bible and can never be erased. It is written forever, so believe it today.

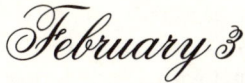

"And he shall bring it to pass" (Psalm 37:5).

*I*t is impossible for the Lord to fight our battles for us when we insist upon trying to fight them ourselves.

A young man, who was struggling to let the Lord have His way in his life, knelt to pray. He had been advised to "Let God do the work for him." But as he was kneeling he cried, "I want to let God have His way, but I can't."

The day before he had cut out of pasteboard the letters, LET GOD and tacked them on the wall. He rose from his knees and

with a feeling of defeat and despair he left the room and slammed the door with a bang, saying, "I can't Let God."

On his return to his room, he was startled to note that the slam of the door had loosened the letter D on the word *God* causing it to fall to the floor, and changing the motto to LET GO.

"I will, I will, Lord Jesus," he cried and threw himself on his knees at the side of his bed. "I will LET GO, and LET GOD." —*GOSPEL FOR THE YOUTH*[43]

J. H. McConkey once asked a physician friend: "Doctor, what is the exact significance of God's touching Jacob upon the sinew of his thigh?"

He replied, "The sinew of the thigh is the strongest in the human body. A horse could scarcely tear it apart." *God has to break us down at the strongest part of our self-life before He can have His own way of blessing with us.* —J. H. MCCONKEY[44]

This is the day to submit or let go and let God be God. He wants full control of the situation. He does not want to play tug of war with us. He wants us to relax and trust even in the storms of life.

Once there was a king named Jehoshaphat who was in much trouble, so much that he prayed a desperate prayer, saying in II Chronicles 20:12, "O our God, wilt thou not judge them? for we have no might against this great company that cometh against us; neither know we what to do: but our eyes are upon thee."

The enemy that had surrounded them also outnumbered them and could outfight them, but they could not outfight God.

God said in so many words, "Let Go and Let God." He said in II Chronicles 20:15, 17, "Be not afraid nor dismayed by reason of this great multitude; for the battle is not yours, but God's. Ye shall not need to fight in this battle: set yourselves, stand ye still, and see the salvation of the LORD with you . . . fear not, nor be dismayed; to morrow go out against them: for the LORD will be with you."

The day arrived and the army of Jehosaphat went out towards the enemy but instead of being tense and afraid, they were singing praises unto the Lord, saying, "Praise the LORD; for his mercy endureth for ever." And when they began to sing and to praise the Lord, then the Lord set ambushments against the enemy and the Lord caused Jehosaphat to win the battle.

This is what happens when you *let go* and Let GOD!

February 4

"Then they cry unto the LORD in their trouble, and he bringeth them out of their distresses" (Psalm 107:28).

Sometimes life brings great trouble. Psalm 107:27 describes the feeling of the person experiencing problems: "They reel to and fro, and stagger like a drunken man, and are at their wits' end." But there is a God who can bring you out! Do not be discouraged, for as someone has said, "It may be the last key in the bunch that opens the door."

We've all seen someone at a door with a huge ring of keys, patiently trying each one to see which one fit. Finally the right key went in and the door was opened. When you have tried everything and feel like nothing works, just hang in there; a key will fit sooner or later. Don't try to figure everything out, but let each day be a day of trust.

> *He does not lead me year by year*
> *Nor even day by day*
> *But step by step my path unfolds;*
> *My Lord directs my way.*
> *Tomorrow's plans I do not know,*
> *I only know this minute;*
> *But He will say, "This is the way.*
> *By faith now walk in it."*
> *And I am glad that it is so,*
> *Today's enough to bear;*
> *And when tomorrow comes,*
> *His grace shall far exceed its care.*
> *What need to worry then, or fret?*
> *The God who gave His Son*
> *Holds all my moments in His hand*
> *And gives them, one by one.*
> —BARBARA C. RYBERG[45]

One minute at a time, that is all He expects you to do. You can trust one minute at a time. Even at your wits' end, trust God each moment at a time. Don't try to figure the whole thing out. Just say,

"God, You're in charge; I will trust You as a child, believing that You do all things well. All things are in Your hands. I will live each moment knowing that You care and are working things out according to Your will."

Life becomes an adventure when He takes charge of the controls. It is like Him sitting with you while you are riding a roller coaster—up and down—take your breath away—scream, panic, fear, then laughter, another scream—recklessly around the track He steers the little cage you are in. With Him at the controls you are going to come to the end of it safe and sound and everything will be all right. With Him on board all is well.

February 5

"When thou passest through the waters, I will be with thee" (Isaiah 43:2).

*B*elieve not only if the circumstances are favorable, but believe even when they are not.

Sir John Franklin lived an exciting life of adventure in the British Navy, which took him to many parts of the world. As a signal midshipman in the Battle of Trafalgar, he transmitted the memorable message from the flagship, "England expects every man to do his duty." He was a devout Christian and found great strength in reading the Bible. His men said they would rather have him hold a service than most ministers.

After living a long life, his last command was given in 1845. He was to command two ships to look for a passage across the polar seas. Many expeditions were made in the next ten years to learn the fate of Sir John Franklin's ships. Pieces of equipment found on beaches told of shipwreck in the ice seas. One of the books washed ashore was Sir John's Bible with the following verses underlined: Psalm 139:9, 10. "If I take the wings of the morning, and dwell in the uttermost parts of the sea; even there shall thy hand lead me, and thy right hand shall hold me." Isaiah 43:1, 2. "Fear not: . . . When thou passest through the waters, I will be with thee; and through the rivers, they shall not overflow thee."

He lived by these scriptures for many years and when it was time for him to go home, he died by these scriptures.

Jesus said to Peter, "But I have prayed for thee, that thy faith fail not" (Luke 22:32). There is a chance that people can lose their faith when things get tough. The main thing is when you do not understand just hold to the Master's hand, for He never makes any mistakes. Job said in his trouble, "Though he [God] slay me, yet will I trust in him" (Job 13:15). The possibility was there, but Job said in so many words, "If my body dies, my faith will not die." This mortal life is smaller than a grain of sand in comparison to the life which we will live forever.

Trust in the Lord when the going gets rough, for if you keep your faith in God, no matter what happens it will be good. Romans 8:28 states: "And we know that all things work together for good to them that love God, to them who are the called according to his purpose." His purposes and ways are higher than ours but you can rest assured that when you pass through the waters, the Lord shall be with you and lead you to higher ground.

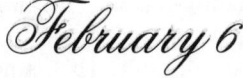

"And his chains fell off" (Acts 12:7).

Difficulty is the very atmosphere and the first stage of a miracle. There had to be a man in prison for an angel to deliver him. Acts 12:7 states: "The angel of the Lord came upon him, and a light shined in the prison: and he smote Peter on the side, and raised him up, saying, Arise up quickly. And his chains fell off."

For the miracle of the chains to fall off, there must first be the initial chaining. Before there was a miracle there was first a difficulty. Oftentimes the sea of life gets very tumultuous and rocks back and forth with disaster.

If your little boat is tossing on the sea of life, rest in the Lord. It is not always easy to rest in the Lord, when the waves are bigger than your head and you are surrounded by storm clouds that threaten your very existence. When it seems like there is no hope, it is time to pray and then rest in God for He will take care of those waves. The key is to not give up on Him.

Years ago the English steamship *Stella* was wrecked on a rocky coast. Twelve women put into a lifeboat, but the boisterous sea immediately carried it away. Having no oars, they were at the mercy of the winds and the waves, and they spent a fearful night being tossed about by the raging tempest.

They probably would have lost hope if it had not been for the spiritual stamina of one of the ladies, Margaret Williams, who was well known for her work in sacred oratorios. Calmly she prayed aloud for divine protection. Then, urging her companions to put their trust in the Lord, she encouraged them by singing hymns of comfort.

Throughout the dark hours her voice rang out across the water. Early the next morning a small craft came searching for survivors. The man at the helm would have missed the women in the fog if he had not heard Miss Williams singing the selection from *Elijah*: "Oh, rest in the Lord, wait patiently for Him!" Steering in the direction of her strong voice, he soon spotted the drifting lifeboat. While many others were lost that night, these trusting few were rescued. —Henry G. Bosch[46]

David sang this song in Psalm 37:5, 7: "Commit thy way unto the Lord; trust also in him; and he shall bring it to pass. Rest in the Lord, and wait patiently for him: fret not thyself."

Are you fretting today about things that are insurmountable and totally impossible to work out? That is normal, but Jesus came so we could live above the human system of failure. He brought newness to life, abundant living, and victory. Greater is His Spirit that is inside of us than all the things that surround us. He is bigger than all the waves, no matter how tall they are. When you are in a life-threatening situation, pray all you can, then rest in the Lord and wait patiently for Him, and while you are waiting instead of fretting, start singing a little song.

"For the former things are passed away" (Revelation 21:4).

Look up! Have hope! There is coming a day not very far away that is spoken of in Revelation 21:4, "And God shall wipe away all

tears from their eyes; and there shall be no more death, neither sorrow, nor crying, neither shall there be any more pain."

This is the day to make plans to go to that place which is called heaven. It will have twelve gates of pearl, streets will be of gold, walls will be of jasper, and the foundations will be garnished with jasper, sapphire, emerald, topaz, and many other jewels. There will be no electricity that can be turned off by storms, for the Lord Jesus will be the light. You will have a new body, one that will never die. Mortals will put on immortality. It is the most important thing in life for which to plan. You will not want to miss going to this city. Life may be tough, but it is only for a moment compared to eternity.

An aged minister was lost on an unpaved, unmarked road in west Texas. He went to a farmhouse to inquire as to how he could reach his destination. A little freckle-faced boy gave the following directions: "Go right on down the big road for several miles. It is plenty sandy and rough. Sometimes you will bog down and get stuck, but keep going until you come to a graveyard. Go right through the graveyard and just on the other side you will come to a paved highway. Turn to the right and the place you are looking for is just around the corner. When you get to the paved road beyond the graveyard, your troubles will be over!"

The old minister thought as he rode along: "I am traveling down the rough road of life. Sometimes it seems that I almost bog down. After I travel life's road for a few more miles, I will come to the graveyard, and then my troubles will all be over, for God's highway and the heavenly home are just the other side of the cemetery."

A BUILDING IN HEAVEN

I've purchased a town lot in heaven
On the city not built with hands
I'm sending material daily to build in that happy land.
I'd like a mansion on Main street,
Where streets are all paved with gold
With a clear view of the pearly gates
Where Christ takes care of the soul.
I want to send good material
That will stand the test of time.
So I'll not be disappointed

When I reach that home sublime.
Prayer is for the foundation,
Faith and love for the walls,
Good deeds for the reinforcement
That will stand when the Savior calls.
By grace we'll enter that City
Washed by the blood of the Lamb who to earth came,
Salvation is free for those,
Who are willing to bear His wonderful name.
Up there we will never know sorrow,
Tears will never dim the eyes,
There we will rest in peace forever
In that happy home on high.
So my friends, start to building
Your home beyond the sky
Where we can all be together
In the sweet by and by.
—AUTHOR UNKNOWN[47]

February 8

"*The fear of the* LORD *prolongeth days*" (Proverbs 10:27).

This happened literally to some Scottish soldiers who were cut off from their company while in fierce engagement with the enemy during World War II. They hid in the loft of an empty house. Death seemed to be inevitable. The Germans were setting fire to surrounding homes and buildings. Nearer and nearer they came to the hiding place of the Scottish lads. Said one of them, "It's time for church, partners. Let's have a wee bit of service here. It may be our last!" He took a New Testament from his pocket and after reading some verses, he said, "I'm not a good hand at this job, but let us finish it off with prayer." After a pause, he began to read reverently and feelingly: "Our Father which art in heaven, Hallowed be thy name." About midway the prayer, they heard a click of heels. They knew the Germans were below, standing reverently at attention! After the prayer, the Scottish lads heard the

door close silently and the sounds of footsteps dying away. —Told by Walter B. Knight[48]

The reverence for God created an atmosphere in which hatred vanished. This is the day to reverence God.

British statesman, W. E. Gladstone, who often served as Prime Minister between 1866 and 1894, once sat in Christ's Church College and talked at some length about happy changes he had witnessed during his lifetime in the lot of the English people. His outlook was so radiantly optimistic that it aroused a challenge. One of the students said, "Sir, are we to understand that you have no anxieties for the future? Are there no adverse signs?" The grand old man of England answered slowly, "Yes, there is one thing that frightens me—the fear that God seems to be dying out in the minds of men."

Hebrews 12:28 instructs us to serve God acceptably with reverence and godly fear.

Proverbs 1:7 says: "The fear of the Lord is the beginning of knowledge."

Proverbs 3:7-8 declares: "Be not wise in thine own eyes: fear the Lord, and depart from evil. It shall be health to thy navel, and marrow to thy bones."

Ecclesiastes 12:13 concludes it well, "Let us hear the conclusion of the whole matter: Fear God, and keep his commandments: for this is the whole duty of man."

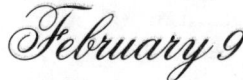

"I will praise the name of God with a song" (Psalm 69:30).

*T*rials are not to harm you but to make you strong. I Peter 5:10 says, "But the God of all grace, who hath called us unto his eternal glory by Christ Jesus, after that ye have suffered a while, make you perfect, stablish, strengthen, settle you."

One of God's children was passing through the dark waters of sorrow and suffering. "God has forgotten to be gracious to me. I don't understand His judgments," he said. The pastor came to see him. He found him in the back yard, pruning a grapevine of its superfluous twigs and branches. "It is necessary to remove them

so the vine can bring better fruit to maturity." "Does this vine resist and oppose you?" asked the pastor. "Of course not," he said. "Then why should you complain about the chastening hand of God when He does for you what you have done to this vine?" asked the pastor. —Told by Walter B. Knight[49]

"There are two ways of getting out of a trial. One is simply to try to get rid of the trial, and be thankful when it is over. The other is to recognize the trial as a challenge from God to claim a larger blessing than we have ever had, and to hail it with delight as an opportunity of obtaining a larger measure of divine grace." —A. B. Simpson[50]

How are you looking at your trials? Are you seeing them as opportunities to grow or as a heavy weight you can't wait to get rid of?

You never know what God is working out for the good of many. Just as it was said about Joseph during his trial, "Ye meant it unto me evil, but God meant it unto good so that many people could be saved."

When Adoniram Judson was dying, news came to him that some Jews in Turkey had been converted through reading the account of his sufferings in Burma. "This awes me," said Judson to his wife. "This is good news. When I was a young man, I prayed for the Lord to send me to the Jews in Jerusalem as a missionary. But He sent me to Burma to preach and to suffer the tortures of imprisonment. Now because of my sufferings, God has brought some Jews in Turkey to repentance."[51]

This is the day to learn to walk through trials with integrity and grace, to learn of the Lord and become strong. And remember that the brook would lose its song if the rocks were removed and that difficulties can strengthen the mind and spirit if allowed to. So walk today with your hand in the Master's hand and let Him lead you to great things and sing during your trial, and then you will truly know victory.

February 10

"I am come that they might have life" (John 10:10).

There is saving power in Jesus Christ! Al Bryant tells the story about what happened at an open-air gospel meeting where the preacher had asked for testimonies. While this was going on a skeptic was passing by just when the testimony of a saved drunkard was being given. He stopped and listened. The former drunkard was telling how Jesus had wrought a miracle and saved his poor soul.

The skeptic scoffing made a few remarks to those standing near him. He said, "It was nothing more than a dream, religion saving a man in this manner; just a mere dream, and nothing more." No one answered him, but God had his way of dealing with him.

Among the listeners was a little girl about ten years old. She had known the misery of a drunkard's home. She heard the remark of the skeptic and, going up to him, she said, "Please, sir, if it is only a dream, please don't wake him—that is my daddy!"

It is more than a dream; it is a reality. Jesus said in John 3:16: "For God so loved the world, that he gave his only begotten Son, that whosoever believeth in him should not perish, but have everlasting life."

This same salvation power was manifested during one of the wars. The fading sound of "Taps" seemed to echo in a lieutenant's ears. As he sat wearily on his cot, an irresistible urge came upon him that he should go to see his colonel to speak to him about his soul. "It would result only in a reprimand and possibly court-martial to wander about the camp after 'Taps,'" he reasoned as he tried to throw off the feeling. Still the urge persisted. A few minutes later, the lieutenant stood trembling before the barracks where the colonel stayed. "What are you doing here?" the colonel asked. Falteringly the lieutenant told him of the irresistible urge he felt to come to talk to him about the Lord Jesus Christ. Without saying a word, the colonel opened a drawer and took out a revolver. Then he said to the lieutenant: "If you had knocked at my door five minutes later, I couldn't have answered your call. I was about to take my life when you interrupted me. What you have said gives me hope. Come again tomorrow and tell me more about your Christ!" Then he added, "No, I won't use the pistol." —Told by Walter B. Knight[52]

The following morning they both knelt in prayer and the colonel felt a cleansing of his soul.

Wherever you are today, whatever you are doing, come to Jesus Christ and make Him a part of your life, and you will be cleansed, renewed and have abundant life. Jesus said, "I am come that [ye] might have life, and that . . . more abundantly."

February 11

"Be careful for nothing" (Philippians 4:6).

This means not to worry, but to trust God for the answer. Someone once said, *"Worry is the advance interest you pay on troubles that seldom come."*

"Worry, like a rocking chair, will give you something to do, but it won't get you anywhere." —Vance Havner

"What does your anxiety do? It does not empty tomorrow of its sorrow, but it empties today of its strength. It does not make you escape the evil—it makes you unfit to cope with it if it comes." —Maclaren

"The beginning of anxiety is the end of faith. The beginning of true faith is the end of anxiety." —George Mueller

Though all the world be troubled,
And men's hearts faint with fear
At the danger in the distance
And dangers drawing near;
Though every help should fail them
On which their hopes are stayed,
"Let not your heart be troubled,
Nor let it be afraid."

Though all the earth be troubled,
And its foundations shake.
Though raging seas shall thunder,
And mighty mountains quake;
Though lofty walls shall crumble,
And in the dust be laid,
"Let not your heart be troubled,
Nor let it be afraid."

Though all your way be troubled,
And bounds and landmarks lost,
Though on the stormy billows
Your little bark be tossed,
Though all around be changing,
Here let your mind be stayed,
"Let not your heart be troubled,
Nor let it be afraid."
—ANNIE JOHNSON FLINT

Worry is like the couple who started off on a ride to see a friend. The morning was pleasant, and they enjoyed themselves until they happened to remember a certain bridge which was very old and probably unsafe. "I shall never dare to go over that bridge," exclaimed the wife, "and we can't get across the river any other way!" "Oh," said the man, "I forgot that bridge. It is a bad place; suppose it should break through and we should fall into the water and be drowned!" "Or," said the woman, adding to his complaint, "suppose you should step on a rotten plank and break your leg; what would become of me and the baby?" "I don't know," responded the husband, "what would become of any of us, for I couldn't work, and we should all starve to death!"

So the negative worried talk ran on until they reached the spot where the old bridge had stood—and lo, they discovered that since they had been there it had been replaced with a new one! All their anxiety had been useless.

This is the day to quit talking about all the "ifs" and worrying about everything that is facing you, and start talking about the goodness of God and believe that He will do a miracle in your life. He will take care of you if you trust in Him.

February 12

"For a dream cometh through the multitude of business" (Ecclesiastes 5:3).

*T*his is not the day to quit. You can make it! Just don't give up too easily. The old saying, "Try and try again," is not an empty

statement. The first attempt of David Livingstone to preach ended in failure. "Friends, I have forgotten all I had to say," he gasped and in shame stepped from the pulpit! At that moment, Robert Moffat, who was visiting Edinburgh, advised David not to give up. Perhaps he could be a doctor instead of a preacher, he advised. Livingstone decided to be both. When the years of medical study were done, he went to Africa.

Napoleon was number forty-two in his class. Wonder who the forty-one were ahead of him? Sir Isaac Newton was next to the lowest in his class. He failed in geometry because he didn't do his problems according to the book. Oliver Goldsmith was at the bottom of his class before he succeeded.

A six-year-old came home from school one day with a note from his teacher in which it was suggested that he be taken out of school as he was too dumb to learn. His name: Thomas Edison.

It was also a fact that Dr. Wernher von Braun, the missile and satellite expert, flunked math and physics in his early teens. Failure means nothing more than getting up and trying again. The tragedy in life is not that someone would fall down or fail, but that they would stay down when they fell or stop trying on the first, second, or third round.

What if Moses would have given up when he was defeated by the frogs? Frogs in the toilet, frogs in the well, frogs in the bed, frogs in the food, frogs in the clothing, frogs in the water pitchers; there were frogs, frogs and more frogs!

Moses just kept going back. Oh yes, he faced defeat! There were many things that would have caused some men to give up, but not Moses. He was on a mission and there was nothing that could stop him. He finally won when God took a hand in things.

This is what happens. God watches the persistence, faithfulness, and determination of a person and sees if they are big enough to handle what he or she is trying to do. If they are, God will step in and do the thing that will cause success to come.

This is no time to let go of your dream, for dreams come to pass when there is enough work, persistence, prayer and courage to just bore on through every obstacle and hindering force.

Ecclesiastes 5:3 says, "For a dream cometh through the multitude of business." It is time to work, plan and go forward. Don't sit down and die but live, create, and become that person God planned for you to be.

February 13

"The thief cometh not, but for to steal, and to kill, and to destroy" (John 10:10).

Who are you listening to today? There is the voice of doom, voice of deceit, or a voice of hope that is calling to you today. It is a fact that the voice of Satan is a voice of doom and destruction. He comes to kill, steal and destroy, and since he is a liar, he will constantly feed thoughts into your mind to depress or lower your spirits. He is a killer of dreams, a conniver who seeks to demolish everything that is good. He wants people to be down in their spirits and he will pit one person against another. Sometimes he will seek to demoralize a whole town. He tried to do that in 1928 to the inhabitants of Robin Hood's Bay, a village that had eight hundred people in it and was situated on the east coast of England.

There were hundreds of poison-pen letters that were written to different people of that community. As each recipient thought he was the only person being attacked, few if any mentioned the letters until 1948 when it was learned that nearly every villager had received a number of them. All the letters had been abusive and vulgar without justification. They accused the persons of offenses and crimes, including prostitution, incest and other terrible things.

For more than two decades those notes were allowed to spread great unhappiness and even caused three successive ministers of the town's one church to resign and move away. Yet the identity of the writer of the malicious letter was unknown. Satan has agents to do his dirty work but you do not have to succumb to his lies. The Bible says in James 4:7 to resist the devil and he will flee—that means run very quickly. It is when you allow those evil thoughts to reside awhile and then take root and find lodging in your heart that the damage is done.

David said, "Let the words of my mouth, and the meditation of my heart, be acceptable in thy sight, O Lord." It is time to put away from you those distressing evil thoughts, accusations and depressions and let the freshness of God's Word blow a breath of fresh air across a stale mind.

You will be surrounded by things that can distress you, you

will face things that will literally take your breath away, and life can be filled with things and people who are not in touch with God; therefore they will live in the carnal mind and to be carnally minded is death.

Your job is to walk in the Spirit as Romans 8 states, for that is where true life is found. It is time to let the Lord God be your shield and buckler, stand up and listen to the voice of the commander Jesus Christ, for His voice will always bring victory. Do not be destroyed or defeated but *will* yourself to win and go forward in God. You are a winner in Him!

February 14

"And thou shalt love the Lord thy God with all thy heart" (Mark 12:30).

Dr. Howard W. Pope once told the story about a young lady who read a certain book and having completed it, remarked that it was the dullest book she had ever read. Not long after this, she met a certain young man. In the course of time their friendship ripened into love, and they became engaged. During a visit in the home of his fiancée one evening, she said to him, "I have a book in my library which was written by a man whose name and even initials are the same as yours. Is not that a singular coincidence?" "I do not think so," he replied. "Why not?" she asked.

He answered, "For the simple reason that I wrote the book." That night the young lady sat up until the early morning hours to read the book again. When she had completed it, she thought it the most interesting book she had ever read! She now knew and loved the author. —AL BRYANT[53]

The question is, "How well do you know and love the author of the good book—the Bible?" Does it thrill you, or is it boring? Does it bring light to you, or is it dull and uninteresting? The key is falling in love with the author. There was only one author, but many writers. Men of old were moved on by the holy inspiration of God Almighty and wrote as He gave them knowledge and direction. It is not just man's word, it is God's word—undisputable, powerful, and forever settled in heaven.

Isaiah 40:8 says, "The grass withereth, the flower fadeth: but the word of our God shall stand for ever."

It was President Herbert Hoover who said, "The whole of the inspiration of our civilization springs from the teachings of Christ and the lessons of the Prophets. To read the Bible for these fundamentals is a necessity of American life." President Eisenhower also found the Bible to be inspirational. He said, "To read the Bible is to take a trip to a fair land where the spirit is strengthened and faith renewed."[54]

This Book, the Bible, is habit forming. Someone once said regular use causes loss of anxiety, decreased appetite for lying, cheating, stealing, and hating. It increases sensations of love, peace, joy and compassion. It is the only book that will change your life completely and make you inherit eternal life with the Savior—and also make life worth living while on the road of temporal life.

As the young lady fell in love with the author and the book became exciting to her, it is time for each of us this day to fall in love with Jesus, our Lord and our God, and become enriched, inspired, and cleansed by the Book above all books. Put God in your schedule and He will put you in His schedule.

February 15

"The angel of the LORD encampeth round about them that fear him" (Psalm 34:7).

*T*his is the day to seek to do things well all the time, for you always have an audience. The story is told about the minister who worked long into the night on a sermon for his small congregation. His unsympathetic wife chided him for spending so much time on a message that so few would appreciate. To this the minister replied: "You forget, my dear, how large my audience will be!" If angels are looking, nothing on earth that is done for Christ is trivial.

All of us today are being observed right now by heavenly hosts and even more so by the Lord God as stated in II Chronicles 16:9: "For the eyes of the LORD run to and fro throughout the whole earth, to shew himself strong in the behalf of them

whose heart is perfect toward him."

If He is watching it is important to become more aware of our performance. This truth is brought home by the story of another minister, Dr. A. J. Gordon. While preparing his Sunday sermon, he was so tired that he fell asleep in his study. He dreamed that it was the next morning and he was standing behind the pulpit, and the church was packed. A stranger walked in and a deacon let him have his seat. The stranger was so commanding yet attentive, and Gordon found himself as if speaking to him alone. He decided to meet this stranger after church.

As the congregation filed out one by one, the pastor looked in vain for the stranger until everyone was gone. "Do you know him?" he asked the deacon. "Why yes, He is Jesus Christ." "Oh, how I wished I could have talked with Him," Pastor Gordon lamented.

"It is all right, pastor," assured the deacon. "He'll be back next Sunday."

Dr. Gordon awoke realizing in a new way that every time he preached and spoke about Christ that Christ was in the midst and heard every word that was spoken. This dream revived both pastor and church.[55] He started preaching with new power. He established "Salvation Centers" in Boston, gave great sums to missions, to the Jews, to the Chinese. He started a school to train missionaries. All this transpired because of a dream that was so real—it literally changed his life.

Let this day be the day that your life takes on new meaning. It is time to wake up and become aware that you always have an audience and you are being watched daily. This is not the time to live halfhearted and give in to shoddy living. It is the time to give your best to the King of kings. Give Him a performance that will bring a smile to His face. Bring out the best inside of you and live excellently and enjoy the fruits of excellence.

February 16

"Let all . . . anger . . . be put away from you" (Ephesians 4:31).

This is the day to put away anger. Ecclesiastes 7:9 states: "Anger resteth in the bosom of fools." A flash of anger can go through your mind, but if you allow it to *rest* there, that is when the damage is done. James C. Hefley says that the obvious symptoms of sudden anger are often red face, swollen neck veins, clenched fists and a stumbling for words. The angry person's vision may also be blurred, because anger clouds the visual centers of the brain.

Dr. Walter Cannon, pioneer researcher in psychosomatic medicine at Harvard University, describes the symptoms more precisely: "Respiration deepens; the heart beats more rapidly; the arterial pressure rises, the blood is shifted from the stomach and intestines to the heart, central nervous system, and the muscles; the processes of the alimentary canal cease; sugar is freed from the reserves in the liver; the spleen contracts and discharges its contents of concentrated corpuscles and adrenalin is secreted."
—JAMES C. HEFLEY[56]

Anger does all those things to the body which can cause a heart attack or other severe health problem. There is a high cost of anger.

C. E. Macartney says, "*Anger weakens a man. It puts him at a disadvantage in every undertaking in life. When Sinbad and his sailors landed on one of their tropical islands, they saw high up in the trees coconuts which could quench their thirst and satisfy their hunger. The coconuts were far above the reach of Sinbad and the sailors, but in the branches of the trees were the chattering apes. Sinbad and his men began to throw stones and sticks up at the apes. This enraged the monkeys and they began to seize the coconuts and hurl them down at the men on the ground. That was just what Sinbad and his men wanted. They got the apes angry so that the apes would gather their food for them. That is a good illustration of how by indulgence in anger we play into the hands of our foes.*"[57]

Paul admonished in Ephesians 4:31-32: "Let all bitterness, and wrath, and anger, and clamour, and evil speaking, be put away from you, with all malice: And be ye kind one to another, tenderhearted, forgiving one another, even as God for Christ's sake hath forgiven you."

Sometimes a word spoken in the anger of a moment is regretted for a lifetime. It is best to be slow to anger as stated in

Proverbs 15:18: "A wrathful man stirreth up strife: but he that is slow to anger appeaseth strife."

The following poem says it well:

I spoke a word in anger
To one who was my friend,
Like a knife it cut him deeply
A wound that was hard to mend.
That word, so thoughtlessly uttered,
I would we could both forget.
But its echo lives and memory gives
The recollection yet.
How many hearts are broken,
How many friends are lost?
By some unkind word spoken
Before we count the cost!
—C. A. LUFBURROW

Count the cost today. Is prolonged anger worth the agony it causes? Let it go. If you keep it resting inside of you it is like a rattlesnake that will poison you and you will die.

This is the day to put anger away from you and realize that there are greater things to think about, greater dreams to dream, than the wrongs and hurtful things people have done to you. If you have any anger, let it go, ask the Lord to help you get rid of it and then live in joy and peace because you were big enough to be bigger than your anger.

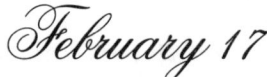
February 17

"*The little foxes, that spoil the vines*" (Song of Solomon 2:15).

The story is told of King Henry VIII of England. He sent a delegation to the Vatican to patch up the political differences between himself and the Pope. The delegation was led by the Earl of Wiltshire, who took along his dog. As was customary at that time, the earl prostrated himself before the Pope and was about to

kiss the Pope's toe. The Pope, willing to receive the homage, thrust his foot toward the earl, and his dog, watching, misunderstood the action and went to the defense of his master. Instead of a kiss, the Pope got a bite on the toe!

This enraged the Swiss Guard and they killed the dog. And this so angered the earl that he refused to proceed with the mission for which he had been sent—and he returned home without having accomplished anything. After his return to England, King Henry VIII took steps to separate England from the jurisdiction of Rome. All because of a dog bite. —*Christian Victory*[58]

There was another man and his wife who were out riding bicycles when a neighbor's dog reached up and bit him high up on the thigh. He said the neighbors were scared they were going to get sued. But the gentleman who had been bitten went and bought a box of candy and took it to the neighbor and said, "I want you to have this. I want to keep you as friends."

Most of the times in life it is a little thing that separates men and women from each other. Jesus said it's the little foxes that spoil the vines.

This is the day to be careful of not letting small, annoying, even hurtful experiences separate you from those you love. Learn to be bigger than the hurt. Many times it is not the actual hurt, but it is the pride involved. Pride was the ingredient that caused Lucifer to be thrown out of heaven. It is still the ingredient that will cause you to be thrown out of a good thing or a good relationship.

It was not the dog bite that caused the big ruckus between England and the Pope—it was the pride involved. The question is, "Are you letting a small thing separate you from someone whom you should not be separated from all because of pride?"

This is the day to be big enough to be humble and let the things go that will cause you more pain in the future. Do it God's way. "Humble yourself and He shall exalt you" is still true. Remember, when you follow the Holy Writ you always rise to a higher level.

February 18

"*The word of our God shall stand for ever*" (Isaiah 40:8).

If you are looking for how to find success today, you will find it in the Bible. "John Wanamaker, one of the country's greatest merchants, said, 'I have of course made large purchases of property in my lifetime . . . and the buildings and grounds in which we are now meeting represent a value of approximately twenty billion dollars.

"'But it was as a boy in the country, at eleven years of age, that I made my biggest purchase. In a little mission Sunday school, I bought from my teacher a small red leather Bible. The Bible cost me $2.75—which I paid in small installments as I saved. That was my greatest purchase, for that Bible made me what I am today.'"[59]

After that statement, the *New York Herald Tribune* captioned its write-up thus: "LATER DEALS IN MILLIONS CALLED SMALL COMPARED WITH BUYING HOLY WRIT AT ELEVEN."

John Wanamaker had it right. You can search the whole world over, but you will not find one thing that is more valuable than the Bible. It is the greatest piece of literature ever written. So closely is the Bible allied with the literature of the world that DeWitt Talmage wrote: *"Every great book that has been published since the first printing press was lifted, has directly or indirectly derived much of its power from the Sacred Oracles. Milton's* Paradise Lost *is borrowed from the Bible; Spencer's writings are imitations of the parables; John Bunyan saw in a dream what John had previously seen in a vision. Walter Scott's characters are Bible men and women under different names. Hobbs stole from this Castle of Truth, the weapons with which he afterward attacked it. The Bible is the fountain of truth from which other good books dip their life."* —HERALD OF HOLINESS[60]

Great writers down through the ages considered the Bible to be the greatest piece of literature ever written, and they were correct in their thinking. The Bible is not just another book. It is the inspired Word of God. It shall forever live. Isaiah 40:8 states: "The grass withereth, the flower fadeth: but the word of our God shall stand for ever."

It is time to not only write from the Word, but it is time to dip into it and learn how to live successfully, happily, peacefully and in triumph! There is no other book that will stand forever! There is no other book that has the power to save men and women. There is no other book that brings a fresh light and inspiration every day to the reader. It never gets old. Every day a new nugget is revealed and new life is infused into the brain. It is time to wake up and read the greatest book ever written, for in it is the way to true life, salvation and peace! Read the Bible and live.

February 19

"And the LORD opened the mouth of the ass, and she said unto Balaam . . ." (Numbers 22:28).

God uses many different people or things to get His message across. He used a donkey to talk to Balaam. He used a rooster's crow to talk to Peter. He used a drunken king to do an astronomical thing. It is reported that this particular king was a habitual drunkard and rumored to be addicted to other vices which could not be mentioned in public. As king of England he married off his children like pawns to suit his foreign policy. He drained the royal treasure to meet the cost of his extravagancies in wine and women.

He was described thus by J. R. Green: "His big head, his slobbering tongue, his goggle eyes, stood out as a grotesque contrast with all that men recalled of Henry and Elizabeth in his gabble, his want of personal dignity, his coarse buffoonery, his drunkenness, his contemptible cowardice."

Yet God in overruling providence used this man to assemble scholars and push through the Authorized Translation of the Bible in 1611—the most influential Bible of all times. His name: King James I.[61]

Who knows why God allowed this king to be instrumental in accomplishing such a great task? Everyone can speculate as to why. Reasons have been given that maybe the king felt so bad in his spirit about the way he was and the way he lived that he didn't want other people to be as miserable as he was down deep inside. He had heard enough truth from the Bible to know that if a person could follow its precepts he could be set free. Although he did not have the discipline or will to rise out of his lustful living, he may have thought, *This will help ease my conscience and my lifestyle if I help others find a better way of living than I myself am living.* Others have speculated that the king was the only man who had the clout and money to hire scholars to do such a large job and God put it in his heart to do so.

The question is, "If God can use a donkey, a rooster, or a drunken king who have not the Spirit of God within them to accomplish His purposes, what can He do through an individual who houses the Spirit of God within him?" There is no limit to what God can do with a surrendered vessel.

This is the day to live totally surrendered to the Lord God, giving yourself to the things that will count for eternity: things that will bless God and others. Let His Spirit flow through you today—don't bottle up the potential, but let it flow until it becomes a river of blessings to others. Do it today!

February 20

"*For the life of the flesh is in the blood*" (Leviticus 17:11).

As life in the natural is in the blood, so is life in the spiritual. There could never have been remission of sins and new life for any man or woman without Christ shedding His blood. Eternal life is attained because of Calvary.

G. Franklin Allee said: "*In the New Testament there are 200 references to the love of God, 290 times when God had declared His love for man. But in the same chapters and the same verses there are more than 1,300 references to the atonement, 1,300 assurances that salvation can be had through the blood of Jesus.*"

In the marketplace of Rotterdam, Holland, there stood for many years an old corner house known as "The House of a Thousand Terrors." During the sixteenth century, the Dutch people rose in revolt against the cruel King Philip II of Spain. Philip sent a great army under the Duke of Alva to suppress the rebellion. Rotterdam held out for a time but finally capitulated. From house to house the victors went, searching out citizens and then killing them in their houses. A group of men, women, and children were hiding in a corner house when they heard soldiers approaching. A thousand terrors gripped their hearts. Then a young man

had an idea. He took a goat in the house, killed it and with a broom swept the blood under the doorway out to the street. The soldiers reached the house and began to batter down the door. Noticing the blood coming out from under the door, one soldier said: "Come away, the work is already done here. Look at the blood beneath the door." And the people inside the house escaped.[62]

A similar thing happened during the reign of Pharaoh when Moses was seeking deliverance for the children of Israel. God told Moses to have the people kill a lamb and take the blood and put it on the doorpost of their home and when the death angel came that night to Egypt, the angel would pass by every house that had the blood applied.

Two thousand years ago, Jesus shed His blood so there could be freedom from and remission of sin. You do not have to kill a lamb or a goat or offer a sacrifice; all you have to do is to come to Jesus, who became the supreme sacrifice for the sins of mankind. Hebrews 9:22 says, "And almost all things are by the law purged with blood; and without shedding of blood is no remission."

The day of destruction will come, and the marching feet of doom are drawing near. This is the day to be sure you have the blood applied to your life by making the gospel of Jesus Christ a part of your life—accepting it with open arms and then you can rest assured that you will live eternally in joy, peace and ecstasy.

"The truth shall make you free" (John 8:32).

James Cash Penney's first venture as a retail proprietor, a butcher shop in Longmost, Colorado, opened in 1899 and failed almost immediately, after he refused to bribe an important local hotel chef with a weekly bottle of bourbon. "I lost everything I had," said Penney, "but I learned never to compromise."

Penney's unwavering faith in the copybook maxims of his youth roused skepticism in a mercenary age, but his credo underlay his success. At his death in 1971, Penney, ninety-five, left a 1,660-store empire that he built without compromising

the stiff principles he had absorbed from three generations of Baptist preacher ancestors. He neither smoked nor drank, and for years demanded the same abstemious conduct from his employees. "I believe in adherence to the Golden Rule, faith in God and the country," he often said. "I would rather be known as a Christian than a merchant." With annual sales of $4.1 billion, J. C. Penney today ranks as the nation's fifth merchandising company. Penney's personal holding of its stock was worth $24 million. Until his final illness, he worked regularly at Penney's mid-Manhattan headquarters, where he kept five secretaries busy with volumes of correspondence. —TIME[63]

We can learn from J. C. Penney today. To operate by Christian principles meant more to him than success. By operating according to the Golden Rule and biblical concepts great success came to him. He failed at first, but he would have failed more if he had not followed the right road in the beginning.

This is the day to stand true to your convictions, follow not the road of compromise, but stick to that which is right, because eventually truth will always triumph.

The following quotation is from the "Cadet Prayer" and is repeated every Sunday in chapel services at West Point: *"Make us choose the harder right instead of the easier wrong, and never to be contented with half truth when whole truth can be won. Endow us with courage that is born of loyalty to all that is noble and worthy, that scorns to compromise with vice and injustice and knows no fear when right and truth are in jeopardy."*[64]

This prayer needs to be repeated for those who desire the way of excellence and true success. Pray it with your children, pray it for your business, and pray it for yourself.

"But there is a spirit in man: and the inspiration of the Almighty giveth them understanding" (Job 32:8).

If you have an idea you think will work or an inspiration to do something good, don't be afraid to venture forth. Sometimes you must step out of the norm to make something happen.

F. W. Woolworth had a big idea. And it was an impatient employer who gave him the chance. Mr. Woolworth was instructed by his employer to gather some remnants from several shelves, make a job lot of them, and get what he could. He did, and then stuck a sign up offering any article for five cents. The rapidity with which the remnants disappeared at the bargain price gave Mr. Woolworth his idea for a five-and-ten-cent store.

The average man would not have seen any idea in the quick sale and would have forgotten the matter as soon as the remnants had been sold. Mr. Woolworth borrowed money to try out his idea, and although it failed to get across in several cities, he stuck to it until he had turned defeat into victory. As a result he accumulated a fortune of some forty million dollars. —E. M. WICKS[65]

All because he dared to take an idea that came to him which was different and make it work. *Woolworth* was not the only one who made a different idea work for him. *Wanamaker* conceived the idea of one price to everybody in his retail stores. That was different, for at the time he put this policy into effect it was directly contrary to accepted practice throughout the country. *Henry Ford* determined to build a light, cheap car for the millions. That was different. His reward came in the greatest automobile output in the world. —HERBERT V. PROCHNOW[66]

Human progress has often depended on the courage of someone who dared to be different. It is not to be different just to be different, but if an idea or inspiration comes to you about something that has not been done before or is different than the accepted norm, do not be afraid to venture forth and make it work.

This concept is shared over and over in the Scripture. God usually told His people to do things that were different. He told Moses to lead people through the Red Sea. If God says something, it will work no matter how different it looks to others. When Moses ventured forth, sure enough it worked because God was with him and had orchestrated the idea.

Jesus told the disciples to bring Him any food they could find amongst the five thousand people. They found a small boy's lunch. Jesus said that was all He needed to feed all the people. What an absurd idea! But it was not absurd with God. Sure enough one lunch fed all the people and they had twelve baskets of food left.

God wants to bring you into a higher level of thinking and production. He wants your thoughts to be in tune with His thoughts. There are miracles waiting for you. There are great

things still before you. Reach for them, step out and follow the inspiration of the Spirit of God. His ideas, inspiration and thoughts always work.

February 23

"If my people, which are called by my name, shall humble themselves, and pray . . . I . . . will heal their land" (II Chronicles 7:14).

*I*n February 1988, Debbie Danowski learned that her two-month-old son, Eric, had a rare and life-threatening disorder affecting his liver. Eight heartbreaking months later, Eric's condition had deteriorated so badly that the child was rushed to Pittsburgh's Children's Hospital, where on October 21 he underwent his first liver transplant. Eric was in a coma and was very frail and the doctors did not even know if he would make it through the transplant, but he did. That was only the beginning of Eric's ordeal, for the liver transplant was unsuccessful. Eric required a second operation in order to survive. His mother felt that something was very wrong and that he would continue to get worse even with another liver transplant. The nurses kept telling her she was wrong, but she had a strong feeling about it.

On March 3 her instincts proved to be correct. Eric underwent his second transplant and serious complications set in. Severe pneumonia struck Eric, coating the child's lungs with heavy mucous, slowly smothering him. Doctors told Debbie that 90 percent of transplant patients who contracted such a virus failed to survive.

Debbie decided to seek help that sidestepped traditional medicine. She visited the *Erie Daily Times* and pleaded with the editors to print a story asking people to pray for her baby boy. Reporter Jack Grazier responded to the young woman's plea. His article appeared in the paper's evening edition. The story began, "Debbie Danowski is asking for your prayers to help her baby live." The story ended with a reminder that Debbie was hoping readers could do for her child what medicine apparently could not: create a healing miracle.

The article ran on Friday. When Debbie arrived at the hospital the following day, she received some extraordinary news. Doctors excitedly told her that Eric's lungs were clearing, his fever had disappeared, and the child's vital signs had greatly improved. One doctor turned to her and said, "As of now, I would say that Eric has beaten the virus."

Eric was labeled the "miracle baby" and before he went home from the hospital had his third liver transplant. Debbie concludes, "Here's a child who had three liver transplants within ten months. He was close to death, in a coma, with two days to live at one point. I think it was the prayer groups who continued to pray for Eric that made his total recovery take place."

The reporter Jack Grazier, who had written the story for Debbie, wrote this after Eric came home from the hospital, "Was it a miracle caused by the power of prayer? I can't say. But I know that this child was dying, that doctors were doing a deathwatch, when people all over this town started praying. Should I ever be in such a life-threatening situation, I hope people put their prayers together for me."

The Scriptures are still true that say, "If my people will humble themselves and pray I will heal and I will answer their prayers." Choose this day to believe in the God who answers prayers.

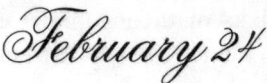

"*He that cometh to God must believe*" (Hebrews 11:6).

Many writers have called today an age of confusion and chaos. Things are not always clear. Where can someone go to find clear answers and positive direction? The only place that is without question is in the Word of God.

The story is told of how over one hundred years ago, William Ramsay, a young English scholar, went to Asia Minor with the expressed purpose of proving that the history given by Luke in his Gospel and in the Acts was inaccurate. His professors had confidently said that Luke could not be right. He began to dig in the ancient ruins of Greece and Asia Minor, testing for ancient terms,

boundaries, and other items which would be a dead giveaway if a writer had invented this history at a later date as claimed. To his amazement, he found that the New Testament Scriptures were accurate to the tiniest detail. So convincing was the evidence that Ramsay himself became a great biblical scholar. —*Science Returns to God*[67]

Sir William Ramsay's books are considered a classic as far as the history of the New Testament is concerned.

What better evidence than this—to prove the rightness of the Bible. If something written so long ago can be proven and verified thousands of years later, that is proof enough that it is not just a book put together by a group of men, but it is put together and authored by God Himself who used men to write what He inspired them to write.

Dr. Robert Dick Wilson, former professor at Princeton Theological Seminary, said, *"After forty-five years of scholarly research in biblical textual studies and in language study, I have come now to the conviction that no man knows enough to assail the truthfulness of the Old Testament. Where there is sufficient documentary evidence to make an investigation, the statements of the Bible, in the original text, have stood the test."*[68]

Dr. J. O. Kinnaman said, "Of the hundreds of thousands of artifacts found by the archaeologists, not one has ever been discovered that contradicts or denies one word, phrase, clause, or sentence of the Bible, but always confirms and verifies the facts of the Biblical record."[69]

In such shaky times, this is no time to argue the authenticity of the Bible, for there is no argument! Hebrews 11:6 says, "He that cometh to God must believe that he is, and that he is a rewarder of them that diligently seek him."

God is, His Word is, and they will always be! Anyone can doubt or argue until he is blue in the face, but his doubts or arguments will never change God or His Word. This is the day to put doubt aside, become a believer in God and reap the benefits that are promised in the irrefutable Word of God.

February 25

"Ask, and it shall be given you" (Matthew 7:7).

Sergeant Felix Jimenez of the Metro-Dade Police in Miami, Florida, wrote an article entitled "Search for the Black Box." The following story is excerpts taken from that story: "I sloshed through the steaming Everglades, desperately searching for a crucial piece of evidence that would help unlock a mystery. It was Sunday, May 26, 1996, fifteen days after ValuJet Flight 592 had crashed in the Florida Everglades, sending 110 passengers to their deaths. I was one of the many police investigating the crash scene. No one really knew what had caused the disaster. But it was believed that the black box, the cockpit voice recorder preserving the flight crew's final words, would provide vital information.

"It was imperative to find the cockpit voice recorder for the National Transportation Safety Board, who was anxiously waiting to study it. Yet, after two weeks of searching amid suffocating humidity under the fierce Florida sun, we had failed to locate it. As I worked I wondered did God allow tragedies such as this one to happen. Late one night, during a break from our work, I reached into my pocket for a daily devotional booklet that had come in the mail. It fell open to a quote from Job 2:10, 'Shall we accept good from God and not trouble?' The message went on to say that we are imperfect and live in an imperfect world, yet God in His perfection will be with us even in times of despair. The words comforted me."

Sergeant Jimenez continued, "I said a prayer for my fellow workers, who were spending twelve-hour days probing in up to three feet of muck, under eighteen inches of water to find bits of the plane. The temperature hovered in the nineties and the murky water was rank with caustic hydraulic fluid and jet fuel. The nauseating stench was so strong that men could work only in forty-minute shifts before collapsing in exhaustion.

"Finding the black box seemed hopeless. Pieces of the plane were scattered over an area of 1800 square feet. At times there seemed to be no rhyme or reason for their location. Naval experts had no success even using detectors that had once located a black box under 7000 feet of ocean. As the days passed searchers were

getting dehydrated and during short breaks lay gasping in air-conditioned tents. I continued praying for everyone as we advanced our search. By the fifteenth day we were reaching our limits. It was 2:30 P.M. and a thunderstorm was muttering on the horizon. I was exhausted and becoming depressed. During a break while leaning on the staff I used to help locate the black box, I realized in all my prayers I hadn't asked God for the obvious. 'God,' I prayed, 'so far I've asked you to keep everyone safe out here, but I haven't asked for your help in finding anything. So now I'm asking. Help us find the recorder.'

"Returning to our labors, I thrust my pole down and struck something hard. Reaching into the muck, I pulled up a mangled container dripping with mud: the black box cockpit voice recorder! I was awestruck. A cheer rose from the men and I could only give God thanks.

"At the end of the day I stood on the levee watching a burnt-orange sun sink beneath the horizon. I thought of the many days we had spent searching for the recorder, how we must have tromped over it many times, and I wondered why its retrieval had taken so long. Amid the low rustle of saw grass and the call of a great white bird, I seemed to hear the response, 'Why did it take you so long to ask?'"

February 26

"Fight the good fight of faith" (I Timothy 6:12).

A Finnish infidel died and left his farm willed to the devil. The courts, after deliberating on such a ridiculous set of circumstances, decided the best way to carry out the wishes of the infidel was to permit the farmland to grow up in weeds and briars, to allow the house and barn to remain unpainted and to rot down, and to permit the soil to erode and wash away. The court said, "The best way to let Satan have it, is to do nothing." —*The Bible Friend*[70]

If you want to gain the victorious life, you must fight for it. Do not lie down and die, but get up and fight. Do not let your life rot away, but make it count for something. Paul said, "I fight." He also said, "Fight the good fight of faith." There are bad fights and there

are good fights. The fight for your faith is a good fight. You must guard as a boxer guards certain parts of his body. You must guard your mind, for that is where all battles are fought and won or lost. Do not just follow the road of least resistance, or let everything go to pot, but take some action. Change some things, stand firm on that which is right and you will win in the end because truth always triumphs.

Many people give up when the going gets tough. When things fall in around their ears, they back up and sit down, afraid to venture forth. The story is told about a member of the Olympic ice-skating team of 1924. Valentine Bialis was acclaimed the fastest man of skates. Everywhere he was honored as king of the ice. Eight years later, as he was preparing to take top honors as ice-skating champion of the world, Valentine Bialis was driving home one dark, drizzly night. The road and his windshield were slowly coating with ice.

Suddenly he heard the screech of a train whistle. He jammed on his brakes and skidded right into the path of an engine. He was rushed to the hospital seriously injured. He came out of the hospital minus a leg. Gone were his hopes of a championship. He tried to make a comeback skating with one wooden leg but it was impossible.

Some time later, however, Bialis appeared in the headline of the paper in a small mid-western town. He had won a local tennis tournament. He had failed to win ice-skating champion of the world because of a freak accident, but he continued to compete in another sport and became tennis champ in the small town where he lived.[71]

This is no time to lie down and die, it is time to keep reaching, keep competing, keep going ahead in God and in the things He has asked you to do. If God is with you and you believe and keep working at your dreams, you will succeed!

February 27

"We are well able to overcome it" (Numbers 13:30).

"JOHN KEATS lived just twenty-six years, yet his poetry will live forever, much of it equal to that of Shakespeare. FRANZ SCHUBERT died at thirty-one. In those thirty-one years he wrote more than 110 musical compositions, more than sixty of them lyric songs.

"Here is a boy so ugly and ridiculously clothed that he was tormented by his schoolmates. He spent his time reading to forget his misery. At eighteen he worked as a bricklayer. But he finally won the acclaim and esteem of England. He was honored by Queen Elizabeth and decorated by King James. His name was BEN JONSON and he was one of the most brilliant playwrights England ever produced.

"Here is a morbid, sensitive son of a poor preacher. He was regarded as a stupid blockhead in the village school. When he finally got a degree from college, he was the lowest on the list. He was rejected for the ministry. He tried law with the same result. He borrowed a suit of clothes to take an examination as a hospital mate, failed, and pawned his clothes. He lived in garrets, failing at everything he tried. Only one thing he wanted to do—write. This he did and rose above the handicaps of illness, poverty, and obscurity to high rank among the greatest writers of all time. His name was OLIVER GOLDSMITH.

"THOMAS EDISON lost most of his hearing at about eight years of age, but he gave us the electric light, phonograph, and over a hundred other useful inventions. There was another man who had terrible hemorrhages of the lungs, and he almost died several times from coughing spells. Yet, while he was an invalid, he gave us at least two masterpieces, one of them *Treasure Island*. He was ROBERT LOUIS STEVENSON." —Author Unknown[72]

Many of the winners of great fame entered the contest with a severe handicap. HOMER was a blind minstrel, and MILTON too was blind. BEETHOVEN was deaf: *"Though so deaf he could not hear the thunder for a token, he made music of his soul, the grandest ever spoken."*[73] ALEXANDER THE GREAT was a hunchback, and so was ALEXANDER POPE. Small in stature was PAUL, NAPOLEON and HORATIO NELSON. SHAKESPEARE on his own testimony was a cripple, and so were SCOTT, BYRON and KELVIN.

When a man or woman is determined nothing can stop them but God. *"Cripple him and you have a SIR WALTER SCOTT; put him in a prison cell and you have a JOHN BUNYAN. Bury*

him in the snows of Valley Forge and you have a GEORGE WASHINGTON. Have him born in abject poverty and you have a LINCOLN. Afflict him with asthma until as a boy he lies choking in his father's arms and you have a THEODORE ROOSEVELT; . . . put him in a grease pit of a locomotive roundhouse and you have a WALTER CHRYSLER; make him a second fiddle in an obscure South American orchestra and you have a TOSCANINI." —PAUL SPEIKER[74]

The question is, "What are you doing with what you have, with where you are or with what you don't have?"

February 28

"All things are possible to him that believeth" (Mark 9:23).

*H*ave you been asked to do something impossible or which you are afraid you do not have the strength or ability to do? There have been men and women down through the ages who have overcome many obstacles simply because they believed.

"*Blind men seldom quote books, but it is not so with Milton. The prodigious power, readiness, and accuracy of his memory, as well as the confidence he felt in it, are proved by his setting himself, several years after he had become totally blind, to compose his* Treatise on Christian Doctrine, *which, made up as it is of Scriptural texts, would seem to require perpetual reference to the Sacred Volume.*

"*A still more extraordinary enterprise was that of the Latin Dictionary—a work which, one would imagine, might easily wear out a sound pair of eyes. After five years of blindness, he undertook these two vast works, along with* Paradise Lost." —JULIUS C. HARE[75]

What is your obstacle today? What hardship are you faced with? Carl C. Williams tells about a boy who lived in his neighborhood. The boy had an unusual mode of transportation. The boy was unusual because he had the misfortune to lose both legs in an accident. His mode of transportation was unusual in that he rode a bicycle. He had a specially constructed bicycle with the seat low-

ered to where he could reach the pedal with his right hand while sitting erect and steering with his left hand. Thus he got along quite well for a person with such a great handicap. By sheer determination that boy had mastered the art of self-propulsion in the face of almost insurmountable obstacles.[76]

Quite a few years ago Jim Ryun was pronounced the world's fast miler. But listen to his story. He was considered too frail and actually eliminated from the track team in his high school freshman year. But he tried again in his sophomore year and convinced track coach Robert Timmons that he had possibilities. Coach Timmons put Jim on a rigorous physical and mental buildup schedule. Jim, after throwing his morning newspaper, would run six miles, the weather notwithstanding. He ran in snow and sleet, dust and fog. Then in the evening he would run some more. Early risers would see his lonely figure cutting across the prairie at the outskirts of Wichita and shake their heads in puzzlement.

Jim took track so seriously that for a while his parents feared he would hurt himself physically. He would vomit after every race and come home at night and flop into bed without eating. But one day, he became the world's fastest miler.[77]

Remember the words of Paul this day in the face of your fear and seemingly impossible odds: "I can do all things through Christ which strengtheneth me" (Philippians 4:13).

"But we have this treasure in earthen vessels" (II Corinthians 4:7).

A remarkable story is told about an exceedingly costly jewel that for many years was considered of no more value than a mere pebble.

Gustaf Gillman, a Chicago lapidary, was at work in his shop, according to the story, when John Mihok, of Omaha, entered. Mihok, who was a laborer, drew out of his pocket a rough red stone and handed it to Gillman. "I want you to cut and polish this," said Mihok. "Where did you get it?" gasped Gillman, as his eyes

almost popped out of his head. "My father picked it up in Hungary fifty years ago," was the reply of Mihok.

"He thought it was a pretty pebble. When I landed in this country, I found it in my case. It has been lying around the house ever since. The children played with it. My last baby cut his teeth on it. One night I dreamed it was a diamond worth a lot of money, but it's not a diamond. It's red."

"No, it's not a diamond, but it is a pigeon blood ruby," said Gillman.

"What might it be worth?" was the question of Mihok.

"I'd say anywhere from one hundred thousand to two hundred and fifty thousand dollars," answered Gillman: and Mihok leaned against the door.

The big, rough stone was cut to a flawless ruby of twenty-three and nine-tenths carats. At that time it was believed to be possibly the largest ruby in the world. —*MOODY MONTHLY*[78]

You may feel today like you are not worth much more than a pebble. You forget that you are a prized ruby in the sight of the Lord Jesus. When He has washed you with His blood and made you His child, you are a bundle of possibilities and great worth to the kingdom of God. You play with that which He has invested in you, as if it were only a worthless pebble. You house within you the greatest treasure on earth, for Paul said about the Holy Spirit, "We have this treasure within." He referred to the people as being earthen vessels which housed a treasure.

Right in your house is a treasure worth more than you are aware. The story is told of Mrs. Rosemary Cattrell, an Edinburgh art teacher. She had a picture which hung on the wall of her modest home for fifteen years. It pictured the temptation of Eve by the devil. She found out the real value of the picture when she decided to sell it to raise a deposit for a car. Her painting was by a sixteenth-century German artist, Hans Baldung. The painting, once valued at fifty dollars, was sold at an auction for $537,600.[79]

For what price are you auctioning off your life? What lies within you that could bless those around you? Are you content to live a mediocre life, going through the motions, and all the while, hiding your treasure?

This is the day to polish the treasure and let the wealth of the Holy Spirit make you rich in Him and then share those riches with those who have not the treasure.

March 2

"The kingdom of heaven is like unto treasure hid in a field" (Matthew 13:44).

Look carefully at the things that other people discard as useless. Look carefully at dead dreams or impossible ventures; there just might be something that could be made worthwhile out of them.

In one of the cathedrals of England there is a beautiful window through which the sunlight streams. It displays the facts and personalities of the Old and New Testaments and the glorious truths and doctrines of the Christian revelation. This window was fabricated by the artist out of broken bits of glass which another artist had discarded.

Sometimes we miss great opportunities simply through ignorance or not knowing the value of valuable things.

Aquilla Webb tells the story about the managers of a Young Men's Christian Association, who once missed a great opportunity by not knowing the value of a certain painting. A friend of the institution had given a picture for the walls of the building, not having suitable room for it in his own home. One day he offered to sell it to them, asking fifty dollars for it. When they declined the offer he said they might have it for twenty-five dollars, but they still declined to purchase it.

Not long afterwards he died. Disposing of the estate, his executors took the picture from the building and sent it to a picture mart. There it was soon recognized as the work of a master and was identified. Thirty-five thousand dollars was offered for it, and later the bid was increased to fifty thousand. Fifty thousand for a picture once offered for twenty-five dollars!

Look not only at opportunities but look also at what you are doing with the things God has given you. What is God asking us to do with the commodities He has provided for us? Sometimes the very things which should be counted dear are counted but light.

In the Christian Businessmen's League paper there appeared the following account of London in 1942. It says, "In 1942, when London was being blitzed, an article appeared in one of the British newspapers, which was widely quoted on this side of the Atlantic. 'We have been a pleasure-loving people, dishonoring God's day, picnicking and bathing—now the seashore is barred; no picnics, no

bathing. We have preferred motor travel to church going—now there is a shortage of motor fuel. We have ignored the ringing of church bells calling us to worship—now the bells cannot ring except to warn us of invasion. We have left our churches half-empty when they should have been well filled with worshippers—now they are in ruins. We would not listen to the way of peace—now we are forced to listen to the way of war. The money we would not give to the Lord's work now is taken from us in higher taxes and high cost of living. The food for which we refused to give God thanks—now is unattainable. The service we refused to give God is now conscripted for our country. Lives we refused to live under God's control—now are under the nation's control. Nights we would not spend watching unto—now are spent in anxious air raid pre-cautions.'"

It is important to treat carefully those things which God has given His children, and remember there are many valuables that are sometimes hidden, waiting to be found.

March 3

"Wait on the LORD" (Psalm 27:14).

*T*he story is told of how some years ago at a resort area along the East Coast, there was a small community having an open town meeting about some financial problems facing their town. Among the two dozen or so people was one man no one seemed to know, who was apparently visiting in that area and had just dropped in on the meeting. He started to make a comment once as various projects were considered, but he was interrupted; so for the rest of the time he kept still, and he left early.

Just as he went out, someone arriving late came in and said breathlessly, "What was he doing here? Is he going to help us?"

The rest said, "Whom are you talking about? Who was that man?"

The person who had just arrived said, "You mean you don't know? That was John D. Rockefeller. His yacht is in our harbor. Didn't you get his help?"

In despair, someone said, "No, we didn't get his help; we didn't know who he was."[80]

Sometimes in our dilemmas, even in our prayer times, Jesus comes into our meetings and into the midst of our problems and tries to help us but we drown Him out by our continual talk about the problem or are so full of ourselves that we do not listen.

Just as Rockefeller probably would have helped that little community, if only they would have let him speak and share, Jesus wants to help with our problems and dilemmas.

Psalm 27:14 says "Wait on the LORD: be of good courage, and he shall strengthen thine heart: wait, I say, on the LORD."

In order to receive answers, when we go to God in prayer, we must learn to listen to the still small voice that comes after the storm of our tears, frustration and supplication.

> *On life's busy thoroughfare,*
> *We meet with angels unaware,*
> *But we are too busy to see or hear,*
> *Too busy to sense that God is near . . .*
> *We are willing to brush off the Savior's touch,*
> *And we tell ourselves there will come a day,*
> *We will have more time to pause on our way,*
> *But before we know it life's sun has set,*
> *And we've passed the Savior, but never met,*
> *For hurrying along life's thoroughfare,*
> *We passed Him by and remained unaware*
> *That within the very sight of our eye,*
> *Unnoticed the Son of God passed by.*
> —HELEN STEINER RICE

The people of the resort community were too busy to listen to Mr. Rockefeller, who could help them. The question is: are we sometimes too busy to listen to God? This is the day to take time to listen to Him.

March 4

"*I have not a cake, but . . . a little oil*" (I Kings 17:12).

God uses little things to bring a miracle: a little oil, a small boy's lunch, or a little slingshot. It does not matter to Him because He is God and can make up the difference.

On the other hand sometimes it is just a little thing that causes defeat or which causes us to not be able to attain success.

James Burns shares the story about Napoleon's defeat. He says, "There is a modern picture by Stanley Berkley, entitled *The Hidden Danger*, which deals with an interesting event at the Battle of Waterloo. This battle decided the fate of Napoleon; upon which issues hung the destinies of Europe and there occurred in it a crucial moment. Throughout the day Napoleon kept his famous cavalry in reserve. They were the finest soldiers in the world, the *Old Guard*, who had never known defeat, and impatiently they awaited the command to charge. Napoleon, seeing the issue going against him, gave at last the order and hurled them against the thin British lines.

"On they came in gallant neck to neck, seemingly invincible. But there was a dip in the road, a sunken part neither they nor Napoleon knew, but of which Wellington had taken advantage by filling it with his sharpshooters. As the thundering lines came on they were met by an unexpected and decimating volley. They wavered for a moment; then forming once more, came on at hand the gallop, but the fire was too deadly, and when the lines were reached their force was spent.

"Waterloo was lost; the fate of Napoleon and Europe was decided by a dip in the road, by that hidden danger on which Napoleon had not counted. This one weak spot ruined him and turned victory into defeat."[81]

Carl C. Williams tells about a man who never quite made it in the invention of the telephone all because of a small thing. He writes, "It is common knowledge that Alexander Graham Bell invented the telephone. What is not so well known is that long before Bell's world-changing invention, a German schoolteacher by the name of Reis almost built a telephone. Mr. Reis's phone would carry the sounds of whistling or humming but would not transmit the human voice. Something seemed to be missing.

"Many years later, Mr. Bell discovered Reis's error. A little screw that controlled the electrodes on Mr. Reis's invention needed an adjustment of one-thousandth of an inch. Mr. Bell discovered this error and turned the screw one-thousandth of an inch and was able to transmit speech loud and clear. This small distance of one-thousandth of an inch made a world of difference—the difference between failure and success."[82]

It is important for people to do their best to live successfully in this life, but more important is to be successful in God's kingdom. That is to live as Christ lived, filled with His Spirit and preparing for that heavenly home. Remember *almost* is not enough. It was King Agrippa who told Paul, "Almost thou persuadest me to be a Christian." Make sure today that it will not be an *almost* with you but that it will be a surety.

March 5

"In all these things we are more than conquerors" (Romans 8:37).

You may be facing a negative situation in your life today, filled with unbelief. If so, do not let it defeat you. There will come open a way for you to prove yourself to be a conqueror over it.

"Years ago when King Humbert of Italy came to the throne, Naples, one of the chief cities of the newly made kingdom, was in a state of barely suppressed insurrection against the monarchy. Politicians were advising stern measures, which Humbert would not allow, when the dread cholera broke out, and raged with sudden deadly fury among the Neapolitans. The young king, fired with the noble resolve to prove to his disloyal subjects his devotion to them, started alone, unmoved by the remonstrances of his ministers; and went through the crowded hospitals of Naples, ministering to his subjects with his own royal hands; and many dying people looked or breathed prayers, and thanked him brokenly for his marvelous self-sacrifice on their behalf.

"After a while the plague was checked, but it left Naples a conquered city; conquered by the love and pity of the king it had once refused; and after, the noble Humbert had no more loyal subjects than those to whom he had proved himself a king indeed." —A. BERNARD WEBBER[83]

King Humbert proved to be a conqueror over the fears that surrounded him simply because he was motivated by love and

devotion. Paul said, "We are more than conquerors through Christ that loved us." You too can be a conqueror today over difficulties, misunderstandings and fear.

It was Benjamin Franklin who tried to help a group of people by giving them some new information about the way they planted in their fields, but they did not believe him. He had learned that plaster sown in the fields would make things grow. He told his neighbors, but they did not believe him and they argued with him to prove that plaster could be of no use at all to grass or grain.

After a little while he allowed the matter to drop and said no more about it. But he went into the field early the next spring and sowed some grain. Close by the path, where men would walk, he traced some letters with his finger and put plaster into them and then sowed his seed in the field.

After two weeks the seed sprang up. His neighbors, as they passed that way, were very much surprised to see, in brighter green than all the rest of the field, the writing in large letters, "This has been plastered." Benjamin Franklin did not need to argue with his neighbors any more about the benefit of plaster for the fields. For as the season went on and the grain grew, these bright, green letters just rose above all the rest until they were a kind of relief-plate in the field: "This has been plastered."[84]

This is the best way to win. Keep on doing what you know to be right without ranting, raving or arguing. Truth always triumphs in the end. This is the day to keep on reaching for greater achievements. It is the day to help people who may seem dubious toward what you are trying to do. It is the day to conquer!

Do not let misunderstanding and prejudice keep you down. If you know you have something that will help people and you are able to perform what you have been asked to do, you rise and go forward with faith, for time and truth are on your side and you will win.

March 6

"*The steps of a good man are ordered by the* LORD" (Psalm 37:23).

*T*his is not the day to give up on a worthy cause in spite of jealousy, hardship or frustration. Have that staying power and you will succeed.

So often in the Christian walk, there are hardships, hindrances by envious people, frustration and setbacks: anything that would tempt you to give up. Dr. Leon Tucker, a gifted preacher, was told about a woman who had been broken by a great tragedy in her life. She had been living under the crushing weight of a heavy burden for so long that praise had given way to complaint. Finally she cried out in bitterness of soul, "Oh, I would to God I had never been made!" In response to her words a friend wisely replied, "Why, my dear child, you are not made yet; you are only being made, and you are quarreling with God's process."

You may be in the midst of a heavy trial, and it has been like a burden on your back for a long time. If you have prayed about it, and nothing has happened, keep praying. The Lord knows where you are. He is making you. One writer said it like this:

> *I know my heav'nly Father knows*
> *The balm I need to soothe my woes,*
> *And with His touch of love divine,*
> *He heals this wounded soul of mine.*
> —AUTHOR UNKNOWN

The Lord is not only able to soothe your woes, but He is right beside you. He is making you into a beautiful vessel of honor.

In order to make Moses ready for His assignment, He let Moses be alienated from his people and taken from a palace to live on the backside of a desert, but God brought him back a victor, with more power than he had in the beginning. God took a Joseph and let him be lied about, sold as a slave and sent to prison, but He was preparing him for the palace to rule and reign. God does not let things happen to you just for them to happen, but when you are God's child, your steps are ordered by the Lord. He has greater things in store for you.

This is no time to give in to quarreling with God, defeat or despair. Victory and success are there; even though sometimes out of reach, they are within reach—in God's time. Just keep keeping on; you shall win.

March 7

"*Whosoever will come after me, let him deny himself, and take up his cross, and follow me*" (Mark 8:34).

Jesus said to take up the cross and lose our life; then and only then would we find true life. A person does not find true growth during prosperity. It is the time of adversity and trials that causes the greater growth. Trials and crosses are among the greatest blessings, for it is only through such disciplinary processes that the character is perfected.

George Matheson, the well-known blind preacher of Scotland wrote years ago, "My God, I have never thanked Thee for my thorn. I have thanked Thee a thousand times for my roses, but never once for my thorn. I have been looking forward to a world when I shall get compensation for my cross, but I have never thought of my cross as itself a present glory. Teach me the glory of my cross; teach me the value of my thorn. Show me that I have climbed to Thee by the path of pain. Show me that my tears have made my rainbow." —MOODY MONTHLY[85]

"*If God sends thee a cross, take it up and follow Him. Use it wisely, lest it be unprofitable. Bear it patiently, lest it be intolerable. If it be light, slight it not. If it be heavy, murmur not.*" —QUARLES

"*The Cross of Christ is the pledge to us that the deepest suffering may be the condition of the highest blessing; the sign not of God's displeasure, but of His widest and most compassionate love.*" —DEAN STANLEY

This is the day to not cry out against the trial, but to learn in the trial. Learn to pray, learn to lean upon the Master, learn about Him in His Word. It is the time to focus our eyes upon Christ and the eternal, bringing ourselves under subjection to the higher will of God for our lives. Things are not allowed to hurt, but for growth.

"*Unloving words are meant to make us gentle, and delays teach patience, and care teaches faith, and press of business makes us look out for minutes to give to God, and disappointment is a special messenger to summon our thoughts to Heaven.*" —E.M. SEWELL

When you are walking through the trial, keep your eyes on

Jesus and allow no doubt to enter your heart. It was Wurmbrand, who was tortured in prison by brutal guards, who said he learned from the guards. "How?" he was asked. He said, "As they allowed no place for Jesus in their hearts, I decided I would leave not the smallest place for Satan in mine."

Remember these words when you are walking through the times of adversity, trial and tears. Keep every inch of your heart occupied by Jesus. Allow no doubt, anger or bitterness to cloud your vision of Him. You are in His hands, He knows where you are, and He does all things well. In your pain, just learn to grow in the grace and knowledge of our Lord Jesus Christ.

March 8

"Be not afraid nor dismayed . . . for the battle is not yours, but God's" (II Chronicles 20:15).

The story of the Alamo is one of sheer courage. When the men who were defending the Alamo found out that no one was coming to help them, the 232 American soldiers realized that they could not hold out forever against the five-thousand-strong Mexican army. General Santa Ana of Mexico had demanded surrender, but Colonel William Travis told his men, "My orders are to hold it." As the American soldiers watched, Colonel Travis drew a line on the dirt floor with his sword. "Any man who wants to escape is free to go now: any who are determined to stay and die in defense of the Alamo will cross this line."

Strong-muscled Davy Crockett boldly stepped across. Others followed, and finally only James Bowie was left, too ill to move by his own strength. He asked to be carried across.

Then Colonel Travis sent the fateful message to the attackers, "We refuse to surrender." The Mexican army attacked on March 6, 1838, and it took three assaults for them to overpower the fort by sheer mass of numbers. The Americans fought back grimly, fiercely, but inevitably all lay dead.

When news of their bravery leaked to American forces, the defenders were inspired to advance. General Sam Houston gave the battle cry: "Victory is certain! Remember the Alamo." The motto

fired the men and they won the victory over the army from Mexico.

Two thousand years ago, Jesus our Lord fought and won a battle at Calvary. He died first at the hand of the enemy but three days later was resurrected. Christians everywhere who are in a battle can triumphantly cry, "Remember Calvary!" Because He lives, we can live also, as the old song declares:

> *Because He lives I can face tomorrow,*
> *Because He lives all fear is gone;*
> *Because I know He holds the future.*
> *And life is worth the living just because He lives.*

This is not the time to give up! Live or die, if you stay with Christ you will win.

Don't run from your calling just because of resistance. Jameson tells the story that during the first persecution of Christians by Emperor Nero, Christians begged Peter not to expose his life, which was considered necessary to the well-being of the church. Finally, Peter consented to depart from Rome, but as he fled along the Appian Way, about two miles from the gates, he was met by a vision of the Savior traveling towards the city.

Struck with amazement, he exclaimed, "Lord, whither goest thou?" The Savior, looking upon him with a mild sadness, replied, "I go to Rome to be crucified a second time," and vanished. Peter immediately turned back and re-entered the city.

Just a story you say; yes, but much truth in it. No matter what you face in the way of adversity, the enemy's tactics or great distress, if God placed you in a certain place, He has a work for you to do. This is no time to vacate the post, no time to surrender to the enemy, but hold fast! As the battle cry went forth in the 1800s, *"Remember the Alamo,"* let the battle cry go forth today, *"Remember Calvary."* Go forward and slack not; God is in charge of the battle.

March 9

"Lo, I am with you alway, even unto the end of the world" (Matthew 28:20).

God will take care of you. A missionary found herself without food or supplies, and among a heathen people. In her distress she claimed the promise of God that He would supply her need. She was also in very poor health. From a businessman in another part of the country came several large boxes of Scotch oatmeal. She already had several cans of condensed milk, so with these two foods, she sustained her life for four long weeks—that is all she ate. It seemed to agree with her and at the end of the four weeks, she felt in excellent health.

In relating the experience some time later to a company of people, which included a physician, she was asked more particularly of the nature of her former illness. The physician said, "The Lord heard your prayer and supplied your need more truly than you realize. For the sickness from which you were suffering, we physicians prescribe a four weeks' diet of nothing but oatmeal gruel for our patients. The Lord prescribed it for you, and saw to it that was all you took. It was the proper remedy."

God is with you today just as He was with the missionary, and He will take care of you!

Dr. Joseph R. Sizoo, who once served as president of New Brunswick Theological Seminary, wrote this testimony in 1942:

"Years ago, in a day of uncertainty and disillusionment, when my whole life seemed to be overwhelmed by forces beyond my control, one morning quite casually I opened my New Testament and my eyes fell upon this sentence, 'He that sent me is with me—the Father hath not left me alone.' My life has never been the same since that hour. Everything for me has been forever different after that. I suppose that not a day has passed that I have not repeated it to myself. Many have come to me for counseling during these years, and I have always sent them away with this sustaining sentence. Ever since that hour when my eyes fell upon it, I have lived by this sentence. I have walked with it and I have found in it my peace and strength. To me it is the very essence of religion. It lies at the rock bottom of everything that makes life worth living. It is the Golden Text of my life."

Jesus said the words over two thousand years ago, "Lo, I am with you always, even unto the end of the world." He is with you in the good times, the bad times, in the hospital room, or driving down the highway. If you can grasp hold of this promise—that Jesus is with you—you will never be alone. He sees all and hears every prayer and is working all things out for your good.

Write it down, put it on the dashboard of your automobile, put it on your refrigerator, but most of all write it in your mind and repeat it often, "The Lord is with me. The Lord is my shepherd. The Lord is a present help in the time of trouble. The name of the Lord is a strong tower and I can run in and be saved." The Lord is with you; just believe it.

March 10

"Thy Father which seeth in secret himself shall reward thee openly" (Matthew 6:4).

Jesus said that when people do good things in secret, God will know about it and reward them. Sharon Addy tells a story that illustrates this in part. Her daughter, Jill, came home from her Sunday school class one blustery morning carrying a small bare tree branch and radiating enthusiasm. "See Mom, I'm giving you a *good deeds tree*. Every time I do something to help you, you're supposed to tape on one of these paper leaves," she said. Sharon gave her daughter Jill a hug and when they got home, she slipped the leaves in a drawer and propped the branch on a windowsill, leaning it against the glass. Some time later it must have slipped out of sight behind the curtain because mother and daughter both forgot about it. Until the next Sunday at the joint service following the adults' and children's Sunday school classes. The teacher asked, "How many boys and girls have leaves on their tree branches?"

With a sinking feeling, Sharon watched Jill's hand shoot up. Jill had been more helpful than usual, but Sharon had forgotten to tape the leaves onto the branch.

After church, Sharon explained to Jill that she had not kept up with her good deeds, but told her the minute they got home she would tape on every leaf she had earned. As soon as they arrived home and hung up their coats, Sharon reached behind the curtain and brought out the branch. Jill began to clap her hands and jump up and down with delight. For the branch was no longer bare, but covered with tiny, bright green *real* leaves: leaves of God's making.

Your life is just like this story. Every single thing you do for God and others in the way of helping them, God is taking notice

and He will reward in His own way. Your living is not in vain. Not only does God reward, but something powerful happens to the person who decides to help others.

The story is told of twenty-nine-year-old Dorothy Dix, a frail schoolteacher, who was given only a slight chance to live. If she survived the lung disease that caused hemorrhaging, her doctors predicted she would be an invalid. She went to England for rest. There she read the New Testament through several times, asking the question, "What would Christ have me to do?" She found the answer when she returned home and a minister asked her to teach the Bible to the women prisoners in the East Cambridge, Massachusetts, jail. She found conditions there at the asylum to be extremely cruel. The determined Miss Dix gathered a mountain of evidence proving cruelty to the mentally ill and came before the Massachusetts legislature. "Gentlemen," she cried, "I call your attention to the state of insane persons confined within the Commonwealth, in cages, closets, cellars, stalls, and pens; chained, naked, beaten with rods and lashed into obedience."

Her speech shook New England. She moved on to other states and found similar conditions. Disregarding ridicule she prodded legislatures into building hospitals and voting reforms. On to Canada, Scotland, England and Italy she marched, calling for action. Finally at eighty she became an invalid. The last five years of her life brought many tributes and distinguished visitors. At her death, a hospital superintendent said of her, "The most useful and distinguished woman America has yet produced has died."[86]

The cause of working for others pulled Dorothy Dix out of her sickbed, and instead of dying or staying an invalid, she became a mighty crusader for over fifty-one years. Jesus' words taken from the book of Matthew are still true today.

March 11

"There is a friend that sticketh closer than a brother" (Proverbs 18:24).

There was a rich man who was not sure who his real friends were and often said that he would divide his fortune among his

friends if only he knew who they were. Years passed. Then the rich man died. His death occurred during a midwinter blizzard. His last request was that the funeral be held at four o'clock in the morning. During his lifetime, many had boasted of being his intimate friends. Only three men and one poor woman turned out to lament his passing and to show their last respects at the graveside. When the rich man's will was read, it directed that his vast fortune be equally divided among those who attended his funeral. —WALTER B. KNIGHT[87]

Sometimes people are like this old man. They are not sure who are their real friends, but there is one friend you never have to wonder about. He is your friend no matter what. That friend who sticks closer than a brother is Jesus. The old hymn, "What a Friend We have in Jesus," reflects this well. This song was not written at a party or in a classroom. It was written by a young man in North America for his mother, who was ill in their native Ireland. In trying to comfort and encourage her, he intended the poem just for her. No one knew about the words of this beloved hymn until a neighbor was visiting and found out.

Born in Ireland, Joseph Scriven graduated from college and was engaged to a beautiful girl. On the eve of their wedding the girl drowned. Overwhelmed with grief, he went to Canada and devoted his life to helping the underprivileged, giving them clothes and sharing his food. If anyone could afford his service, he would not work for him. In 1875, Ira Sankey put out the songbook entitled *Gospel Hymns No. 1* and included "What a Friend We have in Jesus" as the last one in the collection, having recently learned of the almost unknown song. But later, the last hymn became one of his favorites.[88]

The Scripture says Jesus will never leave you nor forsake you. He is truly a friend that is *always* there.

> *It is better to walk in the dark with God*
> *Than to run in the light alone;*
> *Yes better the thorniest path ever trod,*
> *Where the briers are thick, and our feet unshod;*
> *If only we follow his voice and rod,*
> *Than without him to march to a throne.*
> *It is better with him when the billows dash high,*
> *On the breast of the mad Galilee;*
> *Though the Master may sleep, he will wake at our cry,*

Or he'll come on the waves saying: "Peace it is I."
Better this than a calm when he is not nigh,
Or without him to sail a smooth sea.
—ALEXANDER BLACKBURN[89]

With Jesus as your friend you can face any storm, walk through any valley, or climb the highest mountain. He will never let you down, ridicule you, leave you alone, nor cast you aside. For as your Friend, He will always be there.

March 12

"Forgive, and ye shall be forgiven" (Luke 6:37).

Life is too short to lose a friend through unforgiveness. A true friend will forgive, for a friend steps in when others step out.

The story is told of how one night when Mr. Moody was leading the singing and Mr. Sankey was playing the organ, Mr. Moody looked over to Sankey and said, "Excuse me; I see there a friend coming in to the meeting. I offended him today downtown, and I want him to forgive me." Mr. Moody walked down from the platform, and the other man got up from his seat and walked out into the aisle and met Mr. Moody about halfway, and said, "Mr. Moody, I forgive you heartily."

Moody went back to the platform, and an eyewitness said, "I never saw such a meeting; it was wonderful."[90]

Acts 24:16 records the words spoken by Paul when he stood before Felix. He said, "And herein do I exercise myself, to have always a conscience void of offence toward God, and toward men."

Only people who are *big* in their spirit learn to forgive.

At Cambridge, Massachusetts, in 1775, General George Washington discovered that his army was completely out of powder. He sent Colonel Glover to Marblehead for a fresh supply. When Glover returned that evening he found Washington pacing up and down before his headquarters. Without returning Glover's salute, Washington demanded: "Have you got the powder?"

"No sir," replied the colonel.

Washington used some rather severe language, winding up

roughly: "Why did you come back, sir, without it?"

"Sir," said Glover, "there is not a kernel of powder in Marblehead."

Greatly disturbed and embarrassed by the way he had treated Glover, Washington walked up and down for a few minutes and then turned to him, "Colonel Glover, here is my hand, if you will take it and forgive me. The greatness of our danger made me forget what is due to you and to myself."[91] That showed their friendship and respect for one another. They were not to be treated hatefully and rudely. They were supposed to be friends.

If you want to be happy, you will forgive. Dr. Meyer told of a man who went to him and said, "I cannot understand it, sir, but it seems as if God is blotted out of my life. I used to be so happy. I think it has to do with my treatment of my brother. He treated me cruelly over my father's will and I said I would never forgive him. I am sorry I said it, but he has been going from bad to worse. He has lost his wife and child and is now on his deathbed and I cannot go to him because I said I never would." Dr. Meyer said, "Sir, it is better to break a bad vow than to keep it. Go." The man went and the story tells how the smile of God met him there. True happiness and success in life will always have the ingredient of *forgiveness* in them.

March 13

"Stand fast therefore in the liberty wherewith Christ hath made us free" (Galatians 5:1).

The inscription on the Plymouth Rock monument is a challenge to every generation of Americans. It says, *"This spot marks the final resting place of the Pilgrims of the Mayflower. In weariness and hunger and cold, fighting the wilderness and burying their dead in common graves that the Indians should not know how many had perished, they here laid the foundations of a state in which all men for countless ages should have liberty to worship God in their own way. All you who pass by and see this stone remember, and dedicate yourselves anew to the resolution that you will not rest until this lofty ideal shall have been realized throughout the earth."*[92]

 The Pilgrims came to America so they could be free to worship God and not be bound to a creed. They fought for their freedom. General Omar Bradley said this about freedom: "Freedom—no word was ever spoken that has held out greater hope or demanded greater sacrifice. When Martin Luther saw the light and knew that the religious order of the day left something to be desired, he thundered forth the words, 'The truth shall set you free!'"

 "We find freedom when we find God. We lose it when we lose Him." —Paul Scherer

 On the night when the slaves were set free in Jamaica, in 1838, a large mahogany coffin was made and a grave was dug. Into that coffin the liberated slaves threw the reminders of their former life of slavery—whips, torture irons, branding irons, coarse frocks and shirts, fragments of a treadmill, large hats, and handcuffs. The lid of the coffin was screwed down. At the stroke of midnight the coffin was lowered into the grave and buried. Then the liberated natives sang the song:

> *Praise God, from whom all blessings flow;*
> *Praise Him, all creatures here below;*
> *Praise Him above, ye heav'nly host;*
> *Praise Father, Son, and Holy Ghost!*[93]

 Just as the slaves were liberated, so is anyone who finds the saving power of Jesus Christ. He sets men and women free from the bondage of sin. Many things of the former life are discarded, thrown away and buried.

 Freedom in Christ is not to be taken likely. It should be considered precious. Sometimes things that are easily available are taken lightly. Christians everywhere should not take for granted the privilege of religious freedom, but instead stay close to God and follow Him with an intense heart of passion and purity, learning to walk with Him every day of their life.

March 14

"*Charity envieth not*" (I Corinthians 13:4).

*S*o often people want to hear about how they can be successful. But it is difficult for them to recognize or be glad of the success of others. There is a spiteful little word involved: *envy or jealousy*. The Bible says "Jealousy is cruel as the grave." Envy is often the death of success.

A Grecian story depicts the case of a man who killed himself through envy. His fellow citizens had reared a statue to one who was a celebrated victor in the public games. So strong was the feeling of envy which this incited in the breast of one of the hero's rivals that he went forth every night in order, if possible, to destroy that monument. After repeated efforts he moved it from its pedestal, and it fell, but in its fall it crushed him.

Envy is a weapon which shoots at others but wounds itself, for it affects the body as stated in Proverbs 14:30: "A sound heart is the life of the flesh: but envy the rottenness of the bones."

Envy or jealousy was the thing that caused Lucifer to be thrown out of heaven. Ever since then he has tried to put the same feeling in the hearts of all people. The devil will try to get someone to fall, and if he cannot get them any other way, he will try *envy*.

There is a fable wherein the devil once was crossing the Libyan Desert and met a group of friends tempting a holy hermit. They tried seductions of the flesh, used doubts and fears, but to no avail. The holy man was unmoved.

The devil then stepped forward, "Your methods are too crude. Permit me one moment." Going to the hermit, he said, "Have you heard the news? Your brother has been made the Bishop of Alexandria."

According to the fable, a scowl of malignant jealousy clouded the serene face of the holy man.[94]

This same spirit of envy was in the breast of King Saul, the first king of Israel. As long as he was number one everything was all right, but as soon as he heard the women singing, "Saul has killed his thousands, but David his tens of thousands," a fire of jealousy started to rage inside him. The day came when that feeling took action and he threw a javelin at David and David had to flee for his life.

Success is not being able to sit on the throne, for that is where King Saul sat. Success is being able to have a rein on your passions, envy and evil desires, because you have allowed the Lord Jesus Christ to sit upon the throne of your heart. If He truly reigns, then you will be able to rejoice with a brother or sister

when they enjoy success instead of feeling spiteful or discontent at the good fortune or the blessing of another.

True success is being filled with love, for love does not know envy.

March 15

"Therefore, my beloved brethren, be ye stedfast, unmoveable, always abounding in the work of the Lord" (I Corinthians 15:58).

A Southern preacher once divided his church members into five types of bones.

1. *Wishbones*—Folks always wishing for better things, but never willing to work and pray for them.

2. *Jawbones*—The gossiping kind that keeps the church in turmoil.

3. *Funnybones*—like the bone in the elbow that throws a person into a tizzy when it is hurt. They are touchy, wear their feelings on their sleeves, and are always talking about leaving the church.

4. *Drybone*—Orthodox but dead as fossils.

5. *Backbones*—The spiritual support of the church that keeps the body standing.[95]

The need of the hour is for more people to become the backbones of the church. That means that church is more than Sunday religion, but it is religion every day of the week. The church cannot be weak, but it must be able to influence others for God. If not, it will lose its influence.

"If a church has too little influence over a community, it is because the community has too much influence over that church." —Dr. George McDaniel[96]

The church, of course, consists of the people in it.

"In this world, a churchless community where men have abandoned and scoffed at or ignored their religious needs, is a community on the rapid downgrade. Church work and church attendance mean the cultivation of the habit of feeling some responsibility for others. There are enough holidays for most of us. Sundays differ from other holidays in the fact that

there are fifty-two of them every year—therefore, on Sundays go to church. Yes, I know all the excuses. I know that one can worship the Creator in a grove of trees or in a man's own home. But I know, as a matter of cold fact, the average man does not thus worship." —PRESIDENT THEODORE ROOSEVELT[97]

The church is you, as signified in the following poem:

We cannot spell Sunday without U,
We cannot spell church without U
Our church needs U to help:
We are counting on U
—AUTHOR UNKNOWN[98]

It is time for more people to become the backbones of the church of the living God. He doesn't need drybones, jawbones or wishbones; He needs everyone to come alive with fire, purpose and passion.

"The world is being inoculated with a mild form of Christianity which is making us immune to the real thing." —DR. JAMES DEFOREST MURCH[99]

This is the day for the real thing. Nothing else will do. It is time to stand up and be counted for the cause of Christ, to get involved and to make a difference.

March 16

"Forasmuch as ye know that your labour is not in vain in the Lord" (I Corinthians 15:58b).

Sometimes you may feel like your life is unnoticed by the crowds, that your efforts are unrecognized and unappreciated, but payday is not yet. There is coming a day when the great King will sit on His throne and reward you for all the things you did for Him on earth and the things you did for others. To be famous is not the most important thing. The important thing is to do the will of God, affect this world for Him, and to bring others into a relationship with Him.

Babe Ruth, world-famed baseball player, once said about an

aged minister: "Most of the people who have really counted in my life were not famous. Nobody ever heard of them, except those who knew and loved them. I knew an old minister once. His hair was white. His face shone. I have written my name on thousands of baseballs in my life. The old minister wrote his name on just a few simple hearts. How I envy him! He was not trying to please himself. Fame never came to him. I am listed as a famous home-runner, yet beside that obscure minister, who was so good and so wise, I never got to first base!" —AL BRYANT[100]

A faithful missionary was asked: "What pay do you receive for the hardships you undergo and the sacrifices you make, living and working among these people?"

The missionary took from his pocket a letter, worn with much handling, and read two sentences from it, written by a Chinese student: "But for you, I would not have known Jesus Christ, our Savior. Every morning I kneel before God and think of you, thank God for you and pray for you." "That," said the missionary, "is my pay."[101]

In the book, *Legend of the Eagles*, the author George d'Espartes shares a story of how a bridge was built with great sacrifice. In the depth of winter the French army, pressed on all sides by the Cossacks, had to cross a river. The enemy had destroyed all the bridges and Napoleon was almost at his wit's end. Suddenly came the order that a bridge of some sort must be thrown across the river, and the men nearest the water were the first to carry out the almost impossible task. Several were swept away by the furious tide. Others, after a few minutes, sank through cold and exhaustion, but more came, and the work proceeded as fast as possible. At last the bridge was completed and the army reached the opposite bank in safety. Then followed the most dramatic scene, and one of the most touching recorded in the annals of history. When the men who had built the bridge were called to leave the water, not one moved. Clinging to the pillars, they stood silent and motionless, frozen to death. Even Napoleon shed tears. —F. W. BOREHAM[102]

These were the unknown men who helped win a war. How many more are the "unknowns" who daily fight to win the war on earth for the great captain Jesus Christ. Be not weary, but continue on; payday is coming someday soon.

March 17

"If any man serve me, let him follow me; and where I am, there shall also my servant be" (John 12:26).

A century and a half ago there died a humble minister in a small village in Leicestershire, England. He had never attended college and had no degrees. He was merely a faithful village minister. In his congregation was a young cobbler to whom he gave special attention, teaching him the Word of God. This young man was later to be renowned as William Carey, who was known as one of the greatest missionaries of modern times.

This same minister had a son, a boy whom he taught faithfully and constantly encouraged. The boy's character was profoundly affected by his father's life. The son was Robert Hall, known as one of the great public orators of his day, whose sermons influenced the decisions of statesmen and whose character was, as many attest to, as saintly as his preaching was phenomenal. It seemed that the village pastor accomplished little. There were no spectacular revivals, but his faithful witness and godly life had much to do with giving India its Carey and England its Robert Hall.

The kingdom of God on earth is great and vast, and you as God's child have a part to play in it. Not everyone will be the main character in the drama, but all the characters are important. The key is to do what God has asked you to do as well and faithfully as you can and let the influence you bring to others affect them profoundly, so that they will want to give their best to the Lord God also. It is God's kingdom, but each person affects the other.

This is the day to live on the cutting edge, a life of excellence, giving your best to God, and only God knows the depth and the breadth of your influence. As the unknown minister affected India and England through someone other than himself, so can you. What you do for God and what you say are important!

In the 1890s the West was still a wild and uncharted territory. For the most part there were no roads or even trails. For example, from Iowa City, Iowa, to Dubuque, the state capital, a distance of one hundred miles, there was no road, not even a trail. A farmer

who settled in Iowa City, wanting to do something about this, decided to pioneer a path from his newly chosen town to the capital. He hitched up a team of oxen to a plow and started to make a furrow across the wilderness. It took him months to do it. But hardly had he finished when the people of that region began to travel in both directions with that path as their guide. As a result the ground was soon beaten down into a highway, serving travelers from Iowa City to Dubuque.[103]

The apostle Paul stated to those who looked to him for direction, "Follow me as I follow Christ." He started off on a new pathway that was not always known to him, but he had faith in Jesus Christ and a heartfelt love for the things of God. That was all he needed to lead people down an uncharted course towards victory and power.

You are like the farmer today; in the path or the furrows you plow, others will follow. Your duty is not to worry about being great or being known, it is to influence others towards the only great one, the Lord Jesus Christ. He is looking for some pioneers, or some faithful soldiers of the cross, to take up their crosses and follow Him, seeking not to save their life, but to lose it in a cause bigger than themselves. In so doing, true life is found.

"Search the scriptures; for in them ye think ye have eternal life: and they are they which testify of me" (John 5:39).

What do you do with important things or important messages? Does the activity of the moment obscure the urgency of the important?

Archias, the magistrate of Thebes, was sitting with many mighty men drinking wine. A messenger came in bringing him a letter, informing him of a conspiracy against his life and warning him to flee. Archias took the letter but, instead of opening it, put it into his pocket and said to the messenger who brought it, "Business tomorrow." The next day he died. Before he opened the letter the government was captured. When he read the letter it was too late. —*PULPIT TREASURY*[104]

Sometimes people are just like Archias, doing things that make them feel good for the moment but neglecting the urgent and the important.

Just as Archias received an important letter, God has sent the human race a letter that is more important than the letter Archias received. It must be read today before it is too late.

King George V said about God's important letter: "It is my confident hope that my subjects may never cease to cherish their noble inheritance in the English Bible which is the first of national treasures. Its spiritual significance is the most valuable thing the world affords."

"Other books were given for our information. The Bible was given for our transformation." —WALTER B. KNIGHT[105]

This happened in the life of a dear grandmother. Every time a little boy went to a playmate's house, he found the friend's grandmother deeply engrossed in reading her Bible. Finally his curiosity got the better of him. "Why do you suppose your grandmother reads the Bible so much?" he asked. "I'm not sure," said his friend, "but I think it's because she's cramming for her finals." —CARL T. SCHUNEMAN[106]

Paul said it like this: My end is near. II Timothy 4:6 says, "For I am now ready to be offered, and the time of my departure is at hand." He was preparing for his finals: that step over into eternity. The difference between Archias, and the grandmother and Paul is that they read the letter before it was too late.

What are you doing today with the important letter that God has sent to His people? Are you just having a party, ignoring the contents, or are you pausing in your mad rush toward success and search after happiness to read what is written?

It will not only prepare you for the final day of your life, but it will help you be aware of your enemy's tactics and teach you how to fight successfully and win. All the things you are seeking after are in the letter sent from God. Take time to read it today.

March 19

"That we may be able to comfort them which are in any trouble" (II Corinthians 1:4).

    Spurgeon once told of how he was utterly depressed in spirit and soul, discouraged, and failing in health. Just before leaving for a time of recuperation, he preached on "My God, my God, why hast thou forsaken me?" The experience was so sad that he wished it would never happen again.

    Afterwards, a man came to see him. Spurgeon described him later as "one step away from the insane asylum," his head bulging, his hands nervous and spirit totally depressed. The man told Spurgeon that after hearing his sermon, he felt that he was the only one who could understand him and so he had come. Spurgeon comforted him as best he knew how from his own sad experience.

    For five years, Spurgeon did not see the man. But as he stated later, "Just last night I saw him while delivering a lecture to students at the college. It was like night and day. He was completely changed." Spurgeon concluded that he was willing to undergo hundreds of such experiences, now that he knew God permitted it to happen so that he could know and sympathize with people under similar predicaments.[107]

    Paul spoke about this very thing: "Blessed be God, even the Father of our Lord Jesus Christ, the Father of mercies, and the God of all comfort; Who comforteth us in all our tribulation, that we may be able to comfort them which are in any trouble, by the comfort wherewith we ourselves are comforted of God" (II Corinthians 1:3-4). He further stated in verse 7 "that as ye are partakers of the sufferings, so shall ye be also of the consolation."

    When you go through a difficult, painful experience which causes you sorrow, it is not for you alone, but as God gives you comfort and answers, so you are to do the same. Trials and sorrows should not be wasted but should be used to help others along the way.

    Remember that Paul's sweetest epistles were written from prison cells. John Bunyan's *Pilgrim's Progress* came from the Bedford jail. John the Revelator received the Revelation while in exile on the isle of Patmos. Their trials became the seeds for our blessing.

    Our trials are not to strike us down but to put us in a position to see the Lord better and in a new way. It is to make Him come alive in the lives of others around us, as well as ourselves.

    Samuel Brengle wrote a classic, entitled *Helps to Holiness*. How was this written? It was written during a period of convales-

cence after a tough guy threw a brick at the author's head. Mr. Brengle's wife kept the brick and painted a text from the Bible on it found in Genesis 50:20, "But as for you, ye thought evil against me; but God meant it unto good, to bring to pass, as it is this day, to save much people alive."

Remember God uses trials, sorrows and difficulties to let us see Him more clearly, so that we can help others and minister to them of His greatness.

March 20

"What shall we then say to these things? If God be for us, who can be against us?" (Romans 8:31).

Someone once said, "To the Israelites Goliath was too big to hit, but to little David, he was too big to miss." When God is on your side, you always win, so if He is with you, if He is your partner, make your plans as big as you can, for He is able to do exceedingly, abundantly above all you ask or think. David found this out. Everyone in the Israelite camp was hiding and totally afraid, because they had their eyes on the giant instead of the solution to their problem.

Not only did David find out how big his God was, but Daniel also found out that God was bigger than his problems. When he was thrust into the lions' den because of his integrity and his belief, God sent an angel to shut the lions' mouths and all his enemies were thrown into the lions' den and perished.

Joshua found out that God was big enough to tear down the walls of a city that seemed impossible to everyone else. But God spoke a formula to Joshua that worked. The people were to march around Jericho six days without speaking and, on the seventh day, they were to blow the trumpets and shout, and the Lord caused the walls of Jericho to fall down.

Moses found out that God had the power to open a large Red Sea and make water stand upright and also make the water's bed into dry ground so that millions of Israelites could march across.

Paul and Silas found out that their God could send an earthquake and literally shake them free from prison.

Peter found out that God could send an angel and deliver him from a prison.

Noah found out that God kept His word and although he floated alone with his family for over a year, God never forgot about him.

How big is your God today?

When Henry Norris Russell, once a Princeton astronomer, had concluded a lecture on the Milky Way, a woman came to him and asked: "If our world is so little, and the universe is so great, can we believe that God pays any attention to us?"

Dr. Russell replied, "That depends, madam, entirely on how big a God you believe in."[108]

God is God and beside Him there is none else. He created the world out of nothing and spoke the worlds into place. He can do anything. The problem is not with God, the problem is with how much we can believe. Believe Him for great things today, for He is a great God full of glory and power!

"But they that wait upon the LORD shall renew their strength; they shall mount up with wings as eagles" (Isaiah 40:31).

In English the Olympic motto reads: "Swifter, higher, stronger." Interestingly, the Bible also has an Olympic text. It is Isaiah 40:31, "They that wait upon the LORD shall renew their strength; they shall mount up with wings as eagles; they shall run, and not be weary; and they shall walk, and not faint."[109]

Winning in the Olympics is not an easy thing. Each contestant is disciplined to the point of pain. They work out at their particular area of expertise four to six hours per day. They eat certain foods that build up their stamina and strength. They abstain from vices that would destroy their chances to win. They get the right amount of sleep. In short, they live a disciplined life, some of them even giving up their social lives.

Some people read Isaiah 40:31 and all they can see is the floating upward. It is not just a puff of wind and you are up there.

Just as there are disciplines in the Olympics there are disciplines in the Christian walk. It is the discipline of putting God on your daily calendar. It is the discipline of choosing to do what is right and then doing it. The goal must ever be before you, just as it is for the Olympic participants. The goal is pleasing God, finding true life, doing the will of God and of course, making it into the heavenly city and hearing the head Coach say, "Well done, thou good and faithful servant."

In order to go swifter, higher and become stronger in the Lord, we must spend time with Him. It is impossible to soar to the heights and be able to run and not grow weary without spending time in His presence. His Spirit will be transferred to you as you dwell with Him in communication.

"*One day a wanderer found a lump of clay so redolent of sweet perfume. Its odors scented all the room. 'What art thou?' was his quick demand. 'Art thou some gem from Samarkand, or spikenard in this rude disguise or other costly merchandise?' 'Nay, I am but a lump of clay.' 'Then, whence this wondrous perfume, say?' 'Friend, this is the secret I disclose—I have been dwelling with the rose.'*" —PERSIAN FABLE[110]

The same it is with the earthen vessels of mankind. Those who have been dwelling with the sweet *Rose of Sharon* will have the fragrance of His presence.

Not only will the fragrance of His Spirit be there, but the spirit of a winner will transcend into your soul and you will soar swifter, higher and be strengthened.

"*Let not mine enemies triumph over me*" (Psalm 25:2).

H. G. Bosch tells when he was a very young boy, a dear neighbor who lived two doors down the street experienced a great sorrow. She often played and sang at her piano, but after this tragedy struck in her life, the first song with which she would open her daily concert was the lovely hymn, "I Must Tell Jesus." "I must tell Jesus all of my burdens too hard to bear."[111]

When life gets tough, it is essential to tell your troubles to Jesus and then get up and start fighting. Do not lie down and die. You just have to try harder than when everything is easy and rosy.

The story is told by Stan Frager about his daughter Sarah. She was a ten-year-old girl, who was born with a muscle missing in her foot, who had to wear a brace all the time. She went home one beautiful spring day to tell her father she had competed in "field day," where they had lots of races and other competitive events.

Because of her leg support, Stan's mind raced as he tried to think of words of encouragement for his daughter, things he could say to her about not letting this get her down—things he had heard many famous coaches tell the players when they were faced with defeat—but before he could get a word out, Sarah looked up and said, "Daddy, I won two of the races!"

Her father couldn't believe it. And then Sarah said, "I had an advantage."

Stan thought, *They must have given her a head start—some kind of physical advantage.* But before he could say a word, Sarah said, "Daddy, I didn't get a head start; my advantage was I had to try harder."

Sometimes adversity and hardships cause people to work a little harder, re-evaluate, formulate new plans and from somewhere down deep comes that extra determination to make it in spite of the troubles and struggles.

Paul stated in II Corinthians 4:8-9, "We are troubled on every side, yet not distressed; we are perplexed, but not in despair; Persecuted, but not forsaken; cast down, but not destroyed."

"Who shall separate us from the love of Christ? shall tribulation, or distress, or persecution, or famine, or nakedness, or peril, or sword? . . . Nay, in all these things we are more than conquerors through him that loved us. For I am persuaded that neither death, nor life, nor angels, nor principalities, nor powers, nor things present, nor things to come, Nor height, nor depth, nor any other creature, shall be able to separate us from the love of God" (Romans 8:35, 37-39).

Life may have served you a raw and painful deal, and it may look like all is disastrous, but if you will learn, first of all, to tell Jesus about it, and then get that extra "umph" and try a little harder, you will eventually "triumph!" and become more than a conqueror in Christ Jesus.

March 23

"For he is like a refiner's fire" (Malachi 3:2).

Many years ago the goldsmiths had a unique method to determine when the refining fire had purged away all unwanted matter from the precious metal. They would stand patiently and peer intently into the seething, molten mass, meantime making the fire hotter and hotter. At last, a smile of satisfaction would spread across the perspiring face of the goldsmith. He could see his face reflected in the molten mass of gold. Seeing his face mirrored there, he knew that the refining fire had wrought its purifying purpose. Malachi 3:3 states: "And he shall sit as a refiner and purifier of silver: and he shall purify the sons of Levi, and purge them as gold and silver."
—Taken from story told by Rev. R. E. Neighbour, D.D.[112]

Good things are taking place when a Christian is going through struggles and trials. It cannot be seen always by the natural eye, but Job said it well: "When he hath tried me, I shall come forth as gold" (Job 23:10).

Notice the "I shall come forth!" It is a promise of hope: "I shall emerge from this trial. There is an end and it will be different than when I first entered into it. The process will make me pure like gold and more valuable to the kingdom of God."

Good things happen during struggle, as in nature. *"The cocoon of the emperor moth is flask-like in shape. To develop into a perfect insect, it must force its way through the neck of the cocoon by hours of intense struggle. Naturalists explain that this pressure to which the moth is subjected is nature's way of forcing a life-giving substance into its wings. Wanting to lessen the seemingly needless trials and struggles of the moth, an observer said, 'I'll lessen the pain and struggle of this helpless creature!' With small scissors he snipped the restraining threads to make the moth's emergence painless and effortless. The creature never developed wings. For a brief time before its death it simply crawled instead of flying through the air on rainbow-colored wings.*

"Sorrow, suffering, trials, and tribulations are wisely designed to grow us into Christlikeness. The refining and

developing processes are oftentimes slow, but through grace, we will emerge triumphant." —WALTER B. KNIGHT[113]

Psalm 4:1 says, "Thou hast enlarged me when I was in distress."

God sees you during the trial and has His eye on you. He admonishes in I Peter 4:12, "Beloved, think it not strange concerning the fiery trial which is to try you." It may be hot, but God is right there beside you and He will bring you out more valuable than when you went into the trial. So trust in the Lord, during the process.

March 24

"And be ye kind one to another, tenderhearted" (Ephesians 4:32).

Robert Tate Miller tells the story about when he was a small boy. One morning, John Evans shuffled into his life. John was a ragged-looking boy wearing oversized hand-me-down clothes and worn-out shoes. He was the son of migrant workers who had recently arrived at the North Carolina town where Robert lived. Standing at the front of the class by the desk of the teacher, Mrs. Parmele, who was writing his name in the roll book, John shifted nervously from foot to foot. As children sometimes do, whispers of disapproval began drifting from row to row. One of the girls making fun said: "Somebody open a window." The teacher looked up and the murmuring stopped. She then introduced John to the class. He looked around and smiled, hoping somebody would smile back. Nobody did, but John kept on grinning anyway. Robert held his breath hoping Mrs. Parmele wouldn't notice the empty desk next to his, but she did and pointed John in that direction. He looked over at Robert as he slid into the seat, but Robert averted his eyes so John wouldn't think that he had the promise of a new friend. By the end of the first week, John had found himself at the bottom of the social ladder. "It's his own fault," Robert told his mother one evening at dinner. "He barely knows how to count." Robert's mother had grown to know John quite well through Robert's nightly commentary. She always listened patiently, but rarely uttered more than a pensive "Hmmm" or "I see."

One day, John came to Robert and asked if he could sit with him in the lunchroom. Robert feebly said, "Okay," looking around to see if anyone was watching. As Robert watched him eat and listened to him talk, it dawned on him that maybe some of the ridicule heaped on John was unwarranted. He was actually pleasant to be around. After lunch, John and Robert went to play on the bars at the playground. Afterwards while lining up for the march back to class, Robert made up his mind that John would remain friendless no longer. One night he asked his mother, "Why do you think the kids treat John so badly?" "I don't know," she said sadly. "Maybe that's all they know." "Mom," Robert said, "tomorrow is his birthday, and he's not going to get anything. No cake and no presents. Nobody even cares." It was a tradition at Robert's school for a mother to bring cupcakes to the school on her child's birthday and let the class celebrate together.

The next morning Robert told his mother that he did not feel well and wished to stay home. She asked, "Does this have anything to do with John's birthday?" The bright red flush on Robert's cheeks was the only answer she needed. She then asked gently, "How would you like it if your only friend didn't show up on your birthday?" So Robert went to school and wished John a happy birthday.

Later in the day as Mrs. Parmele was writing math equations on the blackboard, Robert heard a familiar sound coming from the hallway. A voice he knew was singing the birthday song. Moments later, she came through the door with a tray of cupcakes aglow with candles. Tucked under her arm was a smartly wrapped present with a red bow on top. Mrs. Parmele's high-pitched voice joined in while the class stared at Robert for an explanation. His mother put the cupcakes and gift on John's desk and said, "Happy birthday, John." He then graciously shared the cupcakes with the class.

Robert says about that day, "Looking back, I can scarcely remember the names of the children who shared that birthday. John Evans moved on shortly thereafter, and I never heard from him again. But whenever I hear that familiar song, I remember the day its notes rang most true in the soft tones of my mother's voice, the glint in a boy's eyes and the taste of the sweetest cupcake." Maybe there is somebody you can be kind to this day who needs someone to care. This is the day to bring some sweetness into the life of someone who needs it very badly.

March 25

"And as ye would that men should do to you, do ye also to them likewise" (Luke 6:31).

An unknown author shares the following story. During the Roosevelt era, times were tough. The president was promising a brighter moon, but the Beasleys hadn't seen it rise over their small town in the Texas panhandle. So when he got the call that his son was ill in California and not expected to live, Bill Beasley didn't know how he was going to scrape together the money for his wife and himself to make the trip. Bill had worked as a trucker his entire life, but he never managed to accumulate any savings. Swallowing his pride, he phoned a few close relatives for help, but they were no better off.

So it was with embarrassment and dejection that Bill Beasley walked the mile from his house to the filling station and told the owner, "The son is really sick, and I've got no cash. Can you trust me for the phone call to California?" "Pick up the phone and talk as long as you need to" was the reply.

As he started to dial, he was interrupted by a voice asking, "Aren't you Bill Beasley?" It was a stranger, jumping from the cab of a truck with out-of-state plates. The young man didn't look familiar, and Bill could only stare at him with a puzzled look and say, "That's right, I am."

"Your son was one of my best pals when we were growing up together. When I went off to college, I lost all track of him." He paused for a moment and then continued, "Heard you say he's sick?"

"Real bad, from what we hear. I'm gonna call and try to make some arrangements for the wife to get out there with him." Then, as a matter of courtesy, he added, "Have yourself a merry Christmas. Wish your daddy was still with us."

Old man Beasley walked into the office of the station and placed his call to the cousin on the West Coast, informing him he or his wife hoped to be out as soon as possible. There was an obvious look of sorrow on the elder citizen's face as he assured the owner that he would pay for the call just as soon as he could. "The call has been paid for. That trucker—the one your son used to pal around with—left me a twenty-dollar bill and said to give you the change when the phone bill comes in. He also left you this envelope."

The old man fumbled as he opened the envelope and pulled out two sheets of paper. One read, "You were the first trucker I ever traveled with, the first my dad trusted enough to let me go along with you when I was barely five years old. I remember you bought me a Snickers bar." The second sheet, much smaller in size, was a signed check with an attached message: "Fill out the amount needed for you and your wife to make the trip, and give your son, my pal, a Snickers bar. Merry Christmas!"

How like the Lord Jesus. When you give anything to Him, He remembers, and then when you are in need, He says, "Here's a blank check, signed with My name on it." Take what you need. As the Lord orchestrated the meeting of the younger man and Mr. Beasley at a crucial time in his life, so the Lord and His angels are there to help you in the time of need. When you are walking through the trial, remember you are not alone. God is with you to help you, sustain you and meet your need. Trust Him today!

March 26

"Now unto him that is able to do exceeding abundantly above all that we ask or think" (Ephesians 3:20).

Nancy Mitchell relates a touching story: One day in a drugstore, the pharmacist handed Nancy her prescription, apologized for the wait, and explained that his register had already closed. He asked if she would mind using the register at the front of the store. She told him not to worry and walked up front, where one person was in line ahead of her, a little girl no more than seven, with a bottle of Children's Motrin on the counter. She clenched a little green and white striped coin purse closely to her chest. The purse reminded Nancy of the days when, as a child, she played dress-up in her grandma's closet. She'd march around the house in oversized clothes, drenched in hats and scarves, talking grown-up talk to anyone who would listen. She remembered the thrill one day when she gave a pretend dollar to someone, and he handed back some real coins for her to put into her special purse. "Keep the change!" he told her with a wink.

Now the clerk rang up the little girl's medicine, while she

shakily pulled out a coupon, a dollar bill and some coins. Nancy watched her blush as she tried to count her money, and Nancy could see right away that the little girl was about a dollar short. With a quick wink to the checker, Nancy slipped a dollar bill onto the counter and signaled the clerk to ring up the sale. The child scooped her uncounted change into her coin purse, grabbed her package and scurried out the door.

As Nancy headed to her car, she felt a tug on her shirt. There was the girl, looking up at her with big brown eyes. She gave Nancy a grin, wrapped her arms around her legs for a long moment then stretched out her little hand. It was full of coins. "Thank you," she whispered.

"That's okay," Nancy answered. Flashing a smile, winking, she said, "Keep the change!"

Many are the times when God's children come up short and the Lord is always there to make up the difference. Then He says, "Keep the change." He always gives more than is needed, for the promise is still true: *He is able to do exceeding abundantly above all that we ask or think*. You can depend on the Lord to keep His Word.

Are you standing in line today, trying to get something that you need and somehow you can't seem to get your answer? Remember, the Lord is right behind you or right by your side, wherever you need Him to be, and He is watching and waiting, seeing when to put that extra something into your hand, just at the right moment. He will not let you down. He does care about you today!

March 27

"*For they perceived that this work was wrought of our God*" (Nehemiah 6:16).

There is an interesting story told about an impossible feat that was accomplished. Engineers were called in to give their ideas on a possible railroad through the Andes Mountains. These men proclaimed the job as an impossible one. Then American engineers were called in to give their opinions whether the railroad could follow along the side of the river Rimac. Even these positive engineers claimed that it could not be done. As a last

resort, a Polish engineer named Ernest Malinowshi was called in. Malinowshi's reputation as an engineer was well known, but he was at that time in his sixtieth year, so the authorities feared to impose such a rigorous task on the man.

Malinowshi assured the representatives of the various countries interested that the job could be done, so in his older years he started the highest railroad in the world.

The railroad began to worm its way across the Andes from Peru with sixty-two tunnels and thirty bridges along its way. One tunnel ran four thousand feet in length, fifteen thousand feet above the level of the sea. Twice, revolutions in some of the countries through which the railroad passed held up construction. Once Malinowshi had to flee Peru and remain in exile for a time, but nothing deterred this aging Pole in completing the engineering feat that became one of the wonders of the world in 1880.
—*Future*[114]

Are you facing something that seems impossible? Take another look. This time ask God to show you the solution. He is the master engineer of all difficult situations. He can make a tunnel for you to go through or a bridge for you to cross over. Whatever it takes for you to make it successfully through life, He can show you the way. There is nothing He cannot do and nothing He cannot handle. Put the impossible situation in the hands of the master engineer, and it will become a wonder to the world. They will not be able to understand how a bad situation could turn out for good, but the Master always makes it so.

Don't know which way to turn? You have tried this remedy or sought after the answer in several different places; try prayer, faith, and let God work it out. He is the master of all things, and when His name is applied to His work, it will be good, for He does all things well.

March 28

"Why sit we here until we die?" (II Kings 7:3).

A friend once showed John Ruskin a costly handkerchief on which a blot of ink had been made. "Nothing can be done with it now," said the owner. "It's absolutely worthless."

Ruskin made no reply but carried the handkerchief away with him. After a time he sent it back, to the great surprise of his friend, who could scarcely recognize it. In a most skillful and artistic way Ruskin had made a design in India ink, using the blot as a basis and making the handkerchief more valuable than ever. —*War Cry*[115]

If you have made mistakes and there are blots on your life, give it to Jesus, the Master, and He will make something beautiful out of the blots and scars. He always makes everything better.

He never makes mistakes. When God made you, He made you for His glory. If His glory is not shining through you, it can, but first you must give Him everything that would obstruct the glory. Life abundantly is yours today—vibrancy, peace, joy, deliverance, dynamic living—it is available, but you have to reach for it.

An advertisement of the Tennessee Gas Transmission Co. pictures four men, the lone survivors of a sea tragedy, afloat in an open lifeboat. They are attempting to catch a few raindrops in a piece of canvas. They were tortured by thirst; yet, where they drifted, the Amazon carried its fresh water many miles to sea. To drink, they had only to lower their buckets.

Lower your bucket today. You are sailing on rough waters, and you might be lost in the sea of life. Everything may be going against you, but where there is God, there is hope. Hope in God. He can make the worthless worth something again. He can give water where seemingly there is none. Your hope is only a prayer away.

The story is told in II Kings 7 of four lepers. There was a famine in the city of Samaria and the Syrian army had surrounded it. The four men said, "If we go into the city, we shall die and if we sit still here, we die also. Now let us fall unto the host of the Syrians. If they save us, we shall live; and if they kill us, we shall but die. Why sit we here until we die? Let us do something."

The Lord was on their side. He had made a sound in the ears of the Syrians as a great host of chariots and horses and they were afraid and fled their camp. So the four lepers found food a plenty and then called into the city and told them of their great find. The gates were opened and everyone ate to his fill.

The question today is, "Why sit here until you die, when there is food a plenty at Father's table?" He will make your life better, more enriched, and take care of your needs. Just do something about it today, for He is waiting even now to be your God, Friend, or whatever you need Him to be.

March 29

"Whatsoever he doeth shall prosper" (Psalm 1:3).

If you want to be rich today, search for God!

Roger Babson, the statistician, was lunching with the President of Argentina. "Mr. Babson," the President said, "I have been wondering why it is that South America with all its natural advantages, its mines of iron, copper, coal, silver and gold; its rivers and great waterfalls which rival Niagara, is so far behind North America."

Babson replied, "Well, Mr. President, what do you think is the reason?"

He was silent for a while before he answered, "I have come to this conclusion. South America was settled by the Spanish, who came to South America in search of gold; but North America was settled by the Pilgrim fathers, who went there in search of God."
—*Christian Digest*[116]

Psalm 1:1-3 enforces this observation: "Blessed is the man that walketh not in the counsel of the ungodly, nor standeth in the way of sinners, nor sitteth in the seat of the scornful. But his delight is in the law of the Lord; and in his law doth he meditate day and night. And he shall be like a tree planted by the rivers of water, that bringeth forth his fruit in his season; his leaf also shall not wither; and whatsoever he doeth shall prosper." That is a strong promise! Whatever a person does, who seeks after God with pleasure and meditates on His Word continually, not allowing the mind to be filled with anything other than the Word or that which strengthens the truth of the Word, is promised to prosper. It is a *shall!* He shall prosper! It is an absolute truth.

"Blessed is the man that feareth the Lord, that delighteth greatly in his commandments. His seed shall be mighty upon earth: . . . Wealth and riches shall be in his house" (Psalm 112:1-3).

Robert Harkness tells about a man who was an atheist all his life. In word and action he said, "There is no God!" One morning he was found dead in his bed. In one hand he held a piece of white paper. On it were written in a scrawling handwriting the following words:

> *I've tried in vain a thousand ways,*
> *My fears to quell, my hopes to raise,*
> *But what I need, the Bible says,*
> *Is ever only Jesus!*
> *I cannot see, I cannot feel,*
> *For light, for life, I must appeal,*
> *In simple faith to Jesus!*[117]

His atheism may have brought him a distorted measure of satisfaction in life, to be able to say, "There is no God," but it failed him in death. When he went into the dark valley of death, he apparently turned to the only One who can help us when it comes time to die.

His life was lived in spiritual poverty. The light was never turned on in his soul. He lived and died without ever becoming rich in God.

What are you choosing today? Are you seeking gold like the early South Americans sought, or are you seeking God like the early Pilgrims did? The blessings and true richness of life are with those who seek the Lord, believe in God, and trust Him with all their heart.

March 30

"Do those things that are pleasing in his sight"
(I John 3:22).

Some people live to please the crowds, others live to please themselves, others live to please or impress a certain group of people, others live to please their Master.

There was once a young man in old Vienna who determined to write a symphony. "He set to work and labored hard; he wrote it and rewrote it. Then he called in some friends and went over it with them; they were loud in their praises. They said: 'It's great, Rudolph; it will make you a great name.' But he was not satisfied with it. He went over it again and again until at last he had finished

it. Then he set the orchestra to work upon it.

"Finally the night came when it was to be given to the public. The great hall was literally packed with people, and as the beauties of the harmony floated out over them it touched a responsive chord in their lives, it melted their hearts and they caught the inspiration of the composer. When the last strain had died out there was a moment's silence, then the great throng went almost wild in the demonstration of their enthusiasm, and hundreds flocked to the stage to congratulate the young musician.

"But he stood there unmoved. After the crowd had passed away somewhat, there came down the aisle an old white-haired man. Going up to the young man, he placed both his hands on his shoulders and said, 'It was well done, Rudolph, it was well done.' Then it was that a smile of satisfaction stole over the face of the young musician. That was his master." —E. A. KRAPP[118]

Just as Rudolph's desire was to please his master, to gain his approval, so must the desire of the Christian be. "What does the Master think?" should ever be our thought.

One of the main ways to please God is for His children to have faith. Hebrews 11:5-6 says: "He [Enoch] had this testimony, that he pleased God. But without faith it is impossible to please him: for he that cometh to God must believe that he is, and that he is a rewarder of them that diligently seek him."

In order to have faith one must transcend from the fleshly realm into the spiritual realm, for Romans 8:8 says, "So then they that are in the flesh cannot please God." Verse 9 further states: "But ye are not in the flesh, but in the Spirit, if so be that the Spirit of God dwell in you."

Faith operates not in tangibles, but intangibles, not the seen but the unseen. Faith does not operate according to facts, but according to that which can be believed.

Because it is impossible to please God without faith, this should be the vibrant desire in the heart of each of His followers: to have faith. Just as Rudolph, the musician, sought to please his master, so must the believer seek to please his heavenly Master by believing that He is and that He rewards them who diligently seek Him. This is the day to please Him and live in the realm of great faith!

March 31

"All his commandments are sure" (Psalm 111:7).

Psalm 111:8 states: "They [His commandments] stand fast for ever and ever, and are done in truth and uprightness." Do you believe in God today or do you doubt His Word? You may not voice your doubts as some do, but there are those who are vocal about their unbelief, but that does not change God one iota.

There was a group of people who thought Jesus could be kept in a grave, but they did not reckon with the power of God and His Word. Caiaphas the high priest and other enemies of Jesus thought that when the tomb in which His body had been laid was made secure, it could not be opened. They had the audacity to plot his death thinking that they had more power than Him. "Then assembled together the chief priests, and the scribes, and the elders of the people, unto the palace of the high priest, who was called Caiaphas, And consulted that they might take Jesus by subtilty, and kill him" (Matthew 26:3-4).

All of their planning had no effect upon the Word. Jesus spoke that He would rise from the grave in three days and it happened just as He spoke it. Matthew 28:2 says, "The angel of the Lord descended from heaven, and came and rolled back the stone from the door, and sat upon it." When Mary Magdalene and the other Mary came to see the sepulcher, the angel told them, "He is not here: for he is risen, as he said. Come, see the place where the Lord lay" (Matthew 28:6).

No matter what anyone says, the Word and power of God are greater than man's word. It is time to believe in God and let Him resurrect things in our life. It is time to bury doubt and let faith be resurrected in us. God is God no matter what anyone thinks, so we might as well start believing and enjoying the Spirit of the Lord working in us and through us.

What is it you need resurrecting today? Jesus said to Martha when He was talking to her about her brother's death, "I am the resurrection, and the life: he that believeth in me, though he were dead, yet shall he live" (John 11:25).

If He is the resurrection, that means that He has the power to resurrect dead things. He can resurrect health back in a sick body,

resurrect love back into a marriage, and resurrect spiritual life back into one who is spiritually dead. He can do all things exceeding abundantly above what we can ask or think.

Believe Him for your answer today. If He can resurrect out of a tomb, He can resurrect anything, no matter how hopeless it may seem to be.

April 1

"Thou wilt shew me the path of life: in thy presence is fulness of joy; at thy right hand there are pleasures for evermore" (Psalm 16:11).

The Lord wants to shine through you, so that others can see His glory! Matthew 5:16 says, "Let your light so shine before men, that they may see your good works, and glorify your Father which is in heaven." It is time to turn the light on and let the world see that light shine.

A Hindu once asked a native Christian of India, "What medicine do you put on your face to make it shine so?" "I don't put anything on it," said the Christian. "Yes, you do. All you Christians do. I've seen shining faces wherever I have met Christians!" Then the Christian said, "I will tell you what 'medicine' makes our faces shine—it is the joy in our hearts because Jesus dwells there."

Rev. Paul Rees told the story about how one Sunday morning a Christian layman from Louisville, Kentucky, walked down the streets in St. Louis, Missouri, trying to find a place of worship. The streets were rather deserted, but he saw a police officer; so he went up to him and said, "Officer, I'm a stranger in St. Louis. I'm a Protestant, and I want to go to church to worship. Could you suggest a place?" The officer said, "I will," and he named a church and gave him directions how to get there. The man thanked him and started to go; then suddenly he stopped, turned around, and said, "By the way, Officer, there must be several churches on your beat. Why have you named this particular one for me to go to?" The officer said, "I'll tell you why! I'm not a very religious man; I'm not a church man. There are several churches on my beat. I'm sending you to this one because I've observed for years that the people who come out of that church are the happiest-looking people in St. Louis!"[119]

Dr. Rees ended the story commenting, "How little those people realized that an ungodly police officer had taken notice of the fact that there was the evidence of the joy of the Lord upon their countenances, as they came out of His sanctuary."

Psalm 126:2 was proven true that day: "Then was our mouth filled with laughter, and our tongue with singing: then said they among the heathen, The LORD hath done great things for them."

Look at what the Lord has done for you this morning and begin to praise the Lord! Let the joy and the glory of the Lord rest upon you. Do not wallow in self-pity, self-absorption, or self-condemnation; get beyond yourself and enter into the presence of the One who gives fullness of joy. This is the day to have joy in its fullness, not partial joy, but full and running over joy so that it affects everyone you meet!

"He that doeth the will of God abideth for ever" (I John 2:17).

George Bernard Shaw once said, "*I am ready to admit after contemplating the world and human nature for sixty years that I see no way out of the world's misery but by the way which would be found by God's will.*"

When Jesus taught the disciples to pray, He started His prayer like this: "Our Father which art in heaven, Hallowed be thy name. Thy kingdom come. Thy will be done in earth, as it is in heaven" (Matthew 6:9-10). It is important for God's will to be done in your life today.

David Livingstone once said, "*I had rather be in the heart of Africa in the will of God than on the throne of England out of the will of God.*"

Dr. James M. Gray related how he saw a painting of a large boat laden with cattle that were being ferried across an angry, swollen river in time of storm. The artist had so cleverly pictured the dark, threatening clouds and the play of the treacherous, jagged lightning that he instantly concluded that the freight of the poor dumb cattle was marked for destruction. But the title of the painting was simply *Changing Pastures*.

Many times Christians imagine that God's plans mean disaster and affliction but He is only "changing pastures" for the good of His children.

"God's will is found by three things which always concur: the inward impulse, the Word of God, and the trend of circumstances. God in the heart, impelling you forward; God in His Book, substantiating whatever He says in the heart; and God in circumstances, which are always indicative of His will. Never act until these three things agree." —Dr. F. B. Meyer[120]

Just where you stand in the conflict,
There is your place;
Just where you think you are useless,
Hide not your face.
God placed you there for a purpose
Whate'er it be;
Think He has chosen you for it,
Work loyally.
Gird on your armor, be faithful
Always your best,
Whate'er it be never doubting,
God's way is best.
Out in the fight or on picket,
Stand firm and true.
There is a work which your Master
Gives you to do.
—Author Unknown[121]

"When typhoons and monsoons occur in the Indian Ocean, these violent cyclonic storms swirl around in a circle. Before navigators learned how to cope with them, there was a frightful loss of ships and lives. In explaining how navigators learned to cope with them, a sea captain said, 'When we run into them we locate the center, and we go around it. We narrow the circle until we get into the center where there is a dead calm. There, we are safe.' This is a parallel of God's will. Christ speaks with finality and authority to us. When we are in the center of His will, we are safe. There He keeps our hearts and minds in *perfect peace*." —Walter B. Knight[122]

To reiterate Mr. Shaw's statement: "The way out of this world's misery is to be in the will of God!" Oh, what a place to be.

April 3

"These that have turned the world upside down are come hither also" (Acts 17:6).

A missionary in India once asked a Hindu, "I want you to teach me your language." "No, I will not teach you my language. You would make me a Christian," said the Hindu. The missionary responded, "You don't understand me. I am only asking you to teach me your language." Replied the Hindu, "No sahib, I will not teach you. No man can live with you and not become a Christian." —WALTER B. KNIGHT[123]

What an influence! The question is, "What kind of influence are you having on the people around you today: in the home, on the job, at the church house, in the marketplaces, or at the store?"

A dying young man, who had made a sordid mess of his life, pleaded with those around him to bury his influence with him, but that was impossible. Influence speaks on and on as stated in Hebrews 11:4: "Abel offered unto God a more excellent sacrifice than Cain, by which he obtained witness that he was righteous, God testifying of his gifts: and by it he being dead yet speaketh."

The story is told of David Brainerd; because of his zeal for missions and outspoken advocacy of missions, he was expelled from Yale College. He became a missionary to the American Indians. After his death, his diary fell into the hands of William Carey, who was so impressed with the life and work of Brainerd that he went as a missionary to India. This is an example of "He being dead yet speaketh."

Alice M. Knight shares the story about a minister's testimony. While giving a challenging message in a Sunday-school conference where many Sunday school teachers were present, a well-known minister told the following story: *"I was a boy from a broken home. I became a member of a Sunday school class in which there were thirteen boys. Five of the boys were from broken homes. They knew little of love and kindness. Our teacher was a big man. He wore a size fourteen shoe. There were no discipline problems in that class—we had respect for that large shoe. Our teacher had never gone beyond the sixth grade in school, but he knew the Lord and he loved the boys in his class. He gave me love that I had never known before. He played with me and with the other boys. All of the thirteen*

boys became Christians. Eleven of them entered into full-time Christian service. How great is the influence of a teacher who knows the Lord and who loves the pupils in his or her class."[124]

What you do, what you say in everyday life will cause people to find true life or to die. It is like the story told about the GI in World War II. It was dark and the colonel and his driver were hurrying along in a jeep, anxious to return to their own lines. Coming to a fork in the road they spied a lone MP stationed there to guide traffic. Getting the necessary directions they were on their way. After a few miles, the driver sensed something wrong and got out to investigate. He walked ahead about thirty feet in the gloom. And there where a bridge should have been, was a yawning drop of several hundred feet. Enraged, the colonel drove back to the MP and demanded an explanation. Wearily, the MP sighed: "I can't understand, sir. I've been sending traffic that way all night and you're the first to complain." —*DIGEST AND REVIEW*[125]

The question is, "Through your influence, are you pointing people in the right or wrong direction?" This is the day to examine your life and realize you are not an island, but what you are affects those around you. It is the duty of all mankind to live justly, serve the Lord and to point others in the right direction. Everyone chooses what kind of influence he will have in life.

"*Blessed are they that have not seen, and yet have believed*" (John 20:29).

*I*n order to believe and have faith, one must leave the safety of the rail and go forward without visible support. It many times means moving in the dark.

"*I said to the man at the gate of the year, 'Give me a light that I may tread safely into the unknown.' He replied, 'Go out into the darkness and put your hand into the hand of God. That shall be to you better than light and safer than a known way.'*" —M. L. HASKINS[126]

"*Faith is to believe what we do not see, and the reward of this faith is to see what we believe.*" —AUGUSTINE[127]

"In the realm of the natural, seeing is believing. In the realm of the spiritual, believing is seeing. Jesus said, 'If thou wouldest believe, thou shouldest see the glory of God' (John 11:40)."
—WALTER B. KNIGHT

When Sir Harry Lauder's only son was killed in World War I, he said to a friend, "When a man comes to a thing like this, there are just three ways out of it—there is drink; there is despair; and there is God. By His grace, the last is for me."

What will it be for you today? When you walk through a difficult time and face pain and anguish, what will you choose? This is the day to choose to have faith in God.

Joseph M. Smith shares how he chose to listen to a voice instead of doubting. One Friday evening in 1967, he finished his day's work as an Air Force chaplain's assistant and headed out to the parking lot. He was looking forward to a weekend of cruising around in his roommate's prized Chevy El Camino, which he had put in his charge while he was out of town. He reached for the door handle. The car had been broken into. A distinctive tachometer, gearshift knob and other pricey accessories were gone. When the base police told Joe not to expect their return, he felt responsible for his friend's loss, so he prayed about it.

The next morning in the chapel parking lot, he felt a hand on his shoulder and he heard a voice say, "Turn around and look in the 1957 Chevrolet." He looked to see who was talking to him. No one was nearby. He took another step and heard the same instruction. More than two hundred cars were parked in the lot, but when he turned, a '57 Chevy was directly in front of him. He glanced in the rear window. There lay the tachometer, gearshift knob and other accessories! By Monday the police had returned his roommate's stolen things and items from other cars as well.

This is what life is all about. There will be adversity and trouble, but in the midst of trouble, pray, and then listen by faith for the answer. God will help you, for He is a present help in the time of trouble!

"The LORD will perfect that which concerneth me" (Psalm 138:8).

Life is filled with vexations and problems; nothing is perfect but God. He is the only One who can perfect the things that concern you, because He is the only One who is perfect. God does not throw trouble and frustration out of your life, but He uses it for your good to help perfect you.

"Toiling through a great hot valley in Ethiopia, far from civilization, we once came with gratitude to the top of a hill, where it was much cooler. Surely the camp would not be far away. The ground was covered with short, dry grass, and after the difficult mountain, we began to rejoice. But we rejoiced too soon. After a short ride everyone began to start itching and smarting in the most intolerable fashion. Even the mules were affected and stamped angrily. A careful examination showed that each seed stem of grass had a myriad of sharp little bayonets that would penetrate the skin and would work up through the clothing, causing intense discomfort. Life's school is full of experiences like that. Not one great trouble, but a thousand little ones cause pain and vexation. Yet this is God's school." —Dr. Thomas A. Lambie[128]

God works things for good in the lives of His children. Sometimes it does not appear that He is working even when He is. He does not always make loud announcements: "You are being worked on today, so beware!" When roads are going to be worked on, there is usually a sign that will announce the days it will be under construction. Not so with God. He is constantly watching His children and will use every opportunity to perfect that which concerns them.

Did the leaves say nothing to you as they murmured when you came hither today? They were not created this spring, but months ago, and the summer just begun will fashion others for another year. At the bottom of every leaf-stem is a cradle, and in it is an infant germ; and the winds will rock it, and the birds will sing to it all summer long; and the next season it will unfold. So God is working for you, and carrying forward to the perfect development all the processes of your lives.
—Henry Ward Beecher[129]

Have peace in your heart knowing that God is working to perfect all that concerns you and when He does it, it is always done well.

April 6

"I have made the earth, and created man upon it: I, even my hands, have stretched out the heavens, and all their host have I commanded" (Isaiah 45:12).

Consider the fact that God guides the great universe. He knows the details of the working of the seas and the weather patterns. Not only does He guide the greater atmosphere that surrounds the earth, but He also guides the birds and the bees in their flights and their daily activities.

"Here is a little bee that organizes a city, that builds ten thousand cells for honey, twelve thousand cells for larvae, a special place for the mother queen, a little bee that observes the increasing heat, and when the wax may melt and the honey be lost, organizes the swarm into squads, puts sentinels at the entrances, glues the feet down, and then, with flying wings, creates a system of ventilation to cool the honey that makes an electric fan seem tawdry—a little honey bee that will include twenty square miles in the field over whose flowers he has oversight. But if a tiny brain in a bee performs such wonders, who are you, that you should question the guidance of God? Lift up your eyes, and behold the hand that supports those stars without pillars, the God who guides the planets without collision." —BEAMS OF LIGHT[130]

Isaiah 40:26 declares: "Lift up your eyes on high, and behold who hath created these things, that bringeth out their host by number: he calleth them all by names by the greatness of his might, for that he is strong in power; not one faileth." This is amazing! God not only created the stars, but He has a name for each of them. "He telleth the number of the stars; he calleth them all by their names" (Psalm 147:4).

This same God, who cares about the universe, cares even more about His children. As He numbered the stars, so He numbers the hair on your head. "But the very hairs of your head are all numbered. Fear ye not therefore, ye are of more value than many sparrows" (Matthew 10:30-31). So why should we not trust Him?

If you are in a quandary and wondering if God really knows what He is doing or if He really cares about your life, rest assured that He knows what He is doing and He does care. The main thing is to learn to trust Him, for He said in Isaiah 45:5-6, "I am the LORD, and there is none else, there is no God beside me: I girded thee, though thou hast not known me: That they may know from the rising of the sun, and from the west, that there is none beside me. I am the LORD, and there is none else." Let this great God direct your steps today.

April 7

"*God is my defence*" (Psalm 59:9).

The sun is always shining no matter how dark the clouds. We used to sing the following old song that says:

> *Back of the clouds the sun is always shining.*
> *Back of the clouds the skies are always blue.*
> *God has prepared a rosy tinted lining*
> *Back of the clouds it's waiting to shine through.*

Once there lived an old woman who was always so cheerful that everyone wondered at her. "But you must have some clouds in your life," said a visitor. "Clouds?" she replied. "Why, of course; if there were no clouds, where would the blessed showers come from?"

> *Be still, sad heart! and cease repining;*
> *Behind the clouds is the sun still shining;*
> *Thy fate is the common fate of all:*
> *Into each life some rain must fall,*
> *Some days must be dark and dreary.*
> —HENRY WADSWORTH LONGFELLOW[131]

Some good advice on how to handle cloudy days is as follows:

> *When troubles come, go at them with songs.*
> *When griefs arise, sing them down.*
> *Lift the voice of praise against cares.*
> —HENRY WARD BEECHER[132]

When the clouds come into your life, it is time to sing about the goodness of the Lord. When grief threatens to overcome you, it is time to sing, "Hallelujah, hallelujah to the Lord."

When David of old was fleeing for his life from the hand of the murderous King Saul, he wrote in Psalm 57, "My soul is among lions. . . . They have prepared a net for my steps; my soul is bowed down: they have digged a pit before me. . . . My heart is fixed, O God, my heart is fixed: I will sing and give praise." Another time when Saul tried to kill him, David wrote, "I will sing of thy power; yea, I will sing aloud of thy mercy in the morning: for thou hast been my defence and refuge in the day of my trouble" (Psalm 59:16).

When the black clouds appear and troubles knock you down, it is no time to sing the blues. It is time to remember that the sun is always shining—the greater Son of God, Jesus Christ is resplendent in power and glory. All power in heaven and earth is in His hands and He is waiting to help you as was stated in Hebrews 4:14 and 16, "Seeing then that we have a great high priest, that is passed into the heavens, Jesus the Son of God. . . . Let us therefore come boldly unto the throne of grace, that we may obtain mercy, and find grace to help in time of need."

> *Be hopeful, friend, when clouds are dark and*
> *days are gloomy, dreary,*
> *Be hopeful even when the heart is sick and*
> *sad and weary.*
> *Be hopeful when it seems your plans are all*
> *opposed and thwarted;*
> *Go not upon life's battlefield despondent and*
> *fainthearted.*
> *And, friends, be hopeful of yourself. Do*
> *bygone follies haunt you?*
> *Forget them and begin afresh. And let no*
> *hindrance daunt you.*
> *Though unimportant your career may seem*
> *as you begin it,*
> *Press on, for victory's ahead. Be hopeful,*
> *friend, and win it.*
> —STRICKLAND GILLIAN[133]

April 8

"Thou art my help and my deliverer; O LORD" (Psalm 70:5).

Once there was a printer who lived in a large city and who had an impressive trademark. He put it on every package that was sent from his company. It was simply a circle within which were his name and the words, "I never disappoint."

Life is filled with disappointments, but there is no disappointment in Jesus, as the old song goes. New cars get smashed. There is disappointment. Children disobey and there is disappointment. Relationships become strained, there is hurt, and then the scars remain.

GOD SEES THE SCARS
When some friend has proved untrue
betrayed your simple trust;
Used you for his selfish ends and trampled in the dust
The past, with all its memories and all its sacred ties,
The light is blotted from the sky
for something in you dies.

Bless your false and faithless friend, just smile
and pass along.
God must be the judge of it;
He knows the right from wrong.
Life is short, don't waste the hours by
brooding on the past;
His great laws are good and just;
Truth conquers at the last.

Red and deep our wounds may be
but after all the pain
God's own finger touches us and we are healed again.
With faith restored, and trust renewed
we look towards the stars.
The world will see the smiles we have
but God will see the scars.

—AUTHOR UNKNOWN[134]

Even though there is disappointment in a relationship, God will heal the wound if we will let Him. God is not the cause of the problem; He is the solution. He is not the one who disappoints; He is the one who can deliver.

Many times disappointments can lead to greater things in our lives if we will look up to the Master who is in control. It was Lord Clive, as a young man, who set out from his British home for India, when the ship upon which he sailed was caught in a terrific storm. Continuous adverse gales drove it far off the course, until it barely made it into a South American harbor. There he had to remain for many months before being able to get passage to India. But during the long wait he acquired the Portuguese language. This qualified him when he did reach India to take an important position with the East India Company, ultimately resulting in his being appointed by the crown as Governor General of India. —PRAIRIE OVERCOMER[135-136]

The upsets of life and disappointments can be the stepping stones that lead to greater things. Just stay close to the One who will never disappoint you and He will always cause you to rise to a higher level; for He is faithful, true and just.

April 9

"My Father giveth you the true bread from heaven" (John 6:32).

"Religion is meant to be bread for daily use, not cake for special occasions," someone once wrote.

Babcock said it like this. "Christianity is not a voice in the wilderness, but a life in the world. It is not an idea in the air but feet on the ground, going God's way. It is not an exotic to be kept under glass but a hardy plant to bear twelve months of fruits in all kinds of weather. Fidelity to duty is its root and branch. Nothing we can say to the Lord, no calling Him by great or dear names, can take the place of the plain doing of His will. We may cry out about the beauty of eating bread with Him in His kingdom, but it is wasted breath and a rootless hope, unless we plow and plant in His kingdom here and now. To remember Him at His table and to forget Him at ours, is to have invested in bad securities. There is no

substitute for plain, every-day goodness."[137]

It is time for Christians to have everyday goodness; to live right, to wake up to the possibilities around us and to have a true revival: the kind that causes people to love one another. Someone once wrote that it all depended on a two-letter word called IF. It goes like this:

If all the sleeping folk—will wake up;
And all the lukewarm folk—will fire up;
And all the dishonest folk—will confess up;
And all the disgruntled folk—will sweeten up;
And all the discouraged folk—will cheer up;
And all the depressed folk—will look up;
And all the estranged folk—will make up;
And all the gossipers will hush up—;
And all the members will pray up—
WE WILL HAVE A REVIVAL AND IT WILL CONTINUE IN OUR CHURCH AND COMMUNITY.
—Author Unknown[138]

Every community needs to get back to the basics of life. It's not the flowery speeches; it's the everyday living that is needed. It's not the pomp and the parade; it's the pulsating love and kindness.

"Religion is the spice which is meant to keep life from corruption." —Francis Bacon

That's the revival that is needed: a religion that keeps one from corruption, bitterness, unkindness, hate, malice and resentment.

It's time to put the bread of His Word on the table: the table of our heart, and eat until it fills us with the Lord's goodness.

Let us pass that bread around today and let the bread of the Word cause us to live as shining lights showing forth just plain ole goodness in a dark and corrupt world. And add a little spice while you're at it.

April 10

"For to be carnally minded is death; but to be spiritually minded is life and peace" (Romans 8:6).

*D*o you ever feel like you are alive physically, but dead inside to the things of the Spirit? There is a better way to live.

Henry Ward Beecher once wrote the following: *"Now, take a man that is spiritually dead. Pinch his conscience; he does not start. Bring before him the law, and let it thunder in his ears; it makes no impression upon him. Pierce him with the sword of the Spirit; he does not feel it; he is not susceptible to fear; he has no moral sensibility. A man that is spiritually dead is not alive to Divine influences."*[139]

Decades ago Charles Bradlaugh, an atheist, challenged Hugh Price Hughes, a godly minister, to debate with him the truth of the Christian faith. The challenge was immediately accepted in these words: "The courts as a rule, in rendering their verdicts, do not rely solely upon the arguments of the lawyers on either side. They carefully scrutinize the evidence offered by those who have first-hand knowledge of the facts. I will bring with me to the debate one hundred men and women who have been saved from lives of sin by the gospel of Jesus Christ. They will give their evidence and you will be allowed to cross-examine them. I will ask that you bring with you one hundred men and women who have been similarly helped by the gospel of infidelity which you preach."[140] The debate was canceled. It was canceled because dead faith has no equal terms with live faith. It cannot even stand on the same ground. There is nothing to argue or debate about.

Charles Bradlaugh would be described as being totally spiritually dead; whereas Rev. Hughes and his one hundred witnesses would be described as people who were seeking to be alive to divine influences.

Something is definitely wrong with anyone who cannot respond to a pinch, feel the pain of being pierced by a sword or be awakened by thunder.

Paul said it like this: "Awake thou that sleepest, and arise from the dead" (Ephesians 5:14). "For yourselves know perfectly that the day of the Lord so cometh as a thief in the night" (I Thessalonians 5:2). "But ye . . . are not in darkness, that that day should overtake you as a thief" (I Thessalonians 5:4). "Therefore let us not sleep, as do others; but let us watch and be sober" (I Thessalonians 5:6).

Which side are you on: those who are spiritually dead or those who are spiritually alive? There is no middle way. None of us can escape the importance of choice. We may think that we can set our lives toward the direction of a middle way by trying to

make the best of both worlds. But no one can sit on the fence for long. He will finally land on one side or the other. It is best to be totally alive to God: His inspiration, deliverance, power and glory and to be totally dead to the things that will enslave and bring evil into our lives.

This is the day to be alive to that which is good and dead to those things which debilitate, and to wake up and sense the sweet fragrance of the presence of the Lord Jesus and be alive to His influence.

April 11

"I have created him for my glory" (Isaiah 43:7).

This is no day to become just a jaded lump of clay filled with depression and discouragement, or suicidal thoughts. This is the day to live up to God's expectancy for you. Consider this: "No scientific instrument is as sensitive to the light as a person's eye. And in the dark, its sensitivity increases 100,000 times; one can detect a faint glow, less than a thousandth as bright as a candle's flame. He can see light from the stars, and the nearest of all stars is 25 billion miles away! Automatically, the muscles of the eye relax so that the lens is small and thick for distant viewing or they stretch the lens to bring into focus. No wonder the eye was the original model for cameras."[141]

Lawrence Galton stated: "Even though your brain will forget more than 90 percent of what you learn during your lifetime, it may still store up as much as ten times more information than there is in the Library of Congress, with its 17 million volumes."[142]

Years ago an issue of *Sunshine Magazine* compared the human mind to a computer. It stated that scientists were asked to determine the size, the cooling system, and the power required to perform electronically the same functions that are automatically accomplished by a person's brain during their lifetime. They decided that if all parts were transistorized and built on a miniature scale like those used in rockets to the moon, the following would be needed:

"A machine the size of the United Nations building in New York; a cooling system with an output equal to Niagara Falls; and

a power source that would produce as much electricity as is used in homes and industry in the entire state of California."[143]

The ten major organs in the body perform such unique feats of electric conduction that it would take a big book to explain each one adequately. In the fraction of a second that it takes you to read one word on a page, the marrow in your bones produces over one hundred thousand red blood cells.

You have all that inside of you. You are a wonder and created for His glory! The question is, what are you doing with all this power?

The first thing is to seek to obey Mark 12:30-31, "And thou shalt love the Lord thy God with all thy heart, and with all thy soul, and with all thy mind, and with all thy strength: this is the first commandment. And the second is like, namely this, Thou shalt love thy neighbour as thyself."

These two commandments are said to be the most important ones. When you get the outward look and focus on God and others, suicidal thoughts seem to leave, as well as depression and discouragement. When we are focused only on ourselves we become depressed, because it is opposite of divine instruction.

It is the little everyday things that you do to help lift someone's heavy load, or bring some happiness into the life of one who is downcast. This is what true living is all about, for buildings will crumble, empires will fall, but the human soul will live forever. This is the day to invest in the eternities of tomorrow by using the power that is within you.

"For by thy words thou shalt be justified, and by thy words thou shalt be condemned" (Matthew 12:37).

Jesus stated that words form your destiny. Words are powerful things as depicted in the following poem:

A careless word may kindle strife,
A cruel word may wreck a life.
A bitter word may hate instill.
A brutal word may smite and kill.

A gracious word may smooth the way.
A joyous word may light the day.
A timely word may lessen stress.
A loving word may heal and bless.[144]

BRIDLE YOUR TONGUE
That speech—it hadn't been gone half a minute
Before I saw the cold black poison in it;
And I'd have given all I had, and more,
To have only safely got it back indoor.
I'm now what most folks "Well-to-do" would call.
I feel today as if I'd give it all,
Provided I through fifty years might reach
And kill and bury that half-minute speech.
Boys flying kites haul in their white-winged birds,
You can't do that with flying words.
Careful with fire—is good advice we know:
Careful with words—is ten times doubly so,
Thoughts unexpressed may sometimes fall back dead,
But God Himself can't kill them when they're already said.
—WILL CARLETON[145]

Once words are spoken, it is impossible to gather them back together and extract them from the air. Proverbs 16:27 says, "An ungodly man diggeth up evil: and in his lips there is as a burning fire." It is a fire that destroys, kills, and causes lives to disintegrate.

But just as words of strife can kindle animosity, words can also paint a beautiful picture that evokes peace in the heart of the listener. An unknown author wrote, *"There is a beauty of language, just as there is a beauty of face. There is a harmony of words, just as there is a harmony of sky and stars, green foliage, and crystal waters. There is a delicacy of speech, just as there is a delicacy of tints in the masterpiece on canvas, in the shimmer of light on the dewdrop, in the semi-transparent petal of the woodland flower."*[146]

Once when Thomas A. Edison was being introduced at a dinner, the toastmaster mentioned his many inventions, dwelling at length on the talking machine. The aged inventor then rose to his feet, smiled and said gently to the audience: "I thank the gentleman for his kind remarks, but I must insist upon a correction. God

invented the talking machine. I only invented the first one that can be shut off."

The question today is: what are we doing with the talking machine that God created within us? Do our words help dispel fears or do they generate hate and hopelessness? This is the day to clean out the talking machine and start speaking words that bless; for "a word fitly spoken is like apples of gold in pictures of silver" (Proverbs 25:11).

What shall it be? Will our words be as a devastating forest fire or will they be as apples of gold; rich, valuable and uplifting? Choose your words carefully today for your destiny is determined by them.

April 13

"For unto whomsoever much is given, of him shall be much required" (Luke 12:48).

*T*his is the day to be bigger than you have ever been before, to give of what you have. Someone once wrote, "Refuse to open your purse, and soon you cannot open your sympathy. Refuse to give, and soon you will cease to enjoy that which you have. Refuse to love, and you lose the power to love and be loved. Withhold your affections and you become a moral paralytic. But the moment you open wider the door of your life, you let the sunshine of your life into some soul."[147]

"Have you ever watched a grower irrigate his grove, or a farmer his land? When he opens little gates to irrigation furrows there rushes in a life-giving flow of water which, in time, will result in beautiful trees and nourishing plants. Our lives are like that. Each of us is given a furrow into which flow power, wisdom, energy and health from a divine source. Like the trees and plants, we thrive—or dry up—according to the degree to which our gates are opened. But there is this tremendous difference. God lets every man be the keeper of his own gate!" —UNKNOWN AUTHOR[148]

Luke 6:38 says it like this: "Give, and it shall be given unto you; good measure, pressed down, and shaken together, and running over, shall men give into your bosom. For with the same

measure that ye mete withal it shall be measured to you again."

How much do you want measured back to you?

Aquilla Webb tells of a deacon in a church in Boston, who many years ago said to himself, "I cannot speak in prayer meeting. I cannot do many other things in Christian service, but I can put two extra plates on my dinner table every Sunday and invite two young men who are away from home and ask them to dinner." He did that for more than thirty years and many of the young men whom he invited became Christians. When he died he was to be buried in a city several miles away and because he was a well-known merchant, a special train was chartered to convey the funeral party. It was made known that any of his friends among the young men who had become Christians through his influence would be welcomed in a special car set aside for them. One hundred and fifty of them came and packed that car from end to end in honor of the memory of the man who had preached to them the gospel of the extra dinner plate.

Life can be a rich, full experience filled with friends. You can be blessed with a positive influence if you are willing to open your heart and give what you can to anyone who needs what you have to give. It is not wasted effort, for only what you put into other people and what you do for God really count.

It is time to open the purse of your life and give, for as you give, your own purse grows bigger and bigger, your own life becomes more and more enriched. Now is the time to be bigger in spirit than you have ever been before.

"Therefore I WILL look unto the LORD" (Micah 7:7).

*H*enry Ford said, "Whether you think you can or not, you are right." Before anything is accomplished there must first be a fixed or determined *will* to do it. Your mind has the power to believe and accomplish something, even when it looks impossible to do so. Whatever your mind believes, that is what will take place.

President Abraham Lincoln said, *"Without the Divine Being,*

I cannot succeed. With that assistance, I cannot fail."

God has given each of us a will. What we do with it determines our success or failure. With Him all things are possible. Each day there must be a fixed set of "I wills" established in our mind to do what is right.

> *I will start anew this morning*
> *with a higher, fairer creed,*
> *I will cease to stand complaining*
> *of my ruthless neighbor's greed;*
> *I will cease to sit repining*
> *while my duty's call is clear;*
> *I will waste no moment whining,*
> *and my heart shall know no fear.*
> *I will look sometimes about me*
> *for the things that merit praise;*
> *I will search for hidden beauties*
> *that elude the grumbler's gaze;*
> *I will try to find contentment*
> *in the paths that I must tread;*
> *I will cease to have resentment*
> *when another moves ahead.*
> *I will not be swayed by envy*
> *when my rival's strength is shown.*
> *I will not deny his merit,*
> *but I'll strive to prove my own;*
> *I will try to see the beauty spread*
> *before me, rain, or shine;*
> *I will cease to preach your duty,*
> *and be more concerned with mine.*
> —Author Unknown[149]

It has often been said, "Where's there a will, there's a way." This was demonstrated by one of our presidents. With his six-foot, three-inch frame, and carrying over 210 pounds, former President Lyndon B. Johnson was given some weighty wisdom by his wife. Mrs. Johnson told the President: "You can't run the country if you can't run yourself." The President took her advice and trimmed his weight down to about 187 pounds.

Yes, where there is a will, there is a way. This is the day to establish some "I wills" in our daily life and to seek to follow God's

will, for His ways are above our ways.

The best way to know God's will is to say "I will" to God. When you couple a surrendered will to God's will and then a resolute spirit toward the "will," you have an unbeatable situation. You will win.

As one Arctic explorer answered, when asked what he would do if there was no way to get through to his destination, "If there is no way, I will make a way."

This is the day to formulate some firm "I wills" and be resolute in our decisions, for as Abraham Lincoln said, "With God's assistance, I cannot fail."

"*Now therefore give me this mountain*" (Joshua 14:12).

*T*he poorest man is not he who is without a cent, but he who is without a dream. When Caleb of the Old Testament was eighty years old, he still had his dream. He said, "As yet I am as strong this day as I was in the day that Moses sent me: as my strength was then, even so is my strength now. . . . Now therefore give me this mountain" (Joshua 14:11-12).

No matter what life hands you, or how many times you get knocked down, it is not the time to give up; it is the day to hold on!

"*When you get into a tight place and everything goes against you, till it seems as though you could not hold on a minute longer, never give up then, for that is just the place and time that the tide will turn.*" —Harriet Beecher Stowe[150]

Years ago a Protestant minister by the name of Basil King was well known for his writings. Suddenly his health and eyesight failed. A specialist broke the painful news that he would eventually become blind. What a crushing verdict for a man with all of life before him! Years later King declared: "On the day that I knew I would lose my sight I bought a typewriter." He refused to give up just because his eyes gave out.

President Theodore Roosevelt offers one of the best examples of a man overcoming terrific handicaps. History tells us that even though he was born with weak eyes, he nevertheless became a keen-eyed hunter, a wide-ranged reader, and a skilled naturalist. Although he lost the use of one ear, he could distinguish the calls of many birds. With a body wracked by pain, Roosevelt would keep working at his correspondence until he fainted. He had that pioneer spirit of never giving up but working until he succeeded.

When you are working with something, an idea or dream that others have tossed aside all because it seemed impossible, consider the story of Michelangelo. Agostino d' Antonio, a sculptor of Florence, Italy, worked diligently but unsuccessfully on a large piece of marble. "I can do nothing with it," he finally said. Other sculptors, too, worked with the piece of marble, but they, too, gave up the task. The stone was discarded. It lay on a rubbish heap for forty years. Out strolling one day, Michelangelo saw the stone and the latent possibilities in it. It was brought to his studio. He began to work on it. Ultimately, his vision and work were crowned with success. From that seemingly worthless stone was carved one of the world's masterpieces of sculpture—*David*. —TOLD BY REV. JAMES SEWARD[151]

When Moses, the great deliverer who delivered the Israelites out of the hands of Pharaoh, chose twelve men to go spy out the land of Canaan, he told them, "Be of good courage" and go forward and see what to expect from their enemies. Ten of the men returned with a fearful report and said, "We are not able to fulfill the dream that the Lord promised us." But two of the men, Joshua and Caleb said, "We are well able to take the land." Only two men kept the dream—the others gave up. Because of it they died in the wilderness, but Joshua and Caleb lived to a ripe old age and attained the mountain that was promised to them.

Keep your dream alive today, for nobody can take it from you but yourself. This is not the time to give up, but to press on to victory.

April 16

"With God all things are possible" (Mark 10:27).

It is time to win today—time to accomplish and to seize the day. There have always been those who have seized the day. A sci-

entist once said about Thomas A. Edison, "This poor fellow is wasting his time. Two fundamental laws of physics prove that he is attempting the impossible. The first is that there can be no light without combustion; the second is that no combustion can take place in a vacuum."

But even in the face of these 'impossibilities,' Edison went right ahead and perfected the electric lamp. Harvey was scoffed at when he insisted that blood flowed through the body. Pasteur's theories of germ life were scorned. Langley's plans for a machine which would fly without the help of a balloon were ridiculed. These men were winners in their field.

"You see some fellow reach out and grab an opportunity that the other fellow standing around had not realized was there. Having grabbed it, he hangs on it with a grip that makes the jaws of a bulldog seem like a fairy touch. He calls into his play his breadth of vision. He sees the possibility of the situation, has the ambition to desire it, and the courage to tackle it. He intensifies his strong points, bolsters his weak ones, cultivates those personal qualities that cause other men to trust him and cooperate with him. He sows the seeds of sunshine, of good cheer, of optimism, of unstinted kindness. He gives freely of what he has, both spiritual and physical things.

"He thinks a little straighter, works a little harder and a little longer; travels on his nerve and enthusiasm; he gives such service as his best efforts permit. He keeps his head cool, his feet warm, his mind busy. He doesn't worry over trifles. He plans his work and then sticks to it, rain or shine. He talks and acts like a winner, for he knows in time he will be one. And then—God does all the rest." —AUTHOR UNKNOWN

With God all things are possible! Work hard, plan and do your part. Then the divine Spirit of God will do what seemingly cannot be done. He makes it all fit together. You can accomplish your dreams, climb those mountains and attain.

Remember, Philippians 2:13 states, "It is God which worketh in you."

If God is working inside you, you definitely are going to win; so keep stretching, working, believing and someday it will happen.

April 17

"*Thou shalt find*" (Matthew 17:27).

This is the day to convert problems into opportunities. What is a problem? A problem is "a question proposed for a solution." A problem that occurs is simply a question that life asks you.

Once a Yankee shoe salesman went to Africa and wired his manufacturer, "I want to come home. Nobody wears shoes in this part of Africa." So they brought him home and sent another salesman who shipped back order after order. He wrote the home office, "Everybody here needs shoes."

Both men were asked the question, "What are you as a shoe salesman going to do in a country where no one wears shoes?" One man answered his problem by giving up and coming home. The other man answered his problem by creating a market for that which had no market.

"One way to solve a problem is to lift your conscious mind above the level where you met the problem." Author John Templeton wrote: "*A problem appears as an obstacle that cannot be seen accurately because it dominates our mental landscape. From the meadow the forest may appear ominous and troubling; all the trees seem to block our journey to a desired destination. A lifted consciousness, however, functions like a hot air balloon—when it gets up high enough, the forest is revealed in its entirety, and shown in proper relationship to all its surroundings. Distance and height provide an encompassing perspective that is helpful in showing us how to cope with challenging circumstances.*"

Distance and height: note the two words used to help look at a problem objectively. The best way to obtain this is to obey Hebrews 4:16. "Let us therefore come boldly unto the throne of grace, that we may obtain mercy, and find grace to help in time of need." Problems present needs; therefore, when you enter God's throne room you are distancing yourself from the problem and you are rising into a heavenly realm of grace, power and glory. So the best way to help turn your problem into an opportunity is to go alone into a place of prayer to the Lord and let Him instruct you what to do.

When the disciples needed money to pay taxes, they went to

Jesus and asked Him what to do. He said, go fishing and you will find gold in a certain fish's mouth. Unorthodox, yes, but when God becomes involved with your problem, the answer is not always like you would reason it to be in your own mind. Somehow He always gives the right answers, problems are solved, and He causes new opportunities to arise.

This is the day to not run away from your problems, but run to the problem solver because He always has an answer.

April 18

"He is strong in power" (Isaiah 40:26).

God always gets the last word. More than one hundred years ago an infidel died in Hanover, Germany. Before his death he ordered that above his grave several large slabs of granite should be placed bound together with iron bands, and above it all a huge stone block weighing almost two tons, so it was done. On the stone the inscription was put, "This grave is purchased for eternity; it shall never be opened."

Somehow a little poplar seed was enclosed in the mold within the tomb. God in His power caused it to sprout. A little shoot found a crevice between the iron-bound slabs. Its hidden power in the course of time broke the iron bands asunder and moved every stone out of its original position. The whole structure was displaced completely and the grave was opened. The tree still lives and waves its branches over the rent sepulcher, which the infidel declared should never be opened. It just needed a tiny little seed, one of God's marvels in creation, to answer the challenge of the infidel.

Do not underestimate God as the infidel did. God is bigger than all the intelligence in the world put together. Isaiah said, "Who hath measured the waters in the hollow of his hand. . . ? It is he that sitteth upon the circle of the earth, and the inhabitants thereof are as grasshoppers; that stretcheth out the heavens as a curtain, and spreadeth them out as a tent to dwell in. . . . Lift up your eyes on high, and behold who hath created these things, that bringeth out their host by number: he calleth them all by names by the greatness of his might, for he is strong in power;

not one faileth" (Isaiah 40:12, 22, 26).

God did not strike the infidel dead for challenging Him. He was so secure in His great power that He chose a tiny seed to disprove the infidel. He didn't cause the earth to shake, thunder and lightning to flash across the sky. He did not have to defend His position or authority, because He is without question the highest power.

There was once a Christian woman whose husband died after a long illness. He did not leave her much, but left her all his tools, since he was a carpenter. A neighbor with bad character, shortly after the funeral presented a bill for labor which he said was due him. It was not only beyond the widow's power to pay, but she felt certain her husband had paid the bill. It was useless to argue with the man, because she could not find a receipt. The man said he would take the tools instead of the money he said she owed him. In great distress the widow went to her room to pray as the man waited for her decision. As she came from her room her little daughter, who had been chasing butterflies, came to report that in chasing one into the garage she had crawled behind a truck causing a pile of papers to fall to the floor from above. It proved to be a packet of receipted bills and the first one on top was the answer to her problem. It was the receipt she needed to prove that the neighbor's bill had already been paid.

God used a small butterfly to answer the little widow's prayer. If you will trust Him today, He will get the last word in concerning your situation and it will be a positive one, for He is on your side and working in your behalf. Trust Him today!

"To this end was I born" (John 18:37).

A life without a high aim is like a ship without a rudder. A ship with sails that are properly trimmed can travel in any direction in relation to the wind except directly into it. While the set of the sails determines the most efficient use of the wind, the rudder enables the ship to travel in a specific direction. Without a rudder the ship can do little more than blow helplessly downwind. A rudder is that which guides or governs the course of a person or thing.

It is possible to go through life doing only what is necessary to live and never doing anything that leaves you with a satisfied glow. Many engage in aimless thought and activity rather than steer themselves in a direction they have charted. Like a rudderless ship, they blow helplessly on the winds of circumstance, wasting precious mind energy. Feeling ineffective, they live in a chronic state of unhappiness.

Paul wrote: "I have finished my course" (II Timothy 4:7). He had charted his course; he knew where he was going. He had a mission and it drove him on even when he was beaten, imprisoned and falsely accused. When barriers were put in front of him, when people said, "you can't," and everything went against him, he grabbed hold of the rudder and hung on for dear life. He was determined that nothing would get him off course.

When Jesus stood before Pilate He said, "To this end was I born." He had charted his course. He was on a mission and nothing could stop Him.

If you are going to do anything in life worthwhile, you must have a rudder, that which guides or governs your course. When Thomas Edison invented the light bulb, he tried over two thousand experiments before he got it to work. A young reporter asked him how it felt to fail so many times. He said, "I never failed once. I invented the light bulb. It just happened to be a two-thousand-step process." Edison just grabbed hold of the rudder and kept on course. He knew where he was going and he let nothing stop him.

It is time to reach for the stars, to stretch, to go beyond the incessant activity of doing the necessary things that life requires. You have within you the power to set your course. Aim high, set your sails for success, grasp the rudder and start moving. When you do, you will find the challenge and the happiness that the amazing seas of life and God have in store for you. Grab hold of it today!

"He hath shewed thee, O man, what is good; and what doth the Lord require of thee, but to do justly, and to love mercy, and to walk humbly with thy God?" (Micah 6:8).

The *Baltimore Sun* conducted a contest in which the question was asked: "What would you do if you only had one more year to live?" Mary Davis Reed entered this poem and received the prize for the best answer:

> *If I had but one year to live;*
> *One year to help; one year to give;*
> *One year to love; one year to bless;*
> *One year of better things to stress;*
> *One year to sing; one year to smile;*
> *To brighten earth a little while;*
>
> *One year to sing my Maker's praise;*
> *One year to fill with work my days;*
> *One year to strive for a reward*
> *When I should stand before my Lord,*
> *I think that I would spend each day*
> *In just the very self-same way*
>
> *That I do now. For from afar*
> *The call may come across the bar*
> *At any time and I must be*
> *Prepared to meet eternity.*
> *So if I have a year to live,*
> *Or just one day in which to give*
>
> *A pleasant smile, a helping hand*
> *A mind that tries to understand*
> *A fellow creature when in need;*
> *'Tis one with me—I take no heed.*
> *But try to live each day He sends*
> *To serve my gracious Master's ends.*[152]

This is the day to live with justice, mercy and walk in humbleness before God, for no one knows the last day he has on earth. It is best to be prepared for that which is to come by living God's way now, for it will affect the future life.

April 21

"As my strength was then, even so is my strength now" (Joshua 14:11).

This is the day to look for new opportunities—to slam the door on that which is a failure and go forward in Jesus' name! The following poem encompasses the thought that opportunities do come more than once even when you are older:

OPPORTUNITY
They do me wrong who say I come no more
When once I knock and fail to find you in,
For every day I stand outside your door
And bid you wake, and rise to fight and win.
Wail not for precious chances passed away,
Weep not for golden ages on the wane!
Each night I burn the records of the day;
Laugh like a boy at splendors that have sped,
To vanished joys be blind and deaf and dumb;
My judgments seal the dead past with its dead,
But never bind a moment yet to come.
Tho' deep in mire, wring not your hands and weep:
I lend my arm to all who say, "I can!"
No shamefaced outcast ever sank so deep
But yet might rise and be again a man.
Dost thou behold thy lost youth all aghast?
Dost reel from righteous retribution's blow?
Then turn from blotted archives of the past
And find the future's pages white as snow.
Art thou a mourner? Rouse thee from my spell;
Art thou a sinner? Sins may be forgiven;
Each morning gives thee wings to flee from hell,
Each night a star to guide thy feet to Heaven.
—Walter Malone[153]

This is the time to rise up and follow your dreams, no matter what the excuse not to, for there are many great and wonderful things yet for you to do.

No one is ever too old to take advantage of a new opportunity. Pine not for days gone by. Open your eyes to what is available today. Many people have done great things when most people thought it couldn't be done. Moses was eighty years old when God called him to deliver His people. Socrates gave the world his wisest philosophy at seventy years of age and at an extreme old age learned to play a musical instrument. Plato was only a student at fifty. He did his best after reaching sixty. Franklin did not begin his philosophical pursuits until fifty. He went to France in the service of his country at seventy-eight, and wrote his autobiography in his eighties. Tennyson published his famous "Crossing the Bar" at age eighty-three. George Bernard Shaw wrote some of his famous plays at age eighty. Scott the commentator began study of Hebrew at age eighty-seven. What is it you feel has passed you by? Arise and go for it.

You say, "Opportunity knocked and will not knock again." Maybe the same opportunity you missed will not come again, but there is always another opportunity waiting for you as long as you are alive.

Have the spirit of Caleb who said, "I am as strong this day as I was in the day that Moses sent me: as my strength was then, even so is my strength now. . . . Now therefore give me this mountain."

It is time to climb your mountain, to follow your dream, to do what seems too big to do. You can do it through Christ!

April 22

"Fitly framed together" (Ephesians 2:21).

Have you ever noticed how life comes in pieces, like the pieces of a puzzle? Life is not all dumped on you in one big piece, but it is given one thing at a time. Birth is a piece. You did not have anything to do with that, but all the choices you make concerning each piece that is given to you as you grow older become your response to the "piece" of life that is allotted you. The growing up years, the school years, the courtship years, marriage, then children, jobs, deaths, and every experience, piece by piece life is granted to you.

Someone once wrote the following poem which says it well:

GOD'S MOSAIC
An artist can take a few bits of colored glass,
And fit them together with infinite pains
Into a design of symmetry.
When he is finished, his colors so blend together
That he has created a picture in glass.
It is a mosaic.
You are God's mosaic,
A distinctive, original design.
The way you fit each "piece" of you together:
Your dreams, your education,
Your lifework, and your total personality,
Will determine whether the "Design for Your Tomorrow"
Will be the masterpiece God has in mind.
—AUTHOR UNKNOWN[154]

Fanny Crosby lost her sight when just a little girl, but she refused to let her discouragement overcome her. Out of her tribulation came scores of the sweetest songs of the church. Although she has long ago passed on to her reward, her spirit goes marching on in the songs she wrote. In her blindness she wrote this note of cheer to the discouraged:

Oh, what a happy soul am I!
Although I cannot see,
I am resolved that in this world
Contented I will be;
How many blessings I enjoy
That other people don't!
To weep and sigh because I'm blind
I cannot, and I won't.

What a spirit! She accepted the pieces of life's puzzle with an undaunted attitude. She did not let the devastations of blindness bind her soul and spirit. Although she was chained to a limited vision, she was free in her spirit and soared high above her handicap and blessed a world.

How could she do it? She chose to live each piece of her life led by the Master's hand. Joshua 24:15 said, "Choose you this day

whom ye will serve . . . but as for me and my house, we will serve the LORD."

When you choose the Lord then you can fit each piece together that life gives you in a becoming manner. You can become the masterpiece that God had in mind when He created you. It all starts with your choice.

Will you choose the high road or the low road? Will your life be a puzzle that is fitly formed together or will it be a shambled mess of disoriented pieces? Let God put your life together piece by piece, let Him guide you and help you when you don't know which way to go or what to do, and things will turn out all right every time for He never makes an idle stroke or wastes any movement. Paul said, "And we know that all things [or all pieces of the puzzle] work together for good to them that love God, to them who are the called according to his purpose."

"*Forgetting those things which are behind*" (Philippians 3:13).

"*Y*esterday is already a dream and *tomorrow* is only a vision, but *today* well lived makes every *yesterday* a dream of happiness and every *tomorrow* a vision of hope."

"*There are two days in every week that we should not worry about, two days that should be kept free from fear and apprehension. One is Yesterday with its mistakes and cares, its faults and blunders, its aches and pains. Yesterday has passed forever beyond our control. All the money in the world cannot bring back yesterday. We cannot undo a certain act or take back a word we've said. Yesterday is gone. The other day we shouldn't worry about is Tomorrow—with its impossible adversaries, its burdens, its hopeful promise, and poor performance. Tomorrow's sun will either rise in splendor or behind a mask of clouds, but it will rise and until it does, we have no stake in tomorrow, for it is yet unknown. This leaves only one day—Today. Any person can fight the battle for just one day. It is only when*

we add the burdens of yesterday and tomorrow that we break down. The sadness comes not from the experience of today, but the remorse of bitterness for something which happened yesterday and the dread of what tomorrow may bring."
—AUTHOR UNKNOWN

Jesus said, "Take . . . no thought for the morrow" (Matthew 6:34). Paul wrote in Philippians 3:13, "This one thing I do, forgetting those things which are behind." So if we are not to worry about tomorrow, and are to forget yesterday, that leaves only today. If you can focus upon and live well today, then tomorrow's memory of today will be pleasant without bitterness.

Martin Luther once said, *"Even if I knew that tomorrow the world would go to pieces, I would still plant my little apple tree and pay my debts."*[155]

The old prayer says it well and would be a good prayer to pray today:

> *Lord, for tomorrow and its needs,*
> *I do not pray;*
> *Keep me, my God, from stain of sin,*
> *Just for today!*
> *Now, set a seal upon my lips*
> *For this I pray;*
> *Keep me from wrong, or idle words,*
> *Just for today!*
> *Let me be slow to do my will,*
> *Prompt to obey;*
> *And keep me, guide me, use me, Lord,*
> *Just for today.*
> —AUTHOR UNKNOWN[156]

April 24

"Speak; for thy servant heareth" (I Samuel 3:10).

God inspires, and He speaks instructions. The choice to obey is in the hands of the listener.

Dr. Donald Grey Barnhouse told of a missionary home in the

Congo where a little son was playing in the yard. Suddenly he heard the father's voice. "Philip, obey me instantly! Drop to your stomach!" The boy obeyed without asking a question. "Now crawl toward me as fast as you can!" Again the boy obeyed. "Now stand up and run to me!" The lad obeyed and ended in his father's arms. Only then did he turn to look at the tree by which he had been playing. Hanging from a branch was a fifteen-foot snake. If the boy would have paused to ask, "Why, Dad?" or "Do I have to right now?" he would have been killed by the snake. Instant obedience is a mark of faith and love. Philip knew he could trust his father, so he obeyed his voice.

Sometimes the Lord speaks to his children to do something. Something crucial to the moment, crucial to His kingdom, crucial to their own well-being, but often they ask why or lag behind in the instructions, causing death to the dream the Savior has for them.

The important thing is to follow the instructions, follow the inspiration, the nudge from above. Psalm 18:28 says, "For thou wilt light my candle: the LORD my God will enlighten my darkness." Proverbs 20:27 says, "The spirit of man is the candle of the LORD." David's words could be interpreted as, "Thou will inspire my spirit. God will show me how to light the darkness of boredom, despair and frustration. He will give me an inspiration that will fuse life into me and help other people."

It doesn't matter who you are; what matters is that you listen to the Voice that instructs you what to do. Whether or not you obey will determine whether you realize your dream or if your dreams will die. You do not have to be famous, degreed or rich to hear His voice of inspiration.

When Edison was a train newsboy he had a layover between runs in Detroit, but Edison did not waste time. He went to the library and put in time with books that gave him further information and education. God was lighting his fire. He gave him the inspiration to invent many things, and Edison applied himself and listened. The father of photography was an army officer; of the electrical motor, a bookbinder; of the telegraph, a portrait painter. The inventor of the typewriter was a farmer; a carpenter invented the cotton gin, and the locomotive was invented by a coal miner. These inventors learned to listen to the voice of inspiration which comes from God, and they obeyed in spite of jeers, discouragement and weariness. Because they obeyed, their dreams came into fruition.

You too can listen to the voice of inspiration, follow instructions and see your dreams live instead of die. God is speaking today; are you listening and obeying?

April 25

"*Every man according to their works*" (Revelation 20:13).

*T*he important thing to consider today is the dash that will be between the dates of your birth and death. Consider the following questions:

Is anybody happier
Because you passed his way?
Does anyone remember
That you spoke to him today?
This day is almost over,
And its toiling time is through;
Is there anyone to utter now,
A friendly word for you?
Can you say tonight in passing,
With the day that slipped so fast,
That you helped a single person
Of the many that you passed?
Is a single heart rejoicing,
Over what you did or said?
Does one whose hopes were fading
Now with courage look ahead?
Did you waste the day,
or lose it?
Was it well or poorly spent?
Did you leave a trail of kindness,
Or a scar of discontent?
—AUTHOR UNKNOWN[157]

I read of a pastor who stood to speak at the funeral of his friend. He referred to the dates on her tombstone from the beginning to the end. He noted that first came the date of her birth and the following

date her death, but he said what mattered most of all was the dash between those years. For that dash represents all the time that she spent alive on earth, and only those who loved her knew what that little line is worth.

"For it matters not, how much we own, the cars, the house, the cash. What matters is how we live and love and how we spend our dash. So think about this long and hard, are there things you'd like to change? For you never know how much time is left. (You could be at 'dash mid-range.') If we could just slow down enough to consider what's true and real, and always try to understand the way other people feel. And be less quick to anger, and show appreciation more and love the people in our lives like we've never loved before. If we treat each other with respect, and more often wear a smile, remembering that this special dash might only last a little while. So, when your eulogy is being read with your life's actions to rehash . . . would you be pleased with the things they say about how you spent your dash?"

Jesus said, "What shall it profit a man, if he shall gain the whole world, and lose his own soul?" Gaining possessions and material wealth but losing your soul, losing your friends and losing a relationship with Jesus Christ is like putting water in a bucket with holes in it. It is like planting copper pennies in the ground and expecting them to sprout growth. It is like building a house on the edge of the sandy seashore and when the tide comes in to have it washed away.

What are you writing today concerning the dash which represents your life?

"Reaching forth unto those things which are before" (Philippians 3:13).

Are you dreaming big enough dreams, or are you staying too close to the shore, afraid to venture forth into the storms that accompany deeper depths?

"Disturb us, O Lord, when we are too well pleased with ourselves; when our dreams have come true because we

dreamed too little, when we have arrived in safety because we sailed close to the shore."

"Disturb us, O Lord, when with the abundance of things, which we possess we have lost our thirst for the water of life; when having fallen in love with time we have ceased to dream of eternity; and, in our efforts to build the new earth, have allowed our vision of the new heaven to grow dim."

"Stir us, O Lord, to dream and dare more boldly, to venture on wider seas where storms shall show Thy mastery, where losing sight of land we shall find the stars. In the name of Him who has pushed back the horizons of our hopes and invited the brave to follow Him." —ADDISON H. GROFF

Paul said in Philippians, "reaching forth unto those things which are before, I press toward the mark." Reaching forth means to stretch, to go beyond, to dream bigger, to press, to expend energy, not to be lazy, self-satisfied, but to extend, expand.

Robert G. Lee once wrote: "If you had a bank that credited your account each morning with $86,400.00 that carried no balance from day to day, allowed you to keep no cash in your account, and finally every evening cancelled whatever part of the amount you had failed to use during the day, what would you do? Draw out every cent of course!

"Well, you have such a bank and its name is 'Time.' Every morning it credits you with 86,400 seconds. Every night it rules off—as lost—whatever of this you have failed to invest to good purpose. It carries no balances. It allows no balances. It allows no overdrafts. Each day the bank named 'Time' opens a new account with you. Each night it burns the records of the day. If you fail to use the day's deposits the loss is yours."[158]

When you act upon your dream, when you launch your ship in the sea of life, going forward towards that which you have been destined to do, this is all part of the withdrawal of the cash in the *Bank of Time* that life gives you each day.

May you use this investment wisely! Settle not on beds of ease, taking the lesser road, leaving your gift in the bank to be cancelled at the end of the day with nothing to show for your efforts, but rise and utilize, reach and become, dream and do, for the smallest deed is better than the greatest intention. What are you doing with your very own *Bank of Time*?

April 27

"LORD, make me to know mine end, and the measure of my days" (Psalm 39:4).

Today is the most important day of your life! Why is today important? Because it is the first day of the rest of your life! What you do today will determine what happens tomorrow, what you will become, what you will accomplish, and how much satisfaction you will have.

Do not waste time, one of the most precious commodities that is given to mankind. J. L. Brandt wrote that in the early life of Elihu Burritt, he began to study the ancient languages after his regular day's work was done. He spent his evenings in study as faithfully as his days in work. He was a blacksmith by trade. At the age of fifty he was familiar with almost as many languages as he was years old. He was a blacksmith by day and linguist by night. He became a noted lecturer, philanthropist and author.

There are others who have accomplished things by utilizing the gift of today. Robert Fulton invented the steamboat, and Morse the telegraph, with fragments of time. Paul in about thirty years preached the gospel and planted churches over the whole civilized world. Madame de Genlis composed several of her charming volumes while waiting for the princess to whom she gave music lessons. One of the great chancellors of France wrote a book in the successive intervals of waiting for dinner. J. L. Brandt commented about those who utilize their time well, *"These men and women have coined minutes into hours and hours into day to show what can be done in a brief space of time. They were industrious from morning till night. They were faithful to their highest convictions and the best thought which God gave to them. In this manner they changed time into life and made every moment bring forth fruit."*

The following poem could have been written by many:

ALL I MEANT TO DO
Said yesterday to tomorrow:
"When I was young like you,
I, too, was fond of boasting

Of all I meant to do.
But while I fell a-dreaming
Along the pleasant way,
Before I scarcely knew it
I found I was today!
And as today, so quickly,
My little course was run,
I had not time to finish
One-half the things begun.
Would I could try it over;
But I can ne'er go back;
A yesterday forever,
I now must be alack.
And so, my good tomorrow
If you would make a name
That history shall cherish
Upon its roll of fame,
Be all prepared and ready
Your noblest part to play
In those few fleeting hours
When you shall be today."

—Author Unknown[159]

It was Edward H. Griggs who said, "Fifteen minutes a day devoted to one definite study will make one a master in a dozen years."[160]

On the outer wall of one of the towers of Beverley Minster is a quaint old dial with a message that says: "Now or When?" A simple question it asks, silently, yet continuously—in the morning, at noon, at the setting of the sun—of all the dwellers in that place, of all the strangers who come there, of all the passersby; a simple question but deep with meaning.[161]

Let today be your Now. Do not waste it!

April 28

"Be content with such things as ye have" (Hebrews 13:5).

*B*enjamin Franklin said, "To the discontented man, no chair is easy." Earl C. Willer told about how years ago there appeared in a newspaper a cartoon showing two fields divided by a fence. Both fields were about the same size and each had plenty of the same kind of grass, green and lush. In each field there was a mule, and each mule had his head through the fence eating grass from the other mule's pasture. All around each mule in his own field was plenty of grass, yet the grass in the other field seemed greener or fresher, although it was harder to get. And in the process the mules were caught in the wires and were unable to extricate themselves. The cartoonist put just one word at the bottom of that picture: DISCONTENT.[162]

Once there was a king who was suffering from a painful ailment. His physician told him that the only cure for him was to find a contented man, get his shirt, and wear it night and day. So messengers were sent throughout the king's realm in search of such a man, and they had orders to bring back his shirt.

Months passed, and after a thorough search of the country the messengers returned but without the shirt. "Did you find a contented man in all my kingdom?" the king asked. "Yes, O King, we found one, just one in all thy kingdom," they replied. "Then why did you not bring back his shirt?" the king demanded. "Master, the man had no shirt," was the answer. —*EVANGELISTIC ILLUSTRATION*[163]

Once a bishop of the early church who was a remarkable example of the virtue of contentment was asked his secret. The old man said, "It consists in nothing more than making a right use of my eyes. In whatever state I am, I first of all look up to heaven and remember that my principal business here is to get there."

This is the gist of the whole matter. Our business here on earth is to prepare to get to heaven. Many of the things we strive for and get upset over are not worth the energy spent.

Hebrews 13:5 says, "Let your conversation be without covetousness; and be content with such things as ye have: for he hath said, I will never leave thee, nor forsake thee."

The important thing is to know that God is always with us. He will help us make it through life successfully, for He is on our side. We must relax in God, take our burdens to the Lord, praise Him for all things and do our best to walk with Him through the tornadoes of life, the upsets, the times of want and pressure.

All we really need is God, for if we have Him, He will supply everything else that we need. So relax today, get off the train that is filled with grabbing, anxious, frustrated, discontented people, and get a ticket riding first class with Jesus; for with Him is love, joy, peace, longsuffering, patience, all the things that are not in the discontent. Trust in God today and be content.

April 29

"*He that cometh to God must believe that he is*" (Hebrews 11:6).

The following story was sent to me in an email entitled: "It takes Guts to say *Jesus.*" This is a true story of something that happened just a few years ago at USC. There was a professor of philosophy there who was a deeply committed atheist. His primary goal for one required class was to spend the entire semester attempting to prove that God couldn't exist. His students were always afraid to argue with him because of his impeccable logic. For twenty years, he had taught this class and no one had ever had the courage to go against him. Nobody would go against him because he had a reputation. At the end of every semester, on the last day, he would say to his class of three hundred students, "If there is anyone here who still believes in Jesus, stand up!"

In twenty years, no one had ever stood up. They knew what he was going to do next. He would say, "Because anyone who does believe in God is a fool. If God existed, he could stop this piece of chalk from hitting the ground and breaking. Such a simple task to prove that he is God, and yet he can't do it." And every year, he would drop the chalk onto the tile floor of the classroom and it would shatter into a hundred pieces. All of the students could do nothing but stop and stare. Most of the students were convinced that God couldn't exist. Certainly, a number of Christians had slipped through, but for twenty years they had been too afraid to stand up. Well, a few years ago, there was a freshman who happened to get enrolled in the class. He was a Christian and had heard the stories about this professor. He had to take the class because it was one of the required classes for his major and he was afraid. But for three months that semester, he prayed every morning that he would have the courage to stand up no matter

what the professor said or what the class thought. Nothing they said or did could ever shatter his faith, he hoped.

Finally the day came. The professor said, "If there is anyone here who still believes in God, stand up!" The professor and the class of three hundred people looked at him, shocked, as he stood up at the back of the classroom. The professor shouted, "You fool! If God existed, he could keep this piece of chalk from breaking when it hit the ground!" He proceeded to drop the chalk, but as he did, it slipped out of his fingers, off his shirt cuff, onto the pleats of his pants, down his leg, and off his shoe. As it hit the ground, it simply rolled away, unbroken. The professor's jaw dropped as he stared at the chalk. He looked up at the young man and then ran out of the lecture hall.

The young man who had stood up proceeded to walk to the front of the room and share his faith in Jesus for the next half-hour. Three hundred students stayed and listened as he told of God's love for them and of his power through Jesus.

The Scripture says, "The fool hath said in his heart, There is no God." The choice is yours today. Will you be considered a fool by God or a fool by godless people who say "There is no God"? God always gets the last word. He is alive and well and will be here forever. His power is beyond man's puny mind to comprehend. He is a power to be reckoned with. He is and will always be. This is the day to believe in Him and truly live!

"I will instruct thee and teach thee in the way which thou shalt go" (Psalm 32:8).

It is important to give prudent thought before making a decision about something, for your decision could mean life or death.

Years ago, two men and a youth—Arnold Dobson, Harold Most and his son Harold Jr.—perished in the blasting summer heat of the Death Valley area. Sheriff deputies found their bodies seven, fourteen and seventeen miles from an abandoned car. "They were kind of strung out like a black line. The heat turned them black," said deputy Red Landergram.

In leaving their stranded car to seek help, the three had tragically headed in the wrong direction, going toward a ranch house they had passed thirty miles back. Just a mile in the other direction was a grove of willows and a spring![164]

Once during a lesson in a medical college, one of the students was asked by the professor, "How much is a dose of this?" as he held up a certain drug that could be poison if administered incorrectly. The student answered quickly without thinking his answer through. "A teaspoonful," he replied.

The professor made no comment, but the student, a quarter of an hour later, realized that he had made a mistake, and straightway said: "Professor, I want to change my answer to that question." "It's too late, sir," responded the professor, curtly, looking at his watch. "Your patient has been dead fourteen minutes." —STORY TAKEN FROM *THE INDIAN WITNESS*[165]

Judas, one of the followers of Jesus, hungry for gold, sold Jesus to the leaders of the Sanhedrin. Realizing he had made a wrong decision, he went back to them saying he wanted his money back and that he did not want to sell Jesus. They said, "What's done is done." The torture of Judas's decision weighed heavily upon his mind, until he went and hung himself.

Many years ago a passenger train was rushing into New York as another train was emerging. There was a head-on collision. Fifty lives were lost. An engineer was pinned under his engine, frightfully injured, and tears were running down his cheeks. In his dying agonies he held a piece of yellow paper crushed in his hand, and said: "Take this. This will show you that someone gave me the wrong orders."[166] Someone higher up made a wrong decision, which resulted in the death of innocent people.

One of the main things you can do to protect yourself from making fatal decisions is to cease to run your own life. Proverbs 3:5-7 says, "Trust in the LORD with all thine heart; and lean not unto thine own understanding. In all thy ways acknowledge him, and he shall direct thy paths. Be not wise in thine own eyes."

God has promised His children: "I will instruct thee and teach thee in the way which thou shalt go: I will guide thee with mine eye" (Psalm 32:8).

Instead of just blundering ahead with life or in making decisions, pause and pray and ask for guidance and help in all that you do. God will illuminate your mind to do that which is right and profitable. This is the day to listen to His voice, be guided by His

Word and follow His way. Then, and only then is it possible to avoid costly mistakes. Let Him help you make decisions today!

May 1

"The greatest of these is charity" (I Corinthians 13:13).

The greatest emotion in the world cannot be bought with money.

Dr. Leonard Cammer, a psychiatrist who specialized for many years in treating depressed persons, said, "The human being is the only species that can't survive alone. The human being needs another human being—otherwise he's dead! A telephone call to a depressed person can save a life. An occasional word, ten-minute visit, can be more effective than twenty-four hours of nursing care. You can buy nursing care. You can't buy love."

Money will buy a lot of things, but it can't buy love. Someone once said, "Money will buy a fine dog, but only love will make him wag his tail." It is the same way with people. Money can buy gifts but it cannot force the heart to love. There is nothing more precious than love for each other in a family, a love that causes the heart to beat faster at the thought of coming home.

There is the story of the retreat of ten thousand Greeks under Zenophon. After great hardships and privations, they finally came to the top of a lofty hill from which, in the distance, they saw the blue waves of the Mediterranean. Its gentle wavelets flashed in the light of the morning sun! From thousands of throats rang the joyous shout, "The Sea! The Sea!" In that time of jubilation, battle-wearied soldiers forgot their months of weary marching and nameless privations. Yonder were home and their waiting loved ones!

The loneliest place in the world is the human heart when love is absent. If you have no one to love, no one to return that love, no one to care, it is like living in a cold tomb of death.

That is why the apostle Paul wrote in I Corinthians 13:13, "And now abideth faith, hope, charity, these three; but the greatest of these is charity."

This is the day to guard your relationships with your family.

Many times people are not appreciated the way they should be until they are taken away from us. Let love rule your tongue, let it rule your actions and your attitude. For many times those who are closest and dearest receive the worst treatment.

They say the world is round
And yet I often think it's square,
So many little hurts we get
From corners, here and there.

But there's one truth in life I've found
While journeying East and West;
The only folks we really wound
Are those we love the best.

We flatter those we scarcely know;
We please the fleeting guest,
And deal full many a thoughtless blow
To those we love the best.
—AUTHOR UNKNOWN[167]

This is the day to strive towards having the *greatest of these* to be at work in our life. Love for the husband or the wife, the children or someone else close to you, for love is the greatest thing you can acquire in life. If you have true love you are a millionaire. Foster that love, nurture it and help it to grow, and you will always have the pounding of the heart when you think of home and those you love. To have that is priceless, for money cannot buy love. Those who love deeply never grow old: they may die of old age, but they die young and love makes the journey of life worthwhile.

May 2

"*For God so loved*" (John 3:16).

There is human love, and there is agape love. Francis of Assisi was terrified of leprosy. And one day, full in the narrow path that he was traveling, he saw, horribly white in the sunshine, a

leper! Instinctively his heart shrank back, recoiling from the contamination of that loathsome disease. But then he rallied; and ashamed of himself, ran and cast his arms about the sufferer's neck and kissed him and passed on. A moment later he looked back, and there was no one there, only the empty road in the hot sunlight. All his days thereafter he was sure it was no leper, but Christ Himself whom he had met. —G. K. CHESTERTON[168]

Going beyond our own human love, loving those who are unlovely or those who do not deserve love, is called agape love. It is a love that transcends all other love. It cannot be generated by the human heart alone; it must be kindled by the flame of God's unselfish love. He who knew no sin came to earth to live and die as a man for no other reason than for love. "For God so loved the world, that he gave his only begotten Son, that whosoever believeth in him should not perish, but have everlasting life. For God sent not his Son into the world to condemn the world; but that the world through him might be saved" (John 3:16-17).

God's love is the highest form of love available to man. It is pure, holy and unselfish.

James C. Hefley told the story that when Wycliffe translator Doug Meland and his wife moved into a village of Brazil's Fulnio Indians, he was referred to simply as "the white man."

The term was by no means complimentary, since other white men had exploited them, burned their homes, and robbed them of their lands. But after the Melands learned the Fulnio language and began to help the people with medicine and in other ways, they began calling Doug "the respectable white man."

When the Melands began adapting the customs of the people, the Fulnio gave them greater acceptance and spoke of Doug as "the white Indian."

Then one day, as Doug was washing the dirty, blood-caked foot of an injured Fulnio boy, he overheard a bystander say to another: "Whoever heard of a white man washing an Indian's foot before? Certainly this man is from God!" From that day on, whenever Doug would go into an Indian home, it would be announced: "Here comes the man God sent us."[169]

When the disciples were gathered at the Last Supper, Jesus displayed His greatest love for them and His profound humility when He asked for a towel and a basin of water and began to wash their feet.

Agape love is always characterized by humbleness, selflessness and compassion. Take the time today to pray not only for more human love for your family, friends and neighbors, but pray for the highest form of love to grab hold of your heart and be the motivating factor of your life; for it transcends all other love and will be highly rewarded.

May 3

"Thou shalt love the Lord thy God with all thy heart, and with all thy soul, and with all thy strength, and with all thy mind; and thy neighbour as thyself" (Luke 10:27).

*T*o love the Lord God with all your heart, soul, mind and strength is life's greatest accomplishment on earth!

On his ninety-ninth birthday, Carl J. Printz, for many years the Commissioner from Sweden to Canada, was asked for rules by which such a long and useful life might be achieved. He replied: "I would suggest one definite rule and that is, one must be temperate in all things." Then he added quickly, "Perhaps I should say all but one, for in the Bible you can read the commandments to love the Lord with all your heart, soul and mind, and your neighbor as yourself. These are the only things we can rightly do to excess."[170]

He was of course referring to Mark 12:29-31, "And Jesus answered him, The first of all the commandments is, Hear, O Israel; The Lord our God is one Lord: And thou shalt love the Lord thy God with all thy heart, and with all thy soul, and with all thy mind, and with all thy strength: this is the first commandment. And the second is like, namely this, Thou shalt love thy neighbor as thyself. There is none other commandment greater than these."

Once a young son of Bishop Berkeley asked him the question, "Papa, what do the words 'cherubim and seraphim' mean?" The bishop took time to tell his son that *cherubim* was a Hebrew word meaning knowledge, and the word *seraphim* stood for flame, explaining that it is commonly supposed the cherubim are angels that excel in knowledge and the seraphim are those who excel in love for God.

"Then I hope," the little boy said, "that when I die I will be a seraphim. I'd lot rather love God than to know everything."

Loving God is letting Him have control over your soul, mind, body and spirit. Some theologians call it being "Christ controlled" or "controlled by the Spirit."

A little boy once declared that he loved his mother "with all his strength." He was asked to explain what he meant by "with all his strength." He said: "Well, I'll tell you. You see, we live on the fourth floor of this tenement; and there's no elevator, and the coal is kept down in the basement. Mother is busy all the time, and she isn't very strong; so I see to it that the coal bin is never empty. I lug the coal up four flights of stairs all by myself. And it's a pretty big bin. It takes all my strength to get it up here. Now, isn't that loving my mother with all my strength?" —*GOSPEL HERALD*[171]

Jesus said it like this, "If ye love me, keep my commandments." Love is not just empty words, but it is shown by actions. This day try to have the concept of the little boy who said, "I'd lot rather love God than to know everything." Let your heart get involved with doing the greatest thing that you can do today: loving the Lord thy God with all your heart, soul, mind and strength.

"Though he fall, he shall not be utterly cast down: for the LORD upholdeth him with his hand" (Psalm 37:24).

Once a man named Don Sydall suffered with a nagging backache. So his doctor took an X ray. It showed a bullet in the back which Sydall had been carrying around for thirty-six years without knowing it. "I couldn't believe it," Sydall said. "Now I feel quite proud. Not many people can boast of a bullet they never knew they had." Doctors decided against operating to remove the old wound, probably fired into Sydall during wartime fighting near Dunkirk in 1940.[172]

Another man, Bishop Potter, once riding in the Yosemite Valley, fell from his horse and injured his foot. The foot grew better, but it troubled him for many years. When finally they took

X rays of it, it was discovered that for twenty-five years he had been walking on a broken foot.[173]

Some Christians are like that. They have been in spiritual battles where they received bullets from hell. They have been wounded but healed. They have fallen and broken spiritual limbs, but they have bounced back.

The bullet could not kill them. The broken foot could not keep them from walking. Oh yes, the bullets from the enemy have caused occasional pain, but it has been a reminder to them that they were conquerors. They did not die, but they just kept on living.

It is an established fact: God's children have an enemy. They are in war, for John 10:10 says, "The thief cometh not, but for to steal, and to kill, and to destroy."

The thief will do everything he can to put a spiritual bullet in you trying to kill you, or cause it to fester, infect and pollute your spirit. He wants to depress, discourage and disillusion you. His business is to make you lose hope and give up. But there is hope. Jesus said, "I am come that they might have life, and that they might have it more abundantly" (John 10:10b). The greater power is on your side. You can live, you can walk, and you can go on in spite of what you go through.

You may be down today with some spiritual bullet wounds or some spiritual broken bones, but let your battle cry be what the prophet wrote in Micah 7:8: "Rejoice not against me, O mine enemy: when I fall, I shall arise; when I sit in darkness, the LORD shall be a light unto me."

"Because he hath set his love upon me, therefore will I deliver him" (Psalm 91:14).

*I*n the early spring of 1877, Minnesota farmers surveyed their lands, dreading the first hordes of locusts that had caused such widespread destruction the summer before. Another such plague threatened to destroy Minnesota's rich wheatlands, spelling ruin for thousands of families.

Suddenly Governor John S. Pillsbury proclaimed April 26 a day of fasting and prayer, urging that every man, woman and child ask divine help. A strange hush fell over the land as Minnesotans solemnly assembled to pray. Next morning the run rose in cloudless skies. Temperatures soared to mid-summer heat. The people looked up at the skies in wonder, and to their horror, the warm earth began to stir with the dreaded insects.

This was a strange answer! Three days passed. The unseasonable heat hatched out a vast army of locusts that threatened to engulf the entire Northwest! Then, on the fourth day the sun went down in a cold sky and that night frost gripped the earth. Most of the locusts were destroyed as surely as if fire had swept them away! When summer came the wheat waved tall and green. April 26 went down in history as the day on which a people's prayer had been answered. —Martin M. Hyzer[174]

Henry Bosch shares a remarkable incident which occurred years ago when a Christian called upon God in a time of great danger. A twelve-car passenger train was speeding along in eastern Missouri. On board were hundreds of happy children on their way to a Sunday school picnic. The sky was cloudless when the excursion began, but it wasn't long before they ran into a severe thunderstorm. The heavy downpour caused the concerned engineer to slow down to about thirty-five miles an hour. As the train rounded a curve, the man saw that the switch just ahead had been left wide open. He jammed on the brakes, but he was sure they faced certain disaster. "Stick with it!" he shouted to the fireman. "Hundreds of children are on board!" "I intend to!" came the reply. Then the fireman, who was a Christian, cried, "O God, help us!" His words were drowned out by a thunderclap as a bolt of lightning struck right in front of the engine.

The next thing they knew, they were safely past the danger point. After stopping the train, the men hurried back to find out what had happened. To their amazement they discovered that the lightning had struck the rails and closed the switch. This in turn kept them from being shunted onto a spur which would have caused certain derailment.[175]

The important thing to do today is to pray when you face a crisis or dilemma in which you have no control. The God who rules the universe has total control and will help you when you call on Him, for He said in Psalm 91:15, "He shall call upon me, and I will answer him: I will be with him in trouble; I will deliver him, and honour him."

May 6

"But my God shall supply all your need according to his riches in glory by Christ Jesus" (Philippians 4:19).

If you know the Lord you are a millionaire. A young boy once asked a serious question. "Dad," he asked, "what is a millionaire?" "Well, son," said his father, "it's somebody who has a million dollars." The little boy thought a moment. "Well," he said, his head held proudly, "then I'm a oneaire." —Maxwell Droke[176]

Because of the little boy's ignorance, he thought it was just as great to be a *onenaire* as a millionaire. Many people who know more than the little boy knew want to be a millionaire, but many people are millionaires and do not even realize it.

Once an aged Indian, who was half-naked and famished, wandered into one of the Western settlements and begged for food to keep him from starving. While he eagerly devoured the bread bestowed by the hand of charity, a brightly colored ribbon, from which was suspended a small dirty pouch, was seen around his neck. On being questioned what it was, he said it was a charm given him in his younger days. Upon opening it, they found a faded, greasy paper, which proved to be a regular discharge from the Federal Army, entitling him to a pension for life and signed by General Washington himself.[177] He was rich and well taken care of for life, but yet lived a starving existence.

If you are a Christian, you have a paper which promises you that you will be taken care of for life. God has promised to supply your needs and your wants, for it is written, "God shall supply all your need according to his riches in glory." Thank God he did not say "out of his riches," which would be like a millionaire giving one dollar in the offering plate, as it would be *out of* His riches. "According to" means "in proportion to" and God's provisions come without measure. He is an exceeding abundant God.

You might ask, "What do I have that makes me a millionaire?" First of all you have salvation—hope of eternal life—living in a beautiful place called heaven without any more pain, tears, sickness, or disappointments. When you leave this earth which is just a moment in time, your spiritual riches will carry you upward into

the joys of the Lord. There are other things that make you a millionaire. They are listed below:

> *A love that can never be fathomed;*
> *A life that can never die;*
> *A righteousness that can never be tarnished;*
> *A peace that can never be understood;*
> *A rest that can never be disturbed;*
> *A joy that can never be diminished;*
> *A hope that can never be disappointed;*
> *A glory that can never be clouded;*
> *A light that can never be darkened;*
> *A happiness that can never be interrupted;*
> *A strength that can never be enfeebled;*
> *A purity that can never be defiled;*
> *A beauty that can never be marred;*
> *A wisdom that can never be baffled;*
> *Resources that can never be exhausted.*
> —Author Unknown[178]

These can never be disturbed, touched, clouded, marred, or defiled because they are His joy, His light, His strength, His beauty, His purity, His peace. No one can take them from you because they are not yours—they are His. He gave many gifts and blessings to you when you surrendered your life to Him and accepted His gift of salvation.

You are a millionaire today. When you seem to run out of His blessings, just go back to the Source. He is waiting to give you good things. It is His pleasure!

May 7

"He that is faithful in that which is least is faithful also in much" (Luke 16:10).

Being faithful is doing one's best in all things. Someone may not be as talented or as accomplished as someone else, but he can be just as faithful, in the fact that he is doing his best to

accomplish what life has handed him.

Today is given as a gift from God. Sometimes when we are asked to do things, we do not understand how our part plays into the bigger scheme of things; but to do it is the key. Do it with a smile, love, and excitement, not cynicism and grumbling. Life is too short to be lazy or hateful, or to perform without determination.

Treat life as you want to be treated, with respect, and enthusiasm in people's responses. A pie that is half-baked, a dress that is half-sewn, a car that is half-finished, or a job that is half-done is no good to anyone. To do one's best is to tackle the task with courage and determination, and work until it is finished.

DO YOUR BEST
It takes a little courage
And a lot of self-control,
And some given determination,
If you want to reach a goal.

It takes a deal of striving,
And a firm and stern set chin;
No matter what the battle,
If you're really out to win.

There is a rule in life to guide you,
As you see Prosperity:
Never put your wishbone
Where your backbone ought to be.
—Florence Koba[179]

Jesus talked about three men whose employer gave them each talents when he went away on a journey. To one he gave five talents, to another he gave two, and the other he gave one talent. They were to take their talents and increase them while their master was gone.

The man with the five increased his to ten, the one with two increased his to four, but the one with one hid his talent and did not increase. He refused to do his best because of his fear.

The first two men were rewarded for their faithfulness and endeavors, but the third man was reprimanded harshly in Matthew 25. The master took his talent away from him and gave it to the one who had ten and he cast away the "unprofitable servant" and

did not give him another chance at making good.

Some would feel this was rather harsh, but the point is being made that everyone should do his best to bring increase into his life with that which God has given him.

Seek today to do your best so that you will hear those wonderful words: "Well done, thou good and faithful servant. Enter into the joys of the Lord."

May 8

"I direct my prayer unto thee" (Psalm 5:3).

God wants His children to direct their prayers unto Him. He desires to have communication with them, and His heart is made happy when they talk to Him. It is a privilege to be able to talk to God. He is not one of the gods; He is the only God and He loves it when His children acknowledge Him as so.

"Prayer is the nearest approach to God, and the highest enjoyment of Him, that we are capable of in this life. It is the noblest exercise of the soul, the most exalted use of our best faculties, and the highest imitation of the blessed inhabitants of Heaven." —WILLIAM LAW[180]

There is power in prayer as the following poem depicts:

THE POWER OF PRAYER
Lord, what a change within us one short hour
Spent in Thy presence will avail to make!
What heavy burdens from our bosoms take;
What parched grounds afresh, as with a shower!
We kneel, and all around us seems to lower;
We rise, and all, the distant and the near,
Stands forth in sunny outline, brave and clear!
We kneel, how weak! We rise, how full of power!

Why, therefore, should we do ourselves this wrong
Or others, that we are not always strong;
That we ever overborne with care;
That we should ever weak or heartless be,
Anxious or troubled, when with us is prayer,

And joy and strength and courage are with Thee?
—RICHARD CHEVENIX TRENCH[181]

In His presence is fullness of joy. He gives peace and understanding. There is nothing that He cannot do, so why should not His children go to Him in prayer, since He has all the answers?

This is the day to learn that prayer is the most important thing people can do, for it affects every area of their life. It is the most powerful habit one can acquire, and those who have learned this secret have a power that is beyond comprehension of the human mind. So pray today and find that power!

May 9

"Ye are of more value than many sparrows" (Luke 12:7).

God cares about the tiniest detail of your life. Newberry once wrote, "Up on the lofty snow-clad mountains of the Matterhorn, we were awed by the wondrous works of God in the superb scenery, when a friend took out a pocket microscope, caught a tiny fly, and placed it under the glass. He then reminded us that the legs of the housefly in England were naked, whereas this little fly's were thickly covered with hair. The same God who made those lofty mountains, remembered to make the tiniest of His creatures comfortable." —ADAPTED FROM NEWBERRY[182]

Jesus said in Luke 12:6-7, "Are not five sparrows sold for two farthings, and not one of them is forgotten before God? But even the very hairs of your head are all numbered. Fear not therefore: ye are of more value than many sparrows."

There is not only a God, but He is a personable God who cares and knows all things. Not one thing escapes His eye.

Walter Baxendale wrote of how Galileo, the most profound philosopher of his age, when questioned by the Roman Inquisition as to his belief in the existence of God, replied, pointing to a straw on the floor of his dungeon, that from the structure of that object alone he would infer with certainty the existence of an intelligent Creator.

This Creator said, "I am the L ORD, and there is none else" (Isaiah 45:6). He sees even a piece of straw on the floor and cares about the pieces of your life that seem so insignificant.

When Lindbergh, the aviator, was flying his plane, *Spirit of St. Louis*, midway on his transatlantic flight between New York and Paris, he began to think of the smallness of man and the deficiency of his devices and the greatness and marvels of God's universe.

He thought, "It's hard to be an agnostic here in the *Spirit of St. Louis* when I am so aware of the frailty of man's devices. If one dies, all God's creation goes on existing in a plan so perfectly balanced, so wondrously simple and yet so incredibly complex that it is beyond our comprehension. There's the infinite magnitude of the universe, the infinite detail, and man's consciousness of it all." —WALTER B. KNIGHT[183]

How much more does God care about the details of your life! You are made in His image. You bear His handprints and His likeness. He is involved with you and cares about each and every thing that makes up your life.

May 10

"I will prepare him an habitation . . . and I will exalt him" (Exodus 15:2).

You can sometimes be so busy doing things that you have no time for the more important things as stated in the following poem:

TOO BUSY
Too busy to read the Bible
Too busy to wait and pray!
Too busy to speak out kindly
To someone by the way!

Too busy to care and struggle,
To think of the life to come!
Too busy building mansions,
To plan for the Heavenly Home.

> *Too busy to help a brother*
> *Who faces the winter blast!*
> *Too busy to share his burden*
> *When self in the balance is cast.*
>
> *Too busy for all that is holy*
> *On earth beneath the sky*
> *Too busy to serve the Master*
> *But—not too busy to die.*
> —AUTHOR UNKNOWN[184]

Published in the *New York Times* was the following commentary: *Time hasn't changed a noticeable fraction of a second since the first man stood on two feet and watched the sunrise and had a glimmering of wonder about time. He knew the same span of daylight that we know today and the same year. Grass grew as deliberately then as now, and the berry ripened in its own time. But somewhere along the way man began to count not only the days, but the hours, the minutes, the seconds. Time was unchanged, but man was caught in his own time-traps. The very echoes came to say, "Hurry, hurry, hurry!" And only now and then did anyone stop and ask, "Why, and what for?"*

Back in the pioneer days, if a man missed a stagecoach, for the most part he just shrugged his shoulders and said, "So what? Another one will be along in a couple of weeks." Now, someone has said, "If a man misses even one section of a revolving door in a bank building, he is ready to explode with impatience."

Many people are rushing around so fast that they have no time to speak to a friend, to smile or just stop and pat a dog on the head. Some things are more important than the hurry.

For two years or more Haydn toiled and worked on his grand oratorio. When friends urged him to hurry and bring his task to a close he replied: "I cannot make haste; I am writing for all time." Each day before beginning he knelt and prayed for divine guidance as he wrote.

This is the day to realize that we are living for *all time*. Take advice from an old man who often wept as he wrote about God. The composer, Haydn was not too busy with his great writings, but that he first took time to kneel and pray for divine guidance.

Life would be so much better if all of us took the time each day to pray and give attention to the important things of life.

May 11

"Look not every man on his own things, but every man also on the things of others" (Philippians 2:4).

You never lose when you help others. It is the best investment you can make. Henrietta C. Mears once said, *"The man who keeps busy helping the man below him won't have time to envy the man above him—and there may not be anybody above him anyway."*

You never know how your investment in others will pay off. One of the early founders of the Rothschild House, in his younger days, borrowed a small amount of money from a friend to help him start in business. Without security to give, he got it on the ground of his need. He went to a distant part of Germany, and many years passed. After nearly a century, when the name of the family and the firm had become worldwide, his old benefactor did not even know it was the same youth he had once befriended.

But one day, when he was an old man and his health had broken, his fortune gone, and his family dependent upon him, and the darkest shadows gathering about his life, he received a letter from the Rothschild House in Frankfurt, summoning him to the bank for an important interview. As he entered the private office of the great banker, he was greeted with a welcome he had little expected.

After the old acquaintance had been renewed, the great banker went to his desk and took out a draft for an enormous amount of money amounting to some hundred thousand dollars. He handed it to his old friend, and said, "I have sent for you to pay you the dividends on the stock you entrusted to my banking nearly fifty years ago."

Astounded, the friend refused to take the money, saying that he had no such claim, and could not accept such a gift. "It is not a gift," said the banker, "it is simply the actual profit on the money you gave me, wisely turned over a great many times, until it has actually accumulated this compound interest." —*Gospel Herald*[185]

Your life is much the same way. Whatever you invest in others will be compounding interest until your life's bank account of friends and blessings will accumulate beyond your expectations. Your investment in helping others is the best way to reap good things.

May 12

"And the Lord said unto him, What is that in thine hand?" (Exodus 4:2).

What do you have in your hand today? What is it that God can take and multiply? Whatever you have, with God it is enough, because He makes up the difference. Place it in His hands in faith believing and watch for the miracle. With God involved all things are possible to him that believes.

It is time to place your little bit in the Master's hand and see Him do the multiplication. Remember the little boy's lunch. When the people whom Jesus was teaching out in the desert became hungry, Jesus asked the disciples to get some food for the people. They replied town was too far away and there was nothing available but a little boy's lunch. Jesus said, "Whatever you have it is enough for Me. Bring Me what you have and I will make it enough." Notice, He did not just make it enough, but He made it more than enough. He always gives in abundance. In fact they ended up with more than that with which they had started.

In the beginning they had five loaves and two fishes, but after all the people had eaten their fill, they gathered up the leftovers which amounted to twelve baskets full.

So why should you worry and fret about your needs being met or your problems being solved? Do all you can do with a good attitude, pray about it and leave the miracle to Jesus. You do not have to perform a miracle; you only have to believe that He will do it.

Just put it in the capable hands of the Master, who loves to do things for His children, whatever it is that is bothering or troubling your mind. Did He not say in the Gospels that if a child asked a father for a piece of bread, would the father give the child a stone? Then He went on to say, "How much more will your heavenly Father give unto His children?"

Remember He is not against you; He is for you! He is not out to get you and pour anger upon you; He is there to help you! He is everything you need today. So get up out of the pit of worry; work hard, give your best to everything you do, depend on the Lord and go forward in victory trusting the King of kings to bless and make up the difference.

May 13

"He that hath ears to hear, let him hear" (Matthew 11:15).

What are your ears listening to—what is it that you hear? Dr. Stuart Holden tells of a boy whose father was telling him about the story of Christ standing at the closed door, as depicted by Holman Hunt in his picture, *The Light of the World*. As the father told the boy about the love and patience of this heavenly visitor, the little lad burst out with, "Father, did He get in?" "Well, son, no, I don't think He did." "But why Father? Did they not hear Him knock?" "Well, yes, boy, I think they heard Him knock, but I don't think He got in."

The boy thought a little, "Father, they could not have heard Him, could they? Perhaps they were living down in the cellar, and that's why."

The question is, are you living in the cellar of life not able to hear the promises of Christ or have you come out of the dark cellar into the light? Where is your residence or where are you dwelling?

A hardened unbeliever went one day to see—but not to hear—George Whitefield when he preached outdoors to a great throng. In order to have a good vantage point, he climbed a nearby tree. Putting his fingers in both ears, he began to watch the mighty preacher. Then a persistent fly lit on his nose. He shook his head, but the fly wouldn't move. Just as he removed a hand from an ear to flick the fly away, Whitefield quoted the verse, "He that hath ears to hear, let him hear" (Matthew 11:15). Then he spoke of the willful refusal of many to hear the Spirit's voice. The unbeliever was so impressed by what happened that he opened not only his ears to the gospel, but also his heart. —*Gospel Herald*[186]

The story is told that Hitler's bodyguard, Kurt Wagner, adored

Hitler and reverenced him as a god. At the end of the war, with Hitler a suicide in a Berlin bunker, Kurt's faith was shattered and he planned a suicide. Going for a final cup of coffee, he picked up a discarded gospel tract and read it—first carelessly and then with interest. As a result of reading this gospel tract, he sought out a godly pastor who led him to Christ. Kurt was transformed from a hardened man into a peace-loving man, and he became a new creation in Christ, because he listened to the voice of the Spirit that issued forth from a tract. —CHRISTIAN VICTORY[187]

You become what you listen to or what you allow your ear to hear. To what do you listen? What captivates you? Take your ears out of the garbage cans of society, remove them from the gossip sessions, take them to a higher place—that place where Jesus speaks, lives and breathes His wondrous Spirit into the hearts of the hungry.

Give Him your ear today and He will give you His ear, for I Peter 3:12 says, "For the eyes of the Lord are over the righteous, and his ears are open unto their prayers." If you choose to listen, the Lord will fill your ears with good things and you will be blessed abundantly.

May 14

"That the trial of your faith . . . though it be tried with fire" (I Peter 1:7).

*F*iery trials are to bring you forth as gold; they are not to kill you. It is during the dark trials when the most precious truths are discovered. It is said that the world's best supply of perfume comes from roses on the Balkan Mountains. The flowers from which the lovely fragrance is distilled must be gathered in the darkest part of the night! The laborers therefore start shortly after twelve o'clock and conclude their picking within two hours. The brevity of the work period is based on scientific tests which have proved that during this gloomy interval the blossoms give their most pleasing scent, while forty percent of their aroma disappears in the light of day.[188]

It is during the midnights of life that God can extract the most precious perfume of worship and surrender from His children.

When they are helpless and in pain, and look to Him, He teaches them a better way, for they are forced to take time to pray. It is the pressure of a trial that produces the best Christians.

One writer has explained how God used pressure for the making of the materials for the Old Testament tabernacle. *"Almost all of them were secured through pressure. The metals had to go through fire; the dyes, doubtless, were secured through pressure; the fine linen had to go through many a trying process from the flax stage; the goats had to be prepared to surrender their ornament—hair; the rams and badgers must die; the wood had to be felled and shaped; the oil and spices were secured through pressure and the precious stones, too, were the result of great heat."*[189]

When King George was visiting a pottery plant years ago, two special vases were shown to him. Both were made of the same material and both had been painted in the same style and manner, but one was a beautiful ornament, and the other blurred and unsightly. The reason? One had taken the fire and the other had not! —J. Oswald Sanders[190]

I Peter 1:7 says, "That the trial of your faith, being much more precious than of gold that perisheth, though it be tried with fire, might be found unto praise and honour and glory at the appearing of Jesus Christ."

The trial of your faith is for a reason. It is to bring you into a place of richness and service.

Job, during the worst nightmare of his life, said these famous words, "But he knoweth the way that I take: when he hath tried me, I shall come forth as gold."

If you are in a trial today, and the pressures of life are applied, what are you saying? How are you looking at your trial? Remember, God is with you and is making of you a beautiful vessel for His glory.

May 15

"*It is more blessed to give than to receive*" (Acts 20:35).

This is the day to give not to get, but give to give. Arthur Tonne tells a story how a woman living on a farm in Germany

brought to her minister an amount in German money equivalent to about ten dollars in American money. As she laid down the money she said: "In former years I have had to pay about this amount in medicine. This year there has been no sickness in our family. I want to show my gratitude to the Lord in this way." Some time later this same woman again came to her minister with about five dollars, explaining that many of her neighbors had suffered some losses in a recent windstorm, but that her farm had been spared. She said, "I bring the church and God this donation as an offering of thanks."[191]

Another similar story was told about the parents of a young man who was killed in World War II. They gave their church a check for two hundred dollars as a memorial to their loved one. When the presentation was made, another war mother whispered to her husband, "Let us give the same for our boy." The father said, "Why, what are you talking about? Our boy didn't lose his life." The mother said, "That's just the point. Let us give it because he didn't." —*OTTERBEIN TEACHER*[192]

Paul said in Acts 20:35, "Remember the words of the Lord Jesus, how he said, It is more blessed to give than to receive."

More blessed to give than to receive—how can a giver be blessed? This is illustrated in the story involving raising money for missions. When Chaplain McCabe set out to raise a million dollars for missions he met many disappointments and was often greatly discouraged. One day while going through a mail that was particularly discouraging, he finally came across a letter from a boy, from which fell a badly battered nickel. The letter, in a boyish scrawl, read: "Dear Chaplain McCabe: I'm sure you're going to get a million dollars for missions. And I'm going to help you get it too. So here's a nickel toward it. It's all I've got right now, but if you need any more, you just call on me."

This letter became one of the chaplain's most effective stories in his money-raising campaign, and by it he was eventually able to reach his goal. A boy's gift multiplied and became a million dollars. He helped far more than he knew. —*EVANGELISTIC ILLUSTRATION*[193]

The choice is yours today. Will you join those who give just to give or do you have an ulterior motive in mind: to give to get? The happiest people I know are the givers who just give to give.

May 16

"*And be ye kind one to another*" (Ephesians 4:32).

A child once prayed: "Dear God, make all the bad people good, and make all the good people nice." It is not enough to be a good person. There must be kindness and a spirit of being nice to others. Kindness has its own rewards and is something that is never regretted. Words once spoken are true: "You cannot do a kindness too soon, because you never know how soon it will be too late!"

Kindnesses are never forgotten. Years ago a Missouri country congregation listened to a sermon by a young preacher who had walked twenty miles to deliver it. Tired, hungry, this youth faltered, floundered and failed. The people were disgusted; they did not know he had walked the long weary miles. When the service was over nobody offered him food or shelter; but as he started down the long road with a breaking heart, the janitor asked him to share his humble meal in a nearby shanty.

Years passed. The young exhorter became Bishop Marvin of worldwide reputation, and after a full generation he once more stood in that spot to dedicate a great country church. The whole community was assembled; it was a tremendous event in their lives. When the service was ended, many crowded about offering lavish hospitality, but the bishop waved them all aside and called the old janitor, saying, "When I was here years ago I was none too good for you, and I am none too good for you today." —CHRISTIAN LIFE AND FAITH[194]

Kindness is a perfume that lingers on and on in the memory of the one receiving the kindness.

Kindness makes people feel important. Once when Wesley visited Rathby, to preach in the church, as he ascended the pulpit, a child sat on the steps directly in the way. Instead of asking, "Why is that child allowed to sit there?" he gently took the little one in his arms, kissed her, and then placed her on the same spot where she had been sitting. The marks of kindness always leave another one feeling loved and cared for as the following poem demonstrates:

> *He stopped to pat a small dog's head,*
> *A little thing to do;*

> *And yet, the dog, remembering,*
> *Was glad the whole day through.*
>
> *He gave a rose into the hand*
> *Of one who loved it much;*
> *'Twas just a rose—but oh, the joy*
> *That lay in its soft touch.*
>
> *He spoke a word so tenderly—*
> *A word's a wee, small thing;*
> *And yet, it stirred a weary heart*
> *To hope again, and sing.*
> —Lois Snelling[195]

The commandment given in Ephesians 4:32, which is often overlooked in our busy rush of life, simply says, "Be ye kind one to another, tenderhearted."

Try being kind today. You might be surprised what happens when you become a good Samaritan as happened in the following story. Three men were involved in a street fight in Portsmouth, England. Old John Perett, a good Samaritan, came strolling along and went to the aid of the underdog. He was getting the worst of it when a brawny young sailor jumped in to help him. After the rumpus was over, Old John Perett discovered that the sailor lad's name was Perett also. He turned out to be Old John's son. Twenty-five years before, Old John Perett was at sea when his wife gave birth to a boy. The mother died soon afterward, and John Perett never saw his son. That is, he never did until the day he was kind to a helpless victim. Kindness always increases individuals and lifts them up!

May 17

"*Come before his presence with singing*" (Psalm 100:2).

This is the day to sing a new song. Psalm 100 says, "Make a joyful noise unto the LORD, all ye lands. Serve the LORD with gladness: come before his presence with singing. Know ye that the LORD he is God: it is he that hath made us, and not we ourselves;

we are his people, and the sheep of his pasture. Enter into his gates with thanksgiving, and into his courts with praise: be thankful unto him, and bless his name. For the LORD is good; his mercy is everlasting; and his truth endureth to all generations."

Judaism and Christianity are known to be singing religions. Atheism is songless. It has nothing to sing about. *"The psalm-singing of Christian martyrs going to their deaths in the arena alerted the Roman Empire to the fact that a new and revolutionary force was coming into being. When the pleasure-bent populace saw the Christians singing as they fearlessly entered the amphitheater where hungry lions awaited them, they were filled with awe."*

Anyone who can sing while he knows he is going to be ripped apart by starving lions has to have something deep within his soul not given by man. You, too, can have a song when you are faced with difficult situations and when the enemy comes against you.

Heaven is vibrant with song: Revelation 15:3 states, "And they sing the song of Moses the servant of God, and the song of the Lamb." If heaven is filled with singing, we better start practicing down here. It is a testimony to those who have no song.

Psalm 126:2 says, "Then was our mouth filled with laughter, and our tongue with singing: then said they among the heathen, The LORD hath done great things for them."

Martin Luther said, "Music is a fair and lovely gift of God which has often wakened and moved me to the joy of preaching. . . . Next after theology, I give to music the highest place and the greatest honor. . . . My heart bubbles up and overflows in response to music, which has so often refreshed me and delivered me from dire plagues."[196]

Music that is written about Christian values, God, and His love always is uplifting. So plug your soul into God and start singing a new song.

May 18

"He that giveth unto the poor shall not lack: but he that hideth his eyes shall have many a curse" (Proverbs 28:27).

You make a living by what you get, but you make a life by what you give. Life is made up of incidents. The way you treat people, the attitude with which you address them, the big heart or the stingy heart, life is a series of people meeting and interacting with people. What is your past record of how you treat people? Could the following story be written about you?

Each of the seven children in our family worked in our father's store, "Our Own Hardware-Furniture Store," in Mott, North Dakota. We started working by doing odd jobs like dusting, arranging shelves and wrapping. As we worked and watched, we learned that work was about more than survival and making a sale.

One lesson stands out in my mind. It was shortly before Christmas. I was in the eighth grade and working evenings, straightening the toy section. A little boy, five or six years old, came in. He was wearing a brown tattered coat with dirty worn cuffs. His hair was straggly, except for a cowlick that stood straight up from the crown of his head. His shoes were scuffed and his one shoelace was torn. The little boy looked poor to me—too poor to afford to buy anything. He looked around the toy section, picked up this item and that and carefully put them back in their place.

Dad came down the stairs and walked over to the boy. His steel blue eyes smiled and the dimple in his cheek stood out as he asked the boy what he could do for him. The boy said he was looking for a Christmas present to buy his brother. I was impressed that Dad treated him with the same respect as any adult. Dad told him to take his time and look around. He did.

After about twenty minutes, the little boy carefully picked up a toy plane, walked up to my dad and said, "How much for this, Mister?"

"How much you got?" Dad asked.

The little boy held out his hand and opened it. His hand was creased with wet lines of dirt from clutching his money. In his hand lay two dimes, a nickel and two pennies—twenty-seven cents. The price on the toy plane he'd picked out was $3.98.

"That'll just about do it," Dad said as he closed the sale. Dad's reply still rings in my ears. I thought about what I'd seen as I wrapped the present. When the little boy walked out of the store, I didn't notice the dirty, worn coat, the straggly

hair, or the single torn shoelace. What I saw was a radiant child with a treasure. —TOLD BY LAVONN STEINER

How many such stories could be written today? How many give to others, simply because of the need presented or for the joy of giving? It is a fact: those who give shall not lack, but be blessed abundantly. This is the day to give.

May 19

"So is he that layeth up treasure for himself, and is not rich toward God" (Luke 12:21).

What is your number one goal today—to make money and get rich in material things or to become rich in God? People never have enough money. The more they get, the more they want. Someone asked John D. Rockefeller Sr., "How much money does it take to satisfy a man?" He answered, "Just a little bit more than he has, which means that money is powerless to satisfy those who waste their life acquiring and hoarding it." No amount is ever quite enough.

It was Lord Congelton who once heard a servant say, "Oh, if I only had five pounds! I would be contented." Lord Congelton, who heard her, gave her a five-pound note. She thanked him profusely. As she left him, she said in an undertone, thinking that her benefactor wouldn't hear her, "Why didn't I say ten?"[197]

A London newspaper once said, "Money is the article which may be used as a universal passport to everywhere except heaven, and the universal provider of everything except happiness."

Money can also buy you food, but it cannot buy you an appetite. Andrew Carnegie, the multimillionaire, sat in a dining room in a swanky hotel. Before him was untouched food. His health was failing and his appetite was gone. He chanced to look out of a window and saw a working man sitting on a curbstone, heartily enjoying his noonday lunch. Exclaimed Carnegie: "I'd give a million dollars to have an appetite like that man!"

"Money may buy the husk of many things, but not the kernel. It brings you food, but not appetite; medicine, but not health; acquaintances, but not friends; servants, but not faith-

fulness; days of joy, but not peace or happiness." —HENRIK IBSEN[198]

Jesus talked about a man who had riches in this world only but was not rich toward God or others in the following parable: "The ground of a certain rich man brought forth plentifully: And he thought within himself, saying, What shall I do, because I have no room where to bestow my fruits? And he said, This will I do: I will pull down my barns, and build greater; and there will I bestow all my fruits and my goods. And I will say to my soul, Soul, thou hast much goods laid up for many years; take thine ease, eat, drink, and be merry. But God said unto him, Thou fool, this night thy soul shall be required of thee: then whose shall those things be, which thou hast provided? So is he that layeth up treasure for himself, and is not rich toward God" (Luke 12:16-21).

Jesus further stated: "And seek not what ye shall eat, or what ye shall drink, neither be ye of doubtful mind. For all these things do the nations of the world seek after: and your Father knoweth that ye have need of these things. But rather seek ye the kingdom of God; and all these things shall be added unto you" (Luke 12:29-31).

This is the day to seek to be rich toward God and be truly rich and have the best of both worlds!

May 20

"He staggered not at the promise of God through unbelief; but was strong in faith" (Romans 4:20).

*F*aith sees the invisible, believes the incredible and receives the impossible! Mother Teresa wanted to build a great orphanage. She said to those who ridiculed her, "With three shillings Teresa can do nothing, but with God and three shillings there is nothing that Teresa cannot do!"

The poet John Greenleaf Whittier once wrote, *"The steps of faith fall on the seeming void, but find the rock beneath."*

When God called Abraham out of the city of Ur, He did not tell him where he was going. Abraham just started walking. Seemingly he was stepping out with nothing to support him but God's instructions. He had no destination, he had no blueprint; he had nothing but a word from God. Hebrews 11:8 and 10 substantiate

this: "By faith Abraham, when he was called to go out into a place which he should after receive for an inheritance, obeyed; and he went out, not knowing whither he went. . . . For he looked for a city which hath foundations, whose builder and maker is God."

His type of faith is described in Romans 4:19-21: "And being not weak in faith, he considered not his own body now dead, when he was about an hundred years old, neither yet the deadness of Sara's womb: He staggered not at the promise of God through unbelief; but was strong in faith, giving glory to God. And being fully persuaded that, what he had promised, he was able also to perform."

Not only did Abraham leave his city and venture forth not really knowing where he was going, but after his promised son was born, he was asked by God to offer his son Isaac up as a sacrifice. Abraham was willing to do this and had the lad on the altar when God stopped him. Hebrews 11:17 and 19 tell how he was able to do this: "By faith Abraham, when he was tried, offered up Isaac: and he that had received the promises offered up his only begotten son . . . Accounting that God was able to raise him up, even from the dead."

Abraham had total trust in his God, knowing that God had all power and would do what was right. Maybe you are having trouble with attaining faith and wondering if you have doubt or unbelief. Consider the words of Henry Drummond: "Christ never failed to distinguish between doubt and unbelief. Doubt is *can't believe*. Unbelief is *won't believe*. Whether you have doubt or unbelief, pray the prayer of the man in the Bible when he prayed, 'Lord, help mine unbelief.'"

A schoolmaster gave three of his pupils a difficult problem. "You will find it very hard to solve," he said, "but there is a way." After repeated attempts, one of them gave up in despair. "There is no way!" he declared. The second pupil had not succeeded, yet he was smiling and unconcerned. "I know it can be explained, because I have seen it done." The third worked on, long after the rest had given up. His head ached and his brain was in a whirl. Yet as he went over it again and again, he said without faltering, "I know there is a way, because the master has said it." This is faith: it is a confidence that rests not upon what it has seen, but upon the promises of God.

May 21

"Who against hope believed in hope" (Romans 4:18).

Someone once said, "When fear knocks at the door of the heart, send faith to open it, and you will find there is no one there." Who is knocking on your door today? It does not matter who or what is there, if faith answers the door, a power is already at work to help reduce your problems or take care of them. Faith releases mighty forces to work. Things that seem big diminish in size when the Lord God comes on the scene. He is not the giver of fear, but He gives love, power and a sound mind.

Adeline Perkins tells a story that demonstrates this kind of faith. "Seventy years ago I was quite a little girl, the baby of the family, with an older brother and sister. My father was very ill at the time, and my mother took in sewing of any kind so we could live. She would sew far into the night with nothing but dim gas mantles and an old treadle sewing machine. She never complained even when the fire would be low and the food was very scarce. She would sew until the early hours of morning.

"Things were very bad that particular winter. Then a letter came from where her sewing machine was purchased, stating that they would have to pick up her machine the next day unless payments were brought up to date. I remember when she read the letter I became frightened; I could picture us starving to death and all sorts of things that could come to a child's mind. My mother did not appear to be worried, however, and seemed to be quite calm about the matter. I, on the other hand, cried myself to sleep, wondering what would become of our family. Mother said God would not fail her—that He never had. I couldn't see how God was going to help us keep this old sewing machine.

"The day the men were to come for our only means of support, there was a knock at the kitchen door. I was frightened as a child would be, for I was sure it was those dreaded men. Instead, a nicely dressed man stood at our door with a darling baby in his arms. He asked my mother if she was Mrs. Hill. When she said she was, he said, 'I'm in trouble this morning and you have been recommended by the druggist and grocer down the street as an honest

and wonderful woman. My wife was rushed to the hospital this morning, and since we have no relatives here, and I must open my dentist office, I have nowhere to leave my baby. Could you possibly take care of her for a few days?' He continued, 'I will pay you in advance.' With this he took out ten dollars and gave it to my mother.

"Mother said, 'Yes, yes, I will be glad to do so,' and took the baby from his arms. When the man left, Mother turned to me with tears streaming down a face that looked as though a light was shining on it. She said, 'I knew God would never let them take away my machine.'"

This is what faith is all about. Believing and trusting God even when it looks like there is no way out. Faith just knows!

May 22

"Be not afraid" (Joshua 1:9).

Sometimes it is hard to believe that Jesus is with you. It is like the little boy who was told by his mother to go into the pantry and get her a can of tomato soup. The little boy did not want to go into the pantry alone and he said, "Mommy, it's dark in there, and I'm scared." "It's all right, Johnny," she said. "You go in there and get a can of tomato soup. I need it for a recipe." He said, "But Mommy, it's dark, and I'm too scared to go in there by myself." "It's okay, Johnny," she said again. "Jesus will be in there with you. Now you go and get a can of tomato soup." Johnny went to the door and opened it slowly. When he peeked inside, it was dark, and he was scared. His hands began to tremble, but he got an idea. He said, "Jesus, if You're in there, would You hand me that can of tomato soup?"

There are times when it is difficult to understand that "God is there." When Joshua was afraid, God spoke these words to him: "Be strong and of a good courage; be not afraid, neither be thou dismayed: for the Lord thy God is with thee whithersoever thou goest" (Joshua 1:9).

Whatever you are asked to go through remember that He will be with you until the end of the world. He will never leave you nor forsake you. He does care and He will stand by you. Even when it seems like you are alone and you are asked to walk through a dark trial—He is there.

To every problem there is the existence of a solution. Psalm 95:4 says, "In his hand are the deep places of the earth: the strength of the hills is his also." You may be in a valley, but the valley is in God's hands. You may be walking in the darkness, but He is the Light of the World. Whatever you need it is in His power to give it to you. He may not hand you the can of tomato soup out of the darkened pantry, but He can give you the courage to walk into the darkness and get it.

God allows you to walk through things so you can come forth as gold. He does not allow things to happen to you to be mean, but to bring you to a higher level in Him. He wants to be number one in your life. So when He asks you to do something you would rather not do, or you would rather do something that seems a lot easier, remember whatever it is that you are called to do, He will give you the strength, power, and courage to do it.

He says today, "Be not afraid!" He will always be with you even to the end of the road. You are never alone when you trust in the Lord.

May 23

"Trust in him at all times; ye people, pour out your heart before him: God is a refuge for us" (Psalm 62:8).

If you want to do something great today, pray! Dr. Alexis Carrel, a medical doctor who won a Nobel Prize in physiology, wrote, *"Prayer is the most powerful form of energy that one can generate. The influence of prayer on the human mind and body is as demonstrable as that of secreting glands. Its results can be measured in terms of increased buoyancy, greater intellectual vigor, moral stamina and a deeper understanding of personality. Only in prayer do we achieve that complete harmonious assembly of mind, body and spirit which gives the frail human need its unshakable strength."*[199]

President Wilson discovered this. "In the midst of President Wilson's difficulties in international negotiations he, too, felt the need of divine guidance. When Mr. Wilson arrived at a cabinet meeting his face wore a solemn look. It was evident that serious affairs of the nation were on his mind. He said to the cabinet members: 'I

don't know whether you men believe in prayer or not. I do; let us pray and ask the help of God.' The President of the United States fell upon his knees with the members of the cabinet and offered a prayer to the Almighty for help." —AQUILLA WEBB[200]

Another President learned the power of prayer: "One day a farmer approaching the camp at Valley Forge during the war heard an earnest voice. On coming nearer, he saw George Washington on his knees, his cheeks wet with tears, praying to God. The farmer returned home and said to his wife, 'George Washington will succeed! The Americans will secure their independence!' 'What makes you think so, Isaac?' asked his wife.

"The farmer replied, 'I heard him pray, Hannah, out in the woods today and the Lord will surely hear his prayer.'"

Prayer should be an integral part of our lives: prayer in the morning, prayer at work, prayer in the car, and even prayer in the government. Even Benjamin Franklin recognized this. In 1787 when the Constitutional Convention was on the verge of total failure over certain issues, he said to the body of men, "Gentlemen, I have lived a long time and am convinced that God governs in the affairs of men. If a sparrow cannot fall to the ground without His notice, is it probable that an empire can rise without His aid? I move that prayer imploring the assistance of heaven be held every morning before we proceed to business." The motion carried. From then on prayer was offered each morning. The change after prayer was introduced was so dramatic that in a short while a compromise was reached which is still in effect today. —*THE BIBLE FRIEND*[201]

Jesus said in Luke 18: "Men ought always to pray, and not to faint." Those who have no prayer life, have no spiritual life and are not in touch with truly great things. Their lives are powerless and meaningless, for times of prayer are always seasons of rich refreshing.

Now is the time to pray. It is time to talk to God. Do not settle down and live without His power, but plug into it today!

May 24

"I am doing a great work, so that I cannot come down" (Nehemiah 6:3).

    A dream comes to pass usually after much hard work and faith are applied. Someone once said, "Life is full of hard knocks, but answer them all. One might be opportunity. Some people fail to recognize opportunity because it so often comes to them in overalls and looks like work."

    "Luck is waiting for something to turn up. Labor, with keen eyes and strong will, will turn up something. Luck lies in bed, and wishes the postman would bring him news of a legacy. Labor turns out at six o'clock and with busy pen or ringing hammer lays the foundation of a competence. Luck whines. Labor whistles. Luck relies on chance. Labor depends on character. Luck slips down to indigence. Labor strives upward to independence." —GOBDEN[202]

    It has been told that on Lincoln's birthday an interesting cartoon appeared in a newspaper. It showed a small log cabin at the base of a mountain, and the White House at the top of the mountain. A ladder connected the two buildings. At the bottom of the cartoon were these words: "The ladder is still there!"

    Ecclesiastes 5:3 says, "For a dream cometh through the multitude of business."

    Multitude is not a small thing, but consists of many. Dreams come true many times after hours, days, even years of hard work.

    When Nehemiah had a dream of rebuilding the walls of Jerusalem, it came to pass after much labor, setbacks, and hardship. It did not just appear out of the blue. He first had the inspiration and dream to do it after God put it in his heart. He then began to gather materials and manpower to accomplish it.

    He was constantly being attacked by those who did not want the walls to be rebuilt. They wanted him to stop and they did their best to make him do so, but Nehemiah was determined to do what God had put in his heart to do, and he did it even in the face of opposition and ridicule.

    Be as Nehemiah. Do not give up on your dream! You may be on the verge of your dream coming to pass. Work on, believe, but don't give up. You do what you can do and leave the miracle with God; for He wants you to succeed. While you are working, don't forget to trust Him to see you through.

May 25

"He that followeth me shall not walk in darkness, but shall have the light of life" (John 8:12).

This is the day to shine with light, even in the darkness.

A preacher once related an incident that happened to him while preaching in Soul's Harbor, Columbus, Ohio. He noticed a nurse under deep conviction of sin. She sat night after night the picture of dejection and distress. One night she yielded herself to Christ. The burden of sin fell from her heart. She became radiant. On the way home that night, she stopped at a store to do some shopping. A clerk who had known her for some time said, "Why, you look as if someone had just lighted a candle inside you!" "That's right," said the converted nurse. "What I mean," said the clerk, "is that you look as if you had just fallen in love!" "I have!" exclaimed the nurse. "I have fallen in love with the One who loved me when I didn't love Him—Jesus!" —JOHN LINTON, IN *CHRISTIAN READERS' DIGEST*[203]

The old song says it well:

Sunlight, sunlight in my soul today,
Sunlight, sunlight all along the way;
Since the Savior found me, took away my sin,
I have had the sunlight of His love within.

Dr. Gwynne W. Davidson told about how one evening at dusk, Robert Louis Stevenson stood as a boy at the window of his home and watched the darkness envelop the city. "Robert," his nurse said to him, "come and sit down. You can't see anything out there."

But young Stevenson insisted, "I can see something wonderful. There is a man coming up the street making holes in the darkness." It was the lamplighter.

Jesus Christ is the divine Lamplighter. He came into the world to make holes in the darkness of sin, ignorance and despair, for He said, "I am the light of the world: he that followeth me shall not walk in darkness, but shall have the light of life" (John 8:12).
—GWYNNE W. DAVIDSON, D.D.[204]

A little girl who sat in church one day looked up at her mother and asked, "Who are these people?" She was looking with admira-

tion at the figures on the stained glass windows, which were shining and glorified by the rays of the sun shining through them.

"They are the saints," replied the mother. As they left the church, the little girl said, "Mother, I now know what a saint is: A saint is one through whom the light shines!"

The question is, "Does the light of Christ shine through your life today? Is the light bright enough to beckon others to partake of His glory?"

This is the day to let the Light of the World shine brightly in your heart. Let Him sweep out all the dark corners of your mind. It is time to shine even in the darkness.

May 26

"*Draw nigh to God, and he will draw nigh to you*" (James 4:8).

A pastor once sat in his study meditating upon the words, "The knowledge of Christ Jesus my Lord." Looking out the window, he saw people scurrying hither, thither and yon, like ants disturbed on an anthill. He asked himself, "What knowledge of Christ do these hurrying people have? What knowledge of Him do the people to whom I preach have? What are their innermost attitudes toward Him?" As he pondered these searching questions, he seemed to see in a vision a caller who asked, "Shall I tell you what Christ means to your people?" The caller spoke calmly and solemnly. "Can you?" asked the pastor. "And how did you know what I was thinking about?"

The caller began, "Some of your people think of Christ as they would think of a generous rich uncle. They ask Him for things unceasingly. Others think of Him as a great teacher. They are stimulated intellectually to hear learned discourses about Him. Some think of Him as an errand boy whom they flippantly order to help them."

"Oh, mysterious caller, is this an accurate picture of my people?" asked the minister.

"Yes," said the caller sadly but firmly. Then he concluded, "But to some He is an ever-present, never-failing friend and confidant! To some, He is the fairest among ten thousands and the altogether

lovely One!" As the caller said this, he receded and vanished, disappearing as mysteriously as he had appeared.

"Was I asleep," asked the startled pastor, "or has an angel visited me, or has Christ Himself been here?" —TOLD BY WALTER B. KNIGHT[205]

With which group of people do you fit? Do you look at Christ as being only a rich uncle to ask things for, does He only teach you good things to make you profit by, is He only there at your beck and call to help you when you get in trouble, or has He become your true Friend?

You choose what He becomes to you. He will come to you, if you will take the time to come to Him, as the scripture states: "Draw nigh to God, and he will draw nigh to you."

There was once a wealthy man who died, but no will could be found. The man's wife and only son had preceded him in death, so in due time all of his things were sold at an auction. Everything was disposed of except a picture of the son. Nobody seemed to want it, until an elderly woman approached. Seeing the unsold picture, she pleaded with the auctioneer to let her have it for the few pennies she had. When he gave her the picture, she drew it to her heart. She had been the son's nurse in his infancy and boyhood days. Attached to the back of the painting was an envelope addressed to an attorney. The woman took it to a lawyer. He read it and exclaimed, "Woman, you have a fortune! This is the rich man's will. In it he bequeathed a vast sum of money to anyone who loved his son enough to buy the picture." —TOLD BY WALTER B. KNIGHT[206]

It is the same way with Christ. When He becomes your Friend and you love Him with your whole heart, you become truly rich! He wants to be your Friend today and will be the truest friend you will ever know.

May 27

"I will be with him in trouble" (Psalm 91:15).

When danger comes, there is one who is invisible who is watching over you. During the dark days of World War II, a British liner left an English port, bound for America. The crossing was very dangerous. Secret directions were given to the liner's cap-

tain. They read: "Keep straight on this course. Turn aside for nothing, and if you need help send a wireless message in this code!" After a few days at sea, an enemy cruiser was sighted. The captain of the liner sent a message in the special code. The captain's message, decoded, read, "Enemy cruiser sighted. What shall I do?" Back came the reply from an unseen ship: "Keep straight on: I am standing by." Although no friendly vessel could be seen, the liner kept straight on and at last reached port in safety. Soon afterward, there steamed into the same harbor a British man-of-war. The battleship, though unseen, had been standing by all the time, ready to help in time of need. —From The Sunday School Times[207]

Just as the unseen battleship was there all the time just in case of trouble, God, though unseen, is watching over you. He is there for you to cushion you, to protect you, to help you in the time of trouble.

A minister visited one of his friends in the hospital who had fallen some thirty feet from a scaffold. It was a miracle that no bones were broken and that he was injured only slightly. With a grateful heart he exclaimed, "There is but one explanation of my being alive—God cushioned the fall!"

Deuteronomy 33:27 says, "The eternal God is thy refuge, and underneath are the everlasting arms." He is unseen, but He is always there.

Two missionaries in Malaya walked to a distant village for some money which had been sent to a bank for them. When they were returning to their station, night overtook them. They prayed and committed themselves to God. Then they lay down to sleep on a lonely hillside. Some weeks later a man came to the mission hospital for treatment. He looked intently at the missionary doctor. "I have seen you before," he said. "No, I don't think we have met before," said the doctor. "But we have met before! You were sleeping one night on a hillside. Several of us saw you withdraw some money from the bank. We followed you, intending to rob you when it was dark. But we could not get near you because you were surrounded by soldiers."

"Soldiers!" exclaimed the missionary. "There were no soldiers with us!" The bandit said, "But there were soldiers with you—sixteen of them. Their swords were drawn. We were filled with fear and ran away!"[208]

God sent eight angels apiece to two of His children. He has promised to protect you, if you will pray and trust Him. Psalm

34:7 says, "The angel of the Lord encampeth round about them that fear him, and delivereth them."

May 28

"And what is the exceeding greatness of his power to us-ward who believe, according to the working of his mighty power" (Ephesians 1:19).

God is in charge no matter that the world is in chaos. He has all power in heaven and in earth and knows the end from the beginning. He still holds the key to it all, as the following poem depicts:

GOD STILL HOLDS THE KEY
To a world of bomb and bursting shell,
Sorrow, want and woe no tongue can tell,
Darkness, hunger, death, a living hell,
God still holds the key!

To an age of greed and bitter hate,
To the hearts that bleed, but hope and wait,
While the hour of time is growing late,
God still holds the key!

To the restless heart that knows no peace,
To the darkened life that nothing sees,
To the slaves of sin that need release,
God still holds the key!

To the heathen lands of deepest night,
To the hardened soul devoid of light,
To a holy life, the path of right,
God still holds the key!

To the unknown years that lie before,
To the unsolved problems yet in store,
To an untrod path, a bolted door,
God still holds the key!

To the boundless wealth within His Word,
Where the trusting soul shall find reward,
To the stores of grace yet unexplored,
God still holds the key!
—Haldor Lillenas[209]

Satan caused sin to enter into the human race and brought with him all his debauched ideas of destruction, greed, hate, evil, war and filth. Only God can undo the evil he has done, but God will not force His ideas and ways on mankind. They must choose God's way, if they want to win over evil.

There is coming a day when Satan will be bound and there will be no evil. The lion will lie down with the lamb and all will be peace and blessing, but until then, man must choose whether he is delivered or set free. God holds the key to peace, deliverance, blessing and power: in Him is all power.

Ephesians 1:19, 21, 22 states, "And what is the exceeding greatness of his power to us-ward who believe, according to the working of his mighty power . . . Far above all principality, and power, and might, and dominion, and every name that is named, not only in this world, but also in that which is to come: And hath put all things under his feet."

He not only has power but the Scripture refers to it as mighty power. As things crumble around you, don't give up on God. He is the only one who has all power and can change things. People will self-destruct if they do not walk God's way. You can choose the way of power or destruction. God is the key to blessing and deliverance. If you put your faith in Him, things will turn out good for you, for He will be in charge of your life and He has never lost a battle.

May 29

"O Lord, make haste to help me" (Psalm 40:13).

There is a formula that God has given mankind on how to receive things from Him. He wants us to ask Him for that of which we are in need. He wants us to call upon Him when there

is trouble or distress. The formula is: A. S. K. What does it mean? Ask, seek, knock and you will receive.

I got up early one morning
And rushed right into the day;
I had so much to accomplish
I didn't have time to pray.

Troubles just tumbled about me
And heavier came each task.
"Why doesn't God help me?" I wondered,
He answered, "You didn't ask."

I tried to come into God's presence.
I used all my keys at the lock.
God gently and lovingly chided,
"Why, child, you didn't knock."

I wanted to see joy and beauty,
But the day toiled on grey and bleak,
I called on the Lord for the reason—
He said, "You didn't seek."

I woke up early this morning
And paused before entering the day.
I had so much to accomplish
That I had to take time to pray.
—AUTHOR UNKNOWN[210]

The greatest thing you can do today is to take time to pray: to ask, seek and knock, to talk with the Lord. Something happens to a person who prays consistently every day. There is a marked difference in his attitude and deportment. It affects him, his spirit and very life. This was noticed in Africa many years ago. The earliest African converts to Christianity were earnest and regular in their private devotions. Each one reportedly had separate spots in the thicket where he poured out his heart to God. The several paths to these little Bethels became distinctly marked; and when anyone began to decline in devotions, it was soon apparent to others. They would then kindly remind him, saying, "Brother, the grass grows on your path yonder."

Jesus reminded us in Matthew 7:7: "Ask, and it shall be given you; seek, and ye shall find; knock, and it shall be opened unto you." Sometimes the things people rush about seeking and working for can bring them pain and pressure, instead of relief. This happens when things in their mind become bigger than God and time spent with Him. He is the burden bearer, the lifter of our hearts, the pressure reliever, the constant source of joy and the answer to our problems. If you will take time for a little A.S.K. therapy, you will gain everything you really need. No longer will you wander in a maze of unfulfillment or throb with pressure, but He will relieve you of that. He will teach you how to succeed, He will give you fulfillment, and your life will take on new meaning. He will impart faith and inspiration to you.

The Master is waiting for you to come and talk to Him. Don't let the grass grow on your pathway to Him, for when you are in His presence you are in the power chamber! Why don't you meet with Him today?

May 30

"The fool hath said in his heart, There is no God" (Psalm 53:1).

The truly intelligent know that there is a God. You can choose to be a fool and throw away all of God's blessings or you can choose to believe in God and receive everything you need. Hebrews 11:6 says, "But without faith it is impossible to please him: for he that cometh to God must believe that he is, and that he is a rewarder of them that diligently seek him."

Gandhi was once approached by an atheist with the request to organize and promote an anti-God society. Gandhi replied, "It amazes me to find an intelligent person who fights against something which he does not at all believe exists."[211]

Even those who try not to believe know deep down inside that there is a God.

Dwight D. Eisenhower, former President of the United States, once said, "It takes no brains to be an atheist. Any stupid person can deny the existence of a supernatural power because man's physical senses cannot detect it. But there cannot be ignored the

mystery of first life . . . or the marvelous order in which the universe moves about us. All of these evidence the handiwork of a beneficent Deity. For my part, that Deity is the God of the Bible and Christ, His Son."[212]

It is a fact: there is nothing but misery for an atheist! Thomas Paine, an immigrant to America in 1787, had leaped from obscurity to fame after writing some brilliant pamphlets on freedom. But then he made a fatal mistake. He began to write *The Age of Reason* which scoffed at Christianity. He said about it, "This will destroy the Bible. Within one hundred years, Bibles will be found only in museums or in musty corners of secondhand bookstores." His book was published in 1794, but it brought him so much misery and loneliness that he once said: "I would give worlds if I had them, if only *The Age of Reason* had never been written."[213]

When Thomas Paine died in 1809, the Bible remained a bestseller. No one can win against God. He is alive and powerful and will get the last word in, so learn to trust Him and His Word today!

May 31

"Shall be likened unto a foolish man, which built his house upon the sand" (Matthew 7:26).

Napoleon once said some startling words. He said, "A man is not a man without God. I saw men without God in the reign of terror in 1793. One does not govern such men; he shoots them down." He recognized the degradation that happens when God is erased from the picture and life of men and women.

G. K. Chesterton once said: "It is often supposed that when people stop believing in God, they believe in nothing. Alas, it is worse than that. When they stop believing in God, they believe in anything." When this happens, there is no firm foundation of truth; therefore, anything goes. It is like standing on shifting sand. There is nothing to stand on. It is slippery, changeable and disastrous.

Dostoevski wrote, "If God does not exist, everything is permissible."[214] God demands character, moral purity, love, rightness and kindness. If He is put out of the picture, the very opposite of those things will take over: immorality, hate, wrong, unkindness,

lack of character, low living, fear and hopelessness.

To be an atheist or someone who does not bring God into His rightful position is a step down for that person. It takes away the creativity that could be his. The potential that he could reach is squashed by unbelief. He can only go so far and then the blacker side of evil will reach its tentacles around his life and mind, and seek to squeeze the nectar of peace and the potential of good out of him.

Calvin Coolidge once said: "It is hard to see how a great man can be an atheist. Doubters do not achieve. Skeptics do not contribute. Cynics do not create."[215]

"Atheism never composed a symphony. Never painted a masterpiece. Never dispelled a fear. Never healed a disease. Never gave peace of mind. Never dried a tear. Never established a philanthropy. Never gave an intelligent answer to the vast mystery of the universe. Never gave meaning to man's life on earth. Never built a just and peaceful world. Never built a great and enduring civilization." —CHARLES M. HOUSER[216]

It is time for people to wake up and put God back into the schools, back into the homes, back into the world of entertainment, back into their conversation and lifestyles. The moral fiber of our schools and communities will be destroyed if He is not brought back into a prominent place.

Choose today to lift Him up and follow Him and you will win in the struggle of life. For God is, whether you believe in Him or not! He wants to be a part of your life, not just a part but an integral part of your life!

"All things work together for good" (Romans 8:28).

Sometimes God allows bad things to happen so that a worse thing might not occur. National Geographic News once reported that without an occasional hurricane, the world's weather might be even worse. Fierce tropical storms play a vital part in maintaining the heat balance between the tropic and polar regions. The tropics and subtropics receive more heat from the sun than they lose by radiation; other means are needed to prevent gradual cooling of the

poles and scorching of the equatorial regions. Hurricanes help keep the balance. "If hurricane control was successful and none were allowed to go through their full life cycle," says Gordon E. Dunn, former director of the National Hurricane Center at Miami, "nature would undoubtedly find some other method of maintaining the heat balance, and who can say that this new method might not be even more disastrous than the hurricane?"

There was once a grandfather who had planned to go to a church conference but at the last minute felt ill and decided not to go. While the grandmother was gone, the grandchildren who lived next door decided to go swimming in Grandpa and Grandma's pool. Grandfather, who stayed home because he had not felt well, felt a sudden urge to check the pool in the backyard. When he went to look, sudden fear struck his heart as he saw his granddaughter floating lifelessly in the pool. He went into action, pulled her out, and sent his grandson to call 911, while he did CPR on her. Later, after the granddaughter had pulled through, the doctor said it was the quick reaction of the grandfather that had saved her life.

A little sick feeling, but bad enough for a man to change his plans at the last minute, was actually all in the plan to save his granddaughter's life.

Paul said in Romans 8:28: "And we know that all things work together for good to them that love God, to them who are the called according to his purpose." If you are a Christian and walk with Jesus Christ close enough to trust Him, He will make sure that all things will work together for good for a higher purpose.

Yes, even as hurricanes in the natural can actually work for the good of mankind's welfare, so can spiritual hurricanes work for the good in the life of a Christian and keep something worse from happening. The important thing is to stay close to Jesus in the time of the storm and the purpose of God will be done—His purpose—that is what counts.

"We will remember the name of the LORD our God" (Psalm 20:7).

 *F*aith acts before it sees a sign. In the book, *The Life of Robert and Mary Moffat*, the story is told of how for ten years the early mission in Bechuanaland was carried on without any encouragement. No convert was made. The directors at home began to question the wisdom in continuing the mission. A friend from England sent word to Mrs. Moffat asking what gift she should send to her. And the brave woman wrote back, "Send a communion service; it will be sure to be needed." At last the breath of God moved and six converts made their way to Christ. The gift Mary Moffat had asked for arrived only one day before the communion service that had already been arranged for by faith. If she had not asked by faith before there were converts, there would not have been the gift she had asked for when she needed it.

 In his book, *God will Help Me*, Walter G. Swanson refers to the life of Robert Dollar. He wrote: A keen-eyed young sea captain stood in the lobby of a large hotel in Hong Kong conversing with an Englishman. "So you've come to do business in the Orient? Well, step into the bar and tell me about your plans." "I'm sorry," said the seaman, "but I never partake of alcoholic beverages." The man's face broke into an unbelieving smile. "Entering the Oriental trade without having a Scotch and soda?"

 "Yes, sir!" he replied.

 "Do you expect to be successful without taking your friends into a tavern for a drink? If you do," the Englishman said with a cynical laugh, "God help you!" The young man replied, "God will help me." And he was right.

 Years later, Robert Dollar stood on the tenth floor of the building that bore his name near San Francisco Bay. He was watching the workmen unload cargo from his freighters that had come from all over the world.

 It was his faith in God, not his faith in alcohol that made the difference. He operated according to Psalm 20:7: "Some trust in chariots, and some in horses: but we will remember the name of the L<small>ORD</small> our God." Put your faith in Him today and act according to His power and great things will happen.

 Someone once said, *"Faith is idle when circumstances are right, only when they are adverse is one's faith in God exercised. Faith, like muscle, grows strong and supple with exercise."*[217]

 Exercise your faith today! Act, before you see a sign, and see what God will do!

June 3

"He that is without sin . . . cast a stone" (John 8:7).

John R. Rice tells about how a young lady was brought before the church for discipline because of a violation of the church covenant. It was suggested that she be dropped from the roll of the church. As the debate developed the pastor said, "Let us also call the church treasurer and have him read the record of the giving of every member, and let us vote to drop everyone who has violated God's law against covetousness." That bombshell cleared the air of accusers, as did the reminder of Jesus: "He that is without sin among you, let him first cast a stone at her" (John 8:7).[218]

Pray don't find fault with a man who limps
Or stumbles along the road,
Unless you have worn the shoes he wears
Or struggled beneath his load.

There may be tacks in his shoes that hurt,
Though hidden away from view.
Or the burden he bears, placed on your back,
Might cause you to stumble, too.

Don't sneer at the man who is down today,
Unless you have felt the blow
That caused his fall, or felt the shame
That only the fallen know.

You may be strong, but still the blows
That were his, if dealt to you
In the selfsame way at the selfsame time,
Might cause you to stagger, too.
—Author Unknown[219]

Many times caustic, angry remarks are made about situations, that if the speaker knew the full story, he would refrain his lips from speaking them. Many years ago a Santa Fe train was speeding through Oklahoma. In one of the coaches sat a young woman

desperately trying to take care of a restless baby, whose crying was evidently annoying some of the passengers. Across the aisle sat a stout fellow, a picture of comfort and rich living. He glowered at the woman and shouted: "Can't you keep that child quiet?" On taking a further look at the young lady, he noticed that her dress was one of mourning. Then he heard her say gently, "I cannot help it. The child is not mine. I am doing my best."

"Where is its mother?" asked the portly passenger.

"In her coffin, sir," answered the young lady, "in the baggage car up ahead."

The [eyes of the demanding] fellow filled with tears. He got up, took the babe in his arms, kissed it, and then walked up and down the aisle with the child, trying his best to soothe the motherless little one and make up for his harshness.[220]

Longfellow said, "*If we could only read the secret history of our enemies, we would find in each man's life, sorrow and suffering enough to disarm all hostility.*"

This is the day to obey the words spoken by Jesus, "Judge not, that ye be not judged." They are truth and truth will set you free.

"To morrow go out against them: for the LORD will be with you" (II Chronicles 20:17).

Sometimes when you are fighting the enemy, you have to do things in an unorthodox manner, in order to win. B. F. Coggin shared a story about General MacArthur, who called in one of his Army engineers during the war and asked: "How long will it take to throw a bridge across this stream?" "Three days," the engineer told him. "Good," snapped General MacArthur. "Have your draftsmen make drawings right away." Three days later the general sent for the engineer and asked how the bridge was coming along. "It's all ready. You can send the troops across right now if you don't have to wait for the pictures. They ain't done yet." —B. F. COGGIN[221]

If they would have had to wait for the pictures, they probably would have lost that battle. They had to move quickly with expert precision.

When Joshua was instructed by God to take a certain city named Jericho, there were no long, drawn-out committee meetings with detailed instructions that filled many pages. It was just short instructions and very unorthodox. March around Jericho seven times. For six days, do not say a word or make a sound. On the seventh day, the priests sound the trumpets and everyone give a loud shout, and the walls would fall. As God instructed, it happened. They moved quickly and in seven days, a strong city that no one else had been able to penetrate was destroyed by God's unorthodox manner.

When Jehosophat was surrounded by the enemies who were much greater than his forces, he prayed to God and said, "We do not know what to do, but our eyes are upon Thee. Show us what to do." The Lord answered back, "It is not your battle. It is the Lord's. All you have to do is organize singers and praisers to go forth before the people and let them cry and sing, 'Praise the Lord for His mercy endureth forever.'" They did what must have seemed foolish to the enemy. As the enemy watched, they were stunned as they heard the singing. There were no swords drawn, no cannons, nothing with which to fight, but suddenly God sent ambushments into the camps of the enemies and there were dead corpses everywhere. In fact none escaped. Not only did they win the battle but they also found riches as stated in II Chronicles 20:25: "And when Jehoshaphat and his people came to take away the spoil of them, they found among them in abundance both riches with the dead bodies, and precious jewels, which they stripped off for themselves, more than they could carry away: and they were three days in gathering of the spoil, it was so much."

Romans 8:31 rings loud and clear here, "If God be for us, who can be against us?" God always does things above and beyond what is expected!

"For he that wavereth is like a wave of the sea driven with the wind and tossed" (James 1:6).

If you try to please all of the people all of the time, you end up pleasing no one none of the time. The best thing is to please God and follow your heart.

The story is told about Mullah and his son who were walking along a country road behind their donkey, who was contentedly nibbling grass along the way. Another man, seeing Mullah and his son sweating profusely, remarked, "Look how foolish they are, walking instead of riding." Hearing the remark, Mullah and his son climbed on the donkey and rode through the next village, where they heard an old man exclaim, "They ought to be ashamed, making that poor old donkey carry two riders." Mullah dismounted and walked while the son rode the donkey to the next village. There Mullah heard someone else say, "Poor old man; that boy should be ashamed, making his poor old dad walk!" Then Mullah got on the donkey, while his son dismounted and walked for some distance. Finally, another villager made this observation, "Look at that old man riding, while his son has to walk—how cruel!" Mullah rubbed his beard, shook his head and said to himself, "You can't please any of the people all of the time."[222]

J. H. Dampier tells the story about a man starting in the fish business. He hung out a sign that said, "Fresh Fish for Sale Today," and invited his friends to the opening. They all congratulated him on his enterprise, but one suggested his sign might be improved. Said he: "Why the *Today*? Of course it's today, not yesterday or tomorrow." So the fishmonger removed the word. Another said, "Why the *For Sale*? Everybody knows that." And so off came the words *for sale*. Another complained, "Why the word *Fresh*? Your integrity guarantees every fish to be fresh." Finally only the word *Fish* remained, but an objector said, "Why the sign? I smelled your fish two blocks away!" —J. H. DAMPIER[223]

If you listen to and are influenced by every voice that speaks, you will become confused. A double-minded man is unstable in all his ways. He that wavers is like the waves of the sea.

The best thing to do is first find a quiet place to pray to God. Ask Him for direction, read His Word, wait for that inner peace to come knowing that He has directed your steps. It is a promise: He will direct your steps. Psalm 32:8 gives the following promise: "I will instruct thee and teach thee in the way which thou shalt go: I will guide thee with mine eye."

Look into His face today, listen to His Word and be guided by your heavenly Father who knows the way for you to go. Job said, "He knows the way that I take." He knows, so ask of Him today and let confusion be gone.

June 6

"Perfect love casteth out fear" (I John 4:18).

Love is more powerful than money and prestige. Neil Strait wrote about William Dixon who lived in Brackenthwaite, England, many years ago. He was a widower who had also lost his only son. One day he saw that the house of one of his neighbors was on fire. Although the aged owner was rescued, her orphaned grandson was trapped in the blaze. Dixon climbed an iron pipe on the side of the house and lowered the boy to safety. His hand that held on to the pipe was badly burned.

Shortly after the fire, the grandmother died. The townspeople wondered who would care for the boy. Two volunteers appeared before the town council. One was a father who had lost his son and would like to adopt the orphan as his own. William Dixon was to speak next, but instead of saying anything he merely held up his scarred hand. When the vote was taken, the boy was given to him.[224]

There is nothing more powerful than love, for love does the unexpected!

In 1864, a crowded train was pulling away from Jersey City station when Robert, the son of President Lincoln, jumped aboard. The man lost balance and was falling when a man by the name of Edwin Booth reached out and grabbed him by the coat collar and saved him. Within a week, a letter of thanks came from Washington.

But within less than a year, this man became "Man of Mystery" as he was always in hiding, shameful that his brother, John Wilkes Booth, had killed Lincoln. It was months later that he got enough courage to appear again in his experienced role as an actor and became recognized as the nation's most able performer of Shakespearean roles. He was the first actor to have name and bust in the American Hall of Fame gallery in New York.[225]

Edwin Booth, because of the shame surrounding his family, could have turned into a cynical and bitter man, but instead he reached out and helped someone whose life was in danger. The power of love for another, caring what happened to someone, set him free.

That is what love does: it sets people free from the shackles of jealousy, hate, bitterness and torment. Love liberates. John said in I John 4:18, "There is no fear in love; but perfect love casteth out fear: because fear hath torment."

If you want power in your life and desire to get rid of your fears, then obey the greatest commandment in the Bible: "Thou shalt love the Lord thy God with all thy heart, and with all thy soul, and with all thy mind. This is the first and great commandment. And the second is like unto it, Thou shalt love thy neighbour as thyself" (Matthew 22:37-39).

Jesus knew, when He gave those instructions, that the power of love would set men and women free from themselves and their fears. This is the day to ask Him to help you love as He instructed to love.

June 7

"Wait on the LORD" (Psalm 27:14).

There are times when a person needs to pause for a moment and not always dash madly ahead in the pursuit of life. A runner cannot run forever; he must pause and rest. A singer cannot sing all the time; she must pause and rest her voice. A mother cannot dash madly about all day; she must pause and rest. A Christian must also take some time to pause before the Lord, instead of running at high speed all the way. Pauses are necessary to life.

A rather humorous story proves this. It started at the end of a Sunday morning service in an Ontario church. The choir began the recessional, singing as they marched in perfect unison up the center aisle to the back of the church.

The last young lady in the women's section was wearing a new pair of shoes with needle heels—heels that are so slender they slip through any grating. And in the aisle was grating that covered the hot-air register. Without a thought for her fancy heels, the young woman sang and marched. And the heel of one shoe sank right through a hole in the register grate. Instantly she realized her predicament. She knew she couldn't hold up the whole recessional while she back-stepped to pull out her heel. She did the next best thing in the emergency. Without missing a step she slipped her foot out of her shoe and continued up the aisle. There

wasn't a break in the recessional. Everything moved like clockwork. The first man following that young woman noted the situation and without losing a beat, reached down and picked up her shoe. The entire grate came with it. Startled but still singing, the man continued up the aisle bearing in his hand one grate attached to one shoe. There was never a break in the recessional. Everybody was singing and everything was moving like clockwork. Then in tune and in time to the beat, the next man stepped into the open register. —*THE LUTHERAN*[226]

Sometimes the Lord wants his children to pause, but they keep going to keep up appearances, to not cause a break in the flow of things. Psalm 27:14 instructs: "Wait on the LORD: be of good courage, and he shall strengthen thine heart: wait, I say, on the LORD."

Waiting for God to do something, pauses in life that sometime seem like an eternity, are necessary. Isaiah 26:20 says it well, "Come, my people, enter thou into thy chambers, and shut thy doors about thee: hide thyself as it were for a little moment, until the indignation be overpast." In times when pauses are dictated, use that time to learn of Christ, and let Him heal, soothe, restore and strengthen you.

June 8

"I will trust, and not be afraid" (Isaiah 12:2).

Did you know that you can travel first class or second class to heaven? It has been reported that Dwight L. Moody's favorite verse was Isaiah 12:2, "I will trust, and not be afraid." He used to say, "You can travel first class or second class to heaven. Second class is found in Psalm 56:3. 'What time I am afraid, I will trust.'"

True trust in the Lord will let you rest your case with the Lord, unafraid of the outcome, because you know that He does all things well.

To celebrate an older man's seventy-fifth birthday, an aviation enthusiast offered to take him for a plane ride over the little West Virginia town where he spent all his life. The old man accepted the offer. Back on the ground, after circling over the town twenty minutes, his friend asked, "Were you scared, Uncle Dudley?" "No-o-o,"

was the hesitant answer. "But I never did put my full weight down."

Trusting in God is putting your full weight down. How like Uncle Dudley are some of us! He was up in the air in the airplane, but yet he was holding a part of himself rigid, thinking that if he held himself rigid, not completely relaxing, that if anything would have happened to the plane, he could have prevented it.

It is time to trust and rest in the Lord and not be afraid.

Arthur F. Glasser tells of how on June 25, 1885, James Hudson Taylor at age thirty-three came to the great crisis of his life. The locale was Brighton beach on the south coast of England. There on a quiet Sunday morning he took a step of faith in response to a simple spiritual principle he had just discovered. He was surprised that this truth had so long eluded him. "If we are obeying the Lord, the responsibility rests with Him, not with us!" Months of struggle were over, and the way ahead was clear. To obey the Scriptures and trust God to be faithful to His pledged Word were not rash. Throwing caution and tradition to the winds, Hudson Taylor formed the China Inland Mission.[227]

What a revelation! "If we are obeying the Lord, the responsibility rests with Him, not with us!" Did He not say He would take care of His children, that He would be with them always, that He would be their shield, a tower to run to in the time of trouble, a pavilion, a light in the darkness? With the knowledge that God is always there, why be afraid?

Some scholars believe the following Scripture text to be the middle verse of the Bible. Psalm 118:8 says, "It is better to trust in the Lord than to put confidence in man."

This scripture should also be at the center of our lives, quoted daily, thought upon and acted upon. Say it in the morning, at the noon hour and when you lie down at night. "It is better to trust in the Lord than to put confidence in man." People and things can let you down because of circumstances that arise beyond their control, but God has promised to never let you down. Trust Him today.

"*Meditate therein day and night, . . . and then thou shalt have good success*" (Joshua 1:8).

Did you know that God wants you to be creative and think positive thoughts, and that He wants you to be successful? III John 2 says, "Beloved, I wish above all things that thou mayest prosper and be in health, even as thy soul prospereth."

Joshua 1:8 states that meditation on the Word of God shall bring prosperity and success to a person. This is the day to think successful, creative thoughts.

Murray Spangler, a department store janitor in Canton, Ohio, set out to find a better way to clean floors, even though the dust made him wheeze and cough. He thought, "Why not eliminate the broom, maybe something that would suck up dust?"

Spangler's question led to a crude but workable vacuum cleaner, which he induced an old friend in the leather business to finance. The friend's name was H. W. Hoover. The name Hoover is synonymous with vacuum cleaners, all because a friend dared to think creative thoughts.

A workman one day set a basin of cold water, the interior of which was covered with plaster of Paris, upon a hot stove to warm. After some moments of waiting, to his surprise he discovered that the water was just as cold as ever. Then the man thought, "Plaster of Paris is a perfect non-conductor of heat." Result: Fireproof safes, that became indispensable to every business concern of America. —LUCY E. KEELER[228]

Galileo, under twenty years of age, standing one day in the Metropolitan Church of Pisa, observed a lamp suspended from the ceiling, swinging backward and forward. Thousands had seen it before: but Galileo observed it, and struck by the regularity with which it moved backward and forward, reflected on it, and perfected the method of measuring time by means of a pendulum.[229]

It is time to use your thinking ability to not only create, but to win in the war with the devil, your adversary. A fable is told about an old lion, too weak to hunt or fight for his food, who decided that he must get it by his wits. He lay down in a cave, pretending to be ill, and whenever any animals came to visit him, he seized them and ate them. After many had perished in this way, there was a fox that had seen through the trick that came and stood at a distance from the cave, and inquired how he was. "Bad," the lion answered, and asked why he did not come in. "I would have come in," said the fox, "but I saw a lot of tracks going in and none coming out." —*FABLES OF AESOP*[230]

This is the day to think before walking into a trap, use the brain God gave you to think on how you can make things better. Let the candle of the Lord, His inspiration warm your soul and illuminate your mind to greater things!

June 10

"He will without fail" (Joshua 3:10).

It does not matter where you come from, or what difficulties face you, you have the power to be successful, if you pray and ask God to help you.

C. E. Macartney tells about how early in the last century a minister at Darlington, Pennsylvania, out on his pastoral round, was riding his horse down a country lane. As he drew up before a humble cottage he heard the sound of a woman's voice lifted in earnest prayer. As he listened he heard this widowed mother, with her boys kneeling at her side, earnestly entreating God that he would open a door for the education of these boys, so that they might become good and useful men. The pastor dismounted and went in to speak with the widow who had prayed so earnestly. Struck with the alertness of one of these boys and touched by the woman's petitions, he took the boy with him to the old Stone Academy at Darlington, and there gave him the instruction for which his mother had prayed.

That boy, so handicapped in his birth, and for whom there seemed to be no opportunity, influenced more young minds in America in the last century than any other man. He was William McGuffy, the author of the famous *Eclectic Readers*, which had the extraordinary circulation of a hundred million copies.[231]

John Newton's mother prayed always that her son might be of service to God. Instead of following God's way, John ran away from home, became a sailor and also a very wicked man. But the prayers of John's mother followed him. They followed him to Africa where he sank so low that he was sold for a slave and lived only on crumbs and wild yams. His clothing was reduced to a single shirt which he washed in the ocean. When he finally escaped from slavery, he went to the natives, accepting their base life. But one day a missionary spoke to him about his soul and John Newton gave his heart to Jesus Christ. He became a sea captain and later became a minister. He wrote many hymns. One of the most famous was "Amazing Grace."

In the church of London of which he was the pastor, there is still an epitaph which John Newton wrote for himself. It reads: "Sacred to the memory of John Newton, once a libertine and blasphemer and slave of slaves in Africa, but renewed, purified, pardoned, and appointed to preach that Gospel which he had laboured to destroy!"

It does not matter where somebody has been or what he is involved in, prayer and faith in God can bring him to a place of service to God and living a life that will bless others. This is the day to pray and believe, for all things are possible to him that believeth!

June 11

"The LORD will do wonders among you" (Joshua 3:5).

You may have been assigned an impossible task, but do not listen to the impossibilities. With God all things are possible!

Benjamin P. Browne tells how in the stormy North Sea off the coast of the Netherlands lay a ledge of rocks where many a vessel had been wrecked. Pirates who looted vessels inhabited the island and murdered crews. Finally the Netherlands government determined to rid the island of pirates and assigned Edward Bok's father, a young Dutch lawyer, to do the job.

It was a grim place, barren of trees, of any living green thing, but the young lawyer cleaned up the island and not only decided to make it his home but determined to make the island beautiful. He led seafaring men to inhabit the island and said to them, "We must have trees." They were too busy with their fishing and so he was compelled to say, "I'll have the trees if I must plant them myself."

"Your trees will never live," said the islanders. "The north winds and storms will kill them all." But plant trees he did, a hundred the first year. The second year he planted more, and each year for the fifty years he lived on the island, he planted trees. As

the trees grew tall through the years, the island became a bird sanctuary. In time, bird lovers from all parts of the world came to this island to study the thousands of birds which rested there. Then one night a singular thing happened. A pair of storm-driven nightingales found refuge in the island. In gratitude for their refuge they remained on the island and raised their young nightingales, wherein a few years the island became a colony for nightingales. Throughout Holland and Europe, the fame of the Island of Nightingales spread. American artist, William M. Chase, took his pupils there each year. "In all the world today," he asserted, "there is no more beautiful place."

It changed from a pirate-infested, grim, lonely, treeless, and barren island into one of the greenest, most luscious and beautiful places in the world. All because one man refused to believe those who said it was impossible. He had a dream and an assignment and went to work, making the dream that he had, become a reality.

Anyone can join the crowd and say it cannot be done. It takes someone with a big enough dream inside to buck the tide and go forward and make it happen, even when it looks impossible.

Let the words of Jesus spoken in Mark 9:23 ring in your ears today. "If thou canst believe, all things are possible to him that believeth."

June 12

"Remember how short my time is" (Psalm 89:47).

*D*o you really know what time it is and do you know that what you do with your time affects your eternity?

This story appeared once in the *Reader's Digest* many years ago. The writer wrote: "One evening in Albany, New York, I asked a sailor what time it was. He pulled out a huge watch and replied, 'It's 7:20.' I knew it was later. 'Your watch has stopped, hasn't it?' I asked.

"'No,' he said, 'I'm still on Mountain Standard Time. I'm from southern Utah. When I joined the navy, Pa gave me this watch. He said it'd help me remember home. When my watch says 5 A.M., I know Dad is rollin' out to milk the cows. And any

night when it says 7:30 I know the whole family's around a well-spread table, and Dad's thankin' God for what's on it and askin' Him to watch over me. I can almost smell the hot biscuits. It's thinkin' about those things that makes me want to fight when the goin' gets tough,' he concluded. 'I can find out what time it is where I am easy enough. What I want to know is what time is it in Utah.'"[232]

The question today is, do you know what time it is according to God's time frame? What place do you have your watch set by? Is it set according to the time clock of life on earth or the time clock of eternity? What time is it for you? Is your mind on the important things or on the frivolous things? What is it that keeps you ticking?

Jonathan Edward's resolutions he made for himself to live by would benefit anyone who really knew what God's time clock said. He wrote the following:

Resolved to live with all my might while I do live.
Resolved, never to lose one moment of time, to improve it in the most profitable way I can.
Resolved, never to do anything which I should despise or think meanly of in another.
Resolved, never to do anything out of revenge.
Resolved, never to do anything which I should be afraid to do if it were the last hour of my life.

Dr. Wernher von Braun, well-known for his part in the U.S. space program, says he has "essentially scientific" reasons for believing in life after death. He explained, "Science has found that nothing can disappear without a trace. Nature does not know extinction. All it knows is transformation. If God applies the fundamental principle to the most minute and insignificant parts of the universe, doesn't it make sense to assume that He applies it to the masterpiece of His creation—the human soul?"[233]

The question is, "What am I doing with my time in its relation to eternity?" For that is where everyone will live forever someday. Be sure today to seek to know what time it really is and to do something about the important usage of time which affects the eternal tomorrows!

June 13

"Which laboured with me in the gospel . . . whose names are in the book of life" (Philippians 4:3).

*H*ave you ever wondered if all the good you do for people is really worth it? Does your influence upon them matter?

Many years ago, when a certain preacher died, his relatives found he had neatly tied up the messages he had delivered and placed a card on top of them with this inscription: "Where has the influence gone of all these sermons I have preached?" Underneath he had scribbled in large letters "OVER." After turning the packet of messages over, they found this answer to his question. He had written, "Where are last year's sunrays? They have gone into fruits and grain and vegetables to feed mankind. Where are last year's raindrops? Forgotten by most people, of course, but they did their refreshing work and their influence still abides."[234]

C. E. Macartney wrote about passing through the corridors of a great hospital and seeing a minister whom he had known. He was a man well advanced in years, now broken in health, who for some time had been forced to give up his church, where he had been in unhappy disputes with a few members of his congregation. Mr. Macartney turned to speak with him, expecting to hear from him some word of melancholy reminiscence or present gloom, but received a pleasant surprise. He told him that a woman going by had just turned to speak with him and had told him that long ago a word spoken by him in the pulpit had been the means of bringing her to Christ. He was happy in the knowledge that his shadow had once pointed the way to Jesus Christ.[235]

You never know what person you are having a lasting effect upon, but everything you do or say is influencing someone just as the young boy in the following story was influenced.

The *Christian Herald* once carried an article about a senior executive of one of the largest banks in New York City. He told how he had risen to a place of prominence and influence. At first he served as an office boy. Then one day the president of the company called him aside and said, "I want you to come into my office and be with me each day." The young man replied, "But what could I do to help you, sir? I don't know anything about finances."

"Never mind that, you will learn what I want to teach you a lot faster if you just stay by my side and keep your eyes and ears open!"

"That was the most significant experience of my life," said the now famous banker. "Being with that wise man made me just like him. I began to do things the way he did, and that accounts for what I am today."

The challenge today is to stay close to the Lord Jesus Christ and learn of His ways, so that you will become like Him and influence others to do so also.

June 14

"I have made the earth, and created man upon it: I, even my hands, have stretched out the heavens, and all their host have I commanded" (Isaiah 45:12).

Why worry today? God's in control! The earth moves in at least six different ways, and yet we on earth are not dizzy. The movements are:

#1. The earth spins on its axis, like a top, at the speed of one-third mile per second or one thousand miles per hour. If it were one hundred miles per hour, the earth would alternately freeze and burn.

#2. It weaves slowly back and forth on its axis, tilting to an angle of twenty-three degrees, then swinging slowly back, twice a year. This gives us our seasons.

#3. The earth with the moon is swinging around the sun, once a year at the rate of 18 1/2 miles per second. And it never varies 1/100,000th of a second on this annual trip.

#4. The sun, with all its planets, is on a trip, rushing northward at twelve miles per second.

#5. The nearby stars, with our planetary system, are revolving at 180 miles per second around the Milky Way's center.

#6. The Milky Way, our galaxy, with all its millions of stars, is on a tremendous journey, plunging through space at terrific speed.

God guides and controls them all.[236] Notice that if the earth were as small as the moon, the power of gravity would be too

weak to retain sufficient atmosphere for man's needs; but if it were as large as Jupiter, Saturn, or Uranus, extreme gravitation would make human movement almost impossible. If we were as near to the sun as Venus, the heat would be unbearable; if we were as far away as Mars, we would experience snow and ice every night even in the warmest regions. If the oceans were only one-fourth larger their present dimensions, our annual precipitation would increase fourfold, and this earth would become a vast, uninhabitable swamp!

Water solidifies at thirty-two degrees above zero. It would be disastrous if the oceans were subject to that law, however, for then the amount of thawing in the polar regions would not balance out, and ice would accumulate throughout the centuries! To prevent such a catastrophe, God put salt in the sea to alter its freezing point! —OUR DAILY BREAD[237]

Psalm 104:24 says, "O LORD, how manifold are thy works! in wisdom hast thou made them all: the earth is full of thy riches."

Why worry when God is in charge? He made the earth and the heavens to operate according to His divine plan. He also has created you along with a plan mapped out for you.

He does know how many hairs are on your head, He knows when each sparrow falls to the ground and He is aware of where you are at all times. Isaiah 43:2-3 is full of His promises: "When thou passest through the waters, I will be with thee; and through the rivers, they shall not overflow thee: when thou walkest through the fire, thou shalt not be burned; neither shall the flame kindle upon thee. For I am the LORD thy God."

God who in His wonder created all things, is with you today, so why worry and be afraid?

June 15

"So they strengthened their hands for this good work" (Nehemiah 2:18).

This is the day instead of only talking about a negative situation, to try to do something about it.

A bus driver became annoyed with his job because he had to

wait seven minutes after every run near an open field which litterbugs had made into an unofficial dump. He often thought that somebody should do something about that unsightly mess. One day he himself decided to get out and pick up some of the tin cans and other debris which were lying all around. This improved things so much that he was eager to complete his route and spend all his free moments in cleaning up the area. When spring came, he was so enthusiastic about his project that he decided to sow some flower seeds. By the end of the summer many were riding to the end of the line just to see what the motorman had accomplished by doing what he and others had only talked about before.
—OUR DAILY BREAD[238]

Another man, John B. Hand, who was once a California postman, decided to brighten the drab countryside of South San Francisco. His special delivery route was in that region. He started the practice of casting wild flower seeds along the way as he drove the mail truck over his fifty-mile route in the Los Altos Hills area.

A traveler could see colorful patches of blossom that provided welcome relief from dull, brown landscape. His procedure: As he entered a twenty-five-mile-an-hour zone or slowed for a curve, he scattered seeds. Instead of letting the negative surroundings influence him, he influenced it.[239]

It was the famous preacher, John Wesley, who rode up and down through the English countryside during the last half of the eighteenth century. His soul was touched by the poverty, the drabness, and the ugliness of the village life. One day he hit upon the scheme of distributing flower seeds to the housewives, and offering prizes for the most beautiful gardens, with the result that today the English countryside has the reputation of being the most colorful in the world. One man, almost single-handedly, changed the complexion of the rural districts of an entire nation.
—GLENN STEWART[240]

Not only can one person change things in the natural, there can also be changes made in the way people think and act. You have the ability to be that person today, just as Nehemiah in the Bible was. When he was confronted by a negative situation, he wept and fasted and prayed, but then he decided to do something about it.

God had put in his heart to do something about the deplorable state of the walls of Jerusalem. They had been torn down and run over by the enemy and the people were not safe. God stirred

up Nehemiah's heart to rebuild the walls and he did, but not without obstacles and hindering forces facing him.

This is the day to not look to the left, nor to the right, but go forward and do something about a negative situation, for you can make a difference!

June 16

"*Then ye shall let your children know*" (Joshua 4:22).

America's greatest resource is her children. A child's mind should be cultivated and taught the ways of God, instead of allowing them to grow wild like weeds.

Coleridge was once talking with a man who told him that he did not believe in giving little children any religious instruction whatsoever. His theory was that the child's mind should not be prejudiced in any direction, but when he came to years of discretion he should be permitted to choose his religious opinions for himself. Coleridge said nothing, but after a while he asked his visitor if he would like to see his garden. The man said he would, and Coleridge took him out into the garden, where only weeds were growing. The man looked at Coleridge in surprise, and said, "Why, this is not a garden! There is nothing but weeds here!"

"Well, you see," answered Coleridge, "I did not wish to infringe upon the liberty of the garden in any way. I was just giving the garden a chance to express itself and to choose its own production."[241]

Isn't it strange that we spend so much time on our gardens, our architecture, among other things, but we allow the children to be taught in a careless manner?

Daniel Webster said once, "*If we work upon marble, it will perish; if on brass, time will efface it; if we rear temples, they will crumble into dust; but if we work upon immortal minds, and imbue them with principles, with the just fear of God and love of our fellow men, we engrave on those tablets something that will brighten to all eternity.*"[242]

It is time to engrave great things on the minds of the children, for children are easily taught, are eager to learn and have great

faith. Even they can make a difference by what they believe.

A mother in New England was helping pack a box to be sent to India. Her son, age four, insisted on putting in an offering all his own, a little leaflet entitled "Come to Jesus." He had his mother write his name on it with the little prayer, "May the one who gets this soon learn to love Jesus." When the child's leaflet reached that far-off land it was finally given to a Hindu priest who was teaching the missionaries the language. He took it without looking at it, but on his way back to his mountain home he thought of the leaflet, took it out, and read the writing on the outside. The child's prayer so touched him that he was then eager to read further. He soon gave up his idols and became a devoted missionary to his own people. Fifteen years after that, American missionaries visited his mountain village and there found the converted Hindu priest with a congregation of fifteen hundred people who had learned to love Jesus as their Savior, through the influence and teaching of that leaflet.

This is the day to teach the children the ways of God instead of allowing society to teach them the ways of man, for God's ways are life, truth and liberty.

June 17

"Therefore I love thy commandments above gold; yea, above fine gold" (Psalm 119:127).

Oftentimes there are within the grasp of many people valuable and important things, but they go unrecognized.

One of the first diamonds found on the South African diamond fields was picked up by the child of a small farmer, as he was playing beside a brook near his father's cottage. Some months afterwards a peddler came to the cottage with a pack on his back. As he was displaying his wares, the peddler spied the stone on a shelf in the room. He took it up and examined it, and then asked the mother what she would take for it. She pointed to the child and said laughing, "It belongs to the child, not to me."

The peddler then offered the boy a box of wooden soldiers, worth a few cents, in exchange for the stone, and the child gladly

accepted the offer. That stone was a very precious jewel. The peddler took it to Cape Town, where he sold it for a large sum to a jeweler. When the jeweler sent it to Europe to be sold, he obtained an even larger amount. Neither the child nor its parents were wise enough to know its value. —JAMES E. DENTON[243]

There is a story about certain Brazilian goatherds, who after listening to the fascinating story of a wandering Indian, organized a party to travel on foot to California to dig gold. Each took with him a small leather bag of glasslike rocks with which to play their favorite gambling game. The journey was long and wearisome. Some died on the way, among them an elderly man who gave his son his bag of pebbles as his only possession. In San Francisco the boy discovered that the glasslike pebbles in the bag were really choice diamonds in the rough, which resulted in the organization of a return party to go to Brazil to hunt diamonds.[244]

You may not have a true diamond in the rough sitting on your shelf or a bag of precious stones within your hands, but even more important than these are people: a child, husband, sister, friend, wife, or a mother and father. The list of valuable things is long.

So many people are disenchanted with life. They are searching for gold in all the wrong places. There is something more valuable than gold or diamonds, and it is the revered Word of the God of the universe. His Word is forever settled in heaven and will bring peace, understanding, revelation, knowledge, happiness, wisdom, strength, and direction.

You do not have to search any longer, for the gold is inside the Bible. It is filled with life, power, and vibrant energy. Delve into it today!

"Train up a child in the way he should go" (Proverbs 22:6).

The greatest thing you can do for your children is to teach them the Bible and live its principles.

John Ruskin said, "All that I have ever taught of art, everything that I have written, whatever greatness there has been in any thought of mine, whatever I have done in my life, has simply been

due to the fact that, when I was a child, my mother daily read with me a part of the Bible, and daily made me learn a part of it by heart."[245]

Missionary John G. Paton used to crouch outside his father's bedroom door to hear him pray. He wrote, "If everything else in religion were by some accident blotted out, my soul would go back to those days of reality. For sixty years my father kept up the practice of family prayer. No day passed without it, no hurry for business, no arrival of friends, no trouble or sorrow, no joy or excitement ever prevented us from kneeling around the family altar." —J. A. CLARK[246]

Today's children are tomorrow's adults. It is time to start putting more of the principles of God into our children; to undo what is happening among the youth, the unwanted pregnancies, the killing of classmates, the drugs, the alcoholism, and the suicide attempts. It is the responsibility of the adults to help train the children in the ways that lead to success.

Proverbs 22:6 says, "Train up a child in the way he should go: and when he is old, he will not depart from it."

Someone once said, "It is easier and better to build boys than to repair men."

This is the day to build, to train, to help the children to become better citizens, to know God and do great things. A child is never too young to start training him.

A visitor found a young mother with her baby in her lap and her Bible in her hand. "Are you reading to your baby?" was the humorous question. "Yes," the young mother replied. "But do you think he understands?" "I am sure he does not understand now, but I want his earliest memories to be that of hearing God's Word," the mother replied.

If you are a parent today, ask yourself the questions, "What sounds are my children hearing? What will be the memories that they will remember?" Will it be what much of the entertainment world offers them: the sounds of gunfire, shootings, sneering blasphemy, dirty language, suggestive jokes or tearing down the family?

Socrates said, "Could I climb to the highest place in Athens, I would lift my voice and proclaim—fellow citizens, why do ye turn and scrape every stone to gather wealth, and take so little care of your children, to whom one day you must relinquish it all?"[247]

This is the day to take time to train the children in the ways of God, for the children are who will be the adults tomorrow. What kind of society do we want to live in?

June 19

"The Lord gave the word: great was the company of those that published it" (Psalm 68:11).

This is the day to circulate good Christian literature. Do not keep it to yourself.

Daniel Webster said, "If religious books are not widely circulated among the masses in this country, I do not know what is going to become of us as a nation. If truth be not diffused, error will be. If the evangelical volume does not reach every community, the pages of a corrupt and licentious literature will. If the power of the Gospel is not felt throughout the length and breadth of the land, anarchy and misrule, degeneration and misery, corruption and darkness, will reign without mitigation or end."[248]

Daniel Webster's words written so long ago were like a prophecy. When there is a dearth of good religious books, then there will be degeneration and corruption, for people are what they read or take into their mind. Good religious books are powerful and influence others for the good.

Over two hundred years ago an old Puritan doctor wrote a book entitled *The Bruised Reed*. A copy of it was sold by a poor peddler to a young man whose name was Richard Baxter, who upon reading it, became converted to Christ. Baxter in turn wrote the monumental book, *A Call to the Unconverted*. This book fell into the hands of another young man, Phillip Doddridge. Phillip Doddridge wrote *The Rise and Progress of Religion*.

The book came into the hands of William Wilburforce, and he was converted. Wilburforce became a burning and shining light, and set in motion a social reform which freed all the slaves in the British Empire. In turn, he wrote a book entitled *A Practical View of Christianity*. This book cheered the faith and fired the zeal of a minister, Leigh Richmond, who in turn wrote a book entitled *The Dairyman's Daughter*. A man in the bleak north of Scotland was greatly influenced by this book, and he became a mighty champion of truth until all Scotland rang with the eloquence of Thomas Chalmers. —*CHRISTIAN VICTORY*[249]

Whether you are a writer or not, does not matter. What matters is that good literature should be passed around, talked

about, and given freely to people of all ages.

Dr. Mason Gross, who was president of Rutgers University and chairman of the National Book Committee, told a library group, one of the important battles of today is the battle between books and television. Television, he said, presents a tremendous emotional impact, but a picture does not present a clear thought. He related Mr. Marshall McLuhan's warning about this subject, "Television is making us descend into something like a global village where there will be no more sharpness or elegance to the life of human beings, but instead a great big blob of emotional reactions."[250] The only alternative says Dr. Gross is the printed word, the reading and thinking about what is written in books. This is the day to let good inspirational books be made available to your friends, neighbors and family.

"Take therefore no thought for the morrow" (Matthew 6:34).

The best way to make your dreams come true is to wake up and do something now. Alexander the Great, when asked how he had conquered the world, replied, "By not delaying."

Sometimes people wait too long, and there is only disaster instead of a dream. On the night of the great Yorkshire flood, which caused such disaster some years ago, a man on the reservoir saw the water rise to a dangerous height. He paced up and down for twenty minutes watching, hesitating, and asking himself the question, "Should I give the alarm?" The fatal moment came; the warning had not been given. The waters rushed over the banks and spread destruction everywhere. Decision twenty minutes before would have saved many lives and thousands of dollars worth of property.

The steamship called *Central America*, on a voyage from New York to San Francisco, sprang a leak in mid-ocean. A vessel, seeing her signal of distress, bore down toward her. Perceiving her danger to be imminent, the captain of the rescue ship spoke to the *Central America*, asking, "What is amiss?" "We are in bad repair,

and going down. Lie by till morning!" "Let me take your passengers on board *now*!" said the would-be rescuer. It was night and the captain of the ailing ship did not like to transfer his passengers then, lest some might be lost in the confusion, and thinking that they would keep afloat some hours longer, replied, "Lie by till morning!" Once again the captain of the rescue ship called, "You had better let me take them now." "Lie by till morning" was sounded back through the night. About an hour and half later, her lights were missed. The *Central America* had gone down, and all on board perished. They were lost, all because a captain misjudged the timing. —Leslie Greening[251]

Now is a moment that can never come back to you. This is the day to not delay doing something that will affect your future, your tomorrows, what you will become. *Now* is an important word. Each moment is the meeting place of two eternities.

Benjamin Franklin said, "Dost thou love life? Then do not squander time. For that's the stuff life is made of."

Jesus said, "Do not worry about tomorrow." Invest in the *now* or *today*, for that is the threshold that ushers in tomorrow.

The advertising firm of J. Walter Thompson of Chicago had an ad that said, "You have twenty-four hours to live." Then at the bottom it said, "Today, that is."

The question that was at the bottom of the ad was this, "So what are you doing with your time? Are you helping another human being toward the dignity you want for yourself? Are you doing anything to overcome hate in this world—with love? Break the hate habit; love your neighbor."

"*Satan hath desired to have you, that he may sift you as wheat*" (Luke 22:31).

*I*t is better to stand for what is right than to give in to the taunts of those around you. "Johnny Urso of Halifax, Nova Scotia, was only nine years old, but his playmates dared him to touch a 23,000-volt transmission wire near his home. Young as he was, he knew it was risky and even dangerous. He refused. Again and

again they dared him, calling him coward and chicken. He stood the taunts as long as he could, and then rashly decided to take the dare. As he climbed up the steel pole he was cheered by his companions until he actually began to think that he was really brave. When he got to the top, he looked down at his gang and then quickly touched the powerful wire. The shock threw him several feet higher than the pole and he landed on the network of wires. The rescuers worked an hour before they managed to remove him. Johnny died the next day from third-degree burns."[252]

One of the more heroic stories ever told about standing for right was in the days of the Roman Emperor Nero. There lived and served him a band of soldiers known as the "Emperor's Wrestlers." Fine, stalwart men, picked from the best and the bravest of the land. In the great amphitheater they stood before each contest, before the emperor's throne and sang, "We the wrestlers, wrestling for thee, O Emperor, to win for thee the victory and from thee, the victor's crown." When the great Roman army was sent to fight in faraway Gaul, no soldiers were braver or more loyal than this band of wrestlers led by their centurion Vespasian. But news reached Nero that many Roman soldiers had accepted the Christian faith. Therefore the decree was dispatched to the centurion Vespasian: "If there be any among your soldiers who cling to the faith of the Christian, they must die!" The decree was received in the dead of winter. The soldiers were camped on the shore of a frozen lake. It was with sinking heart that Vespasian read the emperor's message. He called the solders together and asked the question, "Is there any among you who cling to the faith of the Christian? If so, let him step forward." Forty wrestlers instantly stepped forward two paces, respectfully saluted and stood at attention. Vespasian pleaded with them long and earnestly without prevailing upon a single man to deny his Lord. Finally he said, "The decree of the emperor must be obeyed, but I am not willing that your comrades should shed your blood. I am going to order that you march out upon the lake of ice and I shall leave you there to the mercy of the elements." The forty wrestlers were stripped and then, falling into columns of four, marched toward the center of the lake. As they marched, they broke into the chant of the arena, "Forty wrestlers, wrestling for Thee, O Christ, to win for Thee the victory and from Thee, the victor's crown!" Through the long hours of the night Vespasian stood by his campfire and watched. As he waited through the long night, there came to him fainter and fainter the wrestler's song. As morning drew near, one figure, overcome by exposure, crept quietly toward the fire; he had renounced his Lord. Faintly but clearly from the darkness came the song: "Thirty-nine wrestlers, wrestling for Thee, O Christ, to win for Thee the victory and from Thee, the victor's crown!" Vespasian looked at the figure drawing close to the fire, then took off his helmet and clothing and sprang upon the ice, crying, "Forty wrestlers, wrestling for Thee, O Christ, to win for Thee, the victory and from Thee, the victor's crown."

June 22

"Ye are the salt of the earth" (Matthew 5:13).

A Christian is called salt. What is Christianity? Someone wrote: "In the home it is kindness. In business it is honesty. In society it is courtesy. In work it is fairness. Toward the unfortunate it is pity. Toward the weak it is help. Toward the wicked it is resistance. Toward the strong it is trust. Toward the fortunate it is congratulations. Toward the penitent it is forgiveness. Toward God it is reverence and love."[253]

Hudson Taylor said, "If your father and mother, your sister and brother, if the very cat and dog in the house, are not happier for your being a Christian, it is a question whether you really are."[254] The following poem says it like this:

> *Not, how did he die?*
> *But, how did he live?*
> *Not, what did he gain?*
> *But, what did he give?*
>
> *These are the merits*
> *To measure the worth*
> *Of a man as man*
> *Regardless of birth.*
>
> *Not, what was his station?*
> *But, had he a heart?*

*And how did he play
His God-given part?*

*Was he ever ready
With word of good cheer
To bring a smile
To banish a tear?*

*Not, what did the sketch
In the Newspaper say,
But, how many were sorry
When he passed away?*
—Author Unknown[255]

At a meeting some young people were discussing the text found in Matthew, "Ye are the salt of the earth." One suggestion after another was made as to the meaning of "salt" in this verse. "Salt imparts a desirable flavor," said one. "Salt preserves from decay," another suggested. Then a Chinese Christian girl spoke out of an experience none of the others had. "Salt creates thirst," she said, and there was a sudden hush in the room. Everyone was thinking. Have I ever made anyone thirsty for the Lord Jesus Christ?[256]

June 23

"For mine eyes have seen the King" (Isaiah 6:5).

How is your spiritual eyesight today? How do God and His promises look to you? Have you felt a tinge of doubt lately? Have you felt a little let down towards Him, maybe silently being a slight bit critical for the way He did His business or handled a situation? Maybe you have dust on your spiritual glasses.

Katy's mother one morning went to check Katy's room and asked, "Katy, did you forget to open the windows when you swept? This room is very dusty."

"I think there is dust on your eyeglasses, ma'am," she said modestly. Sure enough, the eyeglasses were at fault and not Katy. The mother rubbed them off, and everything looked bright and clean, the carpet like new.

That evening Katy went to her mother and said that the cook had done so and so, and she had said so and so. And when she finished, the mother smiled at Katy and said, "There is dust on your glasses, honey. Rub them off; you will see better."

Let us be careful not to criticize God in our spirits or even criticize another. Let us wipe the dust off our spiritual glasses and see things differently.

This happened to Isaiah. He did not see the Lord in His majesty until a tragedy happened in his life. Then when he went into the Temple, he said, "In the year that king Uzziah died I saw also the Lord sitting upon a throne, high and lifted up, and his train filled the temple. Above it stood the seraphims. . . . And one cried unto another, and said, Holy, holy, holy, is the Lord of hosts: the whole earth is full of his glory. . . . Then said I, Woe is me! for I am undone; because I am a man of unclean lips, and I dwell in the midst of a people of unclean lips: for mine eyes have seen the King, the Lord of hosts" (Isaiah 6:1-3, 5).

Our hearts affect our vision. What is seen and how we see it are determined by what our inner eye sees. Let us see the glory of the Lord in our everyday life. In our homes or driving down the road, let us be aware of the beauty of His holiness. Let His glory fill our hearts and cause us to lift Him up to His rightful position.

Let God be God and glorify Him as such, never being critical of Him or feeling let down by Him. He is your best friend. He loves you more than anybody in the world does. He would never do you wrong. He wants only good for you. Trust Him today and wipe away the distractions and the things that would cause Him to be blurred in your vision. He is still God whether we see Him as such; so we might as well see Him in all His glory!

"Which worketh in me mightily" (Colossians 1:29).

God's power is sufficient, but how many use it? There was once a Welsh woman who lived in a valley far away from any town or city. She was a simple-minded, hard-working person who knew

little about progress. At a great sacrifice to herself, she had electricity installed in her little cottage. "You use the electric lights so little, I wonder if it was worth what it cost you to have them put in," said a neighbor. "Oh, yes," answered the woman, "I switch them on every night to see to light my lamps. Then I switch them off!" Walter B. Knight comments about this story: "Think of it! With great power at her command with the flip of a switch, she continued the weary task of trimming wicks, pouring oil and lighting smelly lamps! Christ's strength is ours for the asking. Yet there are many who continue to serve the Lord in weariness and weakness, sometimes up, but most times down." —TOLD BY WALTER B. KNIGHT[257]

God's power is sufficient, so why not use it today and let it flow through you? Flick on the switch of prayer and begin to pray to God and let Him fill you full and running over with His Spirit, which gives life and power.

A minister was being shown through a large plant where locomotives were built. Pointing at one completed locomotive, the guide said, "This locomotive is the last word in engine building!" The minister exclaimed with admiration, "What a mighty thing!" "Yes," said the guide, "there are three things attending it. It must have power generated by internal combustion of crude oil. It must be on the rails, for its power would bring destruction if it is derailed. It must have a good engineer, for it will run efficiently only when rightly handled." The minister replied, "That's just like a Christian. We are powerful and useful only when we are filled with the fullness of God, walking in His way, and utterly under the Holy Spirit's control!" —TOLD BY WALTER B. KNIGHT[258]

It is time to use the power that is available from God. Paul described it in Colossians 1:29: "Whereunto I also labour, striving according to his working, which worketh in me mightily."

His power is not so that you can barely make it, but to work in you mightily. The might comes through God's Spirit, as told in Ephesians 3:16: "That he would grant you, according to the riches of his glory, to be strengthened with might by his Spirit in the inner man."

It is not by our might, nor by power, but "by my spirit, saith the LORD of hosts" (Zechariah 4:6). This is the day to arise in new faith and let God's power work mightily in you!

June 25

"For when I am weak, then am I strong" (II Corinthians 12:10).

When you are weak, it is important to stay connected to the power!

Years ago, "The Sunday Circle" carried the following story: A delicate little lady, who had obviously seen better days, continued to go to work as a seamstress, although past the traditional three-score and ten years. The daughter of one of the families with which she was employed, marveling at her quiet endurance, asked her one day how she managed to work so hard and so steadily. "Well, my dear," replied the patient voice, "sometimes it seems hard. Often I get up in the morning feeling so weak and faint that it seems impossible to go through the day's work. But, you see, I'm like a tram car before it is connected with the power wire. The first thing I do is to *connect with the Power*. When I have said my prayers, I feel my hand in God's and the power of His Spirit passing into me, and then I can go on and do what I have to do."[259]

Paul described this strength in II Corinthians 12:9-10: "And he said unto me, My grace is sufficient for thee: for my strength is made perfect in weakness. . . . for when I am weak, then am I strong."

The question is asked, Paul, how can you be strong when you are weak? He explained it in Galatians 2:20: "Nevertheless I live; yet not I, but Christ liveth in me: and the life which I now live in the flesh I live by the faith of the Son of God, who loved me, and gave himself for me."

This strength is proven in the story of Dr. F. B. Meyer, who was then an elderly man. He was known as a powerful preacher and was on his last visit to America. A large audience had assembled in a New York City church to hear him speak. Weak and wobbly, Dr. Meyer was helped to the platform by two men, one on either side. Sitting in an elevated chair and with great physical exertion, he began his message. The audience thought, "Will he be able to go through the service?" As he spoke, a miracle of God's enabling power was enacted before their wondering eyes. Dr. Meyer stood to his feet. The heyday and vigor of his earlier years returned, and for over one hour words of graciousness and wisdom flowed from his lips. All left that memorable meeting knowing in their hearts that they had the answer to the ancient question, "Where is the Lord God of Elijah?" and rejoicing in the sure promise of God found in Isaiah 40:29: "He giveth power to the faint; and to them that have no might he increaseth strength."²⁶⁰

You may be weak in yourself today, but if you are connected to the source of power, then you are made strong. This is the day to not only plug in to power but to make it a priority to stay connected.

June 26

"Though I speak with the tongues of men and of angels, and have not charity, I am become as sounding brass, or a tinkling cymbal" (I Corinthians 13:1).

Love makes the difference in everything. Edward E. Plowman shared how love makes a difference in things. Fast work by four hundred Westmont College students saved virtually all valuable records, books, and furniture during a morning fire that gutted the school's administration building. Santa Barbara, California, officials say faulty wiring ignited the fire. Although ceilings collapsed during rescue operations, there were no injuries. Firemen, praising the heroism of students, bitterly contrasted the scene two weeks earlier when riotous arsonists from University of California burned a bank building and drove firemen away. "You kids deserve free tuition for this," the fire chief declared to a drenched, weeping Westmont coed. "No, sir," she replied, "we just love Westmont." Then she returned to study for quarterly finals. —EDWARD E. PLOWMAN²⁶¹

Love made the difference between the two incidents which occurred at the University of California and at Westmont College.

Love is the most powerful force on the face of the earth. Paul described it as being the greatest thing, in I Corinthians 13:13: "And now abideth faith, hope, charity, these three; but the greatest of these is charity [or love]."

Love is kind. It does things to enrich others. There is a beautiful Hebrew legend of two brothers who lived side by side on adjoining lands. One was the head of a large family; the other lived

alone. One night, the former lay awake and thought: "My brother lives alone, he has not the companionship of wife and children to cheer his heart as I have. While he sleeps, I will carry some of my sheaves into his field."

At the same hour, the other brother reasoned: "My brother has a large family, and his necessities are greater than mine. As he sleeps, I will put some of my sheaves on his side of the field." Thus the two brothers went out, each carrying out his purpose and each laden with sheaves. There they met at the dividing line and there they embraced.

Legend says that years later, at this very place stood the Jerusalem Temple, and on the very spot of their meeting stood the Temple's altar.[262]

Love makes the difference in all things. Rabbi Julius Gordon once said, "Love is not blind, it sees more, not less. But because it sees more, it is willing to see less."[263]

What does your thermometer of love read today? Is the ingredient of love the highest emotion in your heart? Does it control your thoughts, actions and motives? Is love, the greatest thing of all, considered to be great by you? Where is love in your life? This is the day to cast your care upon the Lord, give Him your hang-ups, your hates and your selfishness and ask Him to consume you with His love.

May we pray, "Pour it on, Lord, today and pour it in; saturate Your children with the greatest thing of all and let love make a difference in this generation!"

"One chase a thousand, and two put ten thousand to flight" (Deuteronomy 32:30).

One person working alone can make a difference in some things, but how much more wonderful it is, when everyone works together doing their part in helping to make a big difference.

There was once a prince of India who dreamed that he owned a garden more lovely than all the gardens of the world. What made it particularly attractive was a beautiful lake, which was different

from all others in that its water was pure perfume whose fragrance could be caught from every spot in the garden. Upon awaking he decided to make his dream come true. He did not have enough money to fill a lake with perfume. After considerable thought he came upon the idea of inviting every person in the surrounding country to a great party. Each person was to bring a small glass of perfume and empty it into the lake. On the appointed day the roads to the prince's lake were filled with people of all ages, sizes and classes. In the hand of each was a vial of perfume, which each person emptied into the lake. To the surprise of everyone, however, no lovely fragrance came from the lake. The prince did some investigating. He took a sample of the water near the spot where everyone was emptying his perfume. It was just ordinary water. Everyone thought that his little vial of water instead of perfume would make little difference.[264]

Because of this concept, nothing changed, and everything remained the same. The dream for a fragrant lake failed. No one thought his little bit was important, but everyone's little bit would have made a whole lot of difference. If only one person would have done his part, it would not have pervaded the atmosphere of the lake, but if everyone would have cooperated and done what they could, there definitely would have been a difference in the lake.

It is like a penny. One penny is not much, but many pennies can make millions. The heading of a newspaper once read, "Pennies Block Traffic." The article told how in Jessup, Maryland, a truck carrying 4.3 million pennies turned over on an entrance ramp to a highway, dumping copper-filled canvas sacks all over the highway. Traffic was tied up for several hours while police and road crews cleared the road. One penny alone, of course, would not have held up anything, but when 4.3 million pennies were brought together, they stopped traffic.[265]

The power of unified effort is alluded to in the song of Moses. Deuteronomy 32:30 states: "How should one chase a thousand, and two put ten thousand to flight, except their Rock had sold them, and the LORD had shut them up?" One could chase a thousand, but two could put ten thousand to flight.

This is the day to band together, everyone doing their part, and make a big difference in the things that count for eternity.

June 28

"The thief cometh not, but for to steal, and to kill, and to destroy" (John 10:10).

Satan comes to kill your friendships and your relationships, but Jesus comes to heal them.

There were once four bulls which were good friends. They went everywhere together, fed together, and lay down to rest together, always keeping so close to each other that if any danger were near they could all face it at once. Now there was a lion which had determined to have them, but he could never get at them singly. He was a match for any one alone, but not for all four at once. However, he used to watch for his opportunity, and, when one lagged the least bit behind the others as they grazed, he would slink up and whisper that the other bulls had been saying unkind things about him. This he did so often that at last the four friends became uneasy. Each thought the other three were plotting against him. Finally, as there was no trust among them, they went off by themselves, their friendship broken. This was what the lion wanted. One by one he killed them, and made four good meals.[266]

This is the exact tactic used by the enemy of your soul. Jesus described him in John 10:10: "The thief cometh not, but for to steal, and to kill, and to destroy: I am come that they might have life, and that they might have it more abundantly."

I Peter 5:8 says, "Be sober, be vigilant; because your adversary the devil, as a roaring lion, walketh about, seeking whom he may devour."

The lion will stalk you and watch you. Anything you are happy with, he will try to kill. He comes to separate friends, separate husbands and wives, parents and children and even church members from one another. His business is death. He desires to bring death to your marriage, your home, your friendships and your church. Even though he desires it, he cannot do it, unless it is allowed. I Peter 5:9 says that we have power to resist this bearer of bad news. After describing the lion that seeks to devour, he said, "Whom resist stedfast in the faith." James 4:7 also gives instructions to resist. It says, "Submit yourselves therefore to God. Resist the devil, and he will flee from you." There first must be a

submitting of ways and will to God and His Word, then the power is there to resist the devil and he must, he has to flee. Flee means to run for your life, and that is running fast. The lion that stalks your soul and tries to devour your marriage and friendships has to run away from you at top speed. You have that power, when you are submitted to God.

Dr. Wilbur Chapman once said, "The greatness of a man's power is the measure of his surrender."

When you surrender yourself to God, you then have power to defy the forces of evil that would try to destroy your friendships and relationships with others. Listen not to the whispers of the enemy today, but listen to the voice of God, which always builds and restores.

June 29

"Pray without ceasing" (I Thessalonians 5:17).

*I*t is time to pray like we've never prayed before. Contained in the *Bible Friend* were these words: "An hour in prayer can give the believer enough power from God to overcome the second most powerful force in the universe."

Chrysotom once wrote that "The *potency of prayer* hath subdued the strength of fire; it hath bridled the rage of lions, hushed anarchy to rest, extinguished wars, appeased the elements, expelled demons, burst the chains of death, expanded the gates of heaven, quenched diseases, repelled frauds, rescued cities from destruction, stayed the sun in its course, and arrested the progress of the thunderbolt. Prayer is an all-sufficient armor, a treasure undiminished, a mine which is never exhausted, a sky unobscured by clouds, a heaven unruffled by the storm. It is the root, the fountain, the mother, of a thousand blessings . . . Prayer is the foundation of the spiritual building, that which the soul is to the body. The man or woman without prayer is as the fish out of water and gasping for life."

If your family is in trouble, pray, pray, pray. If your life is threatened by disease, pray, pray, pray. If you are facing crisis, it is time to pray.

Bishop Coxe tells of visiting an old feudal castle in England, so

old that one of its towers dated back to the days of King John. When the bishop went down to breakfast, he found the young owner of the castle, his family and servants, assembled for morning prayer conducted by the head of the family. As the bishop lifted his eyes, he noticed high overhead a massive beam that spanned the grand, old hall, and bore in old English the following inscription: *That house shall be preserved and never shall decay. Where the Almighty God is worshipped day by day. AD 1558.*[267] What powerful words preserved since the 1500s.

The following poem says it well:

Happy the home when God is there.
And love fills every breast;
When one their wish, one their prayer,
And one their heavenly rest.

Happy the home where Jesus' name
Is sweet to every ear;
Where children early lisp
His name and parents hold Him dear.

Happy the home where prayer is heard
And praise is wont to rise:
Where parents love the sacred Word,
And live but for the skies.
—AUTHOR UNKNOWN

This is the day to pray as a family. Pray together and love will begin to flow through your home, for when God is included in your plans and activities, great things always begin to happen, because He is great!

June 30

"But whosoever will lose his life for my sake, the same shall save it" (Luke 9:24).

The things we lose or give away are those that we actually keep. Jesus said in Luke 9:23-24, "If any man will come after me,

let him deny himself, and take up his cross daily, and follow me. For whosoever will save his life shall lose it: but whosoever will lose his life for my sake, the same shall save it." Love must be shared, kindnesses must be shown, as the following poem depicts:

> *Love that is hoarded, moulds at last*
> *Until we know some day*
> *The only thing we ever have*
> *Is what we give away.*
> *And kindness that is never used*
> *But hidden all alone*
> *Will slowly harden till it is*
> *As hard as any stone.*
>
> *It is the things we always hold*
> *That we will lose some day;*
> *The only things we ever keep*
> *Are what we give away.*
> —Harold C. Sandall[268]

R. G. LeTourneau, the Christian earthmoving machinery manufacturer who died in 1969, failed often in the earlier years of his career. Ironically, though, he made $35,000 profit one year in the middle of the Depression. Puffed up with pride, he withheld the payment of his $5,000 annual pledge to the Christian and Missionary Alliance in order to reinvest it in the business and give the Lord an even greater share the following year when he anticipated a net profit of $100,000. Within a year, his anticipated $100,000 profit was turned into a $100,000 loss and brought LeTourneau to his knees. Thoroughly chastened and repentant, he pledged not only $5,000 to his church for the year he skipped, but also the same amount for the following year—in the face of a $100,000 debt and no money for payroll. On top of that, his bookkeeper was ready to quit.

From that point on, LeTourneau's fortune changed and within four years, he and his wife founded the LeTourneau Foundation comprised of ninety percent of the stocks of LeTourneau Corp., the earnings of which financed evangelical Christian work worldwide. LeTourneau often said, "It is not how much money I give to God, but how much of God's money I keep for myself."[269] In other words, he was saying that the only thing he really had was what he gave away.

This is the day to release love to others, give of your time, give of your skills; for the things you give to God and others are that which is stored in the bank of heaven. If you want to experience true joy, it is learning to lose yourself in the cause of Christ and giving of all you have to help others and help bring someone to the knowledge of Jesus Christ. When you lay your life on the line for Him and release all you have into His hands, He gives you a glow inside that money cannot place there. This is the day to give, for that is really what you keep forever!

July 1

"Happy shalt thou be" (Psalm 128:2).

"A smile is a light in the window of the face, which signifies the heart is home." Henry Ward Beecher once wrote, "Nothing on earth can smile but man! Gems may flash reflected light, but what is a diamond-flash compared to an eye-flash and a mirth-flash? Flowers cannot smile; this is a charm that even they cannot claim. It is the prerogative of man; it is the color which love wears, and cheerfulness, and joy—these three. It is a light in the windows of the face, by which the heart signifies it is at home and waiting. A face that cannot smile is like a bud that cannot blossom, and dries up on the stalk. Laughter is day, and sobriety is night, and a smile is the twilight that hovers gently between both—more bewitching than either."[270]

"A smile costs nothing, but creates much. It enriches those who receive it without impoverishing those who give it. It happens in a flash, and the memory of it sometimes lasts forever. None are so rich that they can get along without it. And none so poor but are richer for its benefits. It fosters good will in a business. It creates happiness in the home. And is the countersign of friends. It is rest to the weary. Daylight to the discouraged. Sunshine to the sad. And nature's best antidote for trouble." —HENRY H. EVANSEN[271]

A little sympathy will cheer a weary way.
A little kindness lights up a dreary day.

*A very simple, friendly word
will give hope and strength impart,
Or just an understanding smile
revive some fainting heart.
And like a sudden sunlit ray,
Lighting a darkened room,
A sunny spirit may beguile
The deepest depths of gloom.*
—Author Unknown

Walter Baxendale once told about the time he was riding from Franklin, Indiana, on a cold night. He was chilled and so cold he feared that he would freeze. After a while he came across a blacksmith's shop and saw a bright light shining on the forge. Logs were burning and smoldering there and sending up their red flame. He was so cold that he cried. He wanted to get off his horse and warm himself, so he did. After sitting in front of the fire and watching the blacksmith, Walter thought, *It is great comfort just to look at a man who is good-natured,* so he said to the blacksmith, "Well, I feel better just for looking at you," and then he rode on.

There are many people like Walter today riding through life almost frozen to death. They need a warm smile, a good-natured face looking their way. There is a need for smiles and cheers in a dismal world of malice, hate and violence. Won't you be the one who becomes like the blacksmith and build a fire of love that will help warm the world?

"The righteous shall flourish like the palm tree" (Psalm 92:12).

It is much better to be flexible than rigid when life's storms are blown your way. The righteous are likened to the palm tree. They are known for their ability to bend with the wind.

A fable once told how a reed and an olive tree were disputing about their strength and their powers of quiet endurance. When the reed was reproached by the olive for being weak and easily bent by every wind, it answered not a word. Soon afterwards a strong wind began to blow. The reed, by letting itself be tossed about and bent by the gusts, weathered the storm without difficulty; but the olive, which resisted it, was broken by its violence. —AESOP FABLE[272]

A group once visited a stonecutter in a granite shed and learned a lesson from a wise workman. The great block of polished granite was painted over with a thin coating of some rubber combination. The design for the engraving was penciled on the rubber and the workman was cutting away the rubber, leaving the stone exposed. As they watched the worker their curiosity got the better of them and they began to ask questions, for this day he was using compressed air and sand. With the rubber cut away and the granite exposed, the sand was blown on the granite until the design was perfectly etched in the stone. But the rubber was untouched.

It was then that the group learned their lesson. The workman told them that the sand could be blown upon the rubber for an hour without effect, but that when blown upon the stone it would cut a hole through the hardest granite. His explanation was easy— the stone resists stubbornly and is worn away, but the rubber is resilient and receives the shock without damage. The worker said, "That's a good deal like life. The man who is always resisting is the man who is worn out first. The one who is always looking for trouble is always finding it. The stubborn man is always getting harder knocks than the one who accepts his troubles with resiliency of temper. The hot-headed man has a harder time of it than the flexible man." —NORTHWESTERN CHRISTIAN ADVOCATE[273]

The truth told that day by the stonecutter is still true today. Some people refuse to be flexible, to roll with the punches, to flow with it, but instead they clutch tightly, are rigid and stubbornly hold on instead of letting go.

It is like the story told of the monkeys in North Africa. The natives have a very easy way to capture them. A gourd, with a hole just sufficiently large so that a monkey can thrust his hand into it, is filled with nuts and fastened firmly to a branch of a tree at sunset. During the night a monkey will discover the scent of food and its source, and will put his hand into the gourd and grasp a handful of nuts. But the hole is too small for the monkey to withdraw his clenched fist, and he has not sense enough to let go of his bounty so that he may escape. Thus he pulls and pulls without success, and when morning comes he is quickly and easily taken.

It is important today to have the sense to know when to hold

on and when to let go. The important thing is when the wind of adversity blows, to not break under it, but to be flexible, relax, and lean on Jesus. Let it be a learning experience instead of a destroying experience.

July 3

"*O taste and see that the LORD is good*" (Psalm 34:8).

Where Jesus is there is no darkness. His light always penetrates the gloom. Jesus said, "I am the light of the world." Where He is, is Light—great light!

There is an allegory written for children about a cave that lived under the ground, as caves have the habit of doing. It had spent its lifetime in darkness. It heard a voice calling to it, "Come up into the light; come and see the sunshine." The cave retorted, "I don't know what you mean; there isn't anything but darkness." Finally the cave ventured forth and was surprised to see light everywhere. Looking up to the sun, the cave said, "Come with me and see the darkness." The sun asked, "What is darkness?" The cave replied, "Come and see." One day the sun accepted the invitation. As it entered the cave it said, "Now show me your darkness!" But there was no darkness. —*THE SUNDAY SCHOOL TIMES*[274]

This is the way it is with Jesus. Where He is, there is no darkness.

I received the following story in an email: The University of Chicago Divinity School once invited Dr. Paul Tillich to speak to the student body. It was to be an informal lecture outside in a grassy picnic area, with everyone bringing a sack lunch. Dr. Tillich spoke for two hours proving that the resurrection of Jesus was false. He quoted scholar after scholar and book after book. He concluded that since there was no such thing as the historical resurrection, the religious tradition of the church was groundless, emotional mumbo-jumbo, because it was based on a relationship with a risen Jesus, who in fact, never rose from the dead in any literal sense. He then asked if there were any questions. After about thirty seconds, an old preacher with a head of short-cropped, wooly white hair stood up in the back. "Dr. Tillich, I got one ques-

tion," he said as all eyes turned toward him. He reached into his sack lunch and pulled out an apple and began eating it. "Docta Tillich," he said, as he crunched and munched on the apple, "my question is a simple question. Now, I ain't never read them books you read, and I can't recite scriptures in the original Greek. I don't know anything about Niebuhr and Heidegger." He finished the apple and continued talking, "All I wanna know is: This apple I just ate, was it bitter or sweet?"

Dr. Tillich paused for a moment and answered in exemplary scholarly fashion: "I cannot possibly answer that question, for I haven't tasted your apple." The white-haired preacher dropped the core of his apple into his crumpled paper bag, looked up at Dr. Tillich and said calmly, "Neither have you tasted my Jesus." The one thousand in attendance could not contain themselves. They erupted with applause and cheers. Dr. Tillich thanked his audience and promptly left the platform.

The light was greater than the darkness. Psalm 34:8 says, "O taste and see that the LORD is good: blessed is the man that trusteth in him." Trust in the Light today and He will dispel your darkness.

July 4

"A little one shall become a thousand" (Isaiah 60:22).

Little things are very important! A great army, many years ago, invaded Scotland. They crept stealthily over the border and prepared to make a night attack on the Scottish forces. There lay the camp, all silent in the starlight, never dreaming that danger was so near. The Danes, to make their advance more noiseless, came forward barefooted. But as they neared the sleeping Scots, one unlucky Dane brought his foot down squarely on a bristling thistle. A roar of pain was the consequence, which rang like a trumpet through the sleeping camp. In a moment each soldier had grasped his weapon, and the Danes were chased away. The thistle was from that time adopted as the national emblem of Scotland.
—WALTER BAXENDALE[275]

It was just a little thistle, but it saved Scotland from disaster. Someone once wrote: *"Think naught a trifle, though it small*

appear; sands make the mountain, moments make the year, and trifles—life."[276]

The following poem says it well:

ONLY A LITTLE THING
It was only a tiny seed,
Carelessly brushed aside;
But it grew in time to a noxious weed,
And spread its poison wide.

It was only a little leak,
So small you might hardly see;
But the rising waters found the break,
And wrecked the great levee.

It was only a single spark,
Dropped by a passing train;
But the dead leaves caught, and swift and dark
Was its work on wood and plain.

It was only a thoughtless word,
Scarce meant to be unkind;
But it pierced as a dart to the heart that heard,
And left its sting behind.

It may seem a trifle at most,
The thing that we do or say;
And yet it may be that at fearful cost
We may wish it undone someday.
—M. P. Handy[277]

A tiny seed, a little leak, a single spark, a thoughtless word—all good things and all bad things are started with little things. A thought can erupt either into a murder or a kind deed. They both start with a tiny thought. Little things are important

This is the day to give attention to the little things, for wars are won because of little things, lives are saved because of little details, and love is prolonged because of little gestures of kindness.

God cares about a little sparrow. He cares about each hair on your head. He knows each star by name. Little things are important to Him, so should they be to us.

July 5

"All my springs are in thee" (Psalm 87:7).

If you're parched today, there is a well waiting to spring up inside of you! Jesus said in John 4:14: "But whosoever drinketh of the water that I shall give him shall never thirst; but the water that I shall give him shall be in him a well of water springing up into everlasting life."

Jesus promised water inside you, just like a well springing forth. You cannot stop a spring of water. This is proven in the story that as they dug for the dry dock in the navy yard in Brooklyn, they struck a central spring. The engineer said that it had better have some cement put on it to stop it up. They opened a hole and put in some cement; but the next morning the cement was gone, and the spring was boiling again. Then the engineer said there had better be some solid masonry to shut down the spring. So they determined to drive piles down, and fix it. They did drive piles, and fixed it; but the spring bubbled up again, just as if it did not care anything about engineers or engineering. After they had spent some months in trying to stop the spring, they built a curb around it and let it run. —HENRY WARD BEECHER[278]

Nothing could stop the spring of water. That is the same thing that happens when Jesus takes control of your life. He gives you a spring of water and no outside forces can stop the spring; only you can allow it to stop. Bad attitudes can stop it, disobedience, or a lack of faith, so many things can cause the spring to dwindle. This is the day to not let it stop but to let it spring forth. That spring becomes a river.

Jesus said in John 7:38, "He that believeth on me, as the scripture hath said, out of his belly shall flow rivers of living water." This is the day to drink of the Lord's water. It contains blessing, healing, power and forgiveness.

It is said that at St. Margaret's Bay, in the southeast of England, there is a well that is always covered by the sea at high tide. Strangely enough, however, its water remains fresh and pure, uncontaminated by the briny waters of the sea. Fed from the hills above, it has a constant supply of fresh water pouring into it, which effectively prevents the ocean from flowing in.[279]

That is the way it is with God's children. When oceans of problems come crashing into your life, the spiritual water can stay fresh and unpolluted, because the water is fed from above. If you feel parched inside, weary of life and cannot seem to get the victory, why not accept the drink Jesus talked about in John 4 and let Him fill you with an artesian spring of water. This is the day to drink of the water of life and blessing.

July 6

"But the woman . . . came and fell down before him, and told him all the truth" (Mark 5:33).

Matthew 14:12 simply states, "And his disciples came, and took up the body, and buried it, and went and told Jesus." This story concerns the execution of John the Baptist by order of Herod the king. The disciples reacted by going and telling Jesus. When tragedy struck, they told Jesus all about it. Some people may feel that such a reaction is too simple, but that is the beauty of it. We must tell Jesus because He understands the entire circumstance, because He sympathizes, and because He strengthens.

One of the parables that Chinese teachers use is the story of a woman who lost an only son. She was grief-stricken out of all reason. She made her sorrow a wailing wall. Finally she went to a wise old philosopher. He said to her, "I will give you back your son if you will bring me some mustard seed. However, the seed must come from a home where there has never been any sorrow." Eagerly she started her search and went from house to house. In every case she learned that a loved one had been lost. "How selfish I have been in my grief," she said. "Sorrow is common to all."
—*How to Face Life*[280]

Everyone will have sorrow in life. The secret to finding help and consolation is to do as the disciples did when John was executed. They went and told Jesus.

If a person lives long enough, he will realize that life contains sorrow and pain as well as the good times. Hurts will come to all. Ella Wheeler Wilcox once wrote, *"There are times in one's life when all the world seems to turn against us. Our motives are*

misunderstood, our words misconstrued, an unkind word reveals to us the unfriendly feelings of others. The fact is, that it is rare when injustice, or slights, patiently borne, do not leave the heart at the close of the day filled with a marvelous sense of peace—perhaps not at once—but after you've had a chance to reflect a bit. It is the seed God has sown, springing up and bearing fruit. We learn, as the years roll onward and we leave the past behind, that much we had counted sorrow, but proved that God is kind; that many a flower we'd longed for had hidden a thorn of pain, and many a rugged by-path led to fields of ripened grain. The clouds that cover the sunshine; they cannot banish the sun. And the earth shines out the brighter when the weary rain is done."[281]

So when there is sorrow, the hurt is strong and the pain seems not to go away, remember the old song, "I must tell Jesus." Go to Him and realize that the sun will shine once more, and that God is with you no matter where you stand; whether in the shadows, under the cloud, or in the pelting rain. He is there and wants to help you—talk to Him today.

July 7

"Then shall there enlargement and deliverance arise to the Jews from another place" (Esther 4:14).

Mordecai knew that deliverance would come. He believed it and it came to pass, for he said to Esther, "Deliverance shall come." Anyone can be successful if he is willing to believe and persevere.

It is important to have the attitude described in Philippians 4:13, "I can do all things through Christ." If you say, "It can't be done," you never will attempt to do much.

This is the day to believe and say, "It can be done through Christ." All things are possible to those who believe, but belief alone is not enough. It is the perseverance, the continuous efforts, not giving up until it is done as the following poem depicts:

> *Genius, that power which dazzles mortal eyes,*
> *Is oft but perseverance in disguise.*

Continuous effort of itself implies,
In spite of countless falls, the power to rise.
'Twixt failure and success the print's so fine,
Men sometimes know not when they touch the line;
Just when the pearl is waiting one more plunge,
How many a struggler has thrown up the sponge!
As the tide goes clear out it comes clear in;
In business 'tis at turns, the wisest win;
And, oh, how true when shades of doubt dismay,
'Tis often darkest just before the day.
A little more persistence, courage, vim,
Success will dawn o'er failure's cloudy rim.
Then take this honey for the bitterest cup;
There is no failure, save in giving up.
No real fall, so long as one still tries.
For seeming set-backs make the strong man wise,
There's no defeat, in truth, save from within;
Unless you're beaten there, you're bound to win.
—C. C. Cameron[282]

This is not the time to give up. It is the time to believe and persevere. With God on your side you are sure to win.

July 8

"Ah Lord God! . . . there is nothing too hard for thee" (Jeremiah 32:17).

Faith believes, even when there is nothing left to believe in. Ella Wheeler Wilcox wrote those wonderful words of faith:

I will not doubt, though all my ships at sea
Come drifting home with broken masts and sails;
I shall believe the Hand which never fails,
From seeming evil worketh good to me;
And, though I weep because those sails are battered,
Still will I cry, while my best hopes lie shattered,
"I trust in Thee."

> *I will not doubt, though sorrows fall like rain,*
> *And troubles swarm like bees about a hive;*
> *I shall believe the heights for which I strive,*
> *Are only reached by anguish and by pain;*
> *And, though I groan and tremble with my crosses,*
> *I yet shall see, through my severest losses,*
> *The greater gain.*[283]

What a powerful assessment of life! No matter what happens, "I trust in Thee." To trust and believe even when it looks like disaster is the height of faith.

Jesus often said, "If thou canst believe, all things are possible to him that believeth." Why should mankind find it hard to believe in the power of God? Why would they think that it is hard for Him to do things for His children, when He holds all power in heaven and in earth? It is a light thing for Him to do what seems hard to us. Nothing is too hard for Him according to Jeremiah 32:17. The following story proves this:

It was in North Carolina, in 1874 that a congregation wanted to buy a desirable plot of ground to build their church on, but the man who owned it would not sell it to them. The disappointed people built the new church structure on an alternative site but often would look longingly at the original location. Two years after the building was completed, on September 17, 1876, a storm of great violence struck the countryside. Pelting rain, a raging wind and roaring tide combined into a miraculous motive power. The edifice was lifted by the elements as if it had been a scrap of paper. It was airborne a distance of three hundred feet, and although its path was not straight, it found its mark with unerring accuracy. The house of God came to rest upon the exact plot of ground which the worshipers had so ardently desired. The divine transfer awed and thrilled the village and even stilled the objections of the owners. The church still stands on the plot ratified by the hand of God. The name of the church was changed to the Church of Providence and the site has long been acknowledged as holy ground.

If God can cause a storm that can lift a whole church off the ground without breaking into pieces and transport it to a place that is not a straight line, but have some turns which are involved, and allow it to fly through the air to a spot that the church prayed for and asked to buy, but were turned down, then He can do anything!

It does not matter to God how impossible the situation may seem, because with Him there is nothing impossible. Believe Him today no matter what it is, and let Him help you.

July 9

"Them that honour me I will honour; and they that despise me shall be lightly esteemed" (I Samuel 2:30).

Respect and honor God and He will honor you. There is an interesting story surrounding one of the Olympics that prove that this statement is true. For months Eric Liddell trained with the purpose of winning the 100-meter race at the Olympic races of 1924. Many sportswriters predicted he would win. Then Eric learned the 100-meter race was scheduled for Sunday. This posed a problem: Eric believed that he could not honor God by running in the contest on the Lord's Day. His fans were stunned by his refusal. Some who had praised him now called him a fool. But Eric stood firm. Suddenly a runner dropped out of the 400-meter race, scheduled on a weekday. Eric offered to fill the slot, even though this was four times as long as the race for which he had trained. When the race was run, Eric Liddell set a record of 47.6 seconds—the winner.[284]

Eric was the winner all the way around. He won with God and He also won the Olympics because He chose to honor the Word of God.

There have been many people who chose to honor what the Word says, and when they do that they are honoring God. The story is told that when General Grant was in Paris, the President of the Republic invited him to attend the Sunday races. He knew that to refuse an invitation from the President of France would be considered especially discourteous by the French people, and yet he politely declined the invitation, saying, "It is not in accord with the custom of my country, or with the spirit of my religion to spend Sunday in that way. I will go to the house of God."

Having old-fashioned honor of the Sabbath, of God, His Word and godly principles is the only way to true victory in the lives of people. When people leave God out of their lives they become godless, and without godly principles anything can happen.

People need God in order to have true happiness and success. Someone once said, "If God does not exist in your life, everything is permissible."

It was Napoleon who said some startling words. He said, "A man is not a man without God. I saw men without God in the reign of terror in 1793. One does not govern such men, he shoots them down." What Napoleon was saying is that people become like animals who do not honor God and His principles, and those kind of people will stop at nothing, because they do not have a fear of God. This is the day to make sure you honor God and His Word, because that is the only way to true success and victory!

July 10

"The chariots of God are twenty thousand, even thousands of angels; the Lord is among them" (Psalm 68:17).

God sends protection even when we are not aware of it and often sends angels to take care of His children. Carolyn Wheeler from Georgia prayed each morning that God would protect her family. She sent me the following story that proves He answered her prayer. She wrote: "My daughter-in-law was driving home from my house, where she picked up my two grandbabies. The older one was twenty-one months old, the younger seven weeks old. She lost control, slid, and hit a tree on the passenger side of the car. The older child had a cut on his finger. The mother had a broken shoulder and a slight injury to her head. The car was totaled. The seven-week-old baby was thrown twenty feet from the car, but still in his car seat and there was not any dirt or grass stains on his car seat. Neither did the baby have a scratch or bruise. The local newspaper wrote that there was an angel on their shoulders. We give God all the praise for sending His angel to protect them and set our new grandbaby down gently on the ground."

God was certainly watching over Carolyn's family that fateful day. Deuteronomy 33:27 says, "The eternal God is [our] refuge." We *can* go through life unafraid knowing that God is there for us in the times of danger.

Rev. Francis E. Clarke, founder of Christian Endeavor, told of a young man in the Maine woods with his camera for a pleasant outing, who stopped at the entrance of a cavern on a rocky hillside and impulsively thought: "Let us see what kind of a photograph I can get out of that cave." Steadying the camera just a little way from the mouth, he gave the sensitive plate a long time exposure into the darkness of the interior. Then he went heedlessly on his way. When later he developed the plates, a thrill of astonishment passed over him as the exposure of the cave revealed in the center of the opening—but concealed from his eyes by the darkness within—a huge lynx crouched and ready to spring. Danger, disfigurement, perhaps death, had confronted him, yet he had been quite unaware of the peril.[285]

Psalm 91:11-12 came alive in this situation: "For he shall give his angels charge over thee, to keep thee in all thy ways. They shall bear thee up in their hands, lest thou dash thy foot against a stone."

It would be a good thing to take time today to thank God for all the times He has watched over you and kept you from harm and danger. Thank Him for keeping you from what could have been, for He is and will always be there watching over you!

July 11

"He sent his word, and healed them" (Psalm 107:20).

The most powerful thing in the world is the Word of God! The Word of God is likened to fire in Jeremiah, as well as a hammer. Psalms talks about it being a light or lamp. Hebrews 4:12 says, "For the word of God is quick, and powerful, and sharper than any twoedged sword, piercing even to the dividing asunder of soul and spirit, and of the joints and marrow, and is a discerner of the thoughts and intents of the heart."

Can you imagine the power you have in your hands when you hold the Word of God? Tricia Wilson of Lemay, Missouri, sent me the following story that reveals the power of the Word. She writes, "I have been plagued with a severe and progressively worsening

pain in my left leg for the past two years. The doctor accredited it to my right leg being shorter than my left and so I had my shoes built up with no relief. Last night at the women's conference I went to bed with my Bible held to my heart. As the familiar pain awoke me in the early morning hours, I placed my Bible to the spots of pain and prayed and praised the Lord! The pain immediately left! I praised the Lord and read the scriptures in Matthew 8 where Jesus healed many. Then I lay down on my left side, something I have not been able to do for a long time. The pain returned just slightly and each place where the pain was, I would lay the Bible on it and pray and the pain would leave! I accepted my healing and began to praise the Lord loudly and with great pleasure!"

F. W. Farrar once said, *"You might as well quench the sun, and suppose that the world can get along without light, as to think that men or nations can do without God or His Word. The world has no other trumpet of peace save the Holy Scripture for souls at war; no other weapon to slay terrible passions; no other teachings to quench the heart's raging fires."*

There is nothing more powerful than God's Word. The story is told of how in World War II, a fine Christian girl was engaged to a serviceman who was overseas. One morning she received a telegram from the War Department, whose opening words ominously said, "We regret to inform you. . . ." Something snapped in the girl's mind and she lapsed into unconsciousness which lasted for days.

A faithful pastor co-operated with doctors and stood faithfully by, doing his best to bring the girl out of her dazed condition. As he prayed, this thought came to him: "I'm going to read the Word of God to her whether she can hear me or not." He began to read comforting, reassuring verses and chapters. Suddenly the pent-up sorrow and emotions of the girl burst forth into a profusion of tears. Her tears presently ceased. She said to her mother, "It's all right now!" In relating what occurred when the pastor began to read God's healing Word, she said, "At first his voice sounded faraway and unreal. Then, as I listened to the familiar passages, the words came closer and closer. Finally they seemed to reach my heart." —Walter B. Knight[286]

Psalm 107:20 came to life that day. It says, "He sent his word, and healed them, and delivered them." It is time to let the Word help you and heal you today.

July 12

"That ye might be filled with all the fulness of God" (Ephesians 3:19).

Some people are content to have half power, when they could have full power. Ezra G. Roth tells about the first time her family crossed the Rockies by automobile, in a 1916-model car. The steep grade called for all that the old motor could offer. The water in the radiator boiled and several times they were stuck. Only by repeated efforts did they reach the top. There was no margin of power. She said they did not enjoy the mountain scenery under those circumstances. The second time they crossed the same mountains they had a 1922-model car. In comparison with the first experience, they did well. By employing all available power, they kept going, but the strain under which the climb was made took away much of the pleasure of the trip. Much later a third trip carried them over the same Rockies in a new car. That was different. The motor took the mountain climbs easily. They could stop by the roadside and enjoy the scenery. It required less time to travel the same distance and with that margin of power they enjoyed their travels.

When Jesus said, in John 10:10, "I am come that they might have life, and that they might have it more abundantly," He meant just what He said. Some people are content to just barely eke by, when the Lord wants to give them more might than they are experiencing. He wants to give them more power under the hood.

The story is told of how two men were looking out over the sea on a stormy day. One of them said, "I have been watching a steamer fighting her way onward in the face of that terrible wind and those high-crested waves. How she keeps on her course at all is a mystery to me; how does she do it?" The other man answered, "Because the power within her enables her to overcome the opposing forces without."

It is so with God's children. They are hindered by obstacles, thwarted by the keen cutting winds of misfortune; buffeted and bruised by the surging waves of sorrow, bereavement, disappointed hopes; and people wonder how they can keep on their course so bravely. They hold the secret in their hearts; they are conscious of

a power within, one which is not theirs by nature. They have learned to say with the apostle Paul, "I can do all things through Christ which strengtheneth me."

How much power are you allowing to dwell within you to help you through the seas of life or over the steep mountains? God has enough power in His storehouse to enable anyone who wants to, to live an overcoming life and that more abundantly!

July 13

"If thou wouldst believe" (John 11:40).

All things are possible to them that believe. When Thomas A. Edison thought he had discovered the way to record and reproduce the sound of a human voice on a machine, he called in a model maker. Handing the man a rough pencil sketch of his idea, he asked that a working model be built. The model maker surveyed the sketch, then declared, "Impossible. That thing will never work. No one has ever made a machine that could talk." Instead of accepting this verdict, Edison determinedly said, "Build what I have sketched here and let me be the loser if it doesn't work."[287]

Edison believed in his mind that it was possible, and so it became possible.

Jesus said in Mark 9:23, "If thou canst believe, all things are possible to him that believeth."

Often when Jesus was asked to do a miracle for someone, He would say, "Do you believe that I am able to do this?" Most of the miracles were predicated on the belief of the people. This is proven in Mark 6. The Scriptures say that Jesus marveled because of the unbelief of the people and because of their unbelief, he could not do many mighty works, only a few for the ones who believed.

When people believe, they are without fear. They are fueled with trust and assurance that all is well. In the story of the Shunammite woman in the Old Testament, her boy, who had been a miracle child, fell sick and died. She did not panic and give into hysterics, but she answered, "All is well," when her husband asked her where she was going. She was going to where the prophet Elisha was because she believed that a miracle was on its way. She

said to the servant who was driving her to that place, "Go forward and slack not."

When she reached the prophet he saw her coming and told his servant to go and meet her and ask, "Is it well with thee? is it well with thy husband? is it well with the child? And she answered, It is well" (II Kings 4:26). Her belief even in the face of death and tragedy caused another miracle to happen. Her child was brought back to life.

God has the power to restore and bring things back to life that have died. He wants to heal broken relationships, broken hearts and broken dreams, but first there must be a belief that He can and will do it.

Belief manifests itself in speech, actions and choices. Paul said, "I know whom I have believed" (II Timothy 1:12). To know Him is to relax when the trials come. It is to believe that God is working for you, that He is protecting you, and that He is with you. This is the day to choose to believe.

July 14

"I am the LORD thy God which teacheth thee to profit, which leadeth thee by the way that thou shouldest go" (Isaiah 48:17).

The gift of time, once it is gone, can never be resurrected, so use it wisely. Dr. Schofield, one of the Bible translators, once said, "No child of God need ever *kill time*. That ought to be an occupation limited to children of death, not children of life." He told about how a Jewish rabbi once called his attention to the meaning of the Hebrew in Psalm 139:24: "See if there be any wicked way in me, and lead me in the way everlasting." The rabbi pointed out that the Hebrew means not "the everlasting way" but "the way of everlasting things." In other words, Dr. Schofield believes this is a prayer which says in effect: "Lord, enable me to have to do with things that will last, and not fritter away my time on things that are only of transitory value."

"Perhaps we need to bring our daily living, especially some of our *odd minutes* to the test of the Psalmist," he says. It is time to

evaluate how we are spending our time because time on earth is not forever.

> *When as a child I laughed and wept—Time crept!*
> *When as a youth I dreamed and talked—Time walked!*
> *When I became a full-grown man—Time ran!*
> *Then as with the years I older grew—Time flew!*
> *Soon I shall find as I travel on—Time gone!*
> —AUTHOR UNKNOWN[288]

Ralph Waldo Emerson wrote that "One of the illusions of life is that the present hour is not the critical, decisive hour. Write it on our heart that every day is the best day of the year. He only is rich who owns the day, and no one owns the day who allows it to be invaded with worry, fret and anxiety."

> *Time is God's gift to mortal man;*
> *It is that fleeting little span*
> *Between our birth and heaven's door*
> *Where we begin God's evermore*
> *When time is o'er.*
>
> *How then should we our time employ,*
> *In service, or, in passing joy?*
> *Can we afford to throw away*
> *And squander time in passing play,*
> *O men of clay?*
> —DR. R. E. NEIGHBOUR[289]

There is a phrase from Alice M. Muir's summation of what life should consist of that says: "Had I but this one day to live, I'd spend, O God, much time with Thee that Thou might'st plan my day for me. Most earnestly I'd seek to know Thy way that Thou would'st have me go."

There it is, that little jewel of knowledge: "I'd spend, O God, much time with You, so that You could plan my day for me." There is the secret of living life abundantly. It is spending time with God and letting Him help plan your day, listening to His voice, learning of Him, letting Him be in the lead instead of you being in the lead. This is the day to spend time with God, for then you will spend your gift of time well.

July 15

"Beloved, let us love one another" (I John 4:7).

To be able to worship God and Him accept our worship, we must first learn to love one another. A man who had traveled in Europe says that while many of the old cathedrals in France are beautiful on the inside, their exterior is often distasteful because of the art carvings which depict animals with hideous features. Inquiring about this strange custom, he was told that the builders in the Middle Ages wanted these figures to represent man's carnal appetites and prejudices! They were placed there to remind all who came to worship that they should leave bitterness and wrath outside the sanctuary if they hoped to receive God's blessings.

Jesus said the whole law is based on this principle. In Mark 12, he said that the two greatest commandments were to love God, and our neighbor as ourselves. It is imperative to love one another if we expect to be blessed of God. It is impossible to receive the rich blessings of His Spirit if we harbor bad feelings towards another person.

The story is told of how one day a disciple of the Lord declared, "Master, my six brothers are asleep and I alone have remained awake to worship you." God answered, "It would have been better for you to remain asleep, if your worship to God is to be mixed with accusations against your brothers."

Once when Jesus was teaching a multitude, he began to teach what is called the Sermon on the Mount or the Beatitudes in Matthew 5. In this discourse, Jesus made a statement which says, "Therefore if thou bring thy gift to the altar, and there rememberest that thy brother hath ought against thee; Leave there thy gift before the altar, and go thy way; first be reconciled to thy brother, and then come and offer thy gift" (Matthew 5:23-24).

The people could identify with what Jesus was saying, because they were taught to build altars, bring a gift to the Lord and sacrifice it to God. Jesus emphasized the "Before" in offering the gift to God. It is imperative to make sure your heart is right with your brother or sister, and to work at keeping a clean heart if we want the blessings of God upon us.

A missionary once asked a class of young native Christians

the question, "What is true worship?" A shy young man stood and said, "I think I know, but I may not be able to say it so others will understand. Before I knew my Savior, I used to go late to church. But now I love to go real early, sit quietly, think about Jesus and His great love for me!" Then, with tears running down his face, he said, "Oh, I love Him! Because He loves me, and because I love Him, I want to please Him in all I do and say!"

There it is in a nutshell: When we really love Him, we will want to please Him and keep our heart clean from anything that displeases Him. Since God is love, we must learn to love like God and then we will be truly blessed as we worship Him!

July 16

"*Give unto the* LORD *the glory due unto his name: bring an offering, and come into his courts*" (Psalm 96:8).

This is the day to give God not only what is due Him, but to give Him a present. There was once a little girl who was given ten bright new pennies. Instantly she began to part with them. "This one is for Jesus. This one is for you, Mommy. This one is for you, Daddy,"—and so on until she had only one penny left. "And this one is for Jesus," she said. "But you have already given one to Jesus," said the mother. "Yes, Mommy, but that one *belonged* to Jesus. This one is a *present*." —*A* THREEFOLD CORD[290]

If only God's children everywhere had this concept of giving. To give God what belongs to Him and then give Him a present also.

There was once a missionary meeting in a church in Scotland, and the people were greatly moved. They gave generously to send missionaries into God's vineyard. Little Alexander Duff, just ten years old, sat in a pew. His heart was strangely moved. But he had nothing to give. After the offering was taken, the ushers returned to the rear of the church. Little Alexander followed them. Looking into the face of one of the collectors, the lad said, "Please, sir, put the basket low!" The usher, catering to what he thought was a childish whim, put the basket on the floor. "There you are, my boy," he said, smiling. How surprised all were when the boy

stepped into the basket and said, "O God, I have no money to give, but I give myself to the offering." —Told by Walter B. Knight[291]

What an attitude! The giver should feel like it is a privilege to give to God, such as the following story portrays: A wealthy man gave a sizable sum to his church and noticed a poor widow who worked hard to support herself and her six children. Her income was small, but she gave regularly out of her scant earnings. One day the man said to the pastor: "The poor widow ought not to give anything to the church. What she gives represents great sacrifice. I will increase my weekly contributions, adding the amount the widow has been giving on every Lord's Day." The minister told the widow what the wealthy member had said he would do. Tears came to her eyes. She said, "Does he want to take from me the comfort I experience in giving to the Lord? Think how much I owe Him! My health is good. My children keep well. I receive so many blessings that I feel I couldn't live if I did not give my offering to Jesus each week."

Now is the time to examine our attitude towards giving to God and His work and adopt the attitude of the little girl with the extra penny, Alexander Duff and the widow.

July 17

"Looking for that blessed hope" (Titus 2:13).

There is more to life than just a few years on earth; there is life everlasting. While on one of his expeditions to the Antarctic, Sir Ernest Shackleton was once compelled to leave some of his men on Elephant Island, with the intentions of returning for them and carrying them back to England. But he was unavoidably delayed, and by the time he could go for them he found to his dismay that the sea had frozen over and his men were cut off. Three times he tried to reach them, but his efforts ended in failure. Finally, in his last effort, he found a narrow channel through the ice.

Guiding his small ship back to the island, he was delighted to find his men not only alive and well but all prepared to get aboard. They were soon on their way to safety and home. After the excitement ended, Sir Ernest inquired how it was that they were ready

to get aboard so promptly. They told him that every morning their leader rolled up his sleeping bag, saying, "Get your things ready, boys, the boss may come today."

The return of the Lord Jesus to this earth is much more certain than Sir Shackleton's claim to return. —AL BRYANT[292]

Just as the appointed leader of Ernest Shackleton reminded the men that he might come today, the same is true of our Lord and Savior Jesus Christ. He really could come today. Every day we must prepare for the great event of the ages.

Paul declared, "For the Lord himself shall descend from heaven with a shout, with the voice of the archangel, and with the trump of God: and the dead in Christ shall rise first: Then we which are alive and remain shall be caught up together with them in the clouds, to meet the Lord in the air: and so shall we ever be with the Lord. Wherefore comfort one another with these words. But of the times and the seasons, brethren, ye have no need that I write unto you. For yourselves know perfectly that the day of the Lord so cometh as a thief in the night" (I Thessalonians 4:16-18; 5:1-2).

Jesus is coming unexpectedly to many, but for those who say each day, "He may come today," they will be the ones who will be caught up—those who are looking for His appearance as spoken of in Titus 2:12-13: "We should live soberly, righteously, and godly, in this present world; Looking for that blessed hope, and the glorious appearing of the great God and our Saviour Jesus Christ."

Look up today, keep your eyes on the clouds. Someday they will part and you will be out of here. Your ear will hear a trumpet sound. Only the ones who have lived in readiness and preparation for His coming will be able to hear the sound. It will be glorious and wonderful. Be encouraged, and keep your eyes on the goal. It will come to pass!

July 18

"He that keepeth thee will not slumber" (Psalm 121:3).

When you pray, God is with you even when you are not aware of it. God's eyes are constantly upon His children. He watches and

takes care of them, often preventing them from disaster of which they are not even aware.

God took care of a choir and they didn't even know it. It was on March 1, 1950, in Beatrice, Nebraska, that a pastor went to church to prepare for the evening choir practice. Most choir members would arrive between 7:15 and 7:30 P.M. He then went home for a quick supper, was ready to return with his wife and daughter, when it was discovered the daughter's dress was soiled and needed a change which in turn must be ironed. High school sophomore Ladona had trouble with her geometry problems and had to stay to finish the problem. Usually, she would be early for rehearsal. Two sisters were ready to go to church, but the car would not start. They called the geometry girl to pick them up. Mrs. Schuster with a small daughter normally would arrive at 7:20, but that night her elderly mother needed her and so she dropped by her mother's house. A lathe operator wanted to stop putting off an important letter (later, he said, "I didn't know why, but felt this compulsion to finish the letter"), and so he was late. Stenographer Joyce Black feeling "just plain lazy" stayed until the last possible minute. Then she was ready to go when it happened. Machinist Harry Ohl was going to take his two boys to choir practice, since his wife was away, but somehow started talking with someone and when he looked at his watch, it was already too late. Pianist Marilyn Paul decided to come one-half hour earlier. But after supper, she fell asleep and arrived barely on time. Choir director and the mother of the pianist, Mrs. Paul, was late due to her daughter. She had tried unsuccessfully to wake her up before. Two high school girls usually went together. But one was listening to the 7:00-7:30 radio program and that evening broke her usual habit of promptness in order to listen to the end. At 7:25, the West Side Church blew up. Its roof crushed in and its walls fell down due to leaking gas. But the choir members were all late, and this had never happened before.[293]

The Lord was watching over everyone, and they did not even know it. The angels were mighty busy that night. "The angel of the LORD encampeth round about them that fear him, and delivereth them" (Psalm 34:7).

July 19

"Not with eyeservice, as menpleasers; but as the servants of Christ, doing the will of God from the heart" (Ephesians 6:6).

Does God only hear the prayers and the praises that are from the heart? The story is told of how a man once went to church with an angel as his guide. Every seat in the church was filled, but there was something strange about it all. The organist moved his fingers over the keys, but no music came forth from the pipes. The choir arose to sing, and their lips moved, but not a sound was to be heard. The pastor stepped to the pulpit to read the Scriptures, but not a sound was heard. The congregation joined in repeating the prayer, but not a single sound was heard. The pastor again stepped to the pulpit, and went through all the motions of preaching, but the man with the angel heard nothing. So he turned to the angel and said, "What does this mean? I see that a service is being held, but I hear nothing." The angel replied, "You hear nothing because there is nothing to be heard. You see this service just as God sees it. These people are not putting their hearts into it, and so God hears nothing. He hears only that which comes from the heart, and not that which comes from the lips only."

As the angel was speaking, back in the last pew they heard a child saying, "Our Father which art in heaven, Hallowed be thy name." The angel said, "You are hearing the only part of this service that God hears. He hears this little child's prayer because she means what she says and puts her heart and soul in it."
—Taken from *The Gospel for Youth*[294]

If this story were true, I wonder how many prayers and songs offered to God throughout the world are really heard by Him? Jesus did command His followers to love the Lord God with all their heart, soul, mind, and strength. This is a day of inventory—a day to ask ourselves—do we really mean what we say when we pray, when we worship, when we sing, or is it just a ritual, going through the motions, doing it because that is what everyone else is doing? Can we sing to Him and think about tomorrow's duties and the problems that are waiting for us when we get home? What would happen if everyone really gave their heart and soul in worship to the King of kings and not just lip service? What an avalanche of blessings that would flow into our churches and homes. This is the day to begin to praise, sing and worship with our hearts and not with our lips only, but to give God the best, so He will hear us when we call.

Curious as to why her children were whispering, once a mother asked her children what they were playing. "Church," answered the group of youngsters. "You know that you shouldn't whisper in church," said the mother. "Yes, but we're the choir," they said.

The question is, "Are we really giving God our best, or are we distracted and just giving Him a show of lip service?" This is the day to give Him what He deserves, the very, very best.

July 20

"*Blessed be the Lord, who daily loadeth us with benefits*" (Psalm 68:19).

When you walk with God, the blessings outweigh the sorrows. The following poem sent to me in an email explains how blessings outweigh sorrows:

GOD'S BOXES
I have in my hand two boxes
which God gave me to hold.
He said, "Put all your sorrows in the black,
and all your joys in the gold."
I heeded his words, and in the two boxes
both my joys and sorrows I store.
But though the gold became heavier each day
The black was as light as before.
With curiosity, I opened the black,
I wanted to find out why
And I saw, in the base of the box, a hole
Which my sorrows had fallen out by.
I showed the hole to God, and mused aloud,

> *"I wonder where my sorrows could be."*
> *He smiled a gentle smile at me,*
> *"My child, they're all here with me."*
> *I asked, "God, why give me the boxes?*
> *Why the gold, and the black with the hole?"*
> *"My child, the gold is for you to count your blessings,*
> *The black is for you to let go."*

God wants to bear your burdens today. There was once a farmer who was jogging along over a country road in his buckboard, and overtook a fellow who was trudging along with a heavy bundle on his shoulder. "Hop in, neighbor," said the farmer cheerily. "I'll give you a ride."

The traveler clambered into the buckboard, sat down wearily, and placed his burden on his lap. "I am carrying you," said the farmer with a puzzled look on his face, "but you are still carrying your burden!" How like many of God's children. Jesus, the burden bearer, says, "Cast your cares upon me, for I care for you," yet we continue to stay loaded down with the care of all of our troubles.
—Taken from story told by Rev. James Seward[295]

The question is: what are we doing with the two boxes? Are we storing up and counting our blessings in the gold box and letting the sorrows just flow on through the black box, or have we plugged up the hole, so that we are carrying our sorrows and problems also? It is needful to keep that hole open and let the cares of life go straight through the opening and land on God's back; for He has promised to carry them.

It is our choice. We can enjoy the blessings and keep track of them for Psalm 68:19 says, "Blessed be the Lord, who daily loadeth us with benefits, even the God of our salvation," or we can start keeping track of the sorrows in such a way that will load us down and put heavy weights upon us.

Let them go today; transfer them to God's shoulders. Release them into the hand that can do miracles and work all things out for our good! Which load will you carry: the blessing of the Lord who daily loads you with benefits, or the sorrows and troubles that weigh you down? Why not choose the daily load of benefits?

July 21

"If I must needs glory, I will glory of the things which concern mine infirmities" (II Corinthians 11:30).

Many times there are blessings even in our troubles. Henry Bosch shares an interesting story how God shielded former President Theodore Roosevelt from the bullet of a would-be assassin. The Chief of State was very nearsighted and always carried two pairs of glasses, one for close-up work and the other for seeing things at a distance. While speaking in the city of Milwaukee during his last great political campaign, he was shot by a man named Shrenk. Roosevelt was hurt but insisted on finishing his speech. Later, when a surgeon was examining his wound, he discovered that the steel spectacle case in his vest pocket had saved his life, for it had deflected the bullet from his heart.

"That's remarkable!" said the President as he carefully inspected the bent container with its shattered contents. "I've always considered it a nuisance to carry two pairs of glasses, especially those thick heavy ones I kept in that metal case. Yet tonight, God used it to save my life."[296]

Troubles are often blessings in disguise. Dr. Lambie, medical missionary, has forded many swift and bridgeless streams in Africa. The danger in crossing such a stream lies in being swept off one's feet and carried down the stream to greater depths or hurled to death against the hidden rocks. Dr. Lambie learned from the natives the best way to make such a hazardous crossing. The man about to cross finds a large stone, the heavier the better, lifts it to his shoulder, and carries it across the stream as "ballast." The extra weight of the stone keeps his feet solid on the bed of the stream and he can cross safely without being swept away. Dr. Lambie said this: *"While crossing the dangerous stream of life, enemies constantly seek to overthrow us and rush us down to ruin. We need the ballast of burden-bearing, a load of affliction, to keep us from being swept off our feet."* —CHRISTIAN VICTORY[297]

What is ballast? On a ship it is any relatively heavy substance used to maintain a vessel at its proper draft or trim, or to improve its stability. Ballast may be rock, metal, or such like, stowed in holds or other compartments, water in tanks. In the spiritual sense of the word, it gives or helps to maintain stability in character, morals, conduct, or the like. It is to bring steadiness in mind or conduct. So if you are in a situation that seems like you are carrying heavy loads, it could just be a "ballast" that the Lord in His infinite wisdom has allowed you to carry to get you safely to the other side—to the place where there will be no more heavy loads—only glory and peace forevermore!

July 22

"*That ye may know the way by which ye must go*" (Joshua 3:4).

Life is not easy, and sometimes it is hard to find the way, but when God is leading, all is well! "*Life is no straight and easy corridor along which we travel free and unhampered, but a maze of passages, through which we must seek our way—now lost and confused, now checked in a blind alley. But always God will open a door for us, not perhaps one that we ourselves would ever have thought of, but one that will ultimately prove good for us.*"

God does not lay everything out plainly for us to see; He just says, "Follow me." When we follow Him step by step, the way is made plain, the way that we are to go. We cannot know or not always tell exactly what to do, but He knows exactly the way to go if we will but stay close to Him.

There is an interesting story told about John Ting, a man who learned how to follow and obey God's voice. In the time before the communists took over China, John Ting was known as "God's Fool" and was a member of the "Little Flock Evangelists." By his life and his witnessing, he won many Chinese to Christ. He had total faith in God's care, as the following incident shows: One day Ting and his companions arrived at a river which had to be crossed. The river was overflowing its banks and the water was deep. Ting and his companions were being pursued by bandits. The situation seemed humanly hopeless! But Ting said, "Our God is a mighty God. He can open a way for us through the river!" He prayed simply and earnestly: "O Lord, hold back the waters, and

make a way for us to escape from our enemies!" Then he stepped into the raging water which swirled about his knees. He motioned to the others to cross as he bowed his head and prayed silently. For a moment, Ting's companions hesitated. Then, to their amazement, they saw that the water was steadily dropping. In a short while, all had crossed the river to safety! —Told by Walter B. Knight[298]

The God who wrought this miracle in answer to believing prayer, the God who divided the Red Sea for Moses so that His people might pass through safely, still lives! If the way seems rough and unclear today, just follow the Lord and He will make a way where there seems to be no way; for He is the Way Maker.

July 23

"Always in every prayer of mine" (Philippians 1:4).

This is the day to remember to pray, for that is where the power is. For several nights a six-year-old girl threw one shoe under her bed before going to sleep. Her mother asked her why she did that. "My teacher said," was the reply, "that if we have to kneel by our beds to look for our shoes, we'll remember to keep kneeling and say our morning prayers." The little girl was making sure she knelt in prayer. Oh, that we would make sure that we knelt each morning!

C. W. Renwick once said, *"The only footprints on the sands of time, that will really last, are the ones made after kneeprints."*

Robert Lewis of Fredericksburg, Virginia, was George Washington's private secretary. During the first part of the presidency, he said that he accidentally witnessed Washington's private devotions, both morning and evening. He saw him in a kneeling position, with an open Bible before him; and he said that he believed such was his daily practice. His custom was to go to his library at four o'clock in the morning for devotions.[299]

When young America was fighting for her life, George Washington and his soldiers were stationed at Valley Forge, and it was a hard winter. With all the cares and anxieties of that time upon him, he was known to pray to God for help. One day a

farmer approaching the camp heard an earnest voice. On coming nearer, he saw George Washington on his knees, his cheeks wet with tears, praying. The farmer returned home and said to his wife: "George Washington will succeed! George Washington will succeed! The Americans will secure their independence!" "What makes you think so, Isaac?" asked his wife.

The farmer replied: "I heard him pray, Hannah, out in the woods today, and the Lord will surely hear his prayer. He will, Hannah; thee may rest assured He will." —*The Sunday School Times*[300]

And yes, God did hear and answer the prayers of George Washington and many other Americans who prayed.

It is time to pray *always*. Seven days without prayer makes one weak. Jesus said, "Men ought always to pray, and not to faint." A correct deduction of this is that "if you do not pray, you will become weak or faint."

This is the day to pray and win battles, become strong, live in victory and become more than a conqueror through Jesus Christ our Lord!

July 24

"There is a lad here, which hath five barley loaves, and two small fishes: but what are they among so many?" (John 6:9).

*B*e careful of the little things, for they often spell the difference between success and failure. Arthur Tonne relates how Dr. Frederick Fox, who devoted his life to the treatment of snakebites, met his death at Calcutta, India, as the result of experimenting with a snake of the deadly krait variety. In British India this species of snake caused thirty-five thousand deaths every year before he found a cure. To prove the value of his cure Dr. Fox permitted one of these reptiles to inflict five punctures in his arm. With a confident smile he cut out four of the bites, but the fifth one escaped his notice. He quickly applied his remedy but it was too late. He died like thousands of others who had been bitten by the krait, simply because he was careless of just one tiny bite. He missed it and fell down dead. He was playing with death and in his confidence counted only four bites and somehow overlooked the fifth.[301]

When the suspension bridge across the Niagara was to be erected, the question was, how to get the cable over. With a favoring wind, a kite was elevated, which alighted on the other shore. To its insignificant string, a cord was attached, which was drawn over, then a rope, then a larger rope, then a cable strong enough to sustain the iron cable which supported the bridge, over which heavily-laden trains pass in safety.[302] It all started with a small kite.

Years ago when there were knitted stockings, a tall chimney had been completed, and the scaffolding was being removed. One man remained on top to superintend the process. A rope should have been left for him to descend by. His wife was at home doing the washing, when her little boy burst in crying, "Mother, Mother, they've forgotten the rope, and Daddy's going to throw himself down."

She paused, her lips moved in the agony of prayer, and then she rushed forth. A crowd was looking up at the poor man, who was moving round and round the narrow cornice, terrified and bewildered. It seemed as if at any moment he might fall or throw himself down in despair. His wife from below cried out, "Take off thy stockings; unravel the worsted"; and he did so. "Now tie the end to a bit of mortar, and lower gently." Down came the thread and a bit of mortar, swinging backward and forward. Lower and lower it descended, eagerly watched by many eyes; it was now within reach, and was gently seized by one of the crowd. They fastened some twine to the thread, "Now, pull up."

The man got hold of the twine, fastened it and let it down once more and this time some rope came up. He secured the rope tightly and descended to the waiting group of people. "You saved my life, Mary," he cried as he threw his arms around his wife.
—Taken from story told by Newman Hall.[303]

The worsted thread was small, but it was big enough to pull up some twine and the twine was big enough to pull up the rope. Be careful of the little things, they spell the difference between success and failure!

July 25

"The Lord is thy keeper" (Psalm 121:5).

God takes care of His children, even while they are asleep.

Nancy Thompson wrote me the following letter: "In February 1989, my husband Chuck and I had attended a sweethearts' dinner. Earlier in the day I had been doing laundry and when we got home I had one more load to dry. I started the dryer, then Chuck and I got ready for bed. Before we went to bed, the dryer was still going so I decided to turn it off and let the clothes finish drying the next day. I turned the dryer off by opening then closing the door.

"Later that night, while Chuck and I were both sleeping, I felt someone trying to wake me by shaking me. Well, I tried to go into a deeper sleep and said, 'Not now.' I felt the shaking again and I said, 'Okay, I'll open my eyes in a minute.' When I opened my eyes I saw the room was filled with thick smoke. I quickly sat up and shook Chuck, saying, 'Wake up, the house is on fire.' He quickly got up and we crawled to the front door, awakening our dog, Sarah, on our way out. We then put on our coats and went outside. Once outside Chuck saw that there were no flames visible anywhere, so he came back into the house and opened all the windows to air all the smoke out. We waited in the car while the smoke cleared out.

"Chuck had checked the wood stove and thought it had caused all the smoke. The next day when I went to finish drying the clothes I discovered that all the clothes were burned to ashes. When I had opened and closed the dryer door, it had not turned off the heating element, causing the clothes to catch on fire. Thank the Lord that the fire stayed contained in the dryer and that He had His angel to wake me."

Psalm 121:3 says, "He that keepeth thee will not slumber." Verse 5 says, "The LORD is thy keeper." A keeper is someone who watches, guards, maintains, protects and keeps in good condition. Because God does not sleep, we can sleep as David said in Psalm 4:8: "I will both lay me down in peace, and sleep: for thou, LORD, only makest me dwell in safety."

He has promised to send His presence with His children wherever they go as the following poem says so well:

> *My presence shall go with thee*
> *So calm thy troubled fears;*
> *My promise is unchanging*
> *Throughout the changeful years.*

'Mid scenes of gloom and gladness,
When weary or distressed,
My presence shall go with thee,
And I will give thee rest.

My presence shall go with thee!
Most blest assurance here,
While in this lower valley,
Beset by doubt and fear;

No evil shall befall thee,
Close sheltered to my breast;
My presence shall go with thee,
And I will give thee rest.

My presence shall go with thee!
Though in a foreign land,
Afar from home and kindred,
This covenant shall stand.

Nor time nor space can sever,
Love knows not East or West:
My presence shall go with thee,
And I will give thee rest.
—AUTHOR UNKNOWN[304]

July 26

"*Keep me as the apple of the eye*" (Psalm 17:8).

If you are God's child, you are the apple of His eye. God loved the world so much that He sent His only Son into the world to die for them, so that they might live. Those who choose to accept salvation and become His children are very special in God's eye. I received the following story in an email:

A well-known speaker once started off his seminar by holding up a $20 bill. In the room of two hundred people, he asked, "Who would like this new $20 bill?" Hands started going up. He said, "I am going to give this $20 to one of you, but first, let me

do this." He proceeded to crumple the twenty-dollar bill. He then asked, "Who still wants it?" Still the hands were up in the air. "Well," he replied, "what if I do this?" And he dropped it on the ground and started to grind it into the floor with his shoe. He picked it up now all crumpled and dirty. "Now who still wants it?" Still the hands went up into the air. "My friends, you have all learned a very valuable lesson. No matter what I did to the money, you still wanted it because it did not decrease in value. It was still worth $20." The speaker proceeded to speak. He said, "Many times in our lives we are dropped, crumpled and ground into the dirt by the decisions we make and the circumstances that come our way. We feel as though we are worthless. But no matter what has happened or what will happen, you will never lose your value in God's eyes. To Him, dirty or clean, crumpled or finely creased, you are still priceless."

The following phrases are found in Psalms, which describe God's relationship with His children;

Psalm 1:6: "The LORD knoweth the way of the righteous: but the way of the ungodly shall perish."

Psalm 4:3: "But know that the LORD hath set apart him that is godly for himself: the LORD will hear when I call unto him."

Psalm 5:12: "For thou, LORD, wilt bless the righteous; with favour wilt thou compass him as with a shield."

Psalm 7:10: "My defence is of God, which saveth the upright in heart."

Psalm 55:22: "Cast thy burden upon the LORD, and he shall sustain thee: he shall never suffer the righteous to be moved."

Psalm 84:11: "For the LORD God is a sun and shield: the LORD will give grace and glory: no good thing will he withhold from them that walk uprightly."

So many promises, so numerable that it is impossible to quote them all, but in the midst of all the promises to His children, He inserts this phrase, "But he, being full of compassion, forgave their iniquity. . . . For he remembered that they were but flesh" (Psalm 78:38-39).

God loves His children, He is compassionate and patient with them and they are very valuable to Him—the very apple of His eye.

July 27

"Love your enemies" (Matthew 5:44).

It is better to forgive than to harbor hate and resentments. D. M. Panton once told how Maskepetoon, a powerful Indian chief, engaged in savage warfare with his enemies. "One night he heard a missionary speak on the dying Lord's prayer for His enemies, 'Father, forgive them.' The next day Maskepetoon saw the Indian who had murdered his son. Coming face to face with him, Maskepetoon said in a trembling voice, 'You have murdered my son. You deserve to die. You have done me and my tribe the greatest injury that is possible for a man to do. You have broken my heart and destroyed him who was to have succeeded me. But for what I heard from the missionary at the campfire last night, I would now bury this tomahawk in your heart. But the missionary told us that if we want God, the Great Spirit, to forgive us, we must forgive our enemies.' With deep emotion he continued: 'As I hope the Great Spirit will forgive me, I forgive you!' Then, pulling his war bonnet over his face, Maskepetoon bowed over his horse's neck and gave way to his agony in tears!"[305]

Jesus said in Matthew 5:44: "Love your enemies, bless them that curse you, do good to them that hate you, and pray for them which despitefully use you."

This is good medicine—for hate and resentment will destroy the human body and mind. When a person holds hurts within him, he turns into a miserable person as the following story demonstrates: Little Jackie was enjoying playing elevator boy, while his grandfather made some purchases in a large department store. Jackie would say to those entering the elevator, "Up or down?" The operator of the elevator beamed with joy because Jackie was having such a fine time. A sour-faced woman approached the elevator. Little Jackie called out to her, "Up or down?" "Neither one," barked out the woman to Jackie, adding, "Get out of here, you little pest!" Jackie was sorely wounded. With heavy heart and dragging feet, and with tears trickling down his little face, he went and fell into the waiting arms of his grandfather, who saw and heard what had happened. "Why did she call me a little pest, Grandpa?" asked little Jackie. Grandpa tried to explain to Jackie that some-

time in the past the rough-speaking woman must have been hurt, and the hurt had left scars on her soul. "She feels that, by hurting others, the scars on her soul will heal, but that isn't true, Jackie, for when she hurts others, her scars become worse," said Grandpa.

When little Jackie prayed that night he asked God's blessings upon many whom he mentioned by name. "But, dear Lord," he prayed, "don't bless the woman with scars on her soul, because she has put scars on my soul!" Grandpa heard what little Jackie prayed, and he said, "Jackie, if we want to be truly loved by Jesus, and forgiven by Jesus, we must love and forgive others."

Some weeks passed. Grandpa thought little Jackie had forgotten all about the unpleasant experience. But it was not so. One day he came and said, "Grandpa, I am going to love everyone who has scars on her soul. And I am going to love everyone who has put scars on my soul!" —TOLD BY WALTER B. KNIGHT[306]

This is the day to examine our heart and determine as little Jackie to love and forgive anyone who has put scars on our soul, for this is the true road to blessing.

July 28

"The LORD is our king; he will save us" (Isaiah 33:22).

A Christian man who attended the Ecuadorian church was hit from behind by a car while bicycling home from work late one night. The bicycle was crushed and he was severely injured. The driver sped off not wanting to face the penalty for this accident.

The man tried to get up but could not. His head was bleeding, and he was in severe pain and needed help as he could not help himself. On his second attempt to get up, three young men appeared, dressed in shining blue uniforms. Two helped him to his feet and the third retrieved his bicycle for him. Before losing consciousness, he heard the three men say, "Let's go." He remembers nothing from that point until regaining consciousness in the hospital two days later.

While he remained unconscious, the three men took him and

his bike the one mile to his apartment. His family was gone to church that night but the landlord was outside when the four men arrived. She watched as one of them removed a house key from his pocket and opened the locked door. She watched as the two men took the injured brother in and laid him in his own bed. The third man put the bicycle in its spot. She noticed they never came back out of the house. She thought maybe they were relatives.

When the family returned home from church, they found the bicycle in its 'regular parking place,' and his wife found him in his own bed in serious condition. Before taking him to the hospital his wife heard the whole story as told by the landlady. The injured brother recovered with only bruises and scrapes, no broken bones or fractures.

There are no friends of the family who match the description of the three men who helped him that night. The owner of the house has not seen them since. It is easy to believe these "good Samaritans" were angels. After all, not having been to the house before, they knew which apartment to enter, which bed was his and the parking spot for the bicycle. They had a key, went in, and never came out, but were gone when the family returned. This man is convinced they were angels sent by God to help him in the time of need. After all, does not Psalm 91:11 state, "For he shall give his angels charge over thee, to keep thee in all thy ways"?

God is our King, and whatever or whomever He chooses to help us in the time of need is His business. Just trust Him explicitly today!

July 29

"I will call upon the Lord . . . so shall I be saved from mine enemies" (Psalm 18:3).

God, His Word, and His name can literally save your life! The story is told of how the Ibuga Church of Western Tanzania was conducting service outdoors on Easter morning because of the crowd. While they sang and worshiped they had no idea of the calamity that was striking their village. A huge lioness had come from the forest wild and mad and was bent on killing. She dashed from house to house attacking everything in her path. She killed

three goats, a cow, and then a woman and her child! As a cry of anguish arose, the lioness ran off in the direction of the Ibuga Church meeting. The villagers said, "Now the 'Mungu Mwena' (God is good) people will get it, for that lioness is headed directly for them."

The congregation suddenly saw the creature only a few yards away. She stopped and growled furiously. The people were afraid, when suddenly the preacher shouted: "Folks, don't be afraid! The God who saved Daniel from the lions is here. The risen Christ of Easter is here." Then with a God-given faith and authority, he turned to the lioness and said, "You lion, I curse you in the name of Jesus Christ!"

Then the most amazing thing happened. From the scattered clouds, though there had been no rain nor was there any later, a bolt of lightning struck the lioness and she dropped dead in her tracks. The preacher ran and jumped up and down on the carcass and then used it as a platform to preach. —*Convention Herald*

The God who created the world used His power to subdue the lioness as faith uttered words spoken in the name of Jesus! He has all power in heaven and in earth and is able to do the impossible at any time, any place, for anyone who believes in His power.

Psalm 7:2 describes the destruction of a lion: "Lest he tear my soul like a lion, rending it in pieces, while there is none to deliver." There was One to deliver as the preacher cried, "Do not be afraid!"

The Lord is with the righteous as stated in Psalm 37:17-18: "For the arms of the wicked shall be broken: but the LORD upholdeth the righteous. The LORD knoweth the days of the upright: and their inheritance shall be for ever." David continued this psalm in verses 23-25: "The steps of a good man are ordered by the LORD: and he delighteth in his way. Though he fall, he shall not be utterly cast down: for the LORD upholdeth him with his hand. I have been young, and now am old; yet have I not seen the righteous forsaken."

What a comfort! God knows how many days one is to live. He will not let those days be cut short. He orders the steps of His children. He is with them and keeps them in the rough times of life and in the time of trouble. God kept Daniel in his encounter with the lions. When he was thrown into the lions' den, the king could not sleep all night, and when morning came he went to the den to check on Daniel. He was relieved when he heard Daniel say, "My God hath sent his angel, and hath shut the lions' mouths, that they have not hurt me: forasmuch as before him innocency was found

in me; and also before thee, O king, have I done no hurt."

This is the day to trust in God no matter what situation you are thrown into or how much trouble surrounds you. God is able and will help His children when they call on His name!

July 30

"*The righteous cry, and the* LORD *heareth, and delivereth them out of all their troubles*" (Psalm 34:17).

Prayer can make special things happen. Bruce Howell tells an amazing story of what happened in his life when he was in trouble. "In early 1982, while working in El Salvador as a missionary, my wife and I decided to visit our missionary friend Wynn T. Drost, who was then working in Guatemala. He and his family had formerly been missionaries to El Salvador.

"This was during the war in El Salvador when over eighty thousand people lost their lives. The terrorists had a way of stopping the vehicles during the war. They would put large tree trunks or rocks across the roads, often on curves that were on upgrades in the mountains, so that motorists could not go around the blocks but would be forced to stop.

"At the time of our trip from El Salvador to Guatemala, we drove a Toyota Hiace, a four-cylinder van that sat fairly low on the ground. While driving up one side of a mountain, we made a sharp turn and the lights of the van outlined large boulders that the guerrillas had placed across the road to ambush us. We could not go to the right because the road had been cut out of the side of the mountain. We could not go to the left, because there was a several-hundred-foot drop-off. At that moment, the men who were hidden in the bushes were undoubtedly ready to come out to see what they would do to us. All we could do was call on Jesus. As we called out the name of Jesus, we felt the power of God begin to work. We did not see angels, but they were around our car.

"Suddenly the van was lifted up and it seemed as though we flew over the rocks. Then the angels set us down on the other side—and we continued to travel on our way!

"Our van never touched the boulders in the road, and we were

never stopped. The terrorists, I'm sure, were amazed at the flying van that night in 1982!"

Psalm 18:3-4, 6, 9-10 states: "I will call upon the LORD, who is worthy to be praised: so shall I be saved from mine enemies. The sorrows of death compassed me, and the floods of ungodly men made me afraid. . . . In my distress I called upon the LORD, and cried unto my God: he heard my voice out of his temple, and my cry came before him, even into his ears. . . . He bowed the heavens also, and came down: and darkness was under his feet. And he rode upon a cherub, and did fly: yea, he did fly upon the wings of the wind."

Maybe God was flying that night on the wings of the wind and just picked up a van where some people inside were calling for help, took it over the rocks, and set it down on the other side. Who knows how He works? Who can tell of His power and majesty? He is great and awesome and will help anyone who will just pray to Him in the time of trouble.

For He promised in Isaiah 43:2: "When thou passest through the waters, I will be with thee; and through the rivers, they shall not overflow thee: when thou walkest through the fire, thou shalt not be burned; neither shall the flame kindle upon thee." Verse 5 clinches it: "Fear not: for I am with thee."

Wherever you are today, whatever you are involved in, whatever it is that you are going through, God is with you. He is there to help you in the times when everything is broken down, when seemingly everything has fallen apart. When it is impossible to go on, just pray a prayer of faith to the One who loves you most, and He will be there for you to do even the impossible so that you can go forward and win!

"My help cometh from the LORD, which made heaven and earth" (Psalm 121:2).

God can fix anything if we allow Him to do so in His own time. The following email was sent to me and it said the sender was God. The subject was "Life's Problems." The message was as follows: *"Good morning. Today I will be handling all of your problems. Please, remember that I do not need your help. If*

the devil happens to deliver a situation to you that you cannot handle, do not attempt to resolve it. Kindly put it in the SFJTD (something for Jesus to do) box. It will be addressed in MY time, not yours. Once the matter is placed into the box, do not hold on to it or attempt to remove it. Holding on or removal will delay the resolution of your problem. If it is a situation that you think you are capable of handling, please consult my Word and talk it over with me in prayer to be sure that it is the proper resolution. Because I do not sleep nor do I slumber, there is no need for you to lose any sleep.

"Rest, my child. If you need to contact me, I am only a prayer away. As with all good things, please pass this on. Love you! God."

Psalm 37:5 states, "Commit thy way unto the LORD; trust also in him; and he shall bring it to pass." Sometimes we feel our life is "on hold." We are watching, waiting and wondering when God is going do what we have been asking and seeking: when will He "bring it to pass"? One must remember: God's delay is not his denial.

After flying for many years, I have learned that sometimes a plane will get into what is called a "holding pattern." There is a reason. It could be that it is not the safest or best time to land the plane. There may be too much fog, or snow or ice, or air traffic. The captain will not land the plane until it is the right time.

No passenger would even think to rush into the cockpit and tell the pilot to land or tell him, "I'm tired of waiting to land, move over, I'll land this plane." It would be absurd to think that this would happen.

The same way it is in real life. This is the day to commit your desires to the Pilot of your life. He knows what He is doing.

August 1

"Who went about doing good" (Acts 10:38).

*E*verywhere Jesus went He made a difference. He left behind Him a long line of miracles. He gave blind men back their sight, healed a lady with an issue of blood, gave hope to a woman of ill repute, raised a young girl from the dead, and changed the lives of those who obeyed His teachings. Things were never the same

when He came and left. He always lifted people into new dimensions. He gave them hope and love.

If only God's children everywhere would do everything in their power to make a difference in all the lives they touch. Some may feel that the task is too vast and what does it matter what they do? The following story shows the attitude of those who look not at the task, but at the opportunity to make a difference in as many lives as they possibly can:

MAKING A DIFFERENCE

An old man walked the beach at dawn. He noticed a young man ahead of him picking up starfish and flinging them back into the sea. Finally catching up with the youth, he asked him why he was doing this. The answer was that the starfish would die if left until the morning sun.

"But the beach goes on for miles and miles and there are millions of starfish," continued the old man. "How can your efforts make a difference?"

The young man looked at the starfish in his hand and then threw it to safety in the waves.

"I made a difference in that one," he said.

To make a difference in one life is worth more than millions of gold. Jesus illustrated the worth of a soul in Matthew 16:26: "For what is a man profited, if he shall gain the whole world, and lose his own soul? or what shall a man give in exchange for his soul?"

This is the day to make a difference in the life of someone who is in need.

"*Every man according to his several ability*" (Matthew 25:15).

God does not give men and women ability to heap glory on themselves, but He endows them with gifts, talents and abilities to bring glory to Him.

This is proven in I Peter 4:11: "If any man speak, let him speak as the oracles of God; if any man minister, let him do it as of the ability

which God giveth: that God in all things may be glorified through Jesus Christ, to whom be praise and dominion for ever and ever. Amen."

To have ability to do something does not give license to belittle those of lesser abilities or to look down on someone who cannot perform at the same level. Jesus said there would be degrees of talent or ability as depicted in the parable of the talents.

Matthew 25:15 states: "And unto one he gave five talents, to another two, and to another one; to every man according to his several ability."

The same is not expected of all, except one thing, and that is to be faithful. Ability and talent do not excuse unfaithfulness; neither does having no ability excuse unfaithfulness. Everyone is required to be faithful no matter what his capacity for talent may be.

Even the disciples had different gifts, capacities, and abilities. They were not all endowed the same. Acts 11:29 states that each had his own ability: "Then the disciples, every man according to his ability, determined to send relief unto the brethren which dwelt in Judaea."

According to his ability concept should be understood by all. Some people are asked to do things and it does not even bother them, but if others were asked to do the same thing, they would fall apart. It is because God gave different abilities to do different things to everyone.

When God needed someone to stand in the king's palace, he allowed Daniel and his friends to be placed there. Daniel 1:4 states: "Children in whom was no blemish, but well favoured, and skilful in all wisdom, and cunning in knowledge, and understanding science, and such as had ability in them to stand in the king's palace." They had ability to stand in the king's palace for a distinct purpose. That purpose is recorded in the Book of Daniel.

This day, whatever talents and abilities God has given you, use them fully for His glory and be thankful for that which He has given you.

August 3

"Believe ye that I am able to do this?" (Matthew 9:28).

You do not have to understand. You only have to believe! Vincene Parrinello from Escondido, California, shares an experience during her bout with cancer. She would gaze into the mirror and see her haggard face after going through chemotherapy following a double mastectomy for breast cancer in 1991. She looked much older than her thirty-three years and her skin sagged and her face was ashen. One morning, she stepped into her backyard and sat on an oak bench beneath an orange tree. Birds were twittering in the tree branches, the roses were in full bloom and their fragrance mixed with the smell of herbs in her garden. She said amidst all that beauty she felt so sick and ugly, so alone.

Her mother had died of breast cancer, her father of a brain tumor, and she found herself preparing for her own death, but the thought of being taken from her sons was the loneliest thing she could imagine, and on such a bright day, she felt cold deep down inside.

"I must do something positive!" she told herself. Running her fingers over her face, she suddenly recalled her Italian grandmother and how she had given her wonderful facials when she was a little girl. Her grandma had steeped rose petals and herbs in a pot of steaming water, then held her face over the warm vapors. Afterward, when she looked in the mirror, her cheeks were as rosy as the dawn.

"Why not try it?" said Vincene. She thought, *If I could make myself look healthier, maybe I would feel healthier.* So she went outside and got out her mother's old ravioli pot and heated water. Then she gathered herbs and some rose petals from the garden to simmer, and then steamed her face just as her grandma used to do. She then made a paste from the mixture and applied it to her skin. After about ten minutes she rinsed it off and looked in the mirror. The same ravaged face stared back at her. Although the thought crossed her mind that she was a woman who had cancer and looked as if she were going to die, yet for some reason she still cannot explain, she became obsessed with finding a combination of natural ingredients that would make her look better. Every day she would work at it, reading and experimenting. It was if it were the one thing she could do to fight back against the disease, to take back some control of her body and life.

One morning as she knelt in church, her hair had fallen out and she was in much pain, she was crying out, "Why? Tell me why, God?" when suddenly she felt a light touch on her shoulder. She

turned and saw a handsome young man. He asked, "Is there some way I can help?" She shook her head saying, "My whole life is unraveling. I have no faith left. I don't know why I come here any more."

The young man answered, "God is here, and you may feel that your life is unraveling, but it is only the hem that is unraveled, and it can be mended. It is God who is holding your life together now. You must believe that." Vincene answered, "The cancer, the chemo. It's like I'm being eaten alive."

"But you aren't. You must believe this." A strange warmth flowed through her body as he continued speaking, "Out of your experience will come something that will change your life forever and instill in you new faith and hope—not just in yourself, but in God."

"I don't understand," she said. He answered, "You don't have to. Just believe." From that experience Vincene went on to win her battle against cancer and became president of her own skin-care company called Hope Aesthetics.

The truth is still the same: "We don't have to understand, just believe."

August 4

"For thou, LORD, wilt bless the righteous" (Psalm 5:12).

God loves to put a smile on your face and help take away your frustrations. It is His will to bless those who seek after Him and seek to do His will. It does not matter how dark the night, or how despairing the day, true Love, which is God, will find a way to make it better. I John 4:8 declares, "For God is love."

Love will turn the lights back on and bring joy back into the life of those who are going through a trial as the following poem depicts:

> *I never knew a night so black*
> *Light failed to follow on its track.*
> *I never knew a storm so gray*
> *It failed to have its clearing day.*

I never knew such bleak despair
That there was not a rift, somewhere.
I never knew an hour so drear
Love could not fill it full of cheer!
—JOHN KENDRICK BANGS[307]

Did not God's Word say that He would give us the desires of our heart? He doesn't always do it the way we plan or the way we figure He will do it, but if we go to Him daily in prayer and spend time with Him, it is the pleasure of the Lord to do special things for those who love to be with Him.

Psalm 145:19 declares, "He will fulfil the desire of them that fear him." God will give you your desire, if you continue to spend time with Him each day. Not only will He relieve you of your frustration, but He will surround you with favor and blessing as stated in Psalm 5:12: "For thou, LORD, wilt bless the righteous; with favour wilt thou compass him as with a shield."

Prepare yourself today to receive a favor from God. Let Him relieve you of frustration and replace it with a joyful smile that comes from knowing Him.

August 5

"For the preaching of the cross is to them that perish foolishness; but unto us which are saved it is the power of God" (I Corinthians 1:18).

There is power in the preaching of the cross of Jesus Christ. A young man relates the following story that proves this: "In 1967 while taking a class in photography at the University of Cincinnati, I became acquainted with a young man named Charles Murray who also was a student at the school and was training for the summer Olympics of 1968, as a high diver. Charles was very patient with me as I would speak to him for hours about Jesus Christ and how He had saved me. Charles was raised in a home where no one attended any kind of church, so all that I had to tell him was very fascinating. He even began to ask questions about forgiveness of sin. Finally the day came that I put a question to him: I asked if he realized his own need of a Redeemer and if he was ready to trust Christ as his own Savior. I saw his countenance fall and the guilt in his face. But his reply was a strong 'no.' In the days that followed he was quiet and often I felt that he was avoiding me, until I got a phone call and it was Charles. He wanted to know where to look in the New Testament for some verses that I had given him about salvation. I gave him the reference to several passages and asked if I could meet with him. He declined my offer and thanked me for the scripture. I could tell that he was greatly troubled, but I did not know where he was or how to help him.

"Because he was training for the Olympic games, Charles had special privileges at the university pool facilities. Sometime between 10:30 and 11:00 that evening he decided to go swim and practice a few dives. It was a clear night in October and the moon was big and bright. The pool was housed under a ceiling of glass panes so the moon shone bright across the top of the wall in the pool area. No lights were on; all was dark except the light of the moon when Charles climbed to the highest platform to take his first dive. At that moment the Spirit of God began to convict him of his sins. All the Scripture he had read, all the occasions of witnessing to him about Christ flooded his mind. He stood on the platform backwards to make his dive, spread his arms to gather his balance, looked up to the wall and saw his own shadow caused by the light of the moon. It was the shape of a cross. He could bear the burden of sin no longer. His heart broke and he sat down on the platform and asked God to forgive him and save him. Suddenly the lights in the pool area came on. The attendant had come in to check the pool. As Charles looked down from his platform, he saw an empty pool which had been drained for repairs. He had almost plummeted to his death, but the cross had saved him from disaster."

The power of I Corinthians 1:18: "For the preaching of the cross is to them that perish foolishness; but unto us which are saved it is the power of God" was literally proven to be true that night.

August 6

"Thou shalt be missed, because thy seat will be empty" (I Samuel 20:18).

It is important for every Christian to realize how essential a part he plays in God's kingdom. Once when Jonathan was talking to David, he said to him, "To morrow is the new moon: and thou shalt be missed, because thy seat will be empty" (I Samuel 20:18).

An empty seat signifies that someone is missing. Often after a death in a family, everyone is very aware of the empty seat where the family member who passed on once sat. It triggers a lonely, emotional feeling. Empty chairs, empty homes, empty hearts, there is something sad about the vacant place.

THE EMPTY PEW

The empty pew has an eloquent tongue. Though its message is unpleasant, it is one that all may hear.

To the preacher, the empty pew says, "Your sermon is not worthwhile."

To the visitor it whispers, "You see we are not holding our own."

To the treasurer it shouts, "Look out for a deficit."

To the stranger who is looking for a home church it suggests, "You had better wait awhile."

To the members who are present it asks, "Why don't you go gallivanting next Sunday, too?"

The empty pew speaks against the service. It kills inspiration, it smothers hope, and it dulls the fine edge of zeal. The empty pew is a weight; the occupied pew is a wing.

—GOSPEL BANNER[308]

Your occupied place at church at the appointed time, no matter how insignificant you feel, is a *wing* to all those about you. It lifts not only yourself, but it is a lift to those around you.

Your presence at church is important, but your presence at other places is important also as the following tract demonstrates:

THEY WON'T MISS ME

"They won't miss me!" said the mother as she repeatedly left her children for rounds of teas and parties. The devil did not "miss" the children either.

"They won't miss me!" said the soldier as he went AWOL. But he spent thirty days in the guardhouse after that.

"They won't miss me!" said the man on the assembly line, as he slipped away without permission. But that airplane

crashed and killed his brother for lack of a single part.

"They won't miss me!" said the sentry as he slipped away from duty. But the enemy surprised and massacred his comrades that very night.

"They won't miss me!" said the church member as he shed his responsibilities in a day of crisis, and then wondered why his country gave way to softness and demoralization.

"They won't miss me!" said the church member as he omitted worship one Sunday, and then another, for trivial reasons, and then wondered why he no longer enjoyed a victorious Christian life. —THE CHRISTIAN HERALD[309]

You will be missed if you do not carry on faithfully doing the things that you should do and are supposed to do. You are important to everyone around you. Try this day to not be missed, and take the time to reflect how important you are.

August 7

"For ever, O LORD, thy word is settled in heaven" (Psalm 119:89).

Paul Moody, former professor of zoology, University of Vermont, once said: "The more I study science the more I am impressed with the thought that this world and universe have a definite design, and a design suggests a designer."[310]

In 1956, the October 29 issue of *Time* magazine printed this article: "In general science's discoveries rate in many checkable details. Take the case of a Bible-reading British major who surprised and decimated a Turkish force in Palestine in World War I by attacking through the same narrow mountain pass which Saul and Jonathan had used to fall upon the Philistines centuries earlier. The Bible told just where to look to find it: 'And between the passages . . . there was a sharp rock on the one side, and a sharp rock on the other side. . . . The forefront of the one was situate northward over against Michmash, and the other southward over against Gibeah.'"

Years ago Israeli businessman Xiel Federmann began to brood over the account of the destruction of Sodom and Gomorrah:

"and, lo, the smoke of the country went up as the smoke of a furnace," and guessed that this might indicate underground gas—and underground gas meant oil. He was right. In 1953 Israel's first oil well went into operation near the ancient site of Sodom and Gomorrah.[311]

"The fact that the Standard Oil Company discovered oil and is operating wells in Egypt is generally known, but the reason for its going to that ancient land to look for oil is probably not so well-known.

"It is asserted that one of the directors of the company happened to read the second chapter of Exodus. The third verse caught his attention. It states that the ark of bulrushes which the mother of Moses made for her child was 'daubed with slime and with pitch.'

"This gentleman reasoned that where there was pitch, there must be oil, and if there was oil in Moses' time it is probably still there. So the company sent out Charles Whitshott, its geologist and oil expert, to make investigations, with the result that oil was discovered." —*CHICAGO DAILY NEWS*[312]

There have always been those who have tried to refute the Bible and do away with its authenticity, but no one has ever been able to explain away the evidence that is continually found which proves its existence. Find out for yourself the authority of the Bible as you let it be a guiding force in your life, allowing the supernatural power contained in its pages to be a part of your life today.

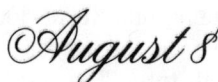

"And Elisha prayed, and said, LORD, I pray thee, open his eyes, that he may see" (II Kings 6:17).

Does it seem like you have not had much sunshine in your life lately, only darkness or hard trials? Have you seemingly been in a dark corridor where you stumble along trying to find your way? You wonder what life is all about, and if there be any joy in the midst of the pain?

There was once an astronomer, Professor Lewis Swift, who was at one time in charge of Warner Observatory of Rochester.

There was also Mundy, a sculptor who was nearly blind, and Dr. Swift determined to make him see a star once more. It was winter and magnificent Sirius, brightest of all the fixed stars, was shining in the south. Dr. Swift took Mundy into a dark alley, set up the instrument, trained it on the star and bade the sculptor to look. He reported he could not see a thing. Then Swift observed that a streetlamp was burning at the corner of the alley. He suspected that even its feeble light was blurring what was left of his friend's sight. He ran and turned it out to perfect the darkness. Then he had Mundy look again through the telescope. It was a thrilling moment when the eye that so long had seen little of earth and nothing of heaven received the flood of light from above. In rapture he exclaimed: "I see it! I see it!"

"*Before one receives heavenly vision sometimes, God often has to deprive him of all earthly lights on which he has depended. When once the mind is set on the things above, there breaks in that light which brings joy eternal.*"

There is the story in II Kings 6 about the servant who was so frightened because of the darkness that had suddenly made him afraid. All he could see was the enemy. He could not see the Lord until his master said, "Fear not: for they that be with us are more than they that be with them." When Elisha prayed for his eyes to be opened, then he saw chariots of fire and horses all around them. What he could not see in the light, he could see in the dark midnight of his life. If there had not been a problem, he never would have needed to see the heavenly host. The dark trial produced the heavenly vision.

If you are in a dark tunnel and storm clouds are surrounding you, pray that the Lord will give you the heavenly vision. Look up, for that is where your help cometh from. The Lord is a present help in the time of trouble and it is in the darkness that the light is revealed.

August 9

"*The fool hath said in his heart, There is no God*" (Psalm 53:1).

There is a God! Be careful of questioning His existence and power. A communist teacher in East Germany once said to a class

of children: "Stand and say, 'There is no God.'" A little eight-year-old girl from a Christian home refused. She was threatened, but she wouldn't say the words. Finally the teacher angrily said, "Go home and write fifty times, 'There is no God,' and give me the paper tomorrow!" That night she sat down and wrote fifty times, in German, "Es gibt doch ein Gott," meaning "There is a God!" The teacher was angry. "When you go home write five hundred times, 'There is no God,' or else!" The "or else" meant terrible punishment. The next day, the father and the little girl went to the superintendent of the school and told him what had happened. "Don't worry," he said to the little girl. "Your teacher was killed in a motorcycle accident last night. The matter is settled. Go to your class."[313]

Recently I received the following email: In Campinas, Brazil, a group of friends, who were drunk, went to pick up a friend. The mother did not want her daughter to go, but her daughter was determined to go, so she accompanied her to the car. While seated in the car, the mother took her daughter's hand and was so worried about the drunkenness of her friends that she said, "My daughter, go with God and may He protect you!" The daughter responded, "Only if He [God] travels in the trunk, 'cause inside here it's already full."

Hours later, news came that her daughter had been involved in a fatal accident, and everyone had died. The car could not be recognized, what type of car it had been, but surprisingly, the trunk remained intact. To their surprise, inside the trunk was a crate of eggs, and none were broken.

God is God and beside Him there is no other. Sometimes He moves swiftly when people jeer and make fun of Him, while other times He moves slowly, but He will not tolerate His name to be mocked. "Be not deceived; God is not mocked" (Galatians 6:7).

This is the day to renew faith in God and allow the wonder of His majesty to fill your mind and His Word to be a daily part of your schedule. He is great and is a power to be reckoned with. Psalm 99:1-3 declares: "The LORD reigneth; let the people tremble: he sitteth between the cherubims; let the earth be moved. The LORD is great in Zion; and he is high above all the people. Let them praise thy great and terrible name; for it is holy."

August 10

"The unsearchable riches of Christ" (Ephesians 3:8).

Many years ago an elderly man living in New Jersey made an unusual discovery as he leafed through an old family Bible. Years earlier, his aunt had died and left it to him. Part of her will read: "To my beloved Steven Marsh I bequeath my family Bible and all it contains, along with the residue of my estate after my funeral expenses and just and lawful debts are paid." When everything had been settled the nephew got a few hundred dollars plus the old Bible mentioned in the will.

After the money was used up, his only support was a small pension, and for more than thirty years he lived in poverty. Then one day he cleaned out his attic in preparation for a move to his son's home where he hoped to spend his old age. There in a trunk was the family Bible he had inherited. Opening it, he was amazed to find bank notes scattered throughout its pages. Within his reach were riches he could have been enjoying all along.[314]

How like some Christians. In the Book of books are many rich promises, but so many live in poverty of soul and spirit when they could be spiritual millionaires.

Much like the ragged man, on a wintry day at twilight, who entered a little music shop on a side street in London. Under his arm was an old violin. "I'm starving," said he to Mr. Betts, the owner of the shop. "Do please buy this old violin so I can get something to eat." Mr. Betts offered him a guinea, worth about five dollars at that time. The man gratefully received it and then shuffled out into the frigid night. When Mr. Betts drew a bow across the strings of the old violin, it produced a rich, mellow tone. How astonished he was! Lighting a candle, he peered intently into the inside of the instrument. There he observed the magic name, Antonio Stradivari, and the date, 1704. He knew instantly that this was the famous violin that had been missing for a hundred years. The attics of Europe had been diligently searched for this missing violin, but in vain. For years the penniless man did not know the value of what he possessed. He lived in poverty on the edge of starvation when he had at his disposal a violin worth thousands of dollars.[315]

This is the day to cash in on the promises of God and to live the abundant life in Christ, living joyously in the presence of the King of kings, and to know that His grace is sufficient for everything you are walking through today.

August 11

"Whereby are given unto us exceeding great and precious promises" (II Peter 1:4).

The Bible is God's love letter to mankind. In it are His promises and truths. He said He would protect and provide for those who followed Him. He said that He would be a Shepherd to His children in the valley, and that He would be a Comforter in times of sorrow, and that He would be a counselor in times of dilemma, and that He would be faithful no matter what. The promises are real and forever written, but many people do not avail themselves of the promises.

The story is told that when Crowfoot, the great chief of the Blackfoot confederacy in southern Alberta, gave the Canadian Pacific Railway permission to cross the Blackfoot land from Medicine Hat to Calgary, he was given in return a lifetime pass. Crowfoot put it in a leather case and carried it around his neck for the rest of his life. There is no record, however, that he availed himself of the right to travel anywhere on the Canadian Pacific Railway.[316]

How many Christians are like Crowfoot? They place the Word of God in a leather case and carry it around for years but never experience the blessings contained in it. God's promises are not for decoration or of only historic value, but they are alive and waiting for someone to put faith in them.

The magnificent nineteenth-century ten-story bank building, known as the "Society of Savings," located in Cleveland, Ohio, was built from unclaimed funds of people. Much of this money was deposited by poor people who died. The directors of the bank, after waiting for years for these depositors to claim that which was theirs, turned the money over to the building of this beautiful bank building.

The unclaimed promises in God's Word are sufficient and are able to build spiritual edifices in life.[317]

God has spoken and His Word will come to pass. Isaiah 55:11 declares: "So shall my word be that goeth forth out of my mouth: it shall not return unto me void, but it shall accomplish that which I please, and it shall prosper in the thing whereto I sent it."

Someone once wrote: *If you have the "blues" read the 27th Psalm. If your pocketbook is empty, read the 7th chapter of Luke. If people seem unkind, read the 13th chapter of Hebrews. If you are discouraged about your work, read the 126th Psalm. If you are all out of sorts, read the 12th chapter of Hebrews.* Whatever you need today, you will find it somewhere in the book of treasures: go find it today in the Holy Bible.

August 12

"Now unto him that is able to do exceeding abundantly above all that we ask or think, according to the power that worketh in us" (Ephesians 3:20).

God always keeps His Word. If He promises something, He will stand behind His promise. There was once a poor philosopher at the court of Alexander who asked for help from him. Alexander gave an order to his treasurer that he should pay the philosopher any amount he asked for. He immediately asked for ten thousand pounds. The treasurer hesitated to pay such an extravagant sum of money, but Alexander replied: "Let the money be instantly paid. I am delighted with this philosopher's way of thinking. He has done me a singular honor. By the largeness of his request, he shows the high idea he has conceived of my wealth and magnificence."

Likewise, God is honored when His children take Him at His Word and believe what He says.

Hudson Taylor, the famous missionary, ventured his life on the promises of God during a crisis in his life. When he first went to China, it was in a sailing vessel. Very close to the shore of cannibal islands the ship was at a standstill and was slowly drifting towards the shore being unable to sail towards their destination

without the wind. Of course, the cannibals were anticipating a feast as they watched the ship slowly approach their island. The captain went to Mr. Taylor and asked him to pray for the help of his God. "I will," said Taylor, "provided you set your sails to catch the breeze." The captain declined to make himself a laughingstock by unfurling in a dead calm. Taylor said, "I will not undertake to pray for the vessel unless you will prepare the sails." So the captain had the sails unfurled. While engaged in prayer, there was a knock at the door of his stateroom. "Who is there?" he asked.

The captain's voice responded, "Are you still praying for wind?" "Yes," he answered.

"Well," said the captain, "you'd better stop praying, for we have more wind than we can manage." —TAKEN FROM *ORIENTAL AND INTERAMERICAN MISSIONARY STANDARD*[318]

Taylor believed that God was able to do exceeding above what he was going to ask Him to do, thereby showing his faith in God's Word by having the captain get the sails ready for the coming wind. He knew before he prayed that God was going to answer his prayer. Today let your faith be steadfast in the Word of God and act accordingly, knowing that God is able to do exceeding above anything that is asked of Him.

"*Who maketh the clouds his chariots*" (Psalm 104:3).

Newscaster Paul Harvey told radio listeners the following remarkable story from World War II: From the island of Guam one of our mighty bombers took off for Kokura, Japan, with deadly cargo. The sleek B-29 turned and circled above the cloud that covered the target for half an hour, three-quarters of an hour, fifty-five minutes, until the gas supply reached the danger point. It seemed a shame to be right over the primary target and then have to pass it up, but there was no choice. With one more look back, the crew headed for the secondary target. Upon arrival, they found the sky clear, "Bombs away!"—the B-29 headed for home.

Weeks later an officer received information from military

intelligence that chilled his heart. Thousands of Allied prisoners of war, the biggest concentration of Americans in enemy hands, had been moved to Kokura a week before the suspended bombing!

"Thank God," breathed the officer. "Thank God for that cloud."

The city which was hidden from the bomber was a prison camp and thousands of Americans are now alive who would have died but for that cloud which rolled in from a sunlit sea.[319]

God made the clouds and is often in the clouds. He controls the clouds. He is in charge of every situation. Psalm 97:1-2 declares: "The LORD reigneth; let the earth rejoice; let the multitude of isles be glad thereof. Clouds and darkness are round about him: righteousness and judgment are the habitation of his throne."

When you are in a tough situation, even a dangerous one, God will come and cover you from the thing that is trying to destroy you. He did this for the children of Israel whom Moses led out of Egypt. Exodus 14, verses 19-20 state: "And the angel of God, which went before the camp of Israel, removed and went behind them; and the pillar of the cloud went from before their face, and stood behind them: and it came between the camp of the Egyptians and the camp of Israel; and it was a cloud and darkness to them, but it gave light by night to these: so that the one came not near the other all the night."

God sent a cloud to separate and keep the enemy from overtaking them, and while the cloud became darkness to the enemy it became a light to God's people.

You may be in a situation where the enemy is trying to overtake and destroy you, but when prayer is made to the delivering God, He will come and cover you. He will put a cloud between you and the object that is determined to destroy you. As you are covered by God's protective cloud, you will emerge the winner.

August 14

"Ask, and it shall be given you" (Luke 11:9).

*E*very day is an adventure in life. With all the negative influences and powers of darkness that be, it is not a good thing to try

to just walk blindly through the maze without asking for God's help. God is waiting for His children to ask for His help. Jesus gave the formula in Matthew 7:7: "Ask, and it shall be given you; seek, and ye shall find; knock, and it shall be opened unto you."

You never know when you are going to need Him in a special way, as once happened to a train engineer. "On the southern road between Atlanta and Birmingham, an engine of a passenger train jumped the track just before it ran onto a high trestle. The engineer slapped on his emergency brakes and reversed his engine. The engine with the train ran out on the trestle. The engine was so neatly balanced that a man could have pushed it off to the gorge below. If it had gone six inches further, it would have gone over and pulled the train with it. It looked like a marvelous providential intervention.

"One of the leading officials of the road said that he went to the engineer and asked what explanation he could give for why the engine did not go over. He replied, 'I don't know whether you are a Christian or not, but I am, and I never go on a run without committing my train and my life into the hands of God. When I saw the danger that day I put on the emergency brakes, reversed the engine and turned my face to God and called for help. I believe it was the hand of God that saved us from a most horrible wreck.'"
—TOLD BY JAMES R. STUART[320]

It does not matter if you are on a plane, a train or in the hospital and even the doctors have given up on you, God is still God and is able to help you. He can do the impossible when He chooses to do so. Dr. Will Mayo of the Mayo Clinic once said, "I have seen patients that were dead by all standards. We knew they could not live. But I have seen a minister come to the bedside and do something for him that I could not do, although I have done everything in my professional power. But something touched some immortal spark in him and in defiance of medical knowledge and materialistic common sense, that patient LIVED!"[321]

Chose not to look at the situation and give up, but look UP to Jesus Christ and follow His advice in the time of need: *Ask and you shall receive, seek and you shall find, knock and it shall be opened unto you.*

God is able! Believe Him for divine intervention in the everyday happenings of life and rest in His promises, submitting our fears to Him and simply believing.

August 15

"I the Lord . . . will keep thee" (Isaiah 42:6).

Charles Spurgeon once wrote: "Faith links me with Divinity. Faith clothes me with the power of Jehovah. Faith insures every attribute of God in my defense. It helps me to defy the hosts of hell. It makes me march triumphant over the necks of my enemies. But without faith how can I receive anything from the Lord?"[322]

Faith is more than just believing God for a miracle; having faith is a way of life. It is walking in His presence believing Him to watch over you and keep you even when you are not aware that you need to be protected by Him.

In the best-selling book *The Hiding Place*, Corrie ten Boom tells of the tense times in Holland during the German invasion. One particular night she tossed restlessly in her bed while war planes flew overhead, shattering the blackness with fiery artillery. After a while she heard her sister downstairs in the kitchen, and because sleep would not come, she went down for a cup of tea. They talked until the night was still again and the sound of fighters died away. Explosions had ripped nearby, but now all was quiet. Stumbling through the darkness to her room, Corrie reached out to pat her pillow before lying down. Suddenly she felt something sharp cutting her hand. It was a jagged piece of metal ten inches long. She cried out for her sister and raced down the stairs with the shrapnel shard in her hand. While Betsie bandaged her hand she kept saying, "On your pillow." Corrie responded, "Betsie, if I hadn't heard you in the kitchen." Betsie replied, "Don't say it, Corrie! There are no *ifs* in God's world. The center of His will is our safety." —C. R. Hembree[323]

Corrie's faith kept her even when she was not aware that she needed to be kept. This same faith kept another couple who lived in a small house with their new baby. For days it had snowed until the roofs of all the homes in that area were heavy with snow. One night a robber entered the home of this Christian couple. As the robber moved about the room where all three were sleeping, the baby began to move and showed signs of awakening. The robber, fearing that the baby might awaken and cry, and thus betray his presence, gently lifted the sleeping infant from his crib and placed him just outside the front door. The baby awakened and began to cry. His crying awakened the father and mother. They ran in the direction where it came from. Just as they ran out the front door, the roof of their home fell in. Later, the robber was found dead beneath the ruins near the things he had stolen.

Their faith in God kept them from evil. God used an evil situation and turned it around for their good. Trust in Him today and let your faith be constant, for He does care about you in everything that happens to you!

August 16

"Men ought always to pray, and not to faint" (Luke 18:1).

*I*f you do nothing else today but pray, you have accomplished a great thing. Jesus said in Luke 18:1, "Men ought always to pray, and not to faint." Throughout the Scriptures prayer is shown to be an essential part of a Christian's lifestyle. It is the way to have power with God. Prayer is the way to God's heart, for He has chosen this to be the way mankind can communicate with Him.

Prayer is a wonderful gift from God to His people. Because of this, there have been millions of disasters averted because of God coming to the rescue of His children in answer to their prayers.

Captain Johnson was serving as chaplain on an island in the South Pacific during World War II. He prepared to go on a bombing raid on enemy-occupied islands several hundred miles away. The mission was a complete success, but on the homeward course the plane began to lose altitude and the engineers faded out. A safe landing was made on a strange island. It was learned later that the enemy was just one-half mile in each direction, yet the landing had gone undetected.

The staff sergeant came to the chaplain and said, "Chaplain, you have been telling us for months of the need of praying and believing God answers prayer in time of trouble, and that He does it right away. We're out of gas, and the base is several hundred miles away, almost surrounded by the enemy."

Johnson began to pray and lay hold of the promises and believed that God would work a miracle. Night came and the chaplain

continued his intense prayer. About 2:00 A.M. the sergeant awakened and felt compelled to walk to the water's edge. He discovered a metal float, which had drifted up on the beach—an octane gas. In a few hours the crew reached their home base safely.

An investigation revealed that the skipper of a U.S. tanker, finding his ship in sub-infested waters, had his gasoline cargo removed, so as to minimize the danger in case of torpedo hit. Barrels were placed on barges and put adrift six hundred miles from where Johnson and the plane crew were forced down. God had navigated one of these barges through wind and current and beached it fifty steps from the stranded men. —EARL C. WILLER[324]

God is still God and can do anything, and He will work wonders to answer His children's intense prayers!

August 17

"I am the first, and I am the last; and beside me there is no God" (Isaiah 44:6).

*T*oday is the day to believe that there is a God and that He is forevermore. Do not join those who do not believe.

George Gallup, founder of the Gallup Statistics, exclaimed: "I could prove God statistically! Take the human body alone. The chance that all the functions of the individual would just happen is a statistical monstrosity!"[325]

The story is told of Kepler, the astronomer who was troubled by one of his friends who denied the existence of God and took the view of the universe which prevails in some circles today, namely, that it came into being of itself by mechanical methods. Kepler, in order to convince his friend, constructed a model of the sun with the planets circling round it. When his friend came into the observatory and saw the beautiful model, he exclaimed with delight, "How beautiful it is! Who made it?" And Kepler carelessly answered, "No one made it: it made itself." His friend looked at him and said, "Nonsense, tell me who made it." Kepler then replied, "Friend, you say that this little toy could not make itself. It is but a very weak imitation of this great universe which, I understood, you believe did make itself." —A. NAISMITH[326]

President Eisenhower once called a person "stupid" if he did not believe in God. Psalm 14:1 declares: "The fool hath said in his heart, There is no God." So to not believe in God puts a person in the class of fools and stupidity.

Thomas Edison said, "No one can study chemistry and see the wonderful way in which certain elements combine with the nicety of the most delicate machine ever invented, and not come to the inevitable conclusion that there is a Big Engineer who is running this universe."[327]

The prophet Isaiah described who the Big Engineer is in Isaiah 40:26, 28: "Lift up your eyes on high, and behold who hath created these things, that bringeth out their host by number: he calleth them all by names by the greatness of his might, for that he is strong in power; not one faileth. . . . Hast thou not known? hast thou not heard, that the everlasting God, the LORD, the Creator of the ends of the earth, fainteth not, neither is weary? there is no searching of his understanding."

"I will instruct thee and teach thee in the way which thou shalt go: I will guide thee with mine eye" (Psalm 32:8).

God gives guidance to those who trust in Him and in His Word. Testifying before the Senate Agriculture Committee on the value of the peanut, George Washington Carver, who as an infant was traded for a broken-down racehorse, said that he got his knowledge of peanuts from the Bible. Asked what the Bible said about peanuts he replied, "The Bible does not teach anything regarding the peanut. But it told me about God, and God told me about the peanut."[328]

The story is told of Admiral Sir Thomas Williams. Many years ago he was in command of a ship crossing the Atlantic. "His course brought him in sight of the island of Ascension, at that time uninhabited and never visited except for the purpose of collecting turtles. The island was barely visible on the horizon, but as Sir Thomas looked at it he was seized by an unaccountable desire to steer towards it. His desire became more and more urgent and distressing,

and foreseeing that it would soon be more difficult to satisfy it, he told his lieutenant to prepare to 'put about ship' and steer in that direction. The officer respectfully protested that changing course would greatly delay them. This only increased the admiral's anxiety, and the ship was steered towards the island.

"All eyes were fixed upon it, and soon something was perceived on the shore. 'It is white—it is a flag—it must be a signal!' someone cried. When they neared the shore they discovered that sixteen men, wrecked on the coast many days before and suffering from hunger, had set up a signal praying to God for help."
—WALTER BAXENDALE[329]

What made the admiral steer his ship in the very opposite direction from what he and his crew wanted was but the supernatural Spirit and guidance from God in answer to someone's prayer.

Alfred Lord Tennyson once wrote these words which sum up the need for prayer:

> *If thou shouldst never see my face again,*
> *Pray for my soul.*
> *More things are wrought by prayer*
> *Than this world dreams of.*
> *Wherefore, let thy voice*
> *Rise like a fountain for me night and day.*
> *For what are men better than sheep or goats*
> *That nourish a blind life within the brain,*
> *If, knowing God, they lift not hands of prayer*
> *Both for themselves and those who call them friend?*
> —ALFRED LORD TENNYSON[330]

This is the day to pray and to find guidance in God's Word; these two things are an unbeatable combination to success and finding true life!

August 19

"Where there is no vision, the people perish" (Proverbs 29:18).

*T*o believe and dream is to live. For without faith a man can do nothing; with it all things are possible. Only he who can see the invisible can do the impossible. Faith sees what others do not see. It enables one to do what those who fear cannot do.

Charles F. Kettering, the noted scientist and inventor, believed the easiest way to overcome defeat was to ignore completely the possibility of failure. Once he was developing this theme in an address delivered at Denison University, Granville, Ohio. He told how he had once given a tough assignment to a young research worker at the General Motors laboratory. Just to see how he would react to a difficult problem, Mr. Kettering forbade him to examine notes on the subject that were filed in the library. These notes were written by expert research men and contained statistics to prove that the assignment was impossible. The young research worker did not know this, of course, so he went to work with confidence that he would succeed. He did succeed, too. He did not know it could not be done—so he did it.
—GOOD BUSINESS[331]

No vision and you perish;
No ideal and you're lost;
Your heart must ever cherish
Some faith at any cost.

Some hope, some dream to cling to,
Some rainbow in the sky,
Some melody to sing to,
Some service that is high.

—HARRIET AUTERMONT

When Henry Ford wanted safety glass for one of his new models he went to his tried and tested engineers for help. All 130 of them knew too many reasons why safety glass could not be produced. Finally, a young engineer, who knew no reason why it could not be done, set to work and developed safety glass.[332]

When Igor Sikorsky was twelve years old, his parents told him that competent authorities had already proved human flight impossible. Yet Sikorsky built the first helicopter. And in his American plant he posted this sign: "According to recognized aero technical tests, the bumblebee cannot fly because of the shape and weight of his body in relation to the total wing area. The bumblebee doesn't

know this, so he goes ahead and flies anyway." —James Hastings[333]

Branch out today in the land of faith, walk with a dream and reach to fulfill it. Believe when there is nothing to believe in, for if God put it in your heart He will help bring it to pass.

Do not give up because others say it cannot be done, but rise and stretch keeping your eyes upon the God of dreams and somehow He will help you win and fulfill them.

August 20

"Be strong and of a good courage" (Joshua 1:6).

Courage is armor a blind man wears;
The calloused scar of outlived despairs;
Courage is Fear that has said its prayers.
    —Karla Baker

One of the amazing stories of sheer courage in the face of tremendous odds is that of Nancy Merki. Stricken with polio at ten, she was condemned to wear heavy braces and later crutches. Yet in four years she became a swimming champion who told President Roosevelt, when he asked her how she had become the youngest champ despite infantile paralysis: "Well, I guess I just kept trying, Mr. President."

Her parents had taken her to a man named Jack Cody, swimming coach at an athletic club in Portland. It took a year to teach her to swim the length of the pool. But she was determined. Finally the coach realized that this young girl was not only interested in swimming as a means of restoring her health and the use of her limbs, she wanted to be a champion. Four years after her paralytic attack, she came in third at a meet in Santa Barbara, California. At the age of nineteen she changed her style of swimming and emerged from the meet as national champion. She just kept trying.[334]

She did what Harriet Beecher Stowe said to do: "When you get into a tight place and everything goes against you, till it seems as though you could not hold on a minute longer, never give up then, for that is just the place and time that the tide will turn."

"A great deal of talent is lost in the world for want of a little

courage. Every day sends to their graves obscure men and women whom timidity prevented from making a first effort; who, if they could have been induced to begin, would in all probability have gone great lengths in the career of fame.

"The fact is that to do anything in the world worth doing, we must not stand back shivering and thinking of the cold and danger, but jump in and scramble through as well as we can."
—SIDNEY SMITH[335]

The story of the twelve spies is famous. Ten were without courage but the other two, Joshua and Caleb, were men of courage. They said, "We are well able to go up and take the land"; whereas the ten weaklings said, "We are not able to go." Which side will you join today, the "we are well able to do it" or the "we are not able to do it" group? God spoke approval of Joshua and Caleb but was angry with the ten men who were without courage.

This is the day to have courage; to go forth even in the face of fears and as we go, God will give strength not of our own and we will win in spite of defeats and threats; for God is able!

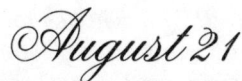

August 21

"To appoint unto them that mourn . . . to give unto them beauty for ashes" (Isaiah 61:3).

*I*f someone's life is in shambles or maybe used up, God can take any life even though it may be broken and torn and make something worthwhile and lovely.

In one of the cathedrals of England there is a beautiful window which the sunlight streams through. It displays the facts and personalities of the Old and New Testaments and the glorious truths and doctrines of the Christian religion. This window was fabricated by the artist out of broken bits of glass which another artist had discarded.[336] You may feel like a discard or not worth much, but when the Master touches your life, He can make it beautiful again as the following reading depicts:

THE TOUCH OF THE MASTER'S HAND
'Twas battered and scarred, and the auctioneer

Thought it scarcely worth his while
To waste much time on the old violin,
But held it up with a smile.
"What am I bidden, good folks," he cried,
"Who will start bidding for me?
A dollar, a dollar"—then, "Two!" he cried,
"Two dollars, and who'll make it three?
Three dollars once; three dollars, twice;
Going for three—" But no,
From the room, far back, a gray-haired man
Came forward and picked up the bow;
Then, wiping the dust from the old violin,
And tightening the loose strings,
He played a melody pure and sweet,
As sweet as a caroling angel sings.
The music ceased, and the auctioneer,
With a voice that was quiet and low,
Said, "What am I bidden for the old violin?"
And he held it up with the bow.
"A thousand dollars, and who'll make it two?
Two thousand! And who'll make it three?
Three thousand, once; three thousand, twice;
And going, and gone!" said he.
The people cheered, but some of them cried,
"We do not quite understand
What changed its worth?"
Swift came the reply;
"The touch of the master's hand."
And many a person with life out of tune,
And battered and scattered with sin,
Is auctioned cheap to the thoughtless crowd,
Much like the old violin.
A "mess of pottage," a glass of wine;
A game and they travel on.
Going once and going twice.
Going and almost gone.
But the Master comes and the foolish crowd
Never can quite understand.
The worth of a soul and the change that's wrought
By the touch of the Master's hand.

—Myra Welch[337]

August 22

"And when they saw him . . . they conspired against him to slay him. And they said one to another, Behold, this dreamer cometh" (Genesis 37:18-19).

Sometimes your dreams might make you the object of ridicule and jealousy, as in the case of a young man who set to work to prevent the repetition of a freight train collision. The result was the invention of the air brake and the beginning of a great industry. Railroad executives took the attitude of Commodore Vanderbilt, who, when George Westinghouse explained the superiority of the air brake over the dangerous hand brakes, exclaimed, "Do you mean to tell me that you expect to stop a train with wind? I have no time to waste on silly fools."

Westinghouse did not give up and complain that his ability was not appreciated. Instead he invented a railroad frog which appealed to the railroad officials and eventually gave him an opportunity to have the air brake tested. That air brake and Westinghouse's system of railway signaling make travel safer.
—HERBERT V. PROCHNOW[338]

Many great people and leaders were ridiculed and talked about before they accomplished their goal. The Wright brothers were considered crazy before they made their airplane fly. Thomas Edison was considered eccentric and at times unreasonable before he invented a light bulb. Fulton was laughed at when he talked about building a boat that was propelled by steam, but while they were laughing he steamed by the negative little group on the banks of the river.

Joseph in the Bible was ridiculed and laughed at by his brothers when he told them about his dreams, but nobody laughed when, thirteen years later, they bowed at his feet, after he had become the most important man in the land next to the king.

Edgar Guest wrote the following poem for those who just go ahead and do it in spite of what the scoffers may say:

Somebody said that it couldn't be done,
But he with a chuckle replied

That "maybe it couldn't" but he would be one
Who wouldn't say so till he'd tried.
So he buckled right in with the trace of a grin
On his face, if he worried he hid it.
He started to sing as he tackled the thing
That couldn't be done and he did it.
Somebody scoffed: "Oh you'll never do that;
At least no one ever has done it"
But he took off his coat and he took off his hat,
And the first thing we knew he'd begun it.
With a lift of his chin and a bit of a grin
Without any doubting or quiddit
He started to sing as he tackled the thing
That couldn't be done and he did it.
There are thousands to tell you it cannot be done,
There are thousands to prophesy failure;
There are thousands to point out to you one by one
The dangers that wait to assail you.
But just buckle in with a bit of a grin,
Just take off your coat and go to it;
Just start to sing as you tackle the thing
That "cannot be done," and you'll do it.

—Edgar A. Guest[339]

August 23

"The LORD is my shepherd; I shall not want" (Psalm 23:1).

Once a pastor in Norfolk, Virginia, phoned the editor of religious news for the newspaper and gave him the topic for his Sunday morning's sermon, "The Lord is my Shepherd." The editor asked, "Is that all?" The pastor replied, "That's enough." The editor, thinking that the words were part of his subject, announced the pastor's topic as follows: "The Lord is My Shepherd: That's Enough!"

To know that the Lord is our protector and provider and is always there to take care of us, helps take away our fears and comforts us in our sorrow. No matter what happens, our times are in His hands. He is taking care of us as the following poem depicts:

MY TIMES ARE IN HIS HANDS
My times are in that mighty hand
That formed the earth, the moon and stars;
That measured oceans, heaven spanned,
And for the sea set doors and bars.

Why should I fear what man can do,
When in that Hand I rest secure?
In life, or death, 'twill bear me through
There I have shelter, safe and sure.

My times are in my Father's Hand,
How could I wish or ask for more?
For He who has my pathway planned,
Will guide me till my journey's o'er.

My times are in my Saviour's Hand,
Nail-pierced upon the cross for me,
And He will lead me to that land,
Where I with Him shall ever be.
—MARGARET K. FRASER[340]

In his book, Walter B. Knight tells about how one morning he received an early morning emergency call to go to a distant hospital. "During the night a heavy fog had blanketed Chicago. As I went to the garage for my car, I became alarmed as I thought upon the shadowy dangers I would encounter on the drive to the hospital. With great apprehension I backed my car into the murky street. As I drove cautiously along I soon observed that the ghostly, indistinct, distant objects became clearly visible when I reached them. My fears subsided. 'How like the will of God!' I said to myself.

"As we move forward the surrounding guideposts are clearly visible. The indistinct, unknown ones shine with light when we approach them. It is step by step that He leads us."[341]

It is good to sing the old song that echoes this sentiment:

I don't know about tomorrow,
I just live from day to day;
I don't borrow from its sunshine,
For its skies may turn to gray.
Many things about tomorrow

I don't seem to understand;
But I know who holds tomorrow,
And I know who holds my hand.

August 24

"*Whosoever will lose his life for my sake shall find it*" (Matthew 16:25).

There was a wealthy nobleman in Italy who had grown tired of life. He had everything one could wish for except happiness and contentment. He said, "I am weary of life. I will go to the river and there end my life." As he walked along, he felt a little hand tugging at his trousers. Looking down, he saw a frail, hungry-looking boy who pleaded, "There are six of us. We are dying for want of food!" The nobleman thought, "Why should I not relieve this wretched family? I have the means." Following the little boy, he entered a scene of misery, sickness and want. He opened his purse and he emptied all of its contents, saying, "I'll return tomorrow, and I will share with you more of the good things which God has given to me in abundance!" He left that scene of want and wretchedness, rejoicing, with no thought of ending his life. —Told by Walter B. Knight[342]

Jesus said it this way, "Whosoever will save his life shall lose it: but whosoever will lose his life for my sake, the same shall save it." A life that is lived selfishly for self alone will be miserable, but a life that is given in living for others, to bless and help them, will find true happiness. When God's love comes into a life, there must be a continuation of that love invested into the lives of others.

There was once a minister who was discussing electricity with an electrician. "Is it true," asked the minister, "that electricity cannot get into you unless it can get out of you?" "That's absolutely right," answered the electrician. "Let me illustrate. When I worked in the coal mines in Pennsylvania, my brother operated one of the coal cars. I was standing on the rear of the car, singing in a carefree manner. Coming to a point where the tracks divided, my head got caught in the overhead frog. There I dangled for a moment, my feet just clearing the ground. That explains my being here today. The high voltage current couldn't get into me because it couldn't get out of me." —TOLD BY WALTER B. KNIGHT[343]

This is how God desires for His love to work. After His love gets inside of us, He wants it to be spread to those around us. His love should not be a dead-end street or kept bottled up inside; it must flow out and help other people.

This generation looks upon a loser with either pity or disgust, but losing one's life for God's sake is a totally different type of losing. It is not losing because of lack of talent; it is losing one's selfish ambition for a higher calling: to do the Master's bidding. This kind of losing is really the way to gain and become truly rich and successful in God. It just takes spiritual understanding to see it.

"*Wait on the LORD, and keep his way*" (Psalm 37:34).

Sometimes waiting is the hardest thing to do. Most people are forever in a hurry. Like the psalmist, they impatiently pray, "O LORD . . . haste thee to help me" (Psalm 22:19).

"*Remember that the cogs of our lives are geared to the cogs of God's workings. The gear teeth of God's plans are stronger than our own. When we speed up while God keeps His own pace we strip our gears. We wear out.*" —WALTER B. KNIGHT[344]

Once a minister, with a group, visited a glacier grotto that was reached by a tunnel bored through solid ice. As the group penetrated into the chilly depths away from the outside sunshine, the light became dimmer and dimmer and when they stood in the narrow chamber at the end of the passage, the darkness was as black as pitch. "Wait," said the guide, "and in five minutes you shall see light clearly." They waited and it was just as he had told them. What happened was this: as the eye got accustomed to its new surroundings, the atmosphere gradually brightened, the walls and roof of the grotto glimmered into pure translucent green, and in the clear soft light that encircled the group they could recognize the faces of their companions and read their guidebooks. This is what waiting can do. It can open our eyes to see the beautiful things of God all around us even in the dark times of our lives, but which only patient waiting eyes can see.

A Christian once visited another Christian who was going through a great trial of distress and affliction, which he bore with such patient and composed resignation. This attitude caused the friend to inquire how he was able to do so. He answered, "The distress I am under is indeed severe; but I find it lightens the stroke very much to creep near to Him who handles the rod."

Learning to wait on God is drawing near to Him and resting in His presence; for even in the trial, in His presence is fullness of joy. To wait patiently is the mark of a true Christian. Learn to rest in God today.

August 26

"O Lord God . . . I have cried day and night before thee: Let my prayer come before thee . . . For my soul is full of troubles" (Psalm 88:1-3).

*I*f you are in trouble today, try praying about it. General Eisenhower once said, "Prayer gives you courage to make the decisions you must make in a crisis and then the confidence to leave the result to a Higher Power."[345]

Dr. Hysloop, psychiatrist, said, "As one whose whole life has been concerned with the sufferings of the mind, I would state that of all the hygienic measures to counteract disturbed sleep, depression of spirits, and all the miserable sequels of a distressed mind, I would undoubtedly give the FIRST place to the simple habit of prayer."[346]

Prayer is powerful! A thrilling incident happened in a little hut in Africa. A missionary awoke suddenly with a feeling of imminent danger. Fear held her in a vise-like grip. The moon's rays shone through the window, but she could see nothing wrong. She continued to have a feeling of great danger so she awoke her husband. They talked in a whisper. Looking beside the bed, they saw a fearsome creature: a giant cobra whose head was raised, ready to strike and inject venom into the flesh of the missionaries. Quickly the husband reached for his rifle and shot the cobra through its head. But that is not the end of the story.

One day while a friend of the missionaries was sweeping the

floor of her Canadian house, she had an irresistible urge to pray for these missionaries. "They are right now in great danger," she said to herself. So she began to pray. Presently God's peace came into her heart. She knew that God had worked in behalf of her faraway friends. Later, when the missionaries told her of their frightful experience, she compared the date and time of the two experiences. The peril of the missionaries and the burden to pray for them corresponded to the minute. —TOLD BY WALTER B. KNIGHT[347]

Someone once said: "Prayer is not overcoming God's reluctance; it is laying hold of His highest willingness."

Learn to pray today and enjoy a life of great victory through the power of the Lord Jesus Christ who is ever present with those who call upon His name!

August 27

"Take no thought for your life" (Matthew 6:25).

There is a difference in thinking seriously about a difficult situation and worrying about the same. To worry is to be full of anxiety and fretfulness. Someone said, "Worry is the advance interest you pay on troubles that seldom come."

"Worry, like a rocking chair, will give you something to do, but it won't get you anywhere." —VANCE HAVNER

It was Maclaren who explained what worry does to an individual: "What does your anxiety do? It does not empty tomorrow of its sorrow, but it empties today of its strength. It does not make you escape the evil: it makes you unfit to cope with it if it comes."[348]

Jesus instructed His followers to not worry in Luke 12:22, 24: "Take no thought for your life, what ye shall eat; neither for the body, what ye shall put on. . . . Consider the ravens: for they neither sow nor reap . . . God feedeth them: how much more are ye better than the fowls?" Jesus stated further in Luke 21:34: "And take heed to yourselves, lest at any time your hearts be overcharged with surfeiting, and drunkenness, and cares of this life."

Having a heart overcharged with the cares of life is what He warned against. It is so much better to take your troubles to the Lord. When life gets fraught with care and the load is more than you can bear, just go to Jesus and let Him make a way where there seems to be no way.

Edward Everett Hale gave good advice about worry: "Never bear more than one trouble at a time. Some people bear three kinds: all they ever had, all they have now, and all they expect to have."[349]

The past is over, cannot be changed; the future is unknown and cannot be lived until it arrives; we have only today, so why not trust today in His hand and not carry all the baggage of yesterday and problems of today on our shoulders. Give it to Jesus.

One of Cromwell's officers was given to the habit of worry and anxious care. One day his godly servant who knew how to live in the today and leave the tomorrow to the care of his Lord said to his worrisome boss, "Master, the Lord ran this world before you came into it," to which Cromwell quickly assented. "You expect Him to run it after you leave it, do you not?" Again Cromwell nodded assent. "Then how would it do to let Him run it while you are in it?"

This is good advice; the Lord ran things before we got here, and He will run them after we leave, so why not let Him be in charge of things while we are here? The one who is in charge must carry the load, so give your burden to the Lord each day and let Him carry it while you rest in His promises. Do all you can do and let Him take care of what you cannot do!

"*The hand of the diligent maketh rich*" (Proverbs 10:4).

This is the day to not rely on luck but on diligence. Proverbs 10:4 states: "He becometh poor that dealeth with a slack hand: but the hand of the diligent maketh rich."

"*Some people fail to recognize opportunity because it so often comes to them in overalls and looks like work.*"

Gobden once wrote: "*Luck is waiting for something to turn up. Labor, with keen eyes and strong will, will turn up something. Luck lies in bed, and wishes the postman would bring him news of a legacy. Labor turns out at six o'clock and with busy pen or ringing hammer lays the foundation of a skill.*"

On Lincoln's birthday an interesting cartoon appeared in a newspaper. It showed a small log cabin at the base of a mountain, and the White House at the top of the mountain. A ladder connected the two buildings. At the bottom of the cartoon were these words: "The ladder is still there!" To climb that ladder, however, means sweat and toil.

The following poem says it well:

I bargained with life for a penny,
And life would pay no more,
However I begged at evening
When I counted my scanty store;
For Life is a just employer,
He gives you what you ask,
But once you have set the wages,
Why, you must bear the task.
I worked for a menial's hire,
Only to learn dismayed,
That any wage I had asked of Life,
Life would have paid.
—Jesse B. Rittenhouse[350]

One step won't take you very far;
You've got to keep on walking;
One word won't tell folks who you are;
You've got to keep on talking;

One inch won't make you very tall;
You've got to keep on growing;
One deed won't do it all;
You've got to keep on going.
—Author Unknown

Once is not enough. You must keep on trying, keep on working, but keep on until you succeed: *Noah Webster* labored thirty-six years writing his dictionary, crossing the Atlantic twice to gather material. *William Cullen Bryant* rewrote one of his poetic masterpieces ninety-nine times before publication, and it became a classic. *Sir Walter Scott* put in fifteen hours a day at his desk, rising at 4:00 o'clock in the morning. He averaged a book every two months. *Adam Clarke* spent forty years writing his commentary on the Holy Scriptures. *George Stephenson* spent fifteen years to

perfect the locomotive. Vulcanization of rubber cost *Charles Goodyear* ten years of study, poverty and public ridicule.

Laziness is no excuse. If you believe something and are willing to work at it until it is successful, nothing can keep you from climbing that same ladder that Abraham Lincoln climbed. Just keep working hard at what God put in your heart to do and eventually it will pay off in rich dividends.

August 29

"I have fought a good fight, I have finished my course, I have kept the faith" (II Timothy 4:7).

Never give up on things that are important to you. McCormick felt discouraged but did not give in to his feelings. McCormick's father was a mechanical genius and invented many farm devices, but he had become the laughingstock of the community on account of his failure to make a grain-cutting device operate successfully. In spite of the discouragements of his father and the ridicule of the neighbors, young McCormick took up the old machine, and after years of experiment and failure, finally succeeded in constructing a reaper which would cut grain. But even then jealous opposition prevented it from being used, and it was only after years of labor to introduce it, and his personal guarantee to each purchaser that it would harvest the crop, that he succeeded in making sales. After long years of waiting, he arranged with a firm in Cincinnati to manufacture one hundred machines, and the famous McCormick reaper was born.[351]

The following poem says it well:

When things go wrong as they sometimes will,
When the road you're trudging seems all uphill.
When the funds are low and the debts are high,
And you want to smile, but you have to sigh,
When care is pressing you down a bit,
Rest, if you must; but don't you quit.
Life is queer with its twists and turns,
As every one of us sometimes learns,

And many a failure turns about
When he might have won had he stuck it out;
Don't give up, though the pace seems slow—
You might succeed with another blow.

Often the goal is nearer than
It seems to a faint and faltering man,
Often the struggler has given up
When he might have captured the victor's cup,
And he learned too late, when the night slipped down,
How close he was to the golden crown.
Success is failure turned inside out—
The silver tint of the clouds of doubt—
And you never can tell how close you are,
It may be near when it seems afar;
So stick to the fight when you're hardest hit—
It's when things seem worst that you mustn't quit.
—AUTHOR UNKNOWN[352]

It was James J. Corbett, former heavyweight champion of the world, who said, "Fight one more round. When your feet are so tired that you have to shuffle back to the center of the ring, fight one more round! When your arms are so tired that you can hardly lift your hands to come on guard, fight one more round! When your nose is bleeding and your eyes are black and you're so tired that you wish your opponent would crack you one on the jaw and put you to sleep—Don't quit—Fight one more round."[353]

Paul uttered those famous words nearly two thousand years ago, "I have fought, I have finished, and I have kept the faith." The principle is still the same. It's not enough to start something; it must be finished. Today just keep on until the taste of victory is in your mouth. It may be nearer than you think.

August 30

"Thou art the God that doest wonders" (Psalm 77:14).

There is an old song that says, "The Lord moves in mysterious ways, His wonders to perform." Major Michael Halt from North Carolina shares how God works in mysterious ways that are sometimes baffling for us, in order to answer our prayers.

He wrote: "The order had come down at last. The ground invasion of Kuwait was about to commence. My battalion would cross the Kuwait border as part of Operation Desert Storm. I was the second in command of 130 brave Marines who were about to face the most daunting challenge of their military lives. We'd already dodged heavy artillery fire and now we'd likely face more dangers, like land mines and oil fires. Thousands of Iraqi troops waited just beyond the Kuwaiti border. It was time for us to make the final strategic push. *Dear God,* I prayed, *help me to lead my troops wisely. Watch over us. Keep us safe.* I walked from one group of Marines to another, talking to them about the mission and trying to keep their spirits up. Hunched against the dry, biting desert winds, we wrote letters home. Maybe our last. Just before dawn the next morning I gave the order to move out. The skies were clear. We slung our gear into our Humvees and began advancing toward the border. I felt a drop of rain, then another. In a matter of minutes it was pouring. The rain came down hard and fast, so thick we could barely make out the desert landscape ahead of us. It went on for days. Each morning we'd awaken soaked to the bone after another night with only camouflage netting for cover. Bad enough we had the enemy to worry about. Now the elements were against us too. I prayed, *Father, please make this rain stop and protect us.* The rain continued to pound us relentlessly until we finally neared the Kuwaiti border. There the battalion halted. On the other side, the enemy waited. Rain or no rain, we'd soon be going in. We awoke on the day of the invasion to clear skies and glorious sunshine. As we closed in on the border, we couldn't help but stare at the astounding sight before us. The torrential rains had washed away the sand to reveal metal disks planted all across our path. It was a Iraqi minefield."

When it seemed like God wasn't listening and prayers were not heard, God was there all the time. In one breath Major Halt had prayed, *stop the rain and protect us*. But God knew in order for the greater miracle to be done (the protection of the men), the rain would have to proceed without stopping. That was God's way of answering prayer. He was there when it seemed like He was not, working all things for their good. God is always great and glorious every day. Whether we are in a crisis or just having an ordinary day, God is there.

August 31

"But the word of the Lord endureth for ever" (I Peter 1:25).

*I*n a shaky world, there is one thing you can put your trust in: that is the Word of God. Isaac Watts once said: "I believe the promises of God enough to venture an eternity on them." Isaiah 40:8 states: "The grass withereth, the flower fadeth: but the word of our God shall stand for ever." It does not matter what happens around you; cling to the Word of God and somehow the God of the Word will see you through. Memorize it, love it, keep the Word close to you in your mind and spirit—you never know when you are going to need it.

Dr. Wilfred T. Grenfell found this to be true. He wrote: "To me the memorizing of Scripture has been an unfailing help in doubt, anxiety, sorrow, and all the countless problems of life. I believe in it enough to have devoted many, many hours of stowing away passages where I can neither leave them behind me nor be unable to get to them. The Word of God is the Christian's best weapon and must be with him always. Facing death alone on a floating piece of ice on a frozen ocean, the comradeship it afforded me supplied all I needed. It stood by me like the truest of true friends that it is. With my whole would I commend to others the giving of some time each day to secure the immense returns that memorizing the Word of God offers and insures."[354]

King George V once said: "It is my confident hope that my subjects may never cease to cherish their noble inheritance in the English Bible which is the first of national treasures. Its spiritual significance is the most valuable thing the world affords."[355]

Realize today that of all the treasures on the earth the Bible is still the greatest treasure one can possess. It is an everlasting source of inspiration, gives hope to the hopeless, and brings light to a darkened mind. It is truly more valuable than gold, fame, or any other great thing the world can offer.

President George Washington once said: *"It is impossible to*

rightly govern the world without God and the Bible."[356] If it is impossible to govern the world without the Bible, even so, it is impossible to successfully govern our own private worlds without the Bible.

President Abraham Lincoln said, "I believe the Bible is the best gift God has ever given to man. All the good from the Savior of the world is communicated to us through this book."[357] Today is the day to take the best gift and hold it close to us and treat it with great respect as we read a word sent from God to us! Get a hold on it and refuse to let go!

September 1

"*No weapon that is formed against thee shall prosper*" (Isaiah 54:17).

It may look like you are hanging by a thread, or you are at the end of the end, but hang on; God's eye is on you and He will not fail you. Just when it looks impossible to hold on, that is when God sends an answer.

"During the siege of Sebastopol, a Russian shell buried itself in the side of a hill without the city, and opened up a spring. A little fountain bubbled forth where the cannon shot had fallen and during the remainder of the siege afforded to the thirsty troops who were stationed in that vicinity an abundant supply of pure cold water. Thus, the missile of death from an enemy, under the direction of an overruling God, proved to be a lifesaver to the parched and weary soldiers of the allies."[358]

You may feel like the enemy is gaining ground and things are getting worse instead of better, but do not give up, for God said in Isaiah 54:17, "No weapon that is formed against thee shall prosper." It may look like things are closing in, but that is when the Lord will help you—in your greatest dilemma.

He said in Isaiah 43:11-13: "I, even I, am the Lord; and beside me there is no saviour. I have declared, and have saved. . . . Yea, before the day was I am he; and there is none that can deliver out of my hand: I will work, and who shall let it?"

The Lord can take a circumstance that seemingly is going to

destroy you, just as the missile would have seemingly destroyed the weary soldiers, and instead of death can give you new life and hope in the midst of a weary situation. Hold to God's unchanging hand. He can guide the missiles, the onslaughts, weapons of death or discouragement and make them a spring that will strengthen you.

Let your dark and bitter times cause you to know Him better, and let them not make you bitter. Seek Him today while you are in the trial because He cares for you whether it looks like He does or not. He does care! He is with you even in the battle; not only while the sun is shining. Why fret, fear, or have despair, when God is on your side? This is the day to put your faith in God and see what He will do in your darkest trial.

September 2

"For thy good" (Deuteronomy 10:13).

*I*n teaching the children of Israel the commandments and statutes of the Lord, Moses made this statement, but it ended with a question mark: Deuteronomy 10:13: "To keep the commandments of the Lord, and his statutes, which I command thee this day for thy good?"

Moses was letting them know that God does not bring evil, but only good for His children; therefore, if evil comes to us, then we need to turn it around for good.

"Whatever evil befalls us, we ought to ask ourselves, after the first suffering, how we can turn it into good. So shall we take occasion, from one bitter root, to raise perhaps many flowers." —Leigh Hunt[359]

Things happen that tempt one to worry and fret and let his mind be disturbed. These are the things that rob a person of peace, the dwelling on and magnifying of trifles that should be forgotten.

"Do not let trifles disturb your tranquility of mind. The little pinpricks of daily life when dwelt upon and magnified, may do great damage, but if ignored or dismissed from thought, will disappear from inanition. Most men have worried about things which never happened, and more men have been killed by worry than by hard work. Life is so great in its opportunities

335

and possibilities, that you should rise confidently above the inevitable trifles incident to daily contact with the world. Life is too precious to be sacrificed for the nonessential and transient. . . . Ignore the inconsequential." —GRENVILLE KLEISER[360]

The right thing to do is to not worry about things that have happened and cannot be changed. They sap strength from your mind, strength that could be applied to productive things. So ignore the things that you have no control over and do not let them dominate your thinking processes. Realize that if it happened, that somehow it will work out for your good, if you do not allow it to kill you in the meantime.

Truth still reigns as stated in Romans 8:28: "And we know that all things work together for good to them that love God, to them who are the called according to his purpose."

If you love God and are doing your best to follow His Word and practices, then nothing can erase the fact that *all things work together for good*.

As has been used before, it is like baking a cake. If each of the ingredients used in the mix were eaten separately it would not taste good, but it is the mixing together of all the ingredients that make it taste good. Some experiences alone are bitter just as the baking powder alone is not good, but together with the other ingredients, it is not bitter but good.

So know today that God is working all things for your good!

"Therefore I love thy commandments above gold; yea, above fine gold" (Psalm 119:127).

Take time today to enjoy one of the greatest gifts God gave to mankind, the Bible. It is a treasure house of truths, a gold mine of beautiful thoughts, and the secret of life. It seems as if some of these secrets are hidden. They must be searched for, studied and then they will spring to life.

Once a man inherited an antique desk and one day by accident he touched a secret spring which opened a hidden drawer. Inside was a great sum of money. The antique desk was valuable,

but the treasure it contained was much more valuable. God's Word is priceless and precious. Unknown spiritual riches await those who will search therein for them as Psalm 19:10 states: "More to be desired are they than gold, yea, than much fine gold: sweeter also than honey and the honeycomb."

The Bible should be prominently placed in the home, not hidden away in some dark, dusty corner, but made an integral part of everyday life. The story is told of how some Christian women met in a home in Hollywood for their weekly Bible study. The leader, standing before the group, said, "Oh my, I came away without my Bible." The hostess hurried away to get her Bible. She looked where she usually kept it, but it wasn't there. She searched for it but couldn't find it. *What will those ladies think of me?* she thought. Running downstairs, she said to the newly employed cleaning woman, "Mattie, have you seen my Bible?" Mattie exclaimed, "Praise the Lord." "Why, what do you mean, Mattie?" Beaming, Mattie said, "The first thing I do when I go to work at a new place is to hide the Bible." "But why?" asked her employer in astonishment. Mattie said, "Just to find out how long it takes the people to miss it. You'll find your Bible in the linen closet under the sheets."

The question is, "Where is your Bible today? Have you read something that will enrich your soul, heart and mind, or is it hidden away in a dark spot waiting to be opened and read so that the riches inside can be enjoyed?"

Most people will pick up the newspaper and read the disheartening news day after day and are made no better for having done so, but who takes the time to be as faithful to read the Book that is full of good news for those who are in love with its Author?

Pick up the Book of books and keep it close to you in a prominent place and let the reading of it become an everyday ritual, and you will experience the promises for this life and the life to come.

"And being fully persuaded that, what he had promised, he was able also to perform" (Romans 4:21).

When God makes a promise, *Faith* believes it, *Hope* anticipates it, and *Patience* waits for it. Life does not always go the way we want it to go, and sorrows come to the best of families, but what God promises, He is able to perform. The key is to trust in Him and believe in His promises no matter what happens, for when God is involved there is no need to understand, only to trust in Him.

It was Victor Hugo who said, *"Have courage for the great sorrows of life and patience for the small ones, and when you have accomplished your daily task, go to sleep in peace. God is awake."* This is true trust, when someone can sleep through the storm, or be at peace when chaos surrounds him, for he knows God is in control.

Some years ago a converted sergeant-major in the Middle East had charge of the locomotive which ran near Cairo. "After his conversion he made it a practice, before starting on each journey, to pray for the safety of the train and of his passengers. On one journey the engine suddenly stopped for no apparent reason. A civil engineer on the train, as well as the engine staff, tried in vain to discover the cause of the breakdown which took place at 3:00 one wet morning. As dawn approached, two workmen came running farther down the line with the news that a rainstorm had made a hole large enough to engulf the whole train had it kept going. 'What luck!' the passengers said. But the driver quietly gave his witness and spoke of the prayer he offered for their safety every time he took his place on the footplate. Strangely enough, as it seemed to the passengers, the engine started without a hitch when the track had been repaired after a fourteen-hour holdup." —*ALLIANCE WEEKLY*[861]

The engineer had learned to trust God to take care of his train and also the passengers. He believed, and God did the rest. Each of us has a way to go, there are pitfalls that are unseen that we know nothing about, but if we pray every day, there is a God who hears and answers prayer when we put our faith and trust in Him to take care of us. He will be with us today and tomorrow as the following poem illustrates:

FAITH FOR TOMORROW
"Tomorrow, friend, will be another day,"
A seer wise of old was wont to say
To him who came at eventide, in grief,
Because the day had borne no fruitful sheaf.

*O Lord of Life, that each of us might learn
From vain todays and yesterdays to turn,
To face the future with a hope newborn
That what we hope for cometh with the morn!*
—Thomas Curtis Clark[362]

This day remember to take the time to pray first and then rest in His promises. We do not always need to know everything; we just need to know God. When we know Him and He becomes involved in our lives, everything is then placed in His hands and He will take care of us. It is a promise!

September 5

"Choose you this day whom ye will serve" (Joshua 24:15).

Be careful of the choices you make today, for choices help to determine destiny. This is proven in the story of David Livingstone, the famed missionary. When his body was brought back from Africa to England, great throngs along the street watched the funeral procession. An elderly man in the crowd burst into sobs. He lamented, "I knew Livingstone when I was a young man. We did things together. We were friends. When he told me of God's call to him to go to Africa, I ridiculed him. I was ambitious. I chose a life of self-ease. I cared only for my own selfish interests. Now, with a misspent life behind me, I acknowledge that Livingstone made a wise choice when he answered and obeyed God's call. I put the emphasis on the wrong world."

Dr. Pierce Harris, one of the pastors in Atlanta, Georgia, went to speak at a prison to some prisoners. The prisoner who introduced him said, "Several years ago, two boys lived in a town in north Georgia. They went to the same school, played together and attended the same Sunday school. One dropped out of Sunday school and said that it was 'sissy stuff.' The other boy kept going. One rejected Christ; the other accepted Him. The boy who rejected Christ is making the introduction today. The boy who accepted

Christ is the honored preacher who will speak to us today."

Where will your choices lead you? What decisions do you face today that will affect your tomorrows? If people knew that they could help shape their future by their choices today, they would be more careful of what they chose. Yes, choices today help mold the tomorrows. It is essential to not just hastily make decisions but to measure our steps, measure our ways and measure carefully our decisions.

This happened in the life of Peter. After he had betrayed the Christ, he could have retreated and let himself become a derelict, but he chose to humble himself and go to an upper room and pray until there came a rushing mighty wind and it filled the house where they were praying. There it was a transformed Peter who became the spokesman on the Day of Pentecost and preached a powerful message of faith and deliverance. All because, even after he failed once, he chose to not stay a failure, but chose to go to the One who could set him free and give him a new life. Whatever you chose yesterday, whether good or bad, remember today is a new day, so choose that which will propel you towards success in God.

September 6

"Praying always with all prayer and supplication in the Spirit" (Ephesians 6:18).

Today is the day to do something that causes the devil to tremble, something that gets God's attention. That something is prayer.

The story is told of how every night a little girl named Mary would kneel at her bedside and pray while Mother stood nearby. One night Mary prayed longer than usual. When she finally arose, Mother asked, "Why did you pray so long tonight?" Said little Mary, "Today in church we sang a song that said, 'Satan trembles when he sees the weakest saint upon his knees.' I wanted to make him tremble longer." —Told by Walter B. Knight[363]

Prayer is such a powerful weapon not only against hell's intentions, but also against depression and sickness. Dr. William Sadler once wrote: "Prayer is a safety valve for the mind and the soul. If Christianity were practically applied to our everyday life it

would so purify and vitalize the race that at least one-half of our sickness and sorrow would disappear."[364] Prayer is powerful!

John R. Mott said, *"Prayer is the greatest force we can wield. It is the greatest talent God has given. He has given it to every Christian. What right have we to leave unappropriated or unapplied the greatest force which God has ordained for the salvation and transformation of men?"*[365]

How is your prayer power today? Have you been to the Master? Did He touch your soul and mind with His presence? David wrote in Psalm 16:11: "Thou wilt shew me the path of life: in thy presence is fulness of joy; at thy right hand there are pleasures for evermore." It is time to go into His presence and enjoy the joy and pleasures of God.

Find a place to pray and pour your heart out to God. Let Him know you love Him, that you trust Him and need Him. As you begin to talk to Him, you will soon feel His presence envelop your soul and a little bit of heaven come into your life. The King of kings comes to visit you in a special way, and the tears will flow as you release your pent-up feelings to the great Counselor—the One who can do all things exceedingly above what you are asking Him to do.

He is saying, "Come unto me, all ye that are weary and heavy laden, and I will give you rest." He is waiting to give you rest for your soul and has gifts to bestow upon you. It just takes stopping what you are doing for a little while and going into His presence to receive His gifts, His blessings, and to experience His presence. This is the day to take time to pray!

"Love your enemies, bless them that curse you, do good to them that hate you" (Matthew 5:44).

*I*f you want to live life to the fullest and be healthy—learn to love everyone. Dr. Andrew Ivy once said, "Religious attitudes of mind help keep men's bodies healthy. Attitudes such as love, faith, hope, unselfishness, forgiveness, tolerance, and a desire for justice and truth set the body at rest and strengthen it physically. Anti-religious attitudes such as hate, envy, jealousy, guilt, vanity,

malice, vindictiveness and selfishness put a strain on the body and are conducive to the development of disease."[366]

Harry Emerson Fosdick wrote, "*Hating people is like burning down your own house to get rid of a rat.*"[367]

Booker T. Washington once said, "I am determined to permit no man to narrow or degrade my soul by making me hate him."[368]

Who would want to hate if it brings darkness, murderous thoughts and degradation as described by Booker T. Washington? This is not the day to burn down your house to get rid of the rat of hate; it is the day to call the exterminators. Save the house, kill the rat. The house is you; the rat is the emotion of hate.

The good news is that if anyone sins by hating, he has an advocate with the Father. They can go to Him in the time of need and He will give them grace to deal with difficult people and help eradicate that poisonous substance out of their brain and body. Hate is a killer and will snuff the life out of someone quicker than anything.

John J. Harrington, national president of the Fraternal Order of Police and a twenty-seven-year veteran of the Philadelphia police force says, "There is hatred today in this country that's growing and growing. Near where I live a man was walking to church and two men came up behind him and cut his throat. Another man was just standing on a street corner when a bunch of kids came along. They said, 'Let's give it to him,' and they killed him. And a little girl was walking up the street from where I live, and a boy just came along and stabbed her. All these things seem to happen for no reason at all—just hatred." —Told by Homer Duncan[369]

Hatred is a murderer. Do not let it rest in your bosom. Fling it from you. Ask the Lord to heal your mind and emotions, to cleanse your physical "house." This is the day to allow no one to degrade you by making you hate them. Be set free and you will live in the sunshine of God's love!

"If ye have faith as a grain of mustard seed . . . nothing shall be impossible unto you" (Matthew 17:20).

When Mary, the mother of Jesus, was told of the miracle birth that she was to experience, she asked, "How can these things be?" It seemed so impossible to her. The angel told Mary in Luke 1:37, "For with God nothing shall be impossible."

The following poem says it well:

He took the loaves and fishes few
And fed the hungry throng.
He saw the mite of faith he had
And made the cripple strong.

He took the lumps of clay and gave
The blind man precious sight.
He, seeing Mary's trust in Him,
Brought Lazarus back to life.

He takes my whispered, silent prayer,
My faith like mustard seed
And makes what once was vague and dim
Reality indeed!
—Chorsten Christensen

It is not a good thing to say that someone cannot do something or that there are limits to what can be done, for it has been proven over and over that this is untrue. There were those who said that it was impossible to build a steamboat, but while they were on the banks of the river lecturing why it could not be done, Fulton steamed by them and gave a blast with his steamboat's horn.

Men and women have been told they would never walk or talk, but they have defied all odds and walked when they should have been in a vegetative state. Dr. Glenn Cunningham was told that his lifeless legs would never walk or run after being burned severely. The doctors at first said he would be a vegetable; then they said he would never walk. He refused to believe what he was told. He determined that he would walk and worked day after day, dragging himself around his yard supported by the white picket fence. He did this until he was finally able to take a few faltering steps. God looked down from heaven and saw his determination and gave him what he believed. Dr. Glenn Cunningham not only believed, but he worked at something that seemed totally impossible and not only did he walk but he ran the world's fastest mile.

It does not matter what you face today, with God all things are possible if you believe. He is sovereign and can make the impossible, possible, for He is God and there are no limits with God. This is the day to trust and believe Him for a miracle!

September 9

"Who is a God like unto thee, that pardoneth iniquity. . . . and thou wilt cast all their sins into the depths of the sea" (Micah 7:18-19).

Where are you today? Do you feel the weight of the world on your shoulders? Are you carrying old sins that haunt you continually? The story is told of how once a Christian visited a minister in his home. As he sat in the minister's study, he began to read one of the minister's books. While reading, he suddenly cried, "Glory! Praise the Lord!" The minister ran into the study, asking, "What is it, man?" The visitor replied, "This book says that the sea is five miles deep!" "Well, what of that?" asked the minister. "Why, the Bible says my sins have been cast into the depth of the sea, and if it is that deep, I'm not afraid of their coming up again!" exclaimed the radiant Christian.

God puts sins in the sea of forgetfulness. He specializes in helping people get rid of their heavy loads and self-inflicted remorse. He came to set the sinner free and when that freedom comes, He expects the sins that were forgiven to stay in the depths of the sea and not come back to haunt the one who has been forgiven.

There was once a man who was deeply convicted of sin and of his need of the Savior. Restlessly he wandered one night along a country road seeking relief for his misery. Wearily he sat beside a hedge. After sitting there for a while, he heard two girls talking on the other side of the hedge. They were discussing a sermon one of them had heard. "I will never forget the thing the minister said in the sermon. It gave me hope and encouragement," one girl said. "What was it?" eagerly inquired the other girl. "The world always says that you make your own bed, and you must lie in it, but One

greater than the world has said, 'Take up thy bed, and walk. Thy sins be forgiven!'" When the distressed man heard those wonderful words, he called upon the author of those words, Jesus, and felt his burden lift.

Do not lie in your bed of sin, remorse, misery and hell, but get out of that bed, and walk in newness of life. Go forward in Christ, and as Paul wrote in Philippians 3:13: "Forget the things of the past and press toward the mark" (my paraphrase). You can have a new goal today, a new life, and a hope that is not of this world. That hope is in Christ. He is waiting to help you get rid of your guilt and pain of the past. Choose to get up and rejoice instead of lying down and dying. This is the day to let go of the past and truly live.

September 10

"The Spirit of the Lord is upon me, because he hath anointed me . . . to preach deliverance to the captives" (Luke 4:18).

The full message of Luke 4:18 is as follows: "The Spirit of the Lord is upon me, because he hath anointed me to preach the gospel to the poor; he hath sent me to heal the brokenhearted, to preach deliverance to the captives, and recovering of sight to the blind, to set at liberty them that are bruised." Jesus wants to set you free!

The story is told of how shortly after Queen Victoria succeeded to the throne of England, the Lord Chamberlain presented to her several documents that required her signature. Among them was a paper pertaining to a man who had committed a crime, and who had been sentenced to death. The queen's signature was needed for his execution to be carried out. "And must I become a party to his death?" asked the eighteen-year-old queen. "I fear it is so, unless Your Majesty desires to exercise her royal prerogative of mercy." To her delight, she was informed that she had the power to pardon the condemned man. "As an expression of the spirit in which I desire to rule, I will exercise my royal prerogative!" she said. She wrote the word "pardoned" on the document and the prisoner was set free. —TOLD BY WALTER B. KNIGHT[370]

Over two thousand years ago, Jesus wrote *pardon* with His blood so that men and women could be free from their sins and the doom of their transgressions. Everyone needs to know about this freedom, this wonderful Light of the World.

There was once an eight-year-old girl who was taken to New York City to see the sights. Along with other places, she was taken to see the Statue of Liberty. She was fascinated with the statue, which has stood for many years at the entrance to New York Harbor, lifting aloft her torch of liberty to enlighten the world. She could not get the scene out of her mind. After the excitement of the day, sleep did not come easily that night. "Daddy," she said, "I am thinking of that beautiful lady out there all by herself, with nobody to help her hold up her lamp. It is dark out there. Shouldn't we be helping Miss Liberty hold up her lamp?"

Jesus needs Christians everywhere to hold up the light of His love to a lost, groping world. He has come to bring liberty, for where the Spirit of the Lord is, there is liberty. Let liberty ring in every burgh, every city, every county, every state, and around the world. Jesus, the Light of the World, has come to bring light and liberty to all. And as the little girl asked her daddy, the question is asked of every Christian, "Shouldn't we be helping to hold up the Light of the World?"

September 11

"*But lay up for yourselves treasures in heaven*" (Matthew 6:20).

Jesus said in Matthew 6:19-20: "Lay not up for yourselves treasures upon earth, where moth and rust doth corrupt, and where thieves break through and steal: But lay up for yourselves treasures in heaven, where neither moth nor rust doth corrupt, and where thieves do not break through nor steal."

The following imaginary story illustrates the laying up of treasures: A millionaire stood at heaven's gate, waiting to be shown his heavenly home. He was taken to a small cottage, located in the midst of other tiny, unpretentious homes. He complained, "Can it be that I, who have lived in a palace on earth midst scenes

of luxury and comfort, must now dwell eternally in this small abode?" Replied the angel, "We built this house out of the material you sent to us while you were on earth! We could have built a palace for you if you had sent us the material with which to build it." —TOLD BY WALTER KNIGHT[371]

A Sunday school teacher wanted to teach the children in her class the difference between tithes and offerings, so she decided to bring each of them a small present as an object lesson. She taught them that they owe God ten percent of everything that comes to them. Tithe is that which is God's and never did belong to them. Offerings are given to God as the need arises; they are a freewill gift. God wants tithes and offerings. The tithe is His; the offering is a gift or present to Him.

Jesus wants our presents today, not just the tithe which already belongs to Him, but He wants something extra. A preacher once preached, "The windows of heaven hinge on the tithe: 'Bring ye all the tithes into the storehouse, . . . and prove me now herewith, saith the LORD of hosts, if I will not open you the windows of heaven' (Malachi 3:10). If we withhold the Lord's tithe, we have no right to pray for open windows and outpoured blessings."

Malachi 3:8 states: "Will a man rob God? Yet ye have robbed me. But ye say, Wherein have we robbed thee? In tithes and offerings." The tithe is His, the offerings are the presents. If we expect to have His blessing, we must give freely without consideration to the cost.

There was once a woman in India who stood by a Buddhist temple that was in process of construction. "What is the cost of the temple?" asked a missionary. "Cost?" asked she of the missionary. "Why, we don't know. It is for our god. We don't count the cost." A god that is dead and they don't count the cost?—how much more should the Christian give abundantly to the cause of the living God? This is the day to give abundantly to the One who gave His all for us. Give and receive blessings beyond understanding.

"These that have turned the world upside down are come hither also" (Acts 17:6).

*T*his is the day to be filled with the Spirit, so that the Spirit can flow through us as in the time of the early church. A preacher once said, "The early Christians were so devoid of any political or worldly pull that they could not stay out of jail. Yet they were so endued with the power of the Holy Spirit that no prison was strong enough to hold them! The apostles met with opposition in most places they visited. Yet one of two things usually occurred wherever they went—a revival or a revolution." Acts 19:18-20 says, "And many that believed came, and confessed, and shewed their deeds. Many of them also which used curious arts brought their books together, and burned them before all men. . . . So mightily grew the word of God and prevailed."

Some people have a hard time understanding the power of the Spirit because they cannot see it. It is like the little boy who asked his father, "Dad, how can I believe in the Holy Spirit when I have never seen it?" The father who was an electrician said, "I'll show you how."

Father and son went to the power plant where they saw many generators. "This is where the power comes from to heat our stove and give us light. We cannot see the power, but it is in that machine and in the power lines," said the father. The son said, "I believe in electricity." "Of course you do, but you don't believe in it because you see it. You believe in it because you see what it can do! Likewise you can believe in the Holy Spirit because you see what He does in people's lives when they are surrendered to Jesus Christ and possess His power." —TOLD BY WALTER B. KNIGHT[372]

It is also like the flying of the kite. A little boy was hanging on to a string for dear life on a very windy day. A man came along and asked him what he was doing. He answered, "I'm flying a kite." The man said, "I don't see a kite," which was hidden behind a cloud. The boy said, "I may not see it, but I feel the tug of it on the end of the string." The Spirit cannot be seen, but it can be felt.

We are not to question, but believe, so as to be filled with the Spirit. I Corinthians 2:9-11 says, "But as it is written, Eye hath not seen, nor ear heard, neither have entered into the heart of man, the things which God hath prepared for them that love him. But God hath revealed them unto us by his Spirit: for the Spirit searcheth all things, yea, the deep things of God. For what man knoweth the things of a man, save the spirit of man which is in him? even so the things of God knoweth no man, but the Spirit of God."

The secret is to be filled with the Spirit and receive the power and revelations that only come from God through His Spirit. Do not try to understand it, just receive it and trust in God!

September 13

"Give, and it shall be given unto you; good measure, pressed down, and shaken together, and running over, shall men give unto your bosom" (Luke 6:38).

Jesus spoke these words of truth over two thousand years ago, and they are still true today. The opposite of giving is to have a miserly spirit, which is mirrored in the story of a stingy member of a rural church who was asked to make a contribution to the church.

The miser owned, among other animals, a calf which he said he was trying to sell. He said, "I'll give something when the calf is sold." On a Sunday night, while the miser was feeding his animals in his barn, some joyful Christians were returning from a church service and as they walked along the road, they began to sing a hymn, "The half has not yet been told." The stingy owner of the calf misunderstood the words of the song. He thought they sang, "The calf has never yet been sold." Conscience stricken he sold the calf and gave the money to the church. —Told by Walter B. Knight[373]

God has ways to talk to all of us, even through a misunderstood phrase.

Another miser who had been converted heard that his neighbors had sustained a great loss. So he said, "I'll go to the smokehouse and get a ham for my needy neighbor." As he walked toward the smokehouse, the tempter seemed to say to him, "Give him half a ham." The struggle was terrific, for covetousness is a sin whose hold is sometimes not easily broken. However, the new convert resolved by God's help to get the victory over the sin of greed. As Satan persisted in his suggestions for half a ham, the man said, "If you don't pipe down, Satan, I'll give him every ham in the smokehouse."[374]

Acts 20:35 states: "It is more blessed to give than to receive." There is a joy in giving that benefits the total person. A Christian

layman discovered this. He had an extensive business, and when the death of some relatives brought great riches to him, he had to make a decision. "Shall I retire from business or continue to work?" was the question he pondered. He decided to continue in business, not for himself but for Christ, saying, "I will trust Him to give me strength to earn money for Him."

Later he testified, "I never knew before what real joy was. Formerly I worked to earn a living for myself. Now I am carrying on the same business as diligently as if for myself, even more so. It is now for Christ and all profits of the business go into the treasure of the Lord."

If you want to know true joy, after becoming a Christian, continue to let the blessings of the Lord flow through you, giving back to Him and giving to others. This is truly the blessed life!

September 14

"Therefore if any man be in Christ, he is a new creature" (II Corinthians 5:17).

Jesus is still the central theme of religion. He is still the central figure of salvation. He still lives. He can do what no one else can do. There was once an alcoholic woman who was gloriously saved. Later, the pastor called on her husband, wanting to win him also to Christ. But the man was bitter. Contemptuously he said of his wife's conversion, "She'll get over it. She'll go back to drinking again." Six months passed. Then the husband went to see the pastor. He said, "I have read all the leading books on the evidences of Christianity, and I can answer their arguments. But for the past six months I have had an open book before me—my wife, whose life has been utterly changed. I have been wrong. There must be something divine about a religion that can take a slave to drink, like my wife was, and change her into the loving, patient, prayerful, singing saint that she now is! I, too, want the thing that has worked the miracle in her life."

Jesus works miracles in people's lives every day. It does not matter how far away from God they are or to what depth they have fallen, He can make anyone a new creature by His marvelous touch.

The story is told of how once on a bitter, cold day in London, an old blind man sat on a little stool near the corner of a street. His fingers were blue with cold. He tried to play a cheap violin. Few paid any attention to him or put any money in his tin cup. Then two well-dressed men stopped. One said in broken English: "No luck, eh? Nobody give money? Make them. Play till they open!" Then he said: "Give me your violin!" The old man gave it to him and he began to play. The cheap violin seemed to come to life. Beautiful, heavenly music flowed from it. Men, women, boys and girls listened spellbound! When the music stopped, a hat was passed. It was filled with money for the blind man. When the stranger returned the violin and bow, the blind man said: "Oh, sir, you have my undying thanks! What's your name?" As the stranger walked away, he said, "My name is Paganini!"[375]

The great and famous violinist had stopped on a street corner to help a poor, unfortunate man. The touch of the master's hand on a cheap violin transformed everything. The miracle of the sound was not in the violin, it was in the master's hand. The same way it is with Jesus Christ. He can transform any life into beautiful music anywhere, anytime, any place, simply by who He is.

September 15

"But whosoever drinketh of the water that I shall give him shall never thirst" (John 4:14).

The battle of El Alamein had raged fiercely through the hours of the day when the heat was most intense on the sands of North Africa. When it seemed that the British had nearly reached the limits of their endurance, with an almost nonexistent water supply, they were suddenly surprised to see large numbers of the elite German army throw up their hands in surrender. They came stumbling in, with parched protruding tongues and thick swollen lips, begging for water, even just a sip.

What had happened was, as they overran the British position, there was a newly constructed water main there, and the German soldiers had shot holes in it and drank deeply. However, the main was not in use for fresh water and was being tested by pumping

seawater through it. What the Germans unwittingly drank was water from the Mediterranean Sea. The more they drank, the greater was their thirst in the battle. Thus was decided the issue of this crucial engagement. —ALBERT MYGATT[376]

There are many water mains in the world today but they are filled with salt water. People are drinking deeply from them, but the more they drink the thirstier they become. There is only one source of clear, sparkling water that satisfies, and that is Jesus Christ. He said to the woman at Jacob's well, "Whosoever drinketh of the water that I shall give him shall never thirst; but the water that I shall give him shall be in him a well of water springing up into everlasting life" (John 4:14).

What source are you drinking from this morning? Is your soul parched, are you stumbling and frantically trying to find something to take away the unquenchable thirst? "There is a way which seemeth right unto a man, but the end thereof are the ways of death" (Proverbs 14:12). But there is another way that is life. "And that they might have it more abundantly" (John 10:10).

"Jesus saith unto him, I am the way, the truth, and the life" (John 14:6). This is the day to drink deeply from the water that He gives, and quit stumbling desperately through life trying all the other things that make you thirsty, even unto death. Today is the day to drink long and hard at this stream of water that has as one of its ingredients eternal life.

It will supply you not only with a drink, but it will become a well of water which will never run dry. The choice is yours: will it be the temporary drink of sin and man's ingenuity that leaves you thirsty and half-dead or will you choose the refreshing, life-giving well of water that is forever satisfying?

September 16

"The effectual fervent prayer of a righteous man availeth much" (James 5:16).

There is power in prayer. James 5:17-18 declares it: "Elias was a man subject to like passions as we are, and he prayed earnestly that it might not rain: and it rained not on the earth by

the space of three years and six months. And he prayed again, and the heaven gave rain, and the earth brought forth her fruit."

Jesus spoke to the multitudes in Matthew 7:7 and encouraged them to pray: "Ask, and it shall be given you; seek, and ye shall find; knock, and it shall be opened unto you." It does not matter what the need is; He is there to help if we will but pray. Reverend Fred Kinzie from Toledo, Ohio, told the following story of how God helped him in a time of trouble:

It had been a long, tiresome day as my wife and I began walking up the west concourse of the St. Louis airport. I noted the time, 11:22 P.M. The plane had parked at the extreme west end of the concourse. It could not have parked any farther away from the luggage carousel.

Upon reaching the baggage carousel, we waited about fifteen minutes for our luggage to arrive. Getting it all together, we started walking toward a taxi stand when my wife turned to me and asked, "Fred, where's your briefcase?"

"Oh, no!" I answered, "I've left it back in the plane. I set it down by my seat next to the window. Our tickets are in it and things I need for tomorrow's board meeting. I've got to go get it."

Pulling all the luggage back near a seat, I told my wife to wait for me as I went back to the plane, hoping the ramp door would not yet be locked.

As I walked back that long concourse it seemed my feet weighed a ton. By the time I got back to the ramp door, it was closed and locked. I asked people in the area if they knew where the man was who had locked the door. No one had seen him. The only thing I thought to do was go back to the baggage area to see if I could find someone there. So I started on that long walk again. It was now 12:15 A.M. Arriving back at the baggage carousel, I found no one around. The place looked deserted. I was so tired after three trips up and down the concourse that I sat to rest for a moment. As I sat there a porter came by to help someone else who had arrived on the same plane as we did. I got to him right away.

He told me where to find the luggage claim area for Eastern Airlines. I went but could find no one there. I reported back to the porter and he said as soon as he took care of his customer, he'd see what he could do.

Shortly thereafter, he came and said we'd go back to the plane. For the fourth time I started walking that long trip to

353

the far end of the concourse. Upon arriving he discovered the ramp door locked and he could find no one in the vicinity who had a key. After he left, I faced that long concourse for the fifth time. I was about two-thirds of the way back when I remembered that probably the best thing I could do was to pray.

I looked up and down that deserted concourse, and not one person was in sight. As I went dragging along, I closed my eyes and prayed desperately, "God, you know the predicament that we're in. Please, put me in touch with the right man to take care of this problem of ours!" It couldn't have taken over ten seconds to pray that prayer.

When I opened my eyes, to my amazement, walking to my left about a step in front of me was a man with an Eastern Airlines emblem on his coat sleeve. I told him we had just arrived and I had left my briefcase on it. It was very important that I have it as my plane tickets and other needed materials were in it.

The end of the story is that he got his briefcase from the plane and said that one thing he is sure of, that God had the airlines official step out beside him at the precise moment when he prayed desperately for help. God is still in the business of answering desperate prayers.

Wherever you are today, just call on Him and He will be there to help you in the darkest night, in those impossible situations that no one can do anything about; that is, anyone but Him. When prayer is made, a signal goes out, an SOS call is placed, and heaven is alerted. Forces are made to work in your behalf. When God gets involved anything can happen, for all power in heaven and in earth is in His hands. Pray to Him today and believe for a miracle!

September 17

"He shall give his angels charge over thee" (Psalm 91:11).

If you are God's child, you need not be afraid. He promised to have His angels encamp round about you. Psalm 34:7 declares: "The angel of the LORD encampeth round about them that fear

him, and delivereth them." Those angels help protect you. The following story bears this out.

Bill Thompson, a missionary to Columbia for many years, once spent the night in a small, primitive farmhouse in the mountains above a village. He was awakened the next morning by a man inspecting the outside of the house.

"Where are the connections for the lights?" the man asked.

"What lights do you mean?" Thompson responded. "There are none here."

"Last night, some hired killers were sent from the village to harm you," the man confessed. "But they saw guards on the roof with bright spotlights, so they did not come near. Where are the wires that powered the lights?"

It was then the missionary's delight to tell the villager about God and His guardian angels.

It is promised in Psalm 91:11: "He shall give his angels charge over thee, to keep thee in all thy ways."

You may not hear the swish of an angel's wing, but if you are God's child, there are angels about you and your family. Carroll McGruder relates in the following story how an angel from God ministered to him during a time of crisis:

"In 1988, I was diagnosed with lymphoma. The doctors termed it aggressive and stage two, and planned aggressive measures of treatment, including several intravenous medications and an additional number of oral medications. I remember the doctors saying, 'We must hit it hard and fast if we have a hope of winning this battle through chemotherapy.'

"Like so many other cancer patients, I bloated, lost my hair, and my personality had severe mood swings, but my faith in God was stable. One night about four months into treatments, I was suffering severely and couldn't sleep. Lying in my bed, I suddenly saw a figure walk down the hall of my house, a man so large that he stooped to avoid touching the ceiling with his head. He came to the bed where I lay and put two massive hands on my chest. Instantly his contact felt like electrical regeneration. Although the current created by his touch seemed to vibrate my whole body from head to foot, it neither awoke my wife nor had any kind of adverse effect on me. For about two to three minutes he stood over me with a confident expression on his face and healing comfort in his hands. Then without saying a word, he turned as though he would walk away and vanished before my very eyes."

God brought healing to Carroll McGruder, and he did not die but has lived many years since this encounter. No matter where you are, no matter how sick you are or how desperate you are, what matters is that God is a part of your life.

This is the day to be aware of God. Look to Him for assistance, pray to Him, love Him, worship Him, talk to Him, and lean on Him. Let God and His angels enter your life, and life will be much brighter, more glorious, and you will have peace in the midst of the storm, for you will know that with God in control, all is well.

September 18

"Take therefore no thought for the morrow" (Matthew 6:34).

Many people have collapsed with nervous and mental troubles because they have failed to obey these words: "Have no thought or anxiety about tomorrow." They are weighted down with the crushing burden of accumulated yesterdays and fearful tomorrows.

Robert Louis Stevenson once wrote, "*Anyone can carry his burden, however hard, from now until bedtime.*" It is time to bury the past instead of letting the past bury you. Do not worry about tomorrow, just live today well.

Mrs. E. K. Shields from Michigan once shared how she was driven to despair because she did not obey the words of Jesus. These are her words: "After my husband died, I had thought that getting back on the road would help relieve my depression, but driving alone and eating alone was not very productive and I found it hard to make my car payments. In the spring of 1938, I was working in Missouri, the schools were poor, the roads bad and I became so lonely and discouraged that at one time I even considered suicide. It seemed that success was impossible. I had nothing to live for. I dreaded getting up each morning and facing life. I was afraid of everything; afraid I could not meet the car payments; afraid I could not pay my room rent; afraid I would not have enough to eat. I was afraid my health was failing and I had to have money for a doctor. All that kept me from suicide were the

thoughts that my sister would be deeply grieved, and that I did not have enough money to pay my funeral expenses. Then one day I read an article that lifted me out of my despondence and gave me the courage to go on living. It was one inspiring sentence that arrested my attention. It said, 'Every day is a new life to a wise man.'"

Mrs. E. K. Shields said she typed that sentence and pasted it on the windshield of her car, where she saw it every minute she was driving. She said she found it wasn't so hard to live only one day at a time. She learned to forget her yesterdays and not be fearful of her tomorrows. Each day she would say to herself, "Today is a new life."

As Mrs. Shields grabbed hold of the truth spoken by Jesus, "Take no thought for tomorrow," it is essential to grab hold of this truth today. Jesus was saying, "Live today and don't worry about tomorrow, plan well, but do not fret, fume and worry." This is the day to live life to the fullest. The old Romans had a word for it, "Seize the day." Today is the day to live life to the fullest through Jesus Christ!

September 19

"We shall reap, if we faint not" (Galatians 6:9).

Are you giving up too soon on something that is important to you? This is no time to quit. After years of progressive hearing loss, by age forty-six German composer Ludwig van Beethoven had become completely deaf. Nevertheless, he wrote his greatest music, including five symphonies, during his later years.

Wilma Rudolph was the twentieth of twenty-two children. She was born prematurely and her survival was doubtful. When she was four years old, she contracted double pneumonia and scarlet fever, which left her with a paralyzed left leg. At age nine, she removed the metal leg brace she had been dependent on and began to walk without it. By age thirteen, she had developed a rhythmic walk, which doctors said was a miracle. That same year she decided to become a runner. She entered a race and came in last. For the next few years every race she entered, she came in last. Everyone told her to quit, but she kept on running. One day she actually won a race. And then another. From then on she won every race she entered. Eventually this little girl, who was told she would never walk again, went on to win three Olympic gold medals. Wilma Rudolph said these words, "My mother taught me very early to believe I could achieve any accomplishment I wanted to. The first was to walk without braces."

This is no time to quit. You can achieve your dream.

Louis L'Amour, successful author of over one hundred western novels with over two hundred million copies in print, received 350 rejections before he made his first sale. He later became the first American novelist to receive a special congressional gold medal in recognition of his distinguished career as an author and contributor to the nation through his historically based works.

In 1953, Julia Child and her two collaborators signed a publishing contract to produce a book tentatively titled *French Cooking for the American Kitchen*. Julia and her colleagues worked on the book for five years. The publisher rejected the 850-page manuscript. Child and her partners worked for another year totally revising the manuscript. Again the publisher rejected it. But Julia Child did not give up. She and her collaborators went back to work again, found a new publisher and in 1961—eight years after beginning—they published *Mastering the Art of French Cooking*, which has sold more than one million copies. In 1966, *Time* magazine featured Julia Child on its cover. Julia Child was at the top of her field for over thirty years, all because she refused to give up.

Galatians 6:9 says it well: "And let us not be weary in well doing: for in due season we shall reap, if we faint not." This is no day to faint; this is the day to fly!

September 20

"*Nothing . . . impossible*" (Luke 1:37).

Years ago, Brutus Hamilton, coach of the U.S. Olympic team, compiled a list of what he considered to be the "ultimate" in track and field performances. He said that no one, out of confidence based on long experience, would ever run the 100-yard dash in

less than 9.2 seconds or the mile in less than 3 minutes 57.8 seconds. No one would ever put the shot more than 62 feet, throw the discus more than 200 feet, do better than 7 feet 1 inch high jump, 27 feet in the long jump, or 16 feet in the pole vault. Since then, in every case, someone has.[377]

The public thought the Wright brothers were crazy when they thought they could fly in the air like the birds. Today everyone is flying in airplanes because a few believed that it was not impossible.

Most people thought it was impossible to build a machine that would enable voices to be heard around the world; today most of the world have telephones because someone believed that it could be done.

Gideon, just a poor farmer, was asked by God to be the leader to help bring deliverance to the Israelites. He called the men together who would help fight and thirty-two thousand men responded, but God told him he had too many. So Gideon proceeded to tell them that if they were afraid and felt like they could not win to go home. Twenty-two thousand men went home. They did not believe.

This left Gideon with ten thousand men and God told him he still had too many, so he gave them the water test. If they drank water from the brook as a dog laps, and one hand kept near their sword, they were chosen to fight with him, but if they were lax and lay down, so that the enemy could come on them unaware, they were sent home. After all the testing and going through God's requirements were finished, Gideon was left with three hundred men. But with God all things are possible. God gave the instructions on how to win and Gideon and his men did exactly what they were told to do and they won the battle.

It does not matter if someone says something cannot be done, or if it looks foolish to believe the impossible, for with God nothing shall be impossible. In every generation there have been those who have won over insurmountable odds. Everything was against them and to the human eye it appeared to be impossible, but some unseen force propelled them forward to victory and success.

This is the day to believe that all things are possible if God is on your side. If He places a dream in your heart, then go forward and join those who have in the past gone beyond the normal and accomplished what seemed to be an impossible thing. For with God, nothing shall be impossible!

September 21

"This is the victory that overcometh the world, even our faith" (I John 5:4).

Borghild Dahl, who was nearly blind for half a century, refused to be pitied or considered different. She had only the use of one eye, and it was so covered with dense scars that she had to do all her seeing through one small opening in the left of the eye.

She dreamed of becoming a college professor in spite of her handicap. She threw herself into her dream with gusto. She did her reading at home, holding a book of large print so close to her eyes that her eyelashes brushed the pages. She earned two college degrees: an A.B. from the University of Minnesota and a Master of Arts from Columbia University.

She started teaching in the tiny village of Twin Valley, Minnesota, and rose until she became professor of journalism and literature at Augustana College in Sioux Falls, South Dakota. She was involved in teaching, lecturing, and giving radio talks about books and authors. In the back of her mind, there had always lurked a fear of total blindness. In order to overcome this, she adopted a cheerful, almost hilarious attitude towards life. She overcame her fears and depression by working daily towards her dream.

George Frederick Handel, the great musician, lost his health; his right side was paralyzed, his money was gone, and his creditors seized and threatened to imprison him. Handel was so disheartened by his tragic experience that he almost despaired for a brief time. But his faith prevailed, and he composed his greatest work, "The Hallelujah Chorus," which is part of his great *Messiah*.[378] He exemplified what the apostle John wrote in I John 5:4, "This is the victory that overcometh the world, even our faith."

True success is overcoming something that is difficult or is a stumbling block. Booker T. Washington said, *"Success is to be measured not so much by the position that one has reached in life as by the obstacles which he has overcome while trying to succeed."*

If you are put in a prison not of your own making, create something good just as John Bunyan did. He wrote the great work which blesses many still today, *Pilgrim's Progress*. If you are faced with problems that seem insurmountable and keep pressing you down, just keep getting up until you win. It is not the falling down that matters; it is whether you get up and try again that is important. Conquering is overcoming. So if you are a conqueror, you will have to fight something. You will have to battle through the thick and the thin. But in Christ you are more than a conqueror. Winning is not always easy, but you will not lose if you purpose in your heart not to do so.

September 22

"If ye shall ask any thing in my name, I will do it" (John 14:14).

Be encouraged today. God does answer prayer—sometimes in ways you would not think of—but He does hear and answer.

Dan Crawford tells of an experience he and his party had while returning to his African mission field after a furlough. A stream to be crossed was in flood, and there were no boats. Haste in getting back was important. The missionaries camped and prayed. After a time a tall tree which had battled with the river for a century, perhaps, began to totter, and then fell, clear across the stream. "The Royal Engineer of Heaven," Mr. Crawford said, "had laid a pontoon bridge for God's servants."

If you need an answer to something that seems impossible or need direction for a confusing problem, God has chosen the method of asking before receiving. Jesus said in John 14:13-14, "And whatsoever ye shall ask in my name, that will I do, that the Father may be glorified in the Son. If ye shall ask any thing in my name, I will do it."

"Ask, and it shall be given you; seek, and ye shall find; knock, and it shall be opened unto you" (Matthew 7:7). God can do anything without our asking, but He chose this way: ask and ye shall receive.

When Queen Victoria was opening the town hall of Sheffield, the officials had given her a little golden key. She was told, as she sat in her carriage, that she only had to turn the golden key and in a moment the town hall gates of Sheffield would fly open. In obedience

to the authority of experts who gave her the directions, she turned the key, and in a moment, by the action of electric wires, the town hall gates flew open.

Jesus has also given us a key and told us how to use it. His divine power or electricity will start things in motion. All that is required is to ask in faith believing and He will open the gate. He has given the golden key of prayer, and if we use it, the gates of heaven will open.

Pray and believe God for an answer; just ask of Him today.

September 23

"Henceforth there is laid up for me a crown of righteousness" (II Timothy 4:8).

Sometimes in the Christian walk a person will battle weariness. There will be the wanting to run away and get away from it all. During these times it is good to remember that this life is really only a beginning for better things. There is something worth working for and that is being faithful to the Lord Jesus and His work. There is coming a reckoning day and there will be a crown given to those who are faithful. When it is all said and done, when it is all over, there is something wonderful yet to come.

When the great plants of our cities
Have turned out their last finished work;
When our merchants have sold their last yard of silk
And dismissed the last tired clerk;

When our banks have raked in their last dollar
And paid the last dividend;
When the Judge of the earth says: "Close for the night,"
And asks for a balance—WHAT THEN?

When the choir has sung its last anthem,
And the preacher has made his last prayer;
When the people have heard their last sermon
And the sound has died out on the air;

When the Bible lies closed on the altar,
And the pews are all empty of men.
And each one stands facing his record—
And the great Book is opened—WHAT THEN?

When the actors have played their last drama,
And the mimic has made his last fun,
When the film has flashed its last picture,
And the billboard displayed its last run;

When the crowds seeking pleasure have vanished,
And gone out in the darkness again.
When the trumpet of ages is sounded,
And we stand up before Him—WHAT THEN?

When the bugle's call sinks into silence,
And the long marching columns stand still,
When the captain repeats his last orders,
And they've captured the last fort and hill,

And the flag has been hauled from the masthead,
And the wounded afield checked in,
And a world that rejected its Savior,
Is asked for a reason—WHAT THEN?
—J. WHITFIELD GREEN[379]

Seek to not waste time on earth, but give your best. Give to the Lord what is His. Help your fellowman and do everything you can to make a difference in your life and those around you in light of eternity. You will be glad that you can say with Paul, "I've fought a good fight; henceforth a crown is laid up for me. For I have finished my course." Be encouraged! This is only the beginning and the best is yet to come.

September 24

"I will direct all his ways" (Isaiah 45:13).

    Are you in a situation where you feel there is no way out? There is always a way when you trust in God. In one of the wars in France, a citadel was besieged by the enemy and the outworks destroyed. In order that none might escape under cover of the night, the besiegers guarded every foot of the wall. They had the garrison in a net and only waited for the morrow to slaughter them.

    No sound came from the city. Those brave but unfortunate defenders seemed to wait their doom in silence. When the morning came, the enemy with swords drawn rushed in to find the citadel empty! Their astonishment was great. "Where are our foes?" they demanded. And then an opening was found leading down into the sub-cellars, and from these a long subterranean passage led them out a long way from the citadel among quiet green fields and the light of day. It was plain that by this passage, the doors of which stood open, their prey had escaped at night.

    The Scriptures tell us that God will make a way of escape. When it looks like you are surrounded by the enemy and He is ready for the kill, the Lord will lead you out by another way of which the enemy is not aware. Do not despair, but look unto the Way Maker; He can make a way where there is no way.

    It may not look like a very good way, but if it is God's way, it is good even if it looks a little ridiculous, just as some people thought about Joshua's plan of battle. When God told him to have the soldiers march around the walls of Jericho seven times without saying a word, the people on the wall probably looked down and laughed at them thinking them to be a little strange, but when they gave the triumphant shout on the seventh time, they laughed no more, because the walls came tumbling down and God caused a great victory and the children of Israel once more outfoxed the enemy simply by obeying God's plan of action. He can do it! The key is to follow His instructions; there is a way, but He is the one who knows what it is.

    Listen to Him and He will get you out of your difficult situation and teach you how to win over the enemy!

September 25

"This I know; for God is for me" (Psalm 56:9).

*D*o you feel like things are against you or people do not understand you? Psalm 56:9-11 says, "When I cry unto thee, then shall mine enemies turn back: this I know; for God is for me. In God will I praise his word: in the LORD will I praise his word. In God have I put my trust: I will not be afraid what man can do unto me."

You may be placed in a situation that is causing you mental anguish and excruciating pain, but if you will trust in God, He will see you through. He said in Psalm 107:6: "Then they cried unto the LORD in their trouble, and he delivered them out of their distresses."

There was once a lady who was severely depressed by a series of disheartening events. When asked by her pastor how she was weathering the storm of adversity, she answered, "Quite well, under the circumstances."

"Sister," he replied kindly yet firmly, "you'll never make it that way. Get above the circumstances—that's where Jesus waits to help and strengthen you." She took his wise admonition as a word from heaven, and laying aside her sadness and self-pity, she began to praise the Lord. New confidence in God's love and kindness was generated in her soul, and she soon gained the victory of faith.

The story of one of the great presidents of Harvard College, Charles William Eliot, is worth recalling. Born with a serious facial disfigurement, he discovered as a young man that nothing could be done about it, and he must go through life with this mark. It is related that when his mother brought to him the tragic truth, it was indeed the dark hour of his soul. His mother told him, "My son, it is not possible for you to get rid of this handicap. We have consulted the best surgeons, and they say there is nothing that can be done. But it is possible for you, with God's help, to grow a mind and soul so big that people will forget to look at your face." —*THE PULPIT*[380]

That young boy took his mother's advice and instead of hiding his disfigurement and wallowing in self-pity, he grew a big soul and became president of Harvard College. Your situation may be totally different but have the same effect on you, but if you will get up and go forward, even as William Eliot did, God will go with you.

You can overcome, and win every time, for God will help you when you cannot help yourself. This is the day to get above the circumstances, and not stay under them.

September 26

"And all things . . . believing, ye shall receive" (Matthew 21:22).

Are you facing a difficult situation today? It was Hudson Taylor, founder of the China Inland Mission, who was fond of three words: "Impossible, difficult, done." Jesus said in Mark 9:23, "If thou canst believe, all things are possible to him that believeth."

The power of belief is an incredible power. It can make things happen. If you believe it strongly enough, it will be as Hudson Taylor said. First it is impossible, secondly it is difficult, but finally it is done.

When you ask in wisdom for things that are appropriate you stand on solid ground to receive your answer. In other words, you would not ask for a tree to be turned into a dog; that is absurd—even though God could do it. He does not waste His time doing magical tricks. Even though He is mighty, great, and magnificent; He is also in the business of helping His children.

Belief based on sound judgment will cause those impossibilities to become possible through the Lord Jesus Christ. Your mind can become a seedbed for negative thoughts and actually produce negative situations, because that is what you believe to be, or you can do what Matthew 21:22 says and believe for things to be better by exercising faith and belief in God. Jesus said, "And all things, whatsoever ye shall ask in prayer, believing, ye shall receive."

If one does not believe this scripture, then he will live in a lower level of living and experience the results of doubt and pessimism. Proper response to the Word of God and belief in it will help change things.

Whom will you join today? The multitudes of scoffers, unbelievers, and doubters, or will you join those who have decided to believe God to help in all things? You can have your prayers answered, you can have your health back, you can be strong, your business can flourish, your finances can be straightened out and blessed.

With God there is no impossible situation; it is only impossible in the mind. Let the concepts of Christ enter into your thinking today and erase anything that is against the knowledge of God and walk in newness of life.

September 27

"And this is the confidence that we have in him" (I John 5:14).

Such a glorious truth: I John 5:14-15 says, "And this is the confidence that we have in him, that, if we ask any thing according to his will, he heareth us: And if we know that he hear us, whatsoever we ask, we know that we have the petitions that we desired of him."

Years ago a widow living in Glendale, California, owned and operated thirty-five rest homes for missionaries. When this need was laid on her heart, she was led to ask God for fifty thousand dollars with which to erect cottages. She had nothing, but her heart was filled with burning faith.

She was confident that the money would be in her hands and immediately opened her little home to take in missionaries. Meanwhile she continued to pray for the fifty thousand dollars. One day a man called and told her that a lot she owned was oil land. His company wanted to sink a well and pay her royalties. A gusher of five thousand barrels a day came in. Money began to come into her hands. Missionary homes were erected. She received fifty thousand dollars when suddenly the well sanded in. Nothing but salt water would be raised thereafter. God gave her the exact amount she asked for. It was for an unselfish purpose to help others and He honored her faith and charity.

Whatever your need is today, God can put oil in land where there was no oil previously. He can put water in ditches where there is no water without any rain as He did in II Kings 3:16-18. Elisha told the king, "Thus saith the LORD, Make this valley full of ditches. For thus saith the LORD, Ye shall not see wind, neither shall ye see rain; yet that valley shall be filled with water, that ye may drink, both ye, and your cattle, and your beasts. And this is but a light thing in the sight of the LORD."

It does not matter how large the problem is, or how impossible it may seem, it is but a light thing for God to do the things that no one else can do. He is God and beside Him there is none other.

Pray and believe in God; cast not your confidence away. Hold on to His hand and pray prevailing prayers full of faith in Him, for He is not just a king, He is the King of kings with all power and authority. Even with all the power He holds in His hand, yet He cares about your smallest need or greatest need. Just trust in Him today!

September 28

"Casting all your care upon him; for he careth for you" (I Peter 5:7).

God cares for you in the good times and in the bad times, even though you may be tempted to believe that He does not. During the time when Napoleon was emperor of France, he had a great many friends and a great many enemies. He placed in prison many people who were not pleased at the way he did things, and left them there to suffer and sometimes to die. One of the men put in the prison was a man named Charney. He was a very wise man and a good scholar, but he did not believe in God and thought that God had forgotten all about him and so he could forget about God. When things go wrong with some people, they think God doesn't care for them any more. This man wrote on the walls of his prison cell these words, "All things come by chance."

One day when he was walking up and down in his cell, he saw a tiny, green blade breaking through the ground. The ground was hard, but the little green blade had broken the ground quite near the wall and was trying to creep out into the light. He was very much interested in it, because it was the only living thing around, and he cared for it and watered it and it began to grow. It became his little friend and teacher, and he wondered how it came there and how it could be formed and made so very beautiful. After a while a flower came out, and it was white and purple and rose-colored with a beautiful white fringe. The man began to think and wonder and after a while thoughts of God came into his heart and

he rubbed the words that he had written from the wall and wrote there instead, "He who made all things is God."

He felt happier and began to think that if God could care for the little flower in the prison cell and make it so beautiful, He could care for him. But that is not the end of the story. There was another prisoner in that great prison who had a little daughter who came often to see him. The little girl became acquainted with Charney and found out about his love for the little flower, and each day when she came to see her father she visited the flower and its friend and saw how kind he was to it. She told the jailer and the story began to be told from one to another and at last it came to the ears of the emperor's wife, Josephine. When she heard the story, she said that surely the man who could so love a flower could not be a bad man, and she persuaded Napoleon, to allow him to have his liberty. When he left the prison, he carried the flower home with him and planted it in his own garden; for it was his little teacher and had taught him to love God and to trust Him.

Jesus said in Matthew 6:30, "If God [then] so clothe the grass of the field, which to day is, and to morrow is cast into the oven, shall he not much more clothe you, O ye of little faith?"

"Surely he hath borne our griefs, and carried our sorrows" (Isaiah 53:4).

Sometimes life becomes too much, the sorrows weigh heavily, and you feel like you cannot take another step. When you cannot go any further, just let the Lord carry you. Isaiah 53:4 says, "Surely he hath borne our griefs, and carried our sorrows." If he is carrying our sorrows then he is carrying us, because the sorrow is in our heart. The following poem says it well:

FOOTPRINTS IN THE SAND
One night I had a dream—
I dreamed I was walking along the beach with the Lord and
Across the sky flashed scenes from my life.

For each scene I noticed two sets of footprints in the sand,
One belonged to me and the other to the Lord.
When the last scene of my life flashed before us,
I looked back at the footprints in the sand.
I noticed, that many times along the path of my life,
There was only one set of footprints.
I also noticed that it happened at the very lowest
and saddest times in my life.
This really bothered me and I questioned the Lord about it.
"Lord, you said that once I decided to follow you,
You would walk with me all the way,
But I have noticed that during the most troublesome times in
my life, there is only one set of footprints.
I don't understand why in times when I needed you most,
You should leave me."
The Lord replied, "My precious, precious child,
I love you and I would never, never leave you
during your times of trial and suffering.
When you saw only one set of footprints,
it was then that I carried you."
—MARY STEVENSON (1936)

Let Him carry you today. If you cannot take another step, then rest in the arms of the Lord. He will give you rest and courage to take some more steps. Psalm 30:5 says, "Weeping may endure for a night, but joy cometh in the morning."

On a sundial in Brighton, England, are the words of Richard Horne: "*It is always morning somewhere in the world.*" It may be dark and disappointing where you are, but it will not always be so. It is always morning somewhere, and some glad, good day it will be morning everywhere. And suffering is endurable, because it is temporary. God is God of the day and the night. He is always there in the good and the bad times. Do not get mad at Him in the stormy times, but let Him carry you when the load gets too heavy. He is waiting with outstretched hands saying, "Come unto me, all ye that are weary and heavy laden, and I will give you rest." And remember this—what you are going through shall pass, morning is coming. While you are in the dark, life-threatening storm, just rest in Jesus and He will lead you safely through it all.

September 30

"And call upon me in the day of trouble: I will deliver thee" (Psalm 50:15).

*I*f you are oppressed it is time to call on the Lord! Job 35:9-11 talks about a group of people who were oppressed who did not call on the Lord: "By reason of the multitude of oppressions they make the oppressed to cry: they cry out by reason of the arm of the mighty. But none saith, Where is God my maker, who giveth songs in the night; Who teacheth us more than the beasts of the earth, and maketh us wiser than the fowls of heaven?"

It is not enough to cry aloud, but make your cry count. Cry unto the Lord God who can give a song even in the midnight and who is the wisest of them all. He wants you to call on Him. Do not be prideful and feel like you can handle your problems by yourself. You need God; acknowledge it today.

The story is told about a doctor from Edinburgh, Sir James Simpson. In 1847, he discovered that chloroform could be used as an anesthetic to render people insensible to the pain of surgery. From his early experiments, Dr. Simpson made it possible for people to go through the most dangerous operations without fear of pain and suffering. Some people even claim that his was one of the most significant discoveries of modern medicine.

Some years later, while lecturing at the University of Edinburgh, Dr. Simpson was asked by one of his students, "What do you consider to be the most valuable discovery of your lifetime?" To the surprise of his students, who had expected him to refer to chloroform, Dr. Simpson replied, "My most valuable discovery was when I discovered myself a sinner and that Jesus Christ was my Savior."

This is the mark of humility, when we discover that we need Jesus—that we cannot make it successfully through life without Him. True success is not in accumulation of wealth or things, for there are those who have had all of earth's wealth at their fingertips and yet taken their own life.

Jesus will not only take away oppression and will help in the day of trouble, but He will give you true wealth: a home with Him in eternity, peace, joy, fulfillment, love, and many blessings. Let this be the day that you call on Him and invite Him to be a part of your life.

October 1

"Yet I will rejoice in the LORD" (Habakkuk 3:18).

*I*s it possible to have joy when everything has gone wrong, and to rejoice when there is nothing seemingly to rejoice about? It is a strange truth that several times when the word *joy* or *rejoice* is mentioned, it is not associated with good times, but with a trial or disaster. How can this be? The prophet Habakkuk gave a desolate picture of everything being totally gone, but yet he rejoiced: "Although the fig tree shall not blossom, neither shall fruit be in the vines; the labour of the olive shall fail, and the fields shall yield no meat; the flock shall be cut off from the fold, and there shall be no herd in the stalls: Yet I will rejoice in the LORD, I will joy in the God of my salvation" (Habakkuk 3:17-18).

James said it this way, "Count it all joy when ye fall into divers temptations; knowing this, that the trying of your faith worketh patience" (James 1:2-3).

Peter expressed it a little differently but with the same message, "Beloved, think it not strange concerning the fiery trial which is to try you, as though some strange thing happened unto you: But rejoice, inasmuch as ye are partakers of Christ's sufferings; that, when his glory shall be revealed, ye may be glad also with exceeding joy" (I Peter 4:12-13).

All three: Habakkuk, James, and Peter, through the inspiration of the Holy Ghost, gave instruction to *rejoice* or *joy* when things are bad, but how does one do this? How can anyone rejoice when the heart is aching and depression covers him like a suffocating blanket?

Is it really possible to do so? Do you think God would tell His children to do something that was impossible for them to do? No, He would not do that. Paul said, "I can do all things through Christ which strengtheneth me" (Philippians 4:13). It is through His strength that this is possible.

The secret is to tune in to God, listen to His Word, look at His majesty and hold Him in awe! Matthew Henry gives a good definition of joy. It simply means to have a constant delight in God. How? When things are bad, you rejoice in the Lord because you

believe that He is going to make things work out for the better. He is your constant friend and designs no evil for you; only Satan your enemy does that. God is for you and wants to bring good out of evil. He works in His great power sending forth His Spirit and His angels to help you.

The key is to trust in Him even when there is nothing to rejoice about. Yes, even when everything appears to be devastation, that is the time to cry, "God, I trust You and in You I will not be afraid. You are my joy and my salvation, and yes, Lord, You are working things out for my good as I follow Your Word."

October 2

"Let this mind be in you, which was also in Christ Jesus" (Philippians 2:5).

Do not give up today. Josh Billings once said, "Consider the postage stamp: its usefulness consists in the ability to stick at one thing till it gets there." Be like the postage stamp; just hang on until you reach your destination. You may go through the rain, the storm, the wind, and the tunnels, but if you stick to the right thing, you will eventually get where you are going.

It has been said that, "Little minds are tamed and subdued by misfortune; but great minds rise above them." What kind of mind do you have? If you are not satisfied with what you find in yourself, ask the Lord to give you a new mind-set. Paul told us how to do that in Romans 12:2: "And be not conformed to this world: but be ye transformed by the renewing of your mind, that ye may prove what is that good, and acceptable, and perfect, will of God."

I Peter 1:13 admonishes: "Wherefore gird up the loins of your mind." That means that which reproduces itself. You can get a mind-set that says, "I am not giving in to depression. I am going to win. My dreams are before me and they are going to guide me instead of beat me. No matter what comes my way, any adversity or storm, I am going to keep a right spirit and eventually I will get to the place Christ has in store for me."

It is possible to be so engrossed in something that one fails to

notice distracting things. An exaggerated view of this happened in 1933 when Albert Einstein visited Dr. Geno Gutenberg, the senior seismologist at the California Institute of Technology. Einstein was greatly interested in the science of earthquakes and asked many questions as they strolled around the campus. Suddenly an excited professor broke in on their conversation. They looked around to see people rushing from nearby buildings and the earth quaking under their feet.

Gutenberg later confessed that they had become so involved in talking about the science of earth movements that they failed to notice the famous Los Angeles earthquake taking place around them. —*The Scientist*[381]

The challenge is this. Are you going to let circumstances of life affect you, or are you going to affect them with your determined faith? Do not let adversity knock your stamp of faith off, or cause you to tremble, but stick close to Jesus and His Word and you will win!

You may have things go wrong in your life and feel like giving up, but there will be those who will stand in judgment who had many failures and got up and just kept going and won. They became conquerors in the face of defeat. In order to conquer, there must first be a battle. Why would you need to conquer something, if there was not something to overcome?

"I exhort therefore, that, first of all, supplications, prayers, intercessions, and giving of thanks, be made for all men" (I Timothy 2:1).

Dr. Torrey once made the statement: "Talking to men for God is a great thing, but talking to God for men is greater still."

It is a great thing to be an intercessor; to be able to pray for others to succeed in God, to pray that their needs will be met and to pray for great revival. It is so vital to the success of the church worldwide. There must be those who will dedicate themselves to intercession for missionaries, workers, pastors, teachers and saints.

James Gilmore, who was a foreign missionary, felt that mission work could not succeed without prayer by God's children in the homeland. He felt so strong about the need for intercessors that he said, "*Unprayed for, I feel like a diver on the bottom of the river with no connecting line to the surface and no air to breathe; or like a fireman with an empty hose on a burning building. With prayer, I feel like David facing Goliath.*"[382]

There is mighty power that comes from God through the dedication of an intercessor. The story is told about an American minister who became the pastor of a London church. On the first Sunday there were several converts. He preached with such power he had never before experienced. About a year later, he was called to the bedside of an obscure member of his church who told him the following story.

"I should not tell you, pastor," he said, "but I know that my time is come, and I do not want my work to cease when I go. I passed through a period of rebellion and spiritual darkness because of my poverty and lameness. It seemed that there was little that I could do for my Master. But God revealed to me that He had given me the privilege of intercession. Saturday night, before you preached your first sermon, I spent all night in prayer for you; and I have done that every Saturday night since. Someone will take up the work that I am about to lay down, surely."

When the weak voice ceased, the pastor knew what had been the secret of his power. —*The Christian Businessmen's League Bulletin*[383]

An unseen prayer warrior on his knees all night in prayer to God for a minister. God answered that prayer and gave great power and anointing.

If you do nothing else in life, learn to be an intercessor, praying in behalf of other people's needs, praying for the missionaries, moving into a realm of the Spirit where there is spiritual travail and great faith mixed together to bring about mighty miracles and deliverances. This is one of the greatest things you can do. The more intercessors there are, the more prayers will be answered and greater power will be in the church.

Jesus said to always pray and not to faint. If the church is to go forward and not faint, there must be dedicated intercessors. This is the day to pray like never before.

October 4

"For the love of Christ constraineth us" (II Corinthians 5:14).

What the world needs is more love. Paul said the love of Christ constrains us. To constrain means that it holds us back from hate or wrong feelings. It constricts us from doing the wrong thing and makes obeying God's Word a joy.

> *Love makes obedience a thing of joy,*
> *To do the will of one we like to please*
> *Is never hardship, though it tax our strength;*
> *Each privilege of service love will seize.*
>
> *Love makes us loyal, glad to do or go,*
> *And eager to defend a name or cause;*
> *Love takes the drudgery from common work*
> *And asks no rich reward or great applause.*
>
> *Love gives us satisfaction in our task,*
> *And wealth in learning lessons of the heart;*
> *Love sheds a light of glory on our toil*
> *And makes us humbly glad to have a part.*
> *Love makes us choose to do the will of God,*
> *To run His errands and proclaim His truth;*
> *It gives our hearts an eager, lilting song;*
> *Our feet are shod with tireless wings of youth!*
> —Hazel Hartwell Simon[384]

Love covers a multitude of sins. Love is God's approval in our life, for love is of God. Just remember no one can make you hate. Just because others close to you choose to hate, that does not have to affect you.

Love is always the best way. Those who love deeply never grow old; they may die of old age, but they die young. Someone once said, "Love is not blind: it sees more, not less. But because it sees more, it is willing to see less."

How much are you willing to love today? It is no chore to love the whole world. The only real problem sometimes is to love the neighbor next door or those closest to you. Try beaming love to all you meet, and you will be surprised at the return signal. Love is the greatest of all; it always wins.

October 5

"Evening, and morning, and at noon, will I pray, and cry aloud: and he shall hear my voice" (Psalm 55:17).

*T*o have the privilege of being able to approach God in prayer is one of the greatest gifts He has given to anyone who desires to do so. Prayer is not a ritual but it is a time of communication. The best kinds of prayers are those where people take time out to get alone and pray in a quiet place. Prayers can be made all the time, while driving, walking, or whatever one is doing, but there is something special about shutting in with God. It is called "listening in" as the following poem so ably describes it:

> *God has a wireless to everywhere*
> *We call it the Word of God and prayer.*
> *And everyone may daily win*
> *God's choicest gifts by "listening in."*
>
> *First you must shut out every sound*
> *From the heedless world that throngs around.*
> *The devil will use his utmost power*
> *To keep you from having this quiet hour*
>
> *But when you prayerfully read God's Word*
> *The still small voice is clearly heard.*
> *And wondrous peace and power within*
> *Daily results from "listening in."*
> —AUTHOR UNKNOWN[385]

Prayer is not to just talk to God, but it is to listen to what He has to say, and sometimes it takes time to wait for His voice to speak.

"The airplane pilot radios a message to headquarters every hour and receives an answer. Thus he keeps on the beam. Thus he keeps in touch with the control station, receives his orders, and reports his position. He knows that if the station does not hear from him at the appointed time, they will be alerted to his danger.

"As we journey the unseen way of life, fraught with many dangers, are we careful to keep in touch with the unseen control? To turn to Him, relax in Him, let go of tension, give ourselves completely to His strong arms—what a change that would make in our lives!" —MILDRED LONG[386]

October 6

"As an eagle stirreth up her nest" (Deuteronomy 32:11).

You may feel like your world has been turned upside-down today. Things that were comfortable may seem very uncomfortable. It could be that the Lord is stirring your nest. Deuteronomy 32:11-12 says, "As an eagle stirreth up her nest, fluttereth over her young, spreadeth abroad her wings, taketh them, beareth them on her wings: So the LORD alone did lead him."

"The mother eagle had tried by every means to induce the little one to leave the nest, but he was afraid. Suddenly, as if discouraged, she rose well above her eaglet that was poised on the edge of the nest, looking down at the plunge which he dared not take. There was a sharp cry from behind, and the next instant the mother eagle had swooped, striking the nest at his feet, sending his support of twigs and himself with them out into the air together.

"He was afloat on the blue air in spite of himself, and flapped lustily for life. Over him, under him, beside him, hovered the mother on tireless wings, calling softly that she was there. But the awful fear of the depths and the lance tops of the spruces was upon the little one; his flapping grew more wild; he fell faster and faster. Suddenly because of fright, he lost his balance and tipped his head downward in the air. It was all over; he folded his wings to be dashed in pieces among the

trees. Then like a flash the old mother eagle shot under him, his despairing feet touched her broad shoulders, between her wings. He righted himself, rested an instant, found his head; then she dropped like a shot from under him, leaving him to come down on his own wings. A handful of feathers, torn out by his claws, hovered slowly down after them. Then I lost them from sight, and when I found them again with my glass, the eaglet was in the top of a great pine, and the mother was feeding him." —Told by Christabel Gladwell.[387]

There are times when it seems that the nest or the rug has been yanked out from under you, and you are filled with fears; you have never walked this way before. As the mother eagle, the Lord is right there watching and will help you when it seems like all hope is dashed. He will spread His wings and carry you until you learn what He is trying to teach you. Let this be a day of trusting in the Lord even when the way seems scary and unfamiliar. God allowed it for a purpose, and He will never let you be dashed to pieces, but will keep you in the hollow of his hand. Trust in Him today.

October 7

"As we have therefore opportunity, let us do good unto all men" (Galatians 6:10).

Do not wait for that golden opportunity to come to you before you start doing something for the Lord. Many times the opportunities are in little things, or mirrored in common faces that surround you. There is a legend of an artist who long sought for a piece of sandalwood, out of which to carve the mother of Jesus. At last he was about to give up in despair, leaving the vision of his life unrealized, when in a dream he was bidden to shape the figure from a block of oak wood which was destined for the fire. Obeying the command, he produced from the log of common firewood a masterpiece. In like manner many people wait for great and brilliant opportunities for doing the great things of which they dream, while through all the plain, common days, the very opportunities they require for such deeds lie close to them in the simplest and most familiar passing events.

It was Alexander Graham Bell who wrote, "When one door closes, another opens; but we often look so long and so regretfully upon the closed door that we do not see the one which has opened for us." Go on with living today. Reach for the stars right where you are and God will be with you. Just use the talents you have, and you will not feel so keenly your need of more talents. Do not bury your abilities today because you feel they are not as spectacular as someone else's, but give your best to the world and the Lord. Look around you; what can you start with? Do not wait for everything to be in perfect order, or you will never begin.

Look for the opportunity in the small faces around you, in the shut-ins, the hidden things that could just be hiding a diamond in disguise.

Paul said in Galatians 6:10, "As we have therefore opportunity, let us do good unto all men, especially unto them who are of the household of faith." You may not carve a figurine as the sculptor desired to do, but you can carve influence in the hearts of those around you. There are untapped opportunities waiting for you to tap. Take off your dark glasses and see beyond your own thoughts. Bless a world today. Give them Jesus.

> *You think there's no chance for you?*
> *Why, the best books have not been written,*
> *The best race has not been run,*
> *The best score has not been made yet,*
> *The best song has not been sung.*
> *The best tune has not been played yet.*
> *Don't worry and fret, faint hearted,*
> *The chances have just begun.*
> *For the best jobs have not been started,*
> *The best work has not been done.*
> —Author Unknown

October 8

"He that followeth me shall not walk in darkness, but shall have the light of life" (John 8:12).

*J*esus Christ is the answer to your problem today. He can change all things if you will submit your life to Him and His teachings. Clarence Hall, a World War II correspondent, gave this remarkable testimony. "I can never think of the boons and benefits that the Bible invariably brings without thinking of Shimmabuke, a tiny village I came upon as a war correspondent in Okinawa.

"Thirty years before, an American missionary en route to Japan had stopped there just long enough to make two converts: Shosei Kina and his brother Mojon. He left a Bible with them and passed on. For thirty years they had no contact with any other Christian missionary, but they made the Bible come alive! They taught the other villagers until every man, woman, and child in Shimmabuke became a Christian.

"Shosei Kina became the headman of the village, and Mojon the chief teacher. In the school the Bible was read daily. The precepts of the Bible were law in the village. In those thirty years there developed a Christian democracy in its purest form.

"When the American army came across the island, an advance patrol swept up to the village compound with guns leveled. The two old men stepped forth, bowed low, and began to speak. An interpreter explained that the old men were welcoming the Americans as fellow Christians. The flabbergasted GIs sent for their chaplain. He came with officers of the Intelligence Service. They toured the village. They were astounded at the spotlessly clean homes and streets and the gentle ways of the inhabitants. The other villages they had seen were filthy, and the people were ignorant and poverty-stricken.

"Later I strolled through Shimmabuke with a tough army sergeant. He said, 'I can't figure it out—this kind of people coming from a Bible and a couple of old guys who wanted to be like Jesus Christ. Maybe we have been using the wrong kind of weapons to make the world over.'"[388]

John 8:12 states: "Then spake Jesus again unto them, saying, I am the light of the world: he that followeth me shall not walk in darkness, but shall have the light of life." Just as Jesus changed a whole village and gave them truth, inspiration, knowledge, and hope, He can do the same for anyone who will allow Him to do so. He is everything anyone needs. This is the day to walk in light!

October 9

"But they that wait" (Isaiah 40:31).

Noise, confusion, stress, and pressure are on every hand. How can people find rest when there is so much required of them? This question can be answered by relating the story of an incident that occurred with the steel mill workers. Frederick W. Taylor worked for a large steel mill during the Spanish-American War in 1896. He was an ambitious young executive and was one of the first to apply scientific methods—as then known—to study the productivity of manual labor. In those days there were no cranes to load steel bars onto railroad cars. It was backbreaking manual work and after some experimentation, Taylor concluded that the men could do more work if they took rest pauses at definite intervals.

He offered some of the workers a dollar a day if they would try his new method. Under this system, a whistle was blown after the men had carried iron for twelve minutes. At this whistle they were to sit down and rest. After three minutes' rest, the whistle was blown again as a signal for the men to resume work.

The result—the amount of iron carried increased from twelve and a half to forty-seven tons a day! This seeming miracle ushered in the era of rest pauses, the forerunner of today's coffee breaks.[389]

The world does not need more coffee breaks—it needs more prayer breaks. Prayer is rest. Waiting on the Lord gives you strength. Isaiah 40:31 says, "But they that wait upon the Lord shall renew their strength; they shall mount up with wings as eagles; they shall run, and not be weary; and they shall walk, and not faint."

Are you tired of life riding you? You cannot seem to get everything done that needs to be done? Are you always rushing here and there and never getting ahead? The secret is to take rest breaks. Wait on the Lord in prayer. Psalm 46:10 says, "Be still, and know that I am God."

Take time to be still. Pause in your headlong dash through the day, to pray and praise the God who loves you. He then will help you get everything done. New inspiration, strength and power will be yours. You might say, "I'm too busy to pray." Then you are too busy.

Those who have made prayer a part of their life know that prayer clears the atmosphere, stiffens the purpose, and redefines the vision.

Choose today to take time to pray. Put it on your calendar, and you will find that you will get much more done and feel more rested doing it, just as the steel workers did. It works, because when you link up with the eternal God, you are always increased in everything you do. He is a winner and that makes you one when you pray to Him every day!

October 10

"My times are in thy hand" (Psalm 31:15).

David penned those beautiful words in Psalm 31:14-16: "But I trusted in thee, O LORD: I said, Thou art my God. My times are in thy hand: deliver me from the hand of mine enemies, and from them that persecute me. Make thy face to shine upon thy servant: save me for thy mercies' sake." It is good to know that our times are in His hands and He is working all things out for our good as the following poem illustrates:

THE LOOM OF TIME
Man's life is laid in the loom of time
To a pattern he does not see,
While the weavers work and the shuttles fly
Till the dawn of eternity.

Some shuttles are filled with silver threads
And some with threads of gold,
While often but the darker hues
Are all that they may hold.

But the weaver watches with skillful eye
Each shuttle fly to and fro,
And sees the pattern so deftly wrought
As the loom moves sure and slow.

God surely planned the pattern:
Each thread, the dark and fair,
Is chosen by His master skill
And placed in the web with care.

He only knows its beauty,
And guides the shuttles which hold
The threads so unattractive,
As well as the threads of gold.

Not till each loom is silent,
And the shuttles cease to fly,
Shall God reveal the pattern
And explain the reason why

The dark threads were as needful
In the weaver's skillful hand
As the threads of gold and silver
For the pattern which He planned.
—Author Unknown[390]

October 11

"Neither know we what to do: but our eyes are upon thee" (II Chronicles 20:12).

There was once a young man studying for the ministry and he and another young friend were going home for the weekend when suddenly their car stopped on a major highway between Wichita, Kansas, and Dallas, Texas. A brief look under the hood showed something drastically wrong with the distributor. The two young men stood, dejected, nearly broke, miles from the nearest town. One of them prayed that God would help them. He prayed a prayer like Jehoshaphat prayed in II Chronicles 20:12: "We do not know what to do, but our eyes are upon Thee."

A half-hour of helpless waiting had passed when a car pulled over and stopped. It was a young couple with a baby between them on the front seat. The driver poked his head out

of the window and hollered, "Got troubles?"

"Our distributor's haywire," they told him. "Mind if I take a look?" "Don't think it'll do any good. We need a new distributor." "Let me take a look anyway," he said.

He checked it and sure enough that was what they needed. "Maybe you could swap this distributor for another one and save a little money," he ventured. "We only have four dollars between us," they told him. "Maybe I can get you another one free," he said.

They hopped into his car and drove in the opposite direction from which he had come. After a few miles they turned onto a dirt road and soon pulled up next to a farmhouse. The man explained that his in-laws lived there. He got out of the car and went over to the rusting remains of an old 1942 Chevrolet. He shone the flashlight on the remains of the engine and with a grunt of satisfaction he bent over and quickly removed the distributor, then holding it up to the light, compared it with the one taken from the other car. "I thought so. They didn't change them a bit. This old '42 is the same as your '48." He handed the distributor to his young brother-in-law and told him to put a little gasoline in a bucket and wash it off.

They then headed back to the car and he told them that when he had first passed them he went on by because his wife was fearful of them, but then he had a nagging feeling that he should go back and help. When he told his wife, she told him to turn around and go back. When they got to the car, he installed the distributor and the car started right up. "We thought over what had happened. Of the hundreds of cars which passed us on the highway, only one stopped, and that one carried a mechanic who not only had the knowledge, but the flashlight, tools, the willingness to help, plus a father-in-law with a farmyard only a few miles away with a rusty old car which contained just what we needed. We then wondered if the wife changed her mind after we prayed. We just knew she had. Oh yes, God truly answers prayers, sometimes in mysterious ways."

October 12

"He went out, not knowing whither he went" (Hebrews 11:8).

Were you ever blind or did you ever watch a blind person encountering a new situation? They grope, feel, and walk in an unsure manner. They do not really know much about what is going on around them. There was a man who started walking one day away from everything that was familiar. He walked as a blind man into a country and did not even know how to get there. It was blind faith. Genesis 12:1-4: "Now the LORD had said unto Abram, Get thee out of thy country, and from thy kindred, and from thy father's house, unto a land that I will shew thee: And I will make of thee a great nation. . . . So Abram departed, as the LORD had spoken unto him."

Hebrews 11:8 says, "By faith Abraham, when he was called to go out into a place which he should after receive for an inheritance, obeyed; and he went out, not knowing whither he went." It is called blind faith. Just walking in the dark, as far as he knew what he was doing or where he was going. All he had to go on was the voice of God.

You may have sickness, financial difficulty, marital problems or any number of struggles, but with God there can be a change for the better. You may feel like it is dark in your life and you do not know where to go or how you can walk on, but just walk as Abraham walked, simply following the voice of the Lord. Begin reading the Word of God and let the Scriptures ignite in your mind. Walk with faith no matter what you are facing. God is still in charge and He knows every need you have. The Bible says Abraham obeyed the voice of God and went out not knowing whither he went. He did not even know where he was going. All he knew was the voice of God.

He did not know where he was going, but he was not confused. He had confidence. Romans 4:20-21 says, "[Abraham] staggered not at the promise of God through unbelief; but was strong in faith, giving glory to God; and being fully persuaded that, what he had promised, he was able also to perform."

The reason Abraham could walk in blind faith towards an unknown destination, giving up kindred and lands, was he did not give in to the chains of unbelief. Unbelief puts men and women in prisons; prisoners of Satan's lies and tactics. When he comes whispering to you that the Bible is not for you or that it really does not mean what it says, or that it was only for the early church or the apostles, refuse to listen to him. Take authority over your mind and cast down the evil imagination that would take away your faith to believe even when you cannot see anything. Blind faith believes even when there is not a sign, only the Word of God. Believe in it, for it will stand forever and ever!

October 13

"He knoweth them that trust in him" (Nahum 1:7).

The words of the following old song are still true today:

> *When your heart is aching turn to Jesus.*
> *He's the dearest friend that you could know.*
> *He is standing right beside you.*

He is closer than you think today. Jesus really does care. He wants to help you with all your problems. He is the Master, even when it looks like your boat is sinking. He can take the fiercest storm, speak to it, and it has to calm itself. What may look like disaster many times is the thing God uses to save many.

Years ago a fishing fleet went out from a small harbor on the east coast of Newfoundland. In the afternoon there came up a great storm. When night settled not a single vessel of all the fleet had found its way into the port. All night long wives, mothers, children, and sweethearts paced up and down the beach, wringing their hands and calling to God to save their loved ones. To add to the horror of the situation, one of the cottages caught fire. Since the men were all away, it was impossible to save the home.

When the morning broke, to the joy of all, the entire fleet found safe harbor in the bay. But there was one face which was a picture of despair—the wife of the man whose home had been destroyed. Meeting her husband as he landed, she cried, "O husband, we are ruined! Our home and all it contained was destroyed by fire!" But the man exclaimed, "Thank God for the fire! It was the light of our burning cottage that guided the whole fleet into port!" —W. W. WEEKS[391]

God answered their prayer by destroying one of the houses. The more important things were saved by the less important one, for a house can always be rebuilt, but we have only one life. What

seemingly was a disaster proved to be the greatest blessing for the little port city.

Disaster may be sitting on your doorstep and it may look like things are going from bad to worse, but if you trust in God, He promised to help you in your time of distress. Nahum 1:7 says, "The LORD is good, a strong hold in the day of trouble; and he knoweth them that trust in him."

God Himself knows you personally when you trust in Him. What a privilege, to be known by God! To know someone is more than a mere acquaintance. God knows you as a Father or a faithful friend. He is on your side and no matter what happens He will not destroy you or make evil come to you. If you trust in Him He will make all things turn out for your good. Paul said in Romans 8:28, "And we know that all things work together for good to them that love God, to them who are the called according to his purpose." God has a purpose for you and when you are walking through those bitter times, remember that He knows you and is working things out for your good. Trust Him today!

October 14

"For our light affliction . . . is but for a moment" (II Corinthians 4:17).

Sometimes when walking through a trial you may feel like it is forever, but it is only for a season. There was once a nearly illiterate man who could only spell his way through the Bible with great effort and often failed to grasp the full import of the passages he tried to read. Rising to his feet in a testimony meeting where the leader had called upon each one to give his favorite portion of Scripture, the aged brother said, "I get more help from them blessed words, 'And it came to pass,' more than anything else in the Bible."

Asked what he meant, he explained, "When I'm so upset with trouble and pestered with trials, I go to the Bible and begin to read, and I never go far before I come across them words, 'It came to pass' and I say, 'Bless the Lord, it didn't come to stay. It came to pass!'"

Paul said in II Corinthians 4:17, "For our light affliction,

which is but for a moment, worketh for us a far more exceeding and eternal weight of glory."

The trial, anxiety, trouble, and hardship are only for a moment within the framework of life. The hard things of life are what bring out the good, if we allow it. There would be no pearl without the sand getting inside the oyster. That grain of sand is like an irritation, and layers of pearl are excreted until a pearl is formed. Many great things in life have hardship connected with them.

Look at the trial today and say, "This too shall pass." All things eventually pass. It is what we do with the time before it passes that matters. What is our attitude during the trial or difficult moment? Do we use it to shine our spirits or corrode it? Is it a time of reflection, cleansing, and reevaluating our goals?

What you do with the difficulty, hardship, and trouble determines what you become. You can do either of two things: rant, rave, blame, and sputter, or go to the Lord and put yourself into His hand and let Him make of you a beautiful vessel. If you are His child, He is as a loving Father and only allows things to happen to you that will work out for your good—if you turn to Him and pray and trust in Him.

So remember if your heart is heavy, *this too shall pass*, but the question is, "What am I doing with the time before the passing? Is it making me bitter or better?" Each of us chooses the vowel that is placed in the word *btter*. Choose well, for the season or moment of your affliction can be a glorious time, if you put yourself entirely into the Master's hand. Trust Him today, and He will bring you to victory after the minute passes.

October 15

"Sweeter also than honey and the honeycomb" (Psalm 19:10).

The Word of God is often said to be sweet. David said, "The law of the LORD is perfect. . . . More to be desired are they than gold, yea, than much fine gold: sweeter also than honey" (Psalm 19:7, 10).

Why would anyone neglect to read a book that is full of life and has the concepts of success spelled out for him? It is full of instruction and gives light to confusing matters. It is strange that it is often overlooked and replaced by books that are full of froth but do not change the soul.

"Strange it is that so many prefer other books than the Bible; strange that some prefer books with the taint of the gutter in them; strange, very strange, that many are swimming through sewerage to get one drop of truth when the Bible, God's book that is still and will ever be the monarch among the trees, is near at hand. How tragic and sad that some should feed on carrion, or starve, when it is true, as many say, 'O LORD, how sweet are Thy words unto my taste! Yea, sweeter than honey to my mouth! More to be desired are they than gold, yea, than much fine gold, sweeter than honey and the droppings of the honeycomb!' (Psalm 119:103; 19:10)." —R. G. LEE[392]

In France, there once lived a poor blind girl who obtained the Gospel of Mark in raised letters and learned to read it by the tips of her fingers. By constant reading, these became calloused, and her sense of touch diminished until she could not distinguish the characters. One day, she cut the skin from the ends of her fingers to increase their sensibility, only to destroy it. She felt that she must now give up her beloved Book, and weeping, pressed it to her lips, saying, "Farewell, farewell, sweet word of my heavenly Father!" To her surprise, her lips, more delicate than her fingers, discerned the form of the letters. All night she read with her lips the Word of God and was filled with joy[393] over this development.

The Bible was very sweet to her and opened to her a whole new world of miracles, love and the wisdom of God. It is truly sweet especially to those who are in need. The void in this girl's life was filled with the sweetness of God's power.

It is not only sweet, but it is powerful. When Edward VI was crowned King of England, three swords were placed before him as tokens of his power. Said the king: "Bring another sword—'the sword of the Spirit, which is the Word of God!' I need this sword more than any other to overcome evil!"

This is the day to put some sweetness and power into your life. Read the Bible and let it lift you into the heavenly realm that only comes from partaking of its wisdom. "How sweet are thy words unto my taste! yea, sweeter than honey to my mouth!" (Psalm 119:103).

October 16

"He delivered me, because he delighted in me" (Psalm 18:19).

He delivers because it is His delight to do so. If God is excited to deliver His children, why should they worry and fret about the burdens and problems of life? It is not His plan to have His children burdened down with loads of care.

"It has been well said that no man ever sank under the burden of the day. It is when tomorrow's burden is added to the burden of today that the weight is more than a man can bear. Never load yourselves so, my friends. If you find yourselves so loaded, at least remember this: it is your own doing, not God's. He begs you to leave the future with Him, and mind the present." —GEORGE MACDONALD[394]

Leave the yesteryears and the future in God's hands, for one is gone and the other is not yet. That leaves only today, as He asks His children to come to Him and let Him carry their burden. When life surrounds you with things that are frightening and impossible to handle, that is when the story of Daniel becomes relevant.

One evening a mother had been telling her child the story of Daniel when she suddenly realized it might disturb her little daughter's dreams. "I am afraid you will dream of Daniel in the den of lions," she said, but her child replied naively, "If I dream about him, Mother, I shall *leave out the lions*."

This is a lesson for the overanxious. Leave out the lions of care, anxiety, and worry that surround you and put your faith in the God that can shut the lions' mouths.

When Daniel was given his death sentence, he did not panic but instead acted like he always did. He went into his chambers and prayed to his God. This prayer that got him into trouble because of the king's command was also the thing that brought him a miracle. God heard his cry and sent an angel to the lions' den to close their mouths. Daniel rested well that night because his faith was in God and not in the decrees of men. He was a conqueror over that which tried to destroy him.

Paul wrote in Romans 8:37, "In all these things we are more than conquerors through him that loved us." Failure and problems do not mean that life is over. Many times they are the beginning of something greater. God will deliver you because He delights in you!

October 17

"The LORD is nigh" (Psalm 145:18).

When you call up a friend many times he or she is gone or has an answering service. It is difficult to reach people. This is the generation of answering phones that say, "Please leave a message at the sound of the tone." But there is a God who can be reached at all times. He never sleeps, slumbers, or goes on vacation. He is always on call. He said in Psalm 145:18, "The LORD is nigh unto all them that call upon him, to all that call upon him in truth." He did not say a select group would get His attention, He said all that call in truth.

God is nigh. That means He is there listening. Not only listening, but it is a fact that He hears as stated in Isaiah 59:1: "Behold, the LORD'S hand is not shortened, that it cannot save; neither his ear heavy, that it cannot hear." He hears and He does something about it. He is the expert and knows all things.

A man was riding along in a Ford when suddenly something went wrong with it, causing him to stop. He looked at the engine but saw nothing wrong. As he stood there, a car came in sight, so the man waved at him and the car pulled over to the side of the road. Out stepped a tall man. "What seems to be the trouble?" he asked.

"I cannot get this Ford to move," was the reply.

The stranger made a few adjustments beneath the hood and said, "Now start the car." It started!

The grateful man asked, "What is your name, sir?" "My name," answered the stranger, "is *Henry Ford!*"[395]

That is just like Jesus. We get stopped by circumstances and cannot make things move; everything is at a standstill. That is when Jesus shows up, when there is a problem. He has the expertise and knowledge to fix things, and He sets us on our way again.

He is a help in the time of trouble. Sometimes people lose contact with someone they once depended upon, but no one has to lose contact with Jesus. He is nigh even waiting right now to help you.

God does care about those who call on Him. So call today even when it looks hopeless, for He is nigh.

October 18

"But if ye through the Spirit do mortify the deeds of the body, ye shall live" (Romans 8:13).

The way to have total victory in following Christ is to mortify the deeds of the body, or anything that is opposite to His way.

There is no other way to overcome the self-life than through the work of the Holy Spirit constantly applying the meaning of the cross. Without the constant work of the Holy Spirit filling our lives with Himself, we are forever "stirring in the coffin." Our constant consent to His constant application of the deeper meaning of the cross keeps us in the "position of death" that we might constantly know the "power of His Life." —JACK R. TAYLOR[396]

Mortifying the deeds of the body is to put Christ first and our carnal desires second. It is giving Him first place in everything we do, a total dedication of ourselves to Him. It is total commitment to the things of God.

On the night of his graduation from medical college, Dr. Howard A. Kelly, world-famed surgeon and gynecologist, wrote in his diary: "I dedicate myself, my time, my capabilities, my ambition, everything to Him. Blessed Lord, sanctify me to Thy uses. Give me no worldly success which may not lead me nearer to my Saviour!" —ORVILLE S. WALTERS, IN *CHRISTIANITY TODAY*[397]

This attitude should epitomize every Christian. Paul wrote about it often. He said, "I die daily" (I Corinthians 15:31). He lived in a state of death to the carnal man so that the Spirit could live in him and have full reign of his life as stated in Romans 8:5-7, 13: "For they that are after the flesh do mind the things of the flesh; but they that are after the Spirit the things of the Spirit. For to be carnally minded is death; but to be spiritually minded is life and peace. Because the carnal mind is enmity against God: for it is not subject to the law of God. . . . For if ye live after the flesh, ye shall die: but if ye through the Spirit do mortify the deeds of

the body, ye shall live." So by choosing death to the carnal man, one is really choosing true life and is set free from the bonds of the flesh.

> *O grant, Lord Jesus, mine may be*
> *A life surrendered unto Thee;*
> *A vessel need not be of gold,*
> *Need not be strong, or wise or bold,*
> *It must be clean, for Thee to use,*
> *So fill my heart, till all shall see,*
> *A living, reigning Christ in me!*
> —AUTHOR UNKNOWN[398]

"It is a faithful saying: For if we be dead with him, we shall also live with him" (II Timothy 2:11).

October 19

"*Yet if any man suffer as a Christian*" (I Peter 4:16).

In the early days of Christianity, Cyprian wrote the following letter to Donatus:

This is a cheerful world as I see it from my garden, under the shadow of my vines. But if I could ascend some high mountain and look out over the wide lands, you know very well what I would see—brigands on the highways; pirates on the seas; armies fighting, cities burning; in the amphitheatres men murdered to please applauding crowds; selfishness and cruelty, misery and despair under all roofs. It is a bad world.

But I have discovered in the midst of it a quiet and holy people who have learned a great secret. They have found a joy which is a thousand times better than any of the pleasures of our sinful life. They are despised and persecuted, but they care not. They are masters of their own souls. They have overcome the world. These people, Donatus, are the Christians—and I am one of them. —CYPRIAN[399]

The apostle Peter wrote in I Peter 4:14 and 16: "If ye be

reproached for the name of Christ, happy are ye; for the spirit of glory and of God resteth upon you: on their part he is evil spoken of, but on your part he is glorified. . . . Yet if any man suffer as a Christian, let him not be ashamed; but let him glorify God on this behalf."

The early church counted it an honor to suffer for Christ. Acts 5:40-41 gives this account: "And when they had called the apostles, and beaten them, they commanded that they should not speak in the name of Jesus, and let them go. And they departed from the presence of the council, rejoicing that they were counted worthy to suffer shame for his name."

Paul wrote in Romans 8:17 that if we suffer with Him, we will be glorified with Him: "And if children, then heirs; heirs of God, and joint-heirs with Christ; if so be that we suffer with him, that we may be also glorified together."

This is reiterated in II Timothy 2:12: "If we suffer, we shall also reign with him: if we deny him, he also will deny us."

The joy is declared in I Peter 3:14 of those who suffer for righteousness: "But and if ye suffer for righteousness' sake, happy are ye: and be not afraid of their terror, neither be troubled."

The main thing is to be a Christian and walk with God. Whatever the consequences may be does not matter, what matters is that we shine Christ's light everywhere we go. This light will either bring joy and revival, or in some cases it will bring ridicule and suffering. Keep walking forward in the light and someday you will reign forever with the true Light of the World.

"And the disciples were called Christians first in Antioch" (Acts 11:26).

What is a Christian? Someone once wrote the following: "*A Christian is a mind through which Christ thinks; a heart through which Christ loves; a voice through which Christ speaks; a hand through which Christ helps.*"[400]

A good rule for Christian living is contained in the words of Dr. Wilbur Chapman: "The rule that governs my life is this; anything

that dims my vision of Christ, or takes away my taste for Bible study, or cramps my prayer life, or makes Christian work difficult is wrong for me, and I must, as a Christian, turn away from it."

Christians are those who have given their life totally to Jesus Christ and been filled with His Spirit. It is not they who are able to live in victory, but He who lives inside of them. People who are filled with the Spirit of God have a love and excitement for the things of God. Their life is His, their pocketbook is His, their talents are His, and their possessions are His.

True Christians are alive unto God and do not use excuses to stay away from His house or shy away from giving to His causes as the following reading depicts:

JUST SUPPOSE

Just suppose the Lord would begin tomorrow to make people sick as they claim to be on Sunday.
Just suppose the Lord should take away the children whom the parents use as an excuse for staying away from church.
Just suppose the Lord should make the people as poor as they claim to be when asked to help finance His program.
Just suppose the Lord should have everyone stoned to death for covetousness as was Achan.
Just suppose the Lord should let some parents look into the future and see what their example and lax control did for their children.
Just suppose and then, by the help of the Lord go forth and live and serve as if eternity was soon coming.
—Author Unknown[401]

Being a Christian is not always easy to do, but God's grace is sufficient for the hard times. Phillips Brooks once stated it like this, *"Christianity helps us face the music gracefully even when we don't like the tune."*

October 21

"For with thee is the fountain of life" (Psalm 36:9).

    Are you trying to find yourself today or are you trying to find the fountain of life? The twenty-eighth President of the United States made a powerful statement in the following paragraph about the man who has found himself.

    "A man has found himself when he has found his relation to the rest of the universe, and here is the book [the Bible] in which those relations are set forth. And so when you see a man going along the highways of life with his gaze lifted above the road, lifted to the sloping ways in front of him, then be careful of that man and get out of his way. He knows the kingdom for which he is bound. He has seen the revelation of himself and of relations to mankind. He has seen the revelations of his relation to God and his Maker, and therefore he has seen his responsibility to the world. This is the revelation of life and of peace."
—Woodrow Wilson[402]

    David said in Psalm 36:9 that the fountain of life is in God: "For with thee is the fountain of life: in thy light shall we see light." God brings light and life to those who seek Him. President Wilson summed it up by saying that the answers to finding real life are contained in the Bible.

    Psalm 146:8 promises that: "The Lord openeth the eyes of the blind: the Lord raiseth them that are bowed down: the Lord loveth the righteous." Whether your understanding is clouded or you are bowed down in your spirit, the Lord is the one to take the clouds away, and to lift you up, because you are loved by Him.

    God is life and God is light and His Word is light. Psalm 119:105: "Thy word is a lamp unto my feet, and a light unto my path." If you do not know which way to go and are torn up inside because of what is happening around you, then walk with God and He will lead you in the way that you should go.

    I said to a man who stood at the gate of the year: "Give me a light that I may tread safely into the unknown." He replied: "Go out into the darkness and put your hand into the hand of God. That shall be to you better than a light and safer than a known way." —Minnie L. Haskins[403]

    This is the day to put your hand in the hand of God and let Him show you the way of life. You will find yourself as you find Him and grow in knowledge as you study His Word as Psalm 119:130 states: "The entrance of thy words giveth light; it giveth understanding unto the simple."

October 22

"And the LORD caused the sea to go back . . . and made the sea dry land" (Exodus 14:21).

When you come to a place in your life where you are stuck, you cannot go forward because of the obstacle in front of you, and you cannot go backward because of the enemy that is chasing you, that is the time to call on the name of the Lord. This happened to Moses when he cried unto God as stated in Exodus 14:15-16: "And the LORD said unto Moses, Wherefore criest thou unto me? speak unto the children of Israel, that they go forward: But lift thou up thy rod, and stretch out thine hand over the sea, and divide it: and the children of Israel shall go on dry ground through the midst of the sea."

Have you come to the Red Sea place in your life,
Where, in spite of all you can do,
There is no way out, there is no way back,
There is no other way but through?
Then wait on the Lord, with a trust serene,
Till the night of your fear is gone;
He will send the winds, He will heap the floods,
When He says to your soul, "Go on!"

And His hand shall lead you through, clear through,
Ere the watery walls roll down;
No wave can touch you, no foe can smite,
No mightiest sea can drown.
The tossing billows may rear their crests,
Their foam at your feet may break,
But over their bed you shall walk dry-shod
In the path that your Lord shall make.

In the morning watch, 'neath the lifted cloud,
You shall see but the Lord alone,
When He leads you forth from the place of the sea,
To a land that you have not known;
And your fears shall pass as your foes have passed,

You shall no more be afraid;
You shall sing His praise in a better place,
In a place that His hand hath made.
—Annie Johnson Flint[404]

This is the day to go forward and the Lord will make a way where there seems to be no way. He will not lead you into a place that appears to be a disaster, without providing a way of escape. He is with you today, go forward with Him!

October 23

"In every thing give thanks" (I Thessalonians 5:18).

The apostle Paul wrote: "In every thing give thanks: for this is the will of God in Christ Jesus concerning you." To paraphrase it: "Everything is the will of God concerning you, so give thanks no matter what it is." Many things in life will never be understood, but we are instructed to give thanks to God in everything. Joseph, in the Old Testament, was cruelly treated by his brothers and later sent to prison because of lies told about him, and eventually was led to the palace. The vicious trials became the avenue God used for promotion, not for himself alone, but that many people would be saved. "But as for you, ye thought evil against me; but God meant it unto good, to bring to pass, as it is this day, to save much people alive" (Genesis 50:20).

If one person is affected for Christ and eternity, through any trial or tragedy, then it is worth it, for life on earth is only a tiny drop in comparison to the life lived hereafter.

Give thanks in the good times, in the bad times, when you feel like it or when you do not feel like it. God is worthy of all praise as stated by David in II Samuel 22:4: "I will call on the Lord, who is worthy to be praised."

John the Revelator recorded in Revelation 4:11: "Thou art worthy, O Lord, to receive glory and honour and power: for thou hast created all things, and for thy pleasure they are and were created."

"In everything give thanks! In Christian circles it is common to hear expressions of thanks and praise to God for His abundant blessing—and this is right! But did you ever thank God for trouble? Have you ever thanked God for allowing problems and heartaches and difficulties to come your way? In trouble—more than in blessings—I believe we come to know God better and appreciate Him more deeply, for:
Out of the presses of pain,
Cometh the soul's best wine;
And the eyes that have shed no rain,
Can shed but little shine."
—M. R. DeHaan[405]

Spurgeon once wrote the following: "When we bless God for mercies, we prolong them. When we bless God for miseries, we usually end them. Praise is the honey of life which a devout heart extracts from every bloom of providence and grace."[406]

So bless the Lord for mercies and miseries. Praise Him in everything and He will stay right with you through it all because He inhabits the praises of His people.

October 24

"*I told you, and ye believed not*" (John 10:25).

There is a phrase in the Bible that has a chilling effect on me when I read it. Jesus was talking to the Jews at Jerusalem in Solomon's Porch as stated in John 10:25, "Jesus answered them, I told you, and ye believed not: the works that I do in my Father's name, they bear witness of me." For Jesus to say something, and for them not to believe is a sad thing. It is often the same way today. Some people have trouble believing.

In the natural, just put a sign on a freshly painted bench that says, "Do not touch, wet paint," and invariably someone has to touch it, because he is not convinced by the sign.

There is a story of how a wealthy man was converted and because of his newfound love wanted to help people. He posted a sign in a prominent place that said on a given day he would be in

his office down by the lodge gates, from 10:00 A.M until twelve noon. During that time, he would be prepared to pay the debts of all his tenants who brought their unpaid bills with them. For days the notices were the cause of much excitement. People talked of the strange offer and some declared it a hoax. Others were certain "there must be a catch somewhere." A few even thought it indicated that the landlord was going out of his mind, for "who has ever heard of any sane man making such an offer?" When the announced day came, many of the people could be seen making their way to the office, and as the time approached a great crowd had gathered about the door. Promptly at ten the landlord and his secretary drove to the gate, left the carriage and without a word to anyone entered the office and closed the door. Outside a great discussion had begun. Was there something to it? Did he really mean it? If one suggested to someone else to venture, he would be met by the angry response, "I don't owe that much. Let someone else go in first: someone who owes a lot more than I do." Finally when it was nearing 12:00 an aged couple came hobbling along arm in arm. "Is it true, neighbor, that the landlord is paying the debts of all who come today?"

"He hasn't paid one yet," said one. "We think it is just a cruel joke," said another. The old couple's eyes filled with tears. "Is it all a mistake? We hoped it was true and thought how good it would be to be able to die free of debts." Then someone said, "No one has tried yet. Why don't you go in?" The old couple agreed and timidly opened the door and went in the office, where a friendly welcome awaited them. Sure enough the man kept his word, every bill was paid. When the couple started to leave, the secretary said, "You must remain here until noon." The old couple told him that the people outside were waiting for verification that what he had said was true. The landlord said, "They must take me at my word if they want their debts paid." At high noon the couple went out the door and all the people said, "Did he pay?" About that time the landlord walked out and got in his carriage while the people thronged him asking him to pay their bills also. "Sorry," he said, "if you would have believed, they would have been paid. It is too late now."

This is the day to believe what Jesus says. Do not join the crowd of unbelievers, but believe God's Word, for He always pays off with interest included.

October 25

"Behold, I stand at the door, and knock" (Revelation 3:20).

*T*oday is the day to trust in the Lord. Do not lock your heart's door to him. He only comes to help, not to condemn. He said in Revelation 3:20, "Behold, I stand at the door, and knock: if any man hear my voice, and open the door, I will come in to him, and will sup with him, and he with me."

Years ago there was an old woman in great distress because of deep poverty. She was living in a little garret in London, England, and was dreadfully afraid the landlord and the bailiff would come to dispossess her, and perhaps sell her bed from under her because of her debts. It happened that a certain Christian minister heard of her need and worked at getting together enough money to go to her creditor and pay everything. Then with the receipt in his hand he went to see her. Her neighbors knew her only by the name, Old Betty. When the clergyman arrived at the house, he said, "Can you tell me where Old Betty lives?"

They told him to go up the stairs to a certain room; he went up, knocked at the door and waited but there was no answer. He knocked again and still there was no answer. He called, "Old Betty, are you there?" but no answer. He started down the stairs and was going away when the neighbors asked, "Did you find her?" "No, she is evidently not in."

"Oh, she's in all right; she just wasn't going to let you in," they said. "She's afraid to open the door." And so he went up again and knocked and then one of the neighbors called, "Old Betty, let him in; it's the clergyman come to see you." "Oh," the voice came from within. "I thought it was the bailiff and I wasn't going to open it," and she opened the door.

He said, "I have come to tell you that some friends have heard of your need and have paid all your debt. They have asked me to bring you the receipt and here is a little gift to help for the future."

"Just to think," she said, "I locked and bolted the door against you. I was afraid to let you in."

If you have been hurt by other relationships and been fearful to let Jesus into your life, do not be afraid. He has paid all your debts and when He comes in He enriches, He never debases. He lifts you up and gives you so much more. The receipt is His blood. The gifts are His Word and His love. Accept them from Him today. Open your heart's door to Him, have faith in Him, and great things will happen.

October 26

"The LORD is my strength and song, and . . . salvation" (Exodus 15:2).

The Lord is everything you need Him to be. He is especially the three S's: our strength, our song, and our salvation. Moses and the children of Israel sang this song in Exodus 15:2, "The LORD is my strength and song, and he is become my salvation: he is my God, and I will prepare him an habitation." Salvation is the most exquisite gift ever given to mankind. God will go a long way to save someone. He will let strange things happen to get our attention.

The story is told that in one of the rock galleries of Gibraltar, two British soldiers had mounted guard, one at each end of the tunnel. One was a Christian; the other seeking Christ.

It was midnight; and as the soldiers were going their rounds—one meditating on the blood of Christ which had brought him peace, the other brooding over his doubts and fears—suddenly an officer challenged the Christian soldier and demanded the password. "The precious blood of Christ," called out the startled soldier, forgetting the password in the thoughts of his heart. Immediately, however, he corrected himself and gave the correct password and the amazed officer passed on.

But those words had run through the rock galleries, echoed by the solid walls, had struck upon the ear of the doubting, seeking soldier as a message from heaven. It seemed as if an angel had spoken these words direct from the throne—"The precious blood of Christ." —*CHRISTIAN VICTORY*[407]

The blood that was shed was the highest price anyone could pay. The wife of a lawyer once cabled her husband from Europe about a tapestry she had found: the price was twenty-five thousand dollars, and she wanted to know if she should buy it. "No,"

was her husband's reply, "price too high."

But she returned from Europe with the tapestry and when her husband asked why she had disregarded his reply, she showed him the cable. It read: "No price too high."

For man's redemption, God thought no price was too high. Jesus died so we might have life and that more abundantly. And when we accept the gift of salvation, then He becomes our song and He gives us strength.

Yes, the three S's are available to those who will give themselves to Jesus: strength, a song, and salvation. He will save from disaster, financial problems, marriage difficulties, or whatever. It does not matter what it is—Jesus is our salvation.

October 27

"*The lips of the righteous feed many*" (Proverbs 10:21).

A businessman, on his way to a prayer meeting, saw a stranger looking in the window of the church. He invited him to go in with him. "All right," said the stranger. That was the beginning of a Christian life for him and his family. He afterward told the friend: "I lived in this city for seven years before I met you. No one had ever asked me to go to church. I wasn't here three days before the grocer, the dairyman, the insurance man and the politician called on me. You are the first one to invite me to church."

There are many people who need the Lord and words of encouragement today and are just waiting for that to happen. A minister was visiting the sick at a hospital in Chicago. Going from bed to bed, he spoke in behalf of his Master, the Lord Jesus. Nightfall was just coming. The lights in the great ward had not yet been turned on. Coming to the bed of an aged child of God, he introduced himself and spoke kindly to her. Tears of gratitude welled in her eyes as she exclaimed, "Oh, I was just lying here, praying that God would send someone to speak some words of cheer and encouragement!" Her prayer is typical of the prayers of multiplied thousands in the streets, in the homes and in the hospitals: everywhere. Who is waiting for you to ask them to church or

to say an encouraging word about the Lord today? The following poem depicts how every Christian should feel:

> *Oh, that my tongue might so possess*
> *The accent of Christ's tenderness*
> *That every word I breathe should bless!*
>
> *For those who mourn a word of cheer,*
> *A word of hope for those who fear,*
> *And love to all men, far and near.*
>
> *Oh, that it might be said of me,*
> *"Surely thy speech betrayeth thee,*
> *A friend of Christ of Galilee!"*
>
> —AUTHOR UNKNOWN

Dr. F. B. Meyer told the story of two professing Christians who worked for ten years in the same business office. Over the years, neither of them knew that the other was a Christian. Said one of these men to a minister one day, "Wasn't it funny that Bill and I were so intimately related to each other in business, and neither of us knew until today that the other was a Christian!" "Funny?" sadly questioned the minister. "Why, that's not funny. It's tragic!"

The opposite is the story about L. C. Hester of Whitehouse, Texas, who was a plumber. He packed a New Testament with his tools. He was known as the witnessing plumber. A minister said of him: "That witnessing plumber has won hundreds to Christ since he became a Christian."

What will it be for you today? Will you choose to tell others about Jesus and say an encouraging word, or will you keep Him and your good will to yourself? The blessed life is the one who shares.

October 28

"With God" (Mark 10:27).

With God all things are possible. "And Jesus looking upon them saith, With men it is impossible, but not with God: for with God all things are possible" (Mark 10:27). Everything changes

with this little phrase: *with God*!

Years ago a young man began a small cheese business in Chicago. He failed and was deeply in debt. A Christian friend said to him, "You didn't take God into your business. You have not worked with Him." The young man thought, *If God wants to run the cheese business He can do it and I'll work for Him and with Him.* From that moment on God became the senior partner and the young man became the largest cheese concern in the world. The name of that young man was J. L. Kraft, who became president of the Kraft Cheese Company. —WALTER B. KNIGHT[408]

With God he became a success. If people could only learn that there are no failures when God is involved. The only thing that is impossible for Him to do is to fail. He simply cannot fail. This is the day to pray to Him when you face impossible situations as the following story illustrates:

Charles Spurgeon, who maintained a large orphanage in London, once went to Bristol to hold meetings in the three largest churches. One of his goals was to try to raise three hundred pounds which was needed immediately for his orphanage. On the last night of his visit he succeeded in getting the amount and went to bed thanking God. In the night the Spirit seemed to say to him, "Give the three hundred pounds to George Mueller. He needs it for his orphanage at once." He thought, *But what about my need?* It became more and more clear to Spurgeon that God had spoken and he must take the money to Mueller and expect the Lord to meet his own need some other way. The next day he visited Mueller's orphanage where he found him on his knees in earnest prayer with his Bible open before him. Spurgeon put his hand on his friend's shoulder and said, "George, God told me to bring you this three hundred pounds."

"Dear Spurgeon," he answered, "I was just asking the Father for that very sum." The two men rejoiced together and when Spurgeon arrived back at his office in London, he found a letter on his desk. He opened it and found a bank draft for three hundred guineas; this was three hundred pounds and three hundred shillings over the amount he had given away.

When God is included in the scheme of things and prayer is made to Him concerning all things, that is when the answers come. He promised it: "Therefore I say unto you, What things soever ye desire, when ye pray, believe that ye receive them, and ye shall have them."

October 29

"For the word of God is quick, and powerful, and sharper than any twoedged sword" (Hebrews 4:12).

There is nothing as powerful as the Word of God! It is described as being a sword in Hebrews 4:12: "For the word of God is quick, and powerful, and sharper than any twoedged sword, piercing even to the dividing asunder of soul and spirit, and of the joints and marrow, and is a discerner of the thoughts and intents of the heart."

There was once a skeptic who traveled on the same boat with Dr. Malan of Geneva. The preacher and the skeptic got into several discussions and he tried to reason with the preacher. Dr. Malan determined he would not resort to any personal remarks or applications, but would let God's Word be his sole instrument. The skeptic tried to evade his quotations or turn them aside, but Dr. Malan continued to meet him with another. At last the man turned away saying, "Can't you see I don't believe the Bible? What's the use of quoting it to me?" The only reply was a well-chosen verse from the Bible.

Years later Dr. Malan received a letter which read: "You are the man who took the sword of the Spirit and stabbed me though and through. Every time I tried to parry the blade and get you to use your hands instead of the heavenly steel, you simply gave me another stab. You made me feel I was not fighting you but God." At the close of the letter Dr. Malan recognized the name of his Paris-bound friend of years before. He had been serving the Lord for many years.

"It was the Bible that gave fire and nobleness to England's language; it was the Bible that turned a dead oppression into a living church; it was the Bible that put to flight the nightmare of ignorance before the rosy dawn of progress. . . . You might as well quench the sun, and suppose that the world can get along without light, as to think that men or that nations can do without God. The world has no other trumpet of peace save Holy Scripture for souls at war; no other weapon to slay terrible passions; no other teachings to quench the heart's raging fires." —F. W. Farrar[409]

It is time to get the flaming sword not only in our hands, but in our mouth. The Word is fire as stated in Jeremiah 20:9: "But his word was in mine heart as a burning fire shut up in my bones." The Spirit is fire: "He shall baptize you with the Holy Ghost and with fire." Take hold of the fire of faith and burn with it today!

October 30

"*Be still, and know that I am God*" (Psalm 46:10).

*T*o turn aside is to gain. Moses, when he saw the burning bush, said in Exodus 3:3, "I will now turn aside, and see this." Because he turned aside from his normal duties, he saw the Lord. Take time to reevaluate your routine, pause in the mad dash of life, and receive strength from the Master.

> *A moment in the morning,*
> *Ere the cares of day begin,*
> *Ere the heart's wide door is open,*
> *For the world to enter in,*
> *Oh, then alone with Jesus,*
> *In the silence of the morn,*
> *In heavenly, sweet communion,*
> *Let your joyful day be born;*
> *In the quietude that blesses,*
> *With a prelude of repose,*
> *Let your soul be soothed and softened,*
> *As the dew revives the rose.*
> —Author Unknown[410]

This is the day to pause and pray. It is time to let the dew of heaven wash away the smut of the earth. So many times, we do just the opposite as shown in the following poem:

> *We mutter and sputter,*
> *We fume and we spurt;*
> *We mumble and grumble,*
> *Our feelings get hurt;*

> *We can't understand things,*
> *Our vision grows dim,*
> *When all that we need is a moment with Him!*
> —Mary Helen Anderson[411]

Will R. Johnson tells about a gallant officer who was pursued by an overwhelming force, and his followers were urging him to a greater speed when he discovered that his saddle girth was becoming loose. He coolly dismounted, repaired the girth by tightening the buckle, and then dashed away. The broken buckle would have left him on the field a prisoner. The wise delay to repair damages sent him on in safety.

The Christian who is in such haste to get about his business in the morning that he neglects his Bible and his season of prayer and quiet waiting before God, rides with a broken buckle.

What will it be today? Will you turn aside from your normal activities and take time to be revived by the Spirit of the living God? You can be swallowed up by the enemy by riding with a broken buckle, or spirit that is stressed; or you can pause and pray and be renewed in the Lord. It is well worth pausing, for time spent in prayer is an investment in the future. It not only helps now, but also lays up treasures in heaven where moth and rust cannot corrupt or thieves break through and steal.

October 31

"Put on the whole armour of God" (Ephesians 6:11).

Armor denotes that there will be a fight. The rest of this scripture is "that ye may be able to stand against the wiles of the devil." This means that there will be temptations and sin, but we are told to fight. "For we wrestle not against flesh and blood, but against principalities, against powers, against the rulers of the darkness of this world, against spiritual wickedness in high places" (Ephesians 6:12).

Billy Sunday, the baseball evangelist and reformer, never spared himself nor those he wanted to help. He fought against sin and the instigator of sin and thundered against evil from the

Gay Nineties through the Great Depression in America. He preached Christ as the only answer to man's needs until his death in 1935. He had his own way of saying things, no one could say it quite the same way. He was known to have said the following:

"I'm against sin. I'll kick it as long as I've got a foot, and I'll fight it as long as I've got a fist. I'll butt it as long as I've got a head. I'll bite it as long as I've got a tooth. When I'm old and fistless and footless and toothless, I'll gum it till I go home to glory and it goes home to perdition."[412]

Christians everywhere need to have renewed purpose and vision, stand up and fight the devil and fight in the Spirit to regain things that he has taken away from them. They cannot lie down and lay low while Christian moral stances and values are slowly being taken away from them.

Dr. Albert J. Lindsey, in an address before the National Association of Evangelicals back in the early sixties warned about the religious freedoms being taken: "Religious liberty in America is being slowly and surely taken away. There seems to be a code of platitudes that certain people have prepared who, in many cases, make no profession of true Christianity. You either use these platitudes or you are silenced or, if permitted to be heard, smeared as a bigot or fanatic."[413] This was over forty-five years ago. What would he think today?

Today, October 31, has been labeled as "The Devil's Day," because of the witches that are displayed and all the skeletons and such. This is what the devil does: he kills people, he destroys their lives until they become mere skeletons of what they once were. It is time to fight for righteousness and stand up and be counted for God. This is no time to let evil overtake us, but we will fight in the name of the Lord and God will bring victory. We will say with David as he was fighting against the giant: "I come to thee in the name of the Lord of hosts, the God of the armies of Israel, whom thou hast defied. This day will the Lord deliver thee into mine hand; and I will smite thee" (I Samuel 17:45-46).

Put on the armor of the Lord and fight today, for we are promised in I John 4:4: "Ye are of God, little children, and have overcome them: because greater is he that is in you, than he that is in the world."

November 1

"They shall speak of the glory of thy kingdom, and talk of thy power" (Psalm 145:11).

The words *glory, honor, power, majesty,* and *greatness* attempt to describe the Lord. He is magnificent! David's praise includes the majesty of God in Psalm 145:10-12: "All thy works shall praise thee, O Lord; and thy saints shall bless thee. They shall speak of the glory of thy kingdom, and talk of thy power; To make known to the sons of men his mighty acts, and the glorious majesty of his kingdom." There are no words that do Him justice. He is high and lifted up and beyond description. The earth reflects His glory as the writer so capably describes in the following paragraph:

"All nature reflects God's glory. Every mountain tells of his majesty and every crystal stream reminds us of the water of life. Each flower that opens pays homage to the Rose of Sharon and Lily of the Valley. His name is written in the splendor all about us and his voice is heard in the song of the robin or redbird as each new spring arrives. His glory is told in the fragrance of the jasmine and jonquil. The eagle on wing is a reminder of the heights to which we are invited. The music of the tossing waves and their pause at twilight are a part of his orchestra." —Rosalee Mills Appleby[414]

There is none to compare with Him. He alone deserves the glory. His goodness and mercy follow His children all the days of their lives. This is the day to praise Him and talk of His glory.

Praise him for his grace and favor
To our fathers in distress;
Praise him still the same for ever,
Slow to chide and swift to bless.
Praise him! Praise him! Praise him! Praise him!
Glorious in his faithfulness.

Fatherlike, he tends and spares us;
Well our feeble frame he knows;
In his hands he gently bears us,
Rescues us from all our foes.

Praise Him! Praise him! Praise him! Praise him!
Widely as his mercy flows.
—H. F. Lyte[415]

November 2

"I will bless the Lord at all times: his praise shall continually be in my mouth" (Psalm 34:1).

To bless the Lord is to bless self. To bless others is to bless self also, for blessings beget blessings. There is no better time to begin blessing God and others than right now. The tongue should be on fire with blessing and this will set the body on fire with blessings.

Talk happiness. The world is sad enough
Without your woe. No path is wholly rough;
Look for the places that are smooth and clear,
And speak of those, to rest the weary ear
Of Earth, so hurt by one continuous strain
Of human discontent and grief and pain.

Talk faith. The world is better off without
Your uttered ignorance and morbid doubt.
If you have faith in God, or man, or self,
Say so. If not, push back upon the shelf
Of silence, all your thoughts, till faith shall come;
No one will grieve because your lips are dumb.

Talk health. The dreary, never-ending tale
Of mortal maladies is more than stale.
One cannot charm, or interest, or please
By harping on that minor chord, disease.
Say you are well, or all is well with you,
And God shall hear your words and make them true.
—Ella Wheeler Wilcox[416]

It is a profound thought that I can bless the Name of God in prayer. The fact that we can bless God with our mouths is

confirmed in James 3:9, "Therewith bless we God, even the Father." The Psalmist supports this when he says in 103:1-2, "Bless the LORD, O my soul: and all that is within me, bless his holy name. Bless the LORD, O my soul, and forget not all his benefits." And again he says, "Bless the LORD, O my soul. O LORD my God, thou art very great; thou art clothed with honor and majesty" (Psalm 104:1). —JACK R. TAYLOR[417]

This is the day to bless the Lord continually and let His praise be always in our mouths. Then and only then will we be truly blessed of the Lord.

November 3

"Let them give glory unto the LORD" (Isaiah 42:12).

Isaiah 42:10-12 states: "Sing unto the LORD a new song, and his praise from the end of the earth, ye that go down to the sea, and all that is therein; the isles, and the inhabitants thereof. Let the wilderness and the cities thereof lift up their voice . . . let the inhabitants of the rock sing, let them shout from the top of the mountains. Let them give glory unto the LORD, and declare his praise in the islands."

In conversation one day with Professor S. F. B. Morse, the inventor of the telegraph, the Rev. George W. Hervey asked this question: "Professor Morse, when you were making your experiments yonder in your room in the university, did you ever come to a standstill, not knowing what to do next?"

"Oh, yes, more than once," he replied.

"And at such times what did you do next?" the minister asked.

"I may answer you in confidence, sir," said the professor, "but it is a matter of which the public knows nothing. I prayed for more light."

"And the light generally came?"

"Yes, and may I tell you that when flattering honors come to me from America and Europe on account of the invention which bears my name, I never felt I deserved them. I had made a valuable application of electricity not because I was superior to other men, but solely because God who meant it for mankind, must reveal it to someone and was pleased to reveal it to me."

Mr. Morse's first words over the telegraph were: "What God hath wrought." —*MOODY MONTHLY*[418]

As Professor Morse gave glory to God for his invention, the same should be said of all. This is the day to give glory to God for His redemption power, and to thank Him for His goodness. He has given so much, let us praise and give Him honor for such.

"O, the goodness of God! Who can so withstand this great love, that he does not love and praise Thee with all his powers? This work of our redemption makes Thee dear to us above all things. It is a work which has no like; humility unbounded, grace undeserved, a gift without return. This work claims our love, draws our wills gently, and unites our desires firmly and justly to Thee." —JOHN TAULER

November 4

"And the LORD *shall guide thee continually"* (Isaiah 58:11).

Jesus always makes up the lack when we depend upon Him and guides us in all we do. When the disciples were asked by Jesus to get some food to feed the multitudes, they asked Him, "From whence can we get bread out here in the wilderness?" He asked in Mark 8:5, "How many loaves have ye? And they said, Seven." After Jesus had taken the seven loaves, he fed four thousand people and they gathered up the fragments, which were seven baskets full. It is difficult to imagine this. They started with seven small loaves of bread, and from that it was broken into pieces enough to feed four thousand people. After they all had eaten and were full, there were seven baskets left over. They had more after it was all said and done than they had when they started. Whatever you have today, it is enough for Jesus; for He makes up the difference.

Gil Dodds was a minister's boy who came out of Nebraska to step off the fastest mile ever run on an indoor track. At the end of a race the crowd wondered what he would say. When he picked up a microphone to acknowledge their applause, he said: "I thank the Lord for guiding me through the race, and seeing fit to let me win. I thank Him always for His guiding presence." The rafters of Madison

Square Garden must have trembled; these were new words there. He continued, "I don't win those races. God wins them. You see, God has given me all I have. I have one great lack. I didn't have the one thing the coaches say a long-distance runner simply must have. I couldn't spring at the end of the mile. But God took care of that. In place of the sprint he gave me stamina." This was true, for Dodds sprints the whole distance. He sets a killing pace all the way.[419]

What do you need today? Work your hardest, give it all you've got, and then ask God to make up the difference. He can do all things exceeding above what you ask or think. He does not want to help a lazy person, so get up and work. The Bible says, "Go to the ant, thou sluggard." That little ant works and works, but she always has food in the winter. God is on your side, He wants to do for you, but He also wants you to do all you can do. When Jesus raised Lazarus from the dead, He could have rolled the stone away also, but He told the people to do what they could do, and then He would do the rest.

Give Him the glory not only with your words, but also with your works. Matthew 5:16 says, "Let your light so shine before men, that they may see your good works, and glorify your Father which is in heaven."

Work hard, pray, then trust God to fill in all the gaps and supply the lacks, because that is what He majors in—the more impossible it is, the greater the miracle.

> *I may not always know the way*
> *Wherein God leads my feet;*
> *But this I know, that 'round my path*
> *His love and wisdom meet,*
> *And so I rest content to know*
> *He guides my feet where'er I go.*
> —AUTHOR UNKNOWN[420]

November 5

"Praise ye the LORD. O give thanks unto the LORD; for he is good: for his mercy endureth for ever" (Psalm 106:1).

This is the day to glorify God. "In a concert in Chicago, Harry Lauder, Scottish singer and songwriter, sang to an overflowing audience. At the conclusion, the audience stood en masse and applauded uproariously. After the applause subsided, the audience said in unison, 'Thank you! Thank you! Thank you!' Showing splendid humility, Lauder replied, 'Don't thank me! Thank the good God who put the songs in my heart.'"[421]

I Peter 4:11 says, "If any man speak, let him speak as the oracles of God; if any man minister, let him do it as of the ability which God giveth: that God in all things may be glorified through Jesus Christ, to whom be praise and dominion for ever and ever. Amen."

David said in Psalm 24:8, "Who is this King of glory? The LORD strong and mighty, the LORD mighty in battle." And in Psalm 86:12, "I will praise thee, O Lord my God, with all my heart: and I will glorify thy name for evermore."

Glorify Him in the morning, glorify Him at noontime, glorify Him in the nighttime and you will soon find your troubles looking a lot smaller. He will come nigh to you and help you when you praise and glorify Him. From the poorest to the richest it is time for all to give God the glory.

At the end of the Civil War, when the news of Appomattox came, the Secretary of War, Edwin M. Stanton, caused to be displayed from the dome of the Capitol a transparency on which were inscribed these words from Psalm 118:23: "This is the LORD's doings; it is marvellous in our eyes."[422] Verse 24 says, "This is the day which the LORD hath made; we will rejoice and be glad in it."

This day find something in which to be thankful. Look in your house. Is there anything you particularly like—thank God for it! If you have children—start thanking God for the good things about them and pray for the lack. Whatever your life touches, find something to praise and glorify the Lord for, and you will find your life will start to sing back to you.

Anyone can grumble, complain or if he does something worthwhile, take the credit for it, but it is time to give God all the glory. Without Him no one would have the brains to know what or how to do something. He gives life, inspiration, breath, goodness. He is great! We need to talk more about His greatness instead of life's weaknesses. Lift Him up and when you do, you lift your own spirit up. Want to soar like an airplane through the clouds of life? Praise and glorify the Lord every day and it will happen.

November 6

"Trust in the LORD with all thine heart; and lean not unto thine own understanding" (Proverbs 3:5).

To trust God means to give Him the anxiety, the problem or whatever it is that is worrying you. It is the feeling that you are being taken care of by someone bigger than yourself. True trust is to know that God will take care of the problem.

"Keep this for me."
What child has not said this,
And placed a treasure in his Mother's hand
With strict injunction she should keep it safe
Till he return?
He knows with her it will be safe;
No troubled thought or anxious fear besets his mind,
And off he runs light-hearted to his play.

If children can so trust, why cannot we,
And place our treasures, too, in God's safe hand;
Our hopes, ambitions, needs, and those we love,
Just see them, in his all embracing care,
And say with joyous heart, "They are with Thee."
—AUTHOR UNKNOWN[423]

God is in charge, so learn to trust Him. He knows what He is doing! At the turn of the century, a German-Austrian expedition uncovered ancient Jericho, and by 1936, explorations had proceeded far enough for a British expedition to determine that the walls of Jericho had indeed fallen with great violence. Expedition leader John Garstang reported the following: "The space between the two walls is filled with fragments and rubble. There are clear traces of a tremendous fire." Says the Bible, "When the priests blew with the trumpets . . . and the people shouted with a great shout . . . the wall fell down flat. . . . And they burnt the city with fire, and all that was therein." —*TIME*, OCTOBER 29, 1956[424]

God said that it would happen and it did. Thousands of years later, there still remains evidence that this took place just like God said it would.

Make a conscious effort today to leave things in God's hands, after prayer is made, and refuse to worry about the problems you are facing. When a worry pops into your mind, immediately begin to thank the Lord for taking care of that which burdens you. Focus on the One who is the problem solver, and not on the problem.

November 7

"*The LORD of hosts shall reign*" (Isaiah 24:23).

*I*n the song of Moses in Exodus 15:18, he sang, "The LORD shall reign for ever and ever." He is in charge, and that is comfort in these shaky times. God will get the last word, and you can rest assured, all that is going on will be judged by God Himself. There is always a reckoning day. It may look bad all around us, but God still reigns.

On the morning of President Lincoln's death, a crowd of fifty thousand people gathered before the Exchange Building in New York. Feelings ran high, natural enough in the circumstances, and there was danger of its finding expression in violence. Then a well-built man in officer's uniform stepped to the front of the balcony, and in a voice that rang like a trumpet call, cried:

"Fellow citizens! Clouds and darkness are round about Him. His pavilion is dark waters, and thick clouds of the skies. Justice and judgment are the establishment of His throne. Mercy and truth go before His face. Fellow citizens! God reigns! And the Government at Washington still lives!"

Instantly the tumult was stilled, as the people grasped the import of those sublime words. The speaker was General James A. Garfield, himself to become a martyr-president sixteen years later. —MOODY MONTHLY[425]

Even in times of distress the nation was pointed towards God. Their fears were calmed by the Word of God. In the face of evil—there was still hope—because there was God. If you have God you can walk through anything and have peace.

Whatever is going on in your personal world, God still reigns, if you will let Him be in charge of your life. Hand over the controls

to Him; let Him be the leader or the pilot. Work with Him. He can see in every direction, He can see through things, He can see things before they happen. He knows all things, made all things, why not let Him run things?

Augustus, the emperor, heard that a gentleman of Rome, despite a great burden of debt, slept quietly and took his ease. So he desired to buy the bed that he slept on. Needless to say, it was a useless purchase for the great emperor. It was not the bed; it was the faith of the man on the bed that made the difference. The first man had peace with God, so had peace sleeping.

It is not enough to change your surroundings; first of all, change your heart. Let God reign and know peace.

November 8

"Let your light . . . shine" (Matthew 5:16).

This is the day to cleanse ourselves in our spirits, just as we cleanse our bodies with baths and showers. People are so meticulous in their physical grooming. How much more important it is, to be just as meticulous in the cleansing of the heart. We clean our homes; we clean our churches, but what about us? One writer said it like this:

We cleaned our church today,
Wiped all the dust and dirt away,
We straightened papers, washed the floors,
Wiped off the lights and painted doors.

We brushed the dirt stains from the books,
And whisked the cobwebs from the nooks,
We polished windows so we'd see,
The newly greening shrub and tree.

The menfolks, too, raked up the yard,
They laughed and said it wasn't hard,
And, oh, it felt so very good,
To have the place look as it should.

*We said, "How wonderful 'twould be,
If we cleaned out what we can't see,"
Such things as grudges, hates, and lies,
And musty thoughts much worse than flies.*

*If all would let God's Spirit in,
To cleanse each heart from soiling sin,
Ah, then, our church would really shine,
Our fellowship would be divine.*
—AUTHOR UNKNOWN[426]

Jesus declared in Matthew 5:16: "Let your light so shine before men, that they may see your good works, and glorify your Father which is in heaven." Sometimes *heart windows* become so filthy that the light cannot shine through. Jesus likened this kind of person to *white sepulchers* (Matthew 23:27), which indeed appear beautiful outwardly, but within are dead men's bones and all uncleanness. Paul said to do something about that. II Corinthians 7:1 says, "Having therefore these promises, dearly beloved, let us cleanse ourselves from all filthiness of the flesh and spirit, perfecting holiness in the fear of God."

A well-known owner of a chain of hotels endeavors to render the best of service to the guests at his hotels. He often says to his employees, "Remember, my reputation is in your hands!" In a sense, Christ's reputation is in our hands. Others will judge Him by those who profess to know Him and serve Him. Let us shine well today, for we represent the King of kings.

November 9

"*He [God] is kind*" (Luke 6:35).

There is something magical and wonderful about kindness. When Rehoboam ascended to the throne after his father, King Solomon, had died, the older counselors went to him and said, "If thou be kind to this people, and please them, and speak good words to them, they will be thy servants for ever" (II Chronicles 10:7).

Sorry to say he did not heed their advice, but followed the

younger men who laid heavy yokes upon the people and caused division and chaos.

Kindness is giving favor, often undeserved, but the fruits are well worth it. In this day and age of so much technology, there are some people who are so busy they do not have time to be kind or to be a friend.

But no man is an island; we all belong to one another.

"We all belong to each other, but friendship is the especial accord of one life with a kindred life. We tremble at the threshold of any new friendship with awe and wonder and fear lest it should not be real or, believing that it is, lest we should prove ourselves unworthy of the solemn and holy contact of life with life, of soul with soul. We cannot live unworthy lives in the constant presence of noble beings to whom we belong and who believe that we are at least endeavoring after nobleness." —RALPH WALDO EMERSON[427]

Take time this day to be kind and to show interest in your fellowman. May we be too big to be little in our thoughts and actions! Let the kindness of our God envelop us and flow out of us to all we meet as the following poem so ably depicts:

Make me too brave to lie or be unkind.
Make me too understanding, too, to mind
The little hurts companions give, and friends.
The careless hurts that no one quite intends.
Make me too thoughtful to hurt others so.
Help me to know
The inmost hearts of those for whom I care,
Their secret wishes, all the loads they bear,
That I may add my courage to their own.
May I make lonely folks feel less alone,
And happier ones a little happier yet.
May I forget
What ought to be forgotten; and recall,
Unfailing, all
That ought to be recalled, each kindly thing,
Forgetting what might sting.
To all upon my way,
Day after day,
Let me be joy, hope! Let my life sing!
—MARY CAROLYN DAVIES[428]

November 10

"The things which are not seen are eternal" (II Corinthians 4:18).

There is an eternal God with an eternal home prepared for His children, and His promises are eternal. God's love is eternal; faith is eternal, for faith is of God. Paul described it like this in II Corinthians 4:18: "While we look not at the things which are seen, but at the things which are not seen: for the things which are seen are temporal; but the things which are not seen are eternal."

God wants to work powerfully in the daily lives of His children. He desires for them to live in faith. This eternal God with eternal power is looking for someone whom He can work strong in behalf of as stated in II Chronicles 16:9: "For the eyes of the LORD run to and fro throughout the whole earth, to shew himself strong in the behalf of them whose heart is perfect toward him."

On a certain day in a certain year, God's eyes were upon a minister, George Mueller, who was riding on a ship which became shrouded in heavy fog. The captain had been on the bridge for twenty-four hours when Mr. Mueller went to him and said, "Captain, I have come to tell you I must be in Quebec on Saturday afternoon."

"It is impossible," the captain said.

"Very well; if your ship cannot take me, God will find some other way. I have never broken an engagement in fifty-seven years," said Mueller. "Let us go down into the chart room to pray," he concluded.

The captain looked at him and thought, *What lunatic asylum can that man have come from, for I never heard of a thing as this!*

"Mr. Mueller," he said, "do you know how dense this fog is?"

"No," he replied, "my eye is not on the density of the fog, but on the living God who controls every circumstance of my life." After he knelt down and prayed, he told the captain to go open the door and he would find the fog gone.

The captain got up and the fog indeed was gone. On that Saturday afternoon George Mueller kept his promised appointment.[429]

There is a power that is not of man, but is of God. His power

is eternal and there is no limit to what He can do. Today let the eternal God be in your heart, His eternal faith spring up in you, let His love be the guiding star of your life, and seek to take hold of eternal things as the following poem portrays:

ETERNAL VALUES
Whatever else be lost among the years,
God still abides, and love remains the same.
And bravery will glimmer through men's tears,
And truth will keep its clean and upright name.
As long as life lasts there will ever be
Kindness and justice and high loyalty.

In a bewildered world these things will hold
The human heart from darkness and despair.
Old as the sun and moon and stars are old,
Remaining constant, they are ever there,
Lodestars for men to steer their courses by.
The eternal things of life can never die.
—GRACE NOLL CROWELL[430]

November 11

"Be ye thankful" (Colossians 3:15).

The apostle Paul gave instructions on what it means to be a believer with Christ in Colossians 3:12-15: "Put on therefore, as the elect of God, holy and beloved, bowels of mercies, kindness, humbleness of mind, meekness, longsuffering; Forbearing one another, and forgiving one another, if any man have a quarrel against any: even as Christ forgave you, so also do ye. And above all these things put on charity, which is the bond of perfectness. And let the peace of God rule in your hearts, to the which also ye are called in one body; and be ye thankful."

Into the pool of words, he dropped this jewel of advice: *be ye thankful*. To have a thankful heart is to have a grateful heart for all the blessings that are everywhere. Everyone chooses his attitude. They can choose to complain, whine, or be disgruntled, or they can choose to have a grateful heart.

Thou that hast given so much to me,
Give one thing more—a grateful heart;
Not thankful when it pleaseth me,
As if Thy blessings had spare days;
But such a heart, whose pulse may be
Thy praise.

—GEORGE HERBERT[431]

I heard the story about a preacher who was a leper many years ago and a patient in the National Leprosarium at Carville, Louisiana. He was crippled, deformed, and blind. Yet he was cheerful and thankful. He sang hymns of praise and greatly inspired other sufferers. The note of thanksgiving was dominant in his prayers. An old-fashioned radio brought joy to him. He turned it on and off with his lips because his fingers were useless. What an indictment against those who have the use of all their faculties!

Attitude is definitely a choice. Choose today to give thanks for everything that is yours. Give thanks to God for His love, His salvation, and His care. Be thankful to your employer, be thankful to your family, and be thankful to everyone who touches your life. To have a thankful, grateful heart is to have a happy heart.

This is the day to obey Colossians 3:15: "Be ye thankful!"

November 12

"*Look up*" (Luke 21:28).

This is the day to look up! Jesus said in Luke 21:28: "And when these things begin to come to pass, then look up, and lift up your heads; for your redemption draweth nigh." It is time to start practicing the upward look.

'Tis better to hope, though clouds hang low,
And keep the eyes uplifted,
For the sweet blue sky will soon peep through,
When the ominous clouds are rifted.

*There was never a night without a day
Or an evening without a morning,
And the darkest hour, as the proverb goes,
Is the hour before the dawning.*
—AUTHOR UNKNOWN[432]

No matter where you stand today, if you will keep your eyes on Jesus, He will give you enlightenment. When Jesus appointed seventy, and sent them two by two into the cities to do His work, they came back rejoicing. "And the seventy returned again with joy, saying, Lord, even the devils are subject unto us through thy name" (Luke 10:17).

Then Jesus told them they were blessed because they had eyes to see beyond the natural into the spiritual realm: "And he turned him unto his disciples, and said privately, Blessed are the eyes which see the things that ye see: For I tell you, that many prophets and kings have desired to see those things which ye see, and have not seen them; and to hear those things which ye hear, and have not heard them" (Luke 10:23-24).

When we choose to be in His presence we see things that others do not see, and learn of Him. He is a teacher of good things. Someone once said, *"Much kneeling keeps us in good standing with God. We cannot stumble when we are on our knees. A Christian on his knees sees more than the philosopher on tiptoes."*

This is the day to be in the presence of the Lord Jesus. He is the One who gives His children the upward look. When we look to Him, all is well. So look up today and live.

November 13

"Thou art not able to perform it thyself alone" (Exodus 18:18).

If you have Jesus you have everything. Dan Crawford, the successor to David Livingstone, carried a copy of the New Testament in the pocket of his jacket. At the time of his death someone found the following verses penned on the flyleaf of that well-worn Book:

I cannot do it alone!
The waves dash fast and high; the fog comes chill around,
and the light goes out in the sky.
But I know that we two shall win in the end—Jesus and I.
Coward and wayward and weak,
I change with the changing sky; today so strong and brave,
tomorrow too weak to fly.
But He never gives up, so we two shall win—Jesus and I.

Jesus said in Matthew 28:20, "Lo, I am with you alway, even unto the end of the world." He is always there.

One evening Lord Radstock was speaking at a meeting in Woolwich and afterwards nearly missed his train home. He had just time to jump in as the guard blew his whistle. But a young army officer had followed him to the platform and, running up to the carriage window, said to Lord Radstock, "Sir, I heard you speak tonight, but tell me, how can a fellow keep straight?"

The train began to move. Lord Radstock pulled a pencil from his pocket and laid it on the palm of his hand. "Can that pencil stand upright?"

"No," said the young officer.

Lord Radstock grasped the pencil in his hand, and held it up in an upright position. "Ah!" said the young fellow, moving beside the train, "but you are holding it now."

"Yes," said Lord Radstock, "and your life is like this pencil, helpless, but Christ is the hand that can hold you." As the train rounded the curve and was lost to sight, the last thing the young officer saw was Lord Radstock's outstretched hand holding that pencil upright. —*Pioneer Camper*[433]

If you feel you cannot make it or cannot stand—well, that's okay. You are not expected to stand alone. You can stand when He is holding you. Just lean on Jesus for Jesus is the solid rock and nothing can move it. It is dependable as the ocean.

Psalm 18:39 says, "For thou hast girded me with strength unto the battle." Whatever your battle is today, you are not alone. Jesus will fight with you. He will gird you, equip you, and fight for you. He is always there. Start acting like He is there and things will get better.

November 14

"Hope that is seen is not hope" (Romans 8:24).

The apostle Paul wrote in Romans 8:24-25 about seeing what is not seen with the naked eye: "For we are saved by hope: but hope that is seen is not hope: for what a man seeth, why doth he yet hope for? But if we hope for that we see not, then do we with patience wait for it."

There is a dimension that must be attained in order to reach our goals and accomplish that which we desire to do. The eye must see what cannot be seen before it becomes visible. It must see beyond fog, sickness, or impossibilities and grab hold of that which can be attained with faith. Faith knows no obstacles; it only believes.

> *Doubt sees the obstacles,*
> *Faith sees the way!*
> *Doubt sees the darkest night,*
> *Faith sees the day!*
> *Doubt dreads to take a step,*
> *Faith soars on high!*
> *Doubt questions, "Who believes?"*
> *Faith answers, "I!"*
> —GOSPEL BANNER[434]

Florence Chadwick was the first woman to swim the English Channel in both directions. At age thirty-four, she desired to become the first woman to swim from Catalina Island to the California coast.

It was on the Fourth of July in 1952, and the sea was icy and the fog was dense. Sharks would cruise toward her as she swam, only to be frightened away by rifle shots. She struggled on hour after hour while millions watched on national television. Her mother and her trainer offered her encouragement and urged her not to quit, but with only a half mile to go, she asked to be pulled out of the water.

Several hours later, she told a reporter, "Look, I'm not excusing myself, but if I could have *seen* land I might have made it." It was not the cold water, fatigue, or the sharks that defeated her. It

was the fog. She could not see through the denseness. The land and mountains were there even though they were hidden from her view.

The good news is that two months later, she tried again. This time she had her goal clearly pictured in her mind. There was the same dense fog, but she did not give up. She kept swimming in spite of the negative elements that surrounded her. Florence Chadwick became the first woman to swim the Catalina Channel and outdid the men's record by two hours. She just kept going until she reached her goal.

> *So on I go, not knowing,*
> *I would not, if I might;*
> *I'd rather walk in the dark with God*
> *Than go alone in the light;*
> *I'd rather walk by faith with Him,*
> *Than go alone by sight!*
> —AUTHOR UNKNOWN[435]

Jesus pronounced a blessing on those who could see by faith in John 20:29: "Blessed are they that have not seen, and yet have believed."

November 15

"Be of good cheer; it is I; be not afraid" (Matthew 14:27).

Jesus had bade His disciples to get into a ship and sent them ahead of Him to go to the other side, while He sent the multitudes away. When they had left, Jesus went into the mountains to pray. Meanwhile the ship carrying the disciples was now engulfed in a storm. "And in the fourth watch of the night Jesus went unto them, walking on the sea. And when the disciples saw him walking on the sea, they were troubled, saying, It is a spirit; and they cried out in fear. But straightway Jesus spake unto them, saying, Be of good cheer; it is I; be not afraid" (Matthew 14:25-27).

When Jesus came walking toward them, they were afraid and their fears found a voice. When Jesus heard their cries, He said what He seemed to always be saying, "Be not afraid." Their human

hearts were fearful, and He was telling them not to be afraid. The wind was boisterous and the situation was out of their control, so they screamed into the force of the storm. After being with Jesus all this time, they still were afraid and did not even recognize Him. They were troubled and thought they were being visited by a ghost.

It was dark, wet, stormy, and now this, there was seemingly room for fear, but Jesus said, "Fear not," just as He is still saying to His children today. It is the same message. He wants us to know that He is with us, and not to worry, that everything will be all right.

"We can be sure of this, that God will be with us in all the days that lie before us. What may be round the next headland we know not; but this we know, that the same sunshine will make a broadening path across the waters right to where we rock on the unknown sea, and the same unmoving nightly star will burn for our guidance. So we may let the waves and currents roll as they list; or rather, as He lists, and be little concerned about the incidents or the companions of our voyage, since He is with us." —ALEXANDER MACLAREN[436]

Just as Jesus got in the boat with the disciples, He gets involved in our situations. Matthew 14:32 states: "And when they were come into the ship, the wind ceased." *They* meaning Peter and Jesus, for Peter had ventured forth by faith to walk on the waters and he did so for a little bit, until he saw the boisterous waves and then he began to sink, and cried, "Lord, save me."

"And immediately Jesus stretched forth his hand, and caught him, and said unto him, O thou of little faith, wherefore didst thou doubt?" (Matthew 14:31).

This is the day to be of good cheer and have no fear for Jesus is with you and will take you safely to the other side!

November 16

"I called upon the LORD in distress" (Psalm 118:5).

*T*o call upon the Lord is to pray. Not only did the psalmist say he called upon the Lord, but the Lord heard his prayer as stated

in Psalm 118:5-6: "I called upon the LORD in distress: the LORD answered me, and set me in a large place. The LORD is on my side; I will not fear: what can man do unto me?" Prayer invokes God's attention and things begin to happen supernaturally. He called, God answered, and fear left. What a solution to a problem!

The unseen forces are set in motion when people begin to pray. There is a shift in the atmosphere and obstacles crumble under the mighty hand of God. When God is involved through prayer, nothing can get past God, not even a bullet as proven in the following story:

During the Korean War, Heartbreak Ridge, one of the battlegrounds, was bathed in the blood and tears of thousands of American soldiers. One night the battle was unusually intense. The North Koreans were firmly dug into the rock and their positions gave them an advantage against the Allied troops. They kept the night skies lit with flares and the air filled with bullets.

One American soldier worked his way through the maze of enemy fire only to be struck down about fifty meters beyond the enemy's outer lines. Out in the darkness he screamed in pain, begging for someone to rescue him, but nobody moved. His moans and cries for help continued unheeded.

One young man crouched in a foxhole, with his head down, kept lifting his wrist up into the light given by the flares. Suddenly he bolted. Slithering and crawling, he followed the screams until he found his wounded comrade. He struggled until he was able to pull the soldier back through the enemy lines to the safety of the American foxhole.

His sergeant came crawling to find out what gave him the sudden urge for heroics. "What in the world got into you?" he asked. "Why did you take the risk?"

"It wasn't really a risk," the young man replied. "I kept checking my watch until I knew it was safe. You see, Sarge, I left on the hour, because it was 9:00 A.M. back home in Kansas. My mom told me before I left that she would pray for me every morning at 9:00. I knew that God would protect me." His faith was in his mother's prayers and her faith in God.

This is the day to pray, so that the Lord can cause a miracle to happen in your life. Contact with God through prayer gives confidence to the one who prays, so that he can say with the psalmist, "The LORD is on my side; I will not fear!"

November 17

"*He delivereth me from mine enemies*" (Psalm 18:48).

Life is filled with problems. There are pain, heartache, disappointments and sorrow, but more often than not there is good that emerges from the trials of life if one walks with the Lord on a daily basis. He has promised to deliver His children during the difficult times. Sickness, pain and dealing with ornery people can cause trauma, but the psalmist declared in Psalm 18:47-49: "It is God that avengeth me, and subdueth the people under me. He delivereth me from mine enemies: yea, thou liftest me up above those that rise up against me: thou hast delivered me from the violent man. Therefore will I give thanks unto thee, O Lord, among the heathen, and sing praises unto thy name."

Things may look very bad, but look for the blessing in them as illustrated in the following tale:

There is an old Hebrew story that tells of a rabbi journeying on a mule through wild country. His only companion was a rooster whose shrill crowing at sunrise awoke him to his devotions. He came to a village at nightfall and sought shelter, but the inhabitants would offer him nothing. Outside the village he found a cave where he prepared to spend the night. He lit his lamp to read a chapter of his Old Testament before retiring, but a gust of wind blew out the light. During the night a wolf killed his rooster and a lion devoured his mule. He passed a somewhat sleepless night and early the next morning went back to the village to see if he could buy a horse or mule. To his surprise he found no one alive in the whole town. A band of robbers had plundered the town and killed all the people during the night. "Now I understand my troubles," said the rabbi. "If the people had received me, I would have been killed. Had not my rooster and mule been killed, their noise would have revealed my hiding place. God has been good to me."

Often God lets something bad happen so that something worse will not take place as in the story of the rabbi. He also lets bad things happen so that something better can transpire as in the case of Joseph. God knew who could stand the pressure of the pain and rejection that he experienced. It did not crush him; it

only helped prepare him for the position of the highest honor in the land next to the king. What was meant for evil was really meant for good.

No matter what happens, just pray to God and praise Him for taking care of you. Let the scars of life be turned into stars of hope and your tears into shining pearls of faith. When you are connected to God, all is well and everything will turn out for good. He will bring deliverance in His time!

November 18

"Go home to thy friends" (Mark 5:19).

When Jesus delivered the maniac of Gadara from the demons that were tormenting him, he asked Jesus if he could stay with Him. This was the answer he received: "Howbeit Jesus suffered him not, but saith unto him, Go home to thy friends, and tell them how great things the Lord hath done for thee, and hath had compassion on thee" (Mark 5:19).

Jesus knew that the man who had been delivered needed support from people who would understand and rejoice with him, so He sent him to his friends. Jesus emphasized that the Lord had compassion on him. He wanted his friends to know this. Just because he was delivered did not mean that he would be accepted back into his circle. Because Jesus had compassion and showed him kindness, his friends were expected to do likewise.

The Friend who sticks closer than a brother [Jesus] understood the man's need for friends at this vulnerable time in his life. It was a changeover from what he had been doing for so long. He had been dwelling in the tombs, and could not be chained. He was a vagabond who cried out in the nighttime and cut himself with stones. He now had to enter back into normal society and learn how to live all over again. To be able to do this he needed friends.

Everyone needs friends, those who can support and help in moments of emotional trauma and transitional times. To be a friend is a special thing. It is being kind, understanding, and uplifting or just being there in those fragile moments of need.

Time is not wasted when it is spent in helping to nurture and

help someone else to grow and become. However this is done, it could be a song that is sung, words that are written or spoken, an ear that will listen, or whatever is used to lift the spirits of that one. What is done is never lost or wasted as the following poem so ably illustrates:

I shot an arrow into the air,
It fell to earth, I knew not where;
For so swiftly it flew, the sight
Could not follow it in its flight.

I breathed a song into the air,
It fell to earth, I knew not where;
For who has sight so keen and strong
That it can follow the flight of song?

Long, long afterward, in an oak
I found the arrow, still unbroke;
And the song, from beginning to end,
I found again in the heart of a friend.
—Henry Wadsworth Longfellow[437]

This is the day to remember as Jesus showed compassion, kindness, and tender care to this man who had cuts and scars all over his body and was not dressed nicely but looked like a wild man, we must have the same spirit as Christ towards those who need a friend. The results of these attitudes will live long after the song is over and will go on until eternity.

November 19

"They have refreshed my spirit" (I Corinthians 16:18).

Life is to be lived helping others. Romans 14:7 states: "For none of us liveth to himself, and no man dieth to himself." John Donne, English clergyman and poet [1572-1631], penned the words: "No man is an island." We are all part of and belong to

someone else. No one can live like a hermit and please the Lord. There must be purpose and a reason to live, not just exist hiding from realities. Paul said in Galatians 6:10: "As we have therefore opportunity, let us do good unto all men, especially unto them who are of the household of faith."

To do good unto others is a commandment that cannot be ignored. There were two people mentioned in the Bible who gave their whole life helping people. In fact, they were addicted to doing this. I Corinthians 16:15 states: "I beseech you, brethren, (ye know the house of Stephanas, that it is the firstfruits of Achaia, and that they have addicted themselves to the ministry of the saints.)"

To be *addicted* here means that they were obsessed by a burning and passionate desire to help others. They were known for refreshing other people's spirits. Paul continued to explain about them in I Corinthians 16:17-18: "I am glad of the coming of Stephanas and Fortunatus and Achaicus: for that which was lacking on your part they have supplied. For they have refreshed my spirit and yours: therefore acknowledge ye them that are such."

To be able to refresh someone's spirit is one of the greatest things a person can do.

If I can stop one heart from breaking,
I shall not live in vain;
If I can ease one life the aching,
Or cool one pain,
Or help one lonely person
Into happiness again
I shall not live in vain.
—Emily Dickinson[438]

Know this day that what is written in the heart of a friend will never die, or that act of kindness shown to another individual will live forever. For Jesus said when we are kind and do and give to others, we are really doing it unto Him. This is the day to refresh other people's spirits, to be kind and helpful to the needy. In doing so, you will not have lived in vain.

November 20

"Praise ye the Lord: for it is good" (Psalm 147:1).

This is the day to praise the Lord! This commandment is given in Psalm 147:1, 3-5: "Praise ye the Lord: for it is good to sing praises unto our God; for it is pleasant; and praise is comely. . . . He healeth the broken in heart, and bindeth up their wounds. He telleth the number of the stars; he calleth them all by their names. Great is our Lord, and of great power: his understanding is infinite."

Matthew Henry states why it is pleasant and comely: "Praising God is work that is its own wages; it is heaven upon earth; it is what we should be in as in our element. It is comely; it is that which becomes us as reasonable creatures, much more as people in covenant with God. In giving honour to God we really do ourselves a great deal of honour."

Work that is its own wages and *people in covenant with God* are two powerful statements. We are in the element that God created us to live in when we praise the Lord, and are joined together with Him as we give Him praise and honor. Those who praise are forever connected with God! It is an awesome place to be, living in the courts of God, for the one who is praising is elevated to that place.

> *Praise the Lord, for he is glorious!*
> *Never shall his promise fail;*
> *God hath made his saints victorious;*
> *Sin and death shall not prevail.*
> *Praise the God of our salvation;*
> *Hosts on high, his power proclaim;*
> *Heaven and earth, and all creation,*
> *Laud and magnify his name.*
> —Author Unknown[439]

Praise not only changes the one who is praising, but it changes things. Paul and Silas found this out when their backs were bleeding from the beatings they had received. Acts 16:25-26 gives the story: "And at midnight Paul and Silas prayed, and sang praises unto God: and the prisoners heard them. And suddenly there was a great earthquake, so that the foundations of the prison were shaken: and immediately all the doors were opened, and every one's bands were loosed."

Praise loosens bands and sets people free. It is finite man joining with infinite God in a bond that is unbreakable in its power. This is the day to praise the Lord!

November 21

"All the trees of the field shall clap their hands" (Isaiah 55:12).

Clapping shows approval and appreciation and honor. The elements in a clap include joy and excitement. The person or thing clapping is applauding the one who accomplished something. Creation applauds its Creator. They are happy and joyful!

"God has joy in his creation. The abundance is evidence of his overflowing joy. He looks on everything that he has made and sees that it is good. So should we. Creation calls us to join in his praise.

"Creation calls us to awe, reverence, wonder, and worship. Everywhere we turn, we discover some new evidence of God's power and wisdom. We are called to gratitude that he has chosen to make us, to give us life, to give us a chance to share in the wonder of his world." —Joseph F. Green[440]

Psalm 98:1, 4-8 declares: "O sing unto the LORD a new song; for he hath done marvellous things. . . . Make a joyful noise unto the LORD, all the earth: make a loud noise, and rejoice, and sing praise. Sing unto the LORD with the harp; with the harp, and the voice of a psalm. With trumpets and sound of cornet make a joyful noise before the LORD, the King. Let the sea roar, and the fulness thereof; the world, and they that dwell therein. Let the floods clap their hands: let the hills be joyful together."

A beautiful promise is given in Isaiah 55:11-12: "So shall my word be that goeth forth out of my mouth: it shall not return unto me void, but it shall accomplish that which I please, and it shall prosper in the thing whereto I sent it. For ye shall go out with joy, and be led forth with peace: the mountains and the hills shall

break forth before you into singing, and all the trees of the field shall clap their hands."

What a beautiful sight:
Mountains and hills singing
Trees clapping
Sea roaring with praise
Floods clapping their hands
Hills being joyful

This is the day to join with creation and praise our Creator. The Lord deserves the praise. He has done marvelous things and His mercy endures forever to all generations. Today let your spirit clap and applaud the Lord and sing unto Him a new song of thanksgiving and praise. As you clap and sing, you will feel renewed energy and buoyancy as you are lifted into the courts of praise.

November 22

"And the LORD God formed man of the dust of the ground" (Genesis 2:7).

God has the power to create and do whatever He pleases. In the beginning God created heaven and earth. He put on the earth herbs, animals, fowls, oceans, lakes, mountains, and other things. In the heaven He created the stars, moon, galaxies, and all the other wonders. "Thus the heavens and the earth were finished, and all the host of them" (Genesis 2:1).

This was not enough for God. He desired to make man, so He did as stated in Genesis 2:7: "And the LORD God formed man of the dust of the ground, and breathed into his nostrils the breath of life; and man became a living soul." Then God said, "This is not enough, I must make a woman for the man." Genesis 2:21-22 gives that account: "And the LORD God caused a deep sleep to fall upon Adam, and he slept: and he took one of his ribs, and closed up the flesh instead thereof; And the rib, which the LORD God had taken from man, made he a woman, and brought her unto the man."

This is an incredible story of God's awesome power and glory. No one can make man except God. Not only did He take the dust

of the earth to make man, but He also used that same dust and created precious jewels.

"What can mud become when God takes it in hand? Well, what is mud? First of all, mud is clay and sand, and usually soot and a little water. When God takes it in hand He transforms the clay into a sapphire, for a sapphire is just that; and the sand into an opal, for that is the analysis of an opal; and the soot into a diamond, for a diamond is just carbon which has been transformed by God; and the soiled water into a bright snow crystal, for that is what the crystals are when God takes the water up into the heaven and sends it back again." —JOHN RUSKIN[441]

Oh the gifts of God, how marvelous, beautiful and rare! Man was created for His glory: "For I have created him for my glory, I have formed him; yea, I have made him" (Isaiah 43:7).

Psalm 102:18 says, "And the people which shall be created shall praise the LORD." He further states in Isaiah 45:12-13: "I have made the earth, and created man upon it: I, even my hands, have stretched out the heavens, and all their host have I commanded. I have raised him up in righteousness, and I will direct all his ways." If there is any question why anyone should praise the Lord, this alone would give proof. Knowing that God created man and has promised to direct his ways is an astounding truth and promise.

Mankind was born to praise the Lord and bring Him glory. Let us not disappoint our Creator, our God. This is the day to praise the Lord with all our hearts for His incredible power and glory!

November 23

"The word of God is not bound" (II Timothy 2:9).

Nobody can bind the Word of God. It is forever settled in heaven. People have tried to discredit it, burn it, and destroy it, but to no avail. It is written: "So shall my word be that goeth forth out of my mouth: it shall not return unto me void" (Isaiah 55:11). The Word is more powerful than any other word or book that has ever been spoken or written from the beginning of time. It shall stand the test of time as stated in Isaiah 40:8: "The grass withereth, the flower fadeth: but the word of our God shall stand for ever."

The Word of God is not bound. It can cross over any barrier, go into any hospital and heal any disease. He sends His Word and heals as declared in Psalm 107:20: "He sent his word, and healed them, and delivered them from their destructions."

The Word is there when it is needed as described in Psalm 147:15: "He sendeth forth his commandment upon earth: his word runneth very swiftly." It is there for you in the time of need.

The Word gives faith to believe in God and His promises. Romans 10:17 states: "So then faith cometh by hearing, and hearing by the word of God." In order to accept the promises and live with hope in God, there must be the hearing of the Word of God. There must be an acceptance of the Word of God for it to work in the lives of people as depicted in I Thessalonians 2:13: "For this cause also thank we God without ceasing, because, when ye received the word of God which ye heard of us, ye received it not as the word of men, but as it is in truth, the word of God, which effectually worketh also in you that believe." So for the Word to have an effect there must first be belief that it is God's Word.

The Word of God is true and nothing anyone can say will discount it. The crux of the matter is that the people who believe will become the recipients of all of God's promises. A whole new world of blessing is opened unto them, but to those who scoff and question it, they live in a dry desert experience.

A college professor said to a young man on graduation day, "Now, my boy, understand that you are going to launch your craft on a dangerous ocean." "Yes, I know it," said the boy, and taking a Bible out of his pocket and holding it up he added, "but you see, I have a safe compass to steer by."

This is the day to let the Bible be your compass to give you direction, to let it give you faith to be healed and delivered, and to open your eyes to the wonders of God. As it cannot be bound, neither can those who read it and believe!

November 24

"All scripture is given by inspiration of God" (II Timothy 3:16).

The apostle Peter declared in II Peter 1:21: "For the prophecy came not in old time by the will of man: but holy men of God spake as they were moved by the Holy Ghost." The following reading expresses it well:

GOD BREATHED

"The Bible is composed of sixty-six books, attributed to more than forty writers who lived over a period of about fifteen hundred years. They were men of varied interests, education, training, lands. . . . Yet when these men write they all speak of one theme, of one Person, and *none of their statements are contradictory*. There may be apparent contradictions, but they are only apparent. Further study always reveals them as perfectly harmonious.

"Could you get forty physicians covering a period of fifteen hundred years to write on any medical topic and find leather strong enough to bind the book? Or forty lawyers? Or forty engineers? Or forty geologists? Or forty chemists? Or forty farmers? Then what is the explanation here: God! God, the Holy Spirit, breathed through Moses and Joshua and Samuel and David and John and Paul." —MARION McHULL[442]

The truth of the Bible is powerful enough to change men and women, to bring deliverance, to set captives free, to enlighten, to heal, and to give understanding. *"The man who studies the Bible and neglects all other books, will be wiser than the man who studies all other books and neglects the Bible. The man who studies the Bible will have more to say that is worth saying, and that wise people wish to hear."* —R. A. TORREY[443]

Man cannot live by bread alone, "but by every word that proceedeth out of the mouth of the LORD doth man live" (Deuteronomy 8:3). To truly live, one must read the Bible. It opens new worlds of inspiration and hope, and gives answers to problems and dilemmas. There is no book like it and it must be read and shared for the jewels of truth to be realized.

This is the day to praise the Lord for His Word as stated in Psalm 56:4: "In God I will praise his word, in God I have put my trust; I will not fear what flesh can do unto me."

The psalmist David gave us the right thing to do today: "I will worship toward thy holy temple, and praise thy name for thy lovingkindness and for thy truth: for thou hast magnified thy word above all thy name." This is the day to worship God and study His Word that is magnified above His powerful name!

November 25

"I will . . . magnify him with thanksgiving" (Psalm 69:30).

Psalm 95:2 instructs us how to approach the Lord: "Let us come before his presence with thanksgiving, and make a joyful noise unto him with psalms." This is reiterated in Psalm 100:4: "Enter into his gates with thanksgiving, and into his courts with praise: be thankful unto him, and bless his name."

One way to offer this thanksgiving is through song as stated in Psalm 147:7: "Sing unto the LORD with thanksgiving; sing praise upon the harp unto our God." Paul wrote also about singing unto the Lord with thanksgiving in Ephesians 5:19-20: "Speaking to yourselves in psalms and hymns and spiritual songs, singing and making melody in your heart to the Lord; Giving thanks always for all things unto God and the Father in the name of our Lord Jesus Christ."

It is time to sing our thanks unto the Lord, not just a stingy little song, but one of magnitude. We are to abound in our thanksgiving as Paul instructed in Colossians 2:6-7: "As ye have therefore received Christ Jesus the Lord, so walk ye in him: Rooted and built up in him, and stablished in the faith, as ye have been taught, abounding therein with thanksgiving." Abounding with thanksgiving means running over in comparison to a small amount.

Thanksgiving seems to have to do with gratitude for what God has done. It is the enumeration of all that the Lord has wrought. As there is thanksgiving, the mood of the heart will turn to one of thanksgiving. There often must be thanksgiving before there will come a thankful spirit. We are ordered by the will to be thankful for everything. "In every thing give thanks: for this is the will of God in Christ Jesus concerning you" (I Thessalonians 5:18). —JACK R. TAYLOR[444]

There is a legend about two angels who were sent to earth to gather up the prayers of men. One was to fill his basket with the petitions of mankind. The other was to gather their prayers of thanksgiving. Some time later they went back to the Father's house. One had a basket heaped high and running over with the innumerable petitions of men. The other returned with a sad and heavy heart, for his basket was almost empty. The thanks of men were heard rarely on earth even though the angel had searched diligently. —*The Expositor*[445]

This is the day to help fill the basket of thanksgiving. It is a day to magnify the Lord with thanksgiving and forget not His many benefits and blessings. Be thankful unto Him, today!

November 26

"Offer unto God thanksgiving; and pay thy vows unto the most High" (Psalm 50:14).

Governor Bradford of Massachusetts made this first Thanksgiving Proclamation three years after the Pilgrims settled at Plymouth:

"Inasmuch as the great Father has given us this year an abundant harvest of Indian corn, wheat, peas, beans, squashes, and garden vegetables, and has made the forests to abound with game and the sea with fish and clams, and inasmuch as He has protected us from the ravages of the savages, has spared us from pestilence and disease, has granted us freedom to worship God according to the dictates of our own conscience,

"Now I, your magistrate, do proclaim that all ye Pilgrims, with your wives and ye little ones, do gather at ye meeting house, on ye hill, between the hours of 9 and 12 in the day time, on Thursday, November 29th, of the year of our Lord one thousand six hundred and twenty-three and the third year since ye Pilgrims landed on ye Pilgrim Rock, there to listen to ye pastor and render thanksgiving to ye Almighty God for all His blessings."

This was a good thing for Governor Bradford to do, and it was the first Thanksgiving holiday in America, but before this ever was, it was commanded in the Bible to give thanksgiving unto God. Psalm 107:22 states: "And let them sacrifice the sacrifices of thanksgiving, and declare his works with rejoicing."

A Chinese proverb says, "When you drink from the stream

remember the spring." God is our spring; He is the supplier of all good things. Let us not forget to praise Him.[446]

In Deuteronomy 6:12, the children of Israel were admonished not to forget: "Then beware lest thou forget the LORD, which brought thee forth out of the land of Egypt, from the house of bondage."

David reminded himself in Psalm 103:1-5 not to forget what the Lord had done for him: "Bless the LORD, O my soul: and all that is within me, bless his holy name. Bless the LORD, O my soul, and forget not all his benefits: Who forgiveth all thine iniquities; who healeth all thy diseases; Who redeemeth thy life from destruction; who crowneth thee with lovingkindness and tender mercies; Who satisfieth thy mouth with good things; so that thy youth is renewed like the eagle's."

Someone once said, *"A thankful heart is not only the greatest virtue, but the parent of all the other virtues."*[447]

A soldier in the American Third Army was sent to a rest camp after a period of active service. When he returned to his outfit, he wrote a letter to General George Patton and thanked him for the splendid care he had received. General Patton wrote back that for thirty-five years he had sought to give all the comfort and convenience he could to his men, and added that this was the first letter of thanks he had received in all his years in the Army.[448]

Let us be as the one soldier who did not forget to send thanks. As a soldier in the army of the Lord, send up your thanks today!

November 27

"And offer a sacrifice of thanksgiving" (Amos 4:5).

This is the day to offer a sacrifice of thanksgiving. Hebrews 13:15 illustrates how to do this: "By him therefore let us offer the sacrifice of praise to God continually, that is, the fruit of our lips giving thanks to his name." God wants a continual sacrifice of praise from His people—that of giving thanks to His name.

Thanksgiving should not be celebrated once a year on a holiday, but its practice should be included in our daily lives. It is a wonderful thing to celebrate Thanksgiving Day, and honor is

given to President George Washington who decreed the following proclamation:

WHEREAS, It is the duty of all nations to acknowledge the providence of Almighty God, to obey His will, to be grateful for His benefits, and humbly to implore His protection and favor;

WHEREAS, Both the houses of Congress have, by their joint committee, requested me "to recommend to the people of the United States a day of public thanksgiving and prayer, to be observed by acknowledging with grateful hearts the many and signal favors of Almighty God, especially by affording them an opportunity peaceably to establish a form of government for their safety and happiness!"

Now, therefore, I do recommend Thursday, the 26th of November next, to be devoted by the people of the states to the service of that great and glorious Being, who is the beneficent Author of all the good that was, that is, or that will be, that we may then all unite in rendering unto Him our sincere and humble thanks for His kind care and protection of the people of this country.[449]

A THANKFUL HEART
Lord, Thou hast given me a cell
Wherein to dwell,
A little house whose humble roof
Is weatherproof...
Low is my porch as is my fate,
Both void of state,
And yet the threshold of my door
Is worn by the poor
Who hither come and freely get
Good words or meat.
'Tis Thou that crown'st my glittering hearth
With guileless mirth.
All these and better Thou dost send
Me to this end,
That I should render for my part
A thankful heart.
—ROBERT HERRICK[450]

Whether the house described in this poem depicts a natural house or you, the spiritual house, may it be said that others can

JOY HANEY
Package

Diamonds for Dusty Roads HC

70-1567226868.................... $24.99

Power of Speaking Positive

70-1567226558.................... $12.50

Philip's Family & The Early Church

70-1880969122.................... $6.00

Complete Set

70-0757733506.................... $43.49
SALE $30.00

ISBN 0-7577-3350-6

WORD AFLAME PRESS
8855 Dunn Road, Hazelwood, MO 63042
www.pentecostalpublishing.com

come to you and freely get good words. Freely give, freely receive. This is the day to be thankful that God has made it possible for you to be the kind of person who knows how to give to others and make their lives more worthwhile.

November 28

"Giving thanks always for all things" (Ephesians 5:20).

All things means it is conclusive, or one-hundred percent of everything. It is an irrefutable fact that we are to thank God for all things. Whatever comes our way, we must thank God. One writer said, "Thank God for God!" It is a privilege to have access to God's mercies and know that He is watching out for His children. So go ahead and thank Him for whatever He allows to come your way as the following poem illustrates:

I THANK THEE
O Thou whose bounty fills my cup,
With every blessing meet!
I give Thee thanks for every drop—
The bitter and the sweet.

I praise Thee for the desert road,
And for the riverside;
For all Thy goodness hath bestowed,
And all Thy grace denied.

I thank Thee for both smile and frown,
And for the gain and loss;
I praise Thee for the future crown
And for the present cross.

I thank Thee for both wings of love
Which stirred my worldly nest;
And for the stormy clouds which drove
Me, trembling, to Thy breast.

> *I bless Thee for the glad increase,*
> *And for the waning joy*
> *And for this strange, this settled peace*
> *Which nothing can destroy.*
> —CHRISTIAN VICTORY[451]

Matthew Henry, the famous scholar, was once accosted by thieves and robbed of his money. He wrote these words in his diary: *"Let me be thankful first, because I was never robbed before; second, because, although they took my purse, they did not take my life; third, because although they took my all, it was not much; and fourth, because it was I who was robbed, not I who robbed."* —CHURCH OF IRELAND[452]

There is always something to be thankful for, so find that something and begin to give thanks today!

November 29

"I will offer to thee the sacrifice of thanksgiving" (Psalm 116:17).

*P*salm 117:1-2 declares: "O praise the LORD, all ye nations: praise him, all ye people. For his merciful kindness is great toward us: and the truth of the LORD endureth for ever. Praise ye the LORD."

To pray, praise, and offer thanksgiving must be an integral part of one's life in order to live in victory. There are many prayers to pray, but the following prayer prayed by Robert Louis Stevenson is simple and a good one to pray:

"Lord, behold our family here assembled. We thank Thee for this place in which we dwell; for the love that unites us; for the peace accorded us this day; for the hope with which we expect the morrow; for the health, the work, the food, and the bright skies that make our lives delightful; for our friends in all parts of the earth.

"Give us courage, gaiety, and the quiet mind. Spare to us our friends, soften to us our enemies. Bless us, if it may be, in all our innocent endeavors. If it may not, give us the strength to encounter that which is to come, that we be brave in peril,

constant in tribulation, temperate in wrath, and in all changes of fortune, loyal and loving one to another."[453]

The main thing is to praise and offer thanksgiving on a daily basis. To be thankful is to be happy. It is to remember the good things that are constantly taken for granted.

G. K. Chesterton proposed a thought-provoking question concerning this very thing: "When we were children we were grateful to those who filled our stockings with toys at Christmastide. Why are we not grateful to God for filling our stockings with legs?"[454]

The story is told of an incident in Abraham Lincoln's life. "What can I do for you, madam?" he asked an elderly lady who had been ushered into his private office. Placing a covered basket on the table she said, "Mr. President, I have come here today not to ask any favor for myself or for anyone. I heard that you were very fond of cookies, and I came here to bring you this basket of cookies."

Tears trickled down the gaunt face of the great President. He stood speechless for a moment; then he said, "My good woman, your thoughtful and unselfish deed greatly moves me. Thousands have come into this office since I became President, but you are the first one to come asking no favor for yourself or somebody else."[455]

This is the day to go into the presence of the Lord and offer him a basket of cookies freshly prepared in the oven of thankfulness. Give him one by one the many things for which you are thankful.

"Be thankful unto him" (Psalm 100:4).

There was once a good king in Spain called Alfonso XII. It came to the ears of this king that the pages at his court forgot to ask God's blessing on their daily meals, and he determined to rebuke them. He invited them to a banquet which they all attended. The table was spread with every kind of good thing, and the young boys ate with great gusto and enjoyed their meal, but none of them remembered to ask God's blessings on the food.

During the feast a beggar entered, who was dirty and ill-clad. He seated himself at the royal table and ate and drank to his heart's content. At first the pages were amazed, and they expected that the king would order him away. But Alfonso never said a word.

When the beggar had finished he rose and left without a word of thanks. Then the boys could keep silence no longer. "What a despicably mean fellow!" they cried.

But the king silenced them, and in clear, calm tones he said, "Boys, bolder and more audacious than this beggar have you all been. Every day you sit down to a table supplied by the bounty of your heavenly Father, yet you ask not His blessing nor express to Him your gratitude." —JAMES HASTINGS[456]

This is the day to offer thanksgiving for all the good things that the Lord God has provided for His children. David sang in Psalm 9:1: "I will praise thee, O LORD, with my whole heart; I will shew forth all thy marvellous works."

A farmer's wife in Iowa worked hard to prepare good, wholesome meals for a gang of men who worked in the fields. Coming into the dining room from their work, they would sit down and wolf the food without thanking God or the one who had prepared it. "I'll teach them a lesson," she said to herself. One day she put hay and oats on the large dining room table. "What does this mean?" angrily demanded the hungry men as they approached the table. "Some practical joke you have played on us," they said. "This is no joke. This is more than you deserve. During the hot days of the summer I have done my best to give you good, wholesome food, but not one of you has uttered a word of thanks to God or to me," said the woman.

Learn a lesson from King Alfonso and the farmer's wife today. God notices when we fail to thank Him for His many blessings. Take the time to give God thanks for all the good things He provides for you and your family and He will give you even more.

December 1

"Neither be ye of doubtful mind" (Luke 12:29).

A mind full of doubt will never accomplish anything, for the mind rules the body. Jesus told the people that their heavenly Father would take care of them and everything would be all right, and then He inserted the words: "neither be ye of doubtful mind." He knew the tendencies of the human mind to doubt and was

admonishing them not to follow the normal way of thinking, but to have faith in God.

This is the day to believe that you can make it, that you can achieve and be successful as the following poem depicts:

> *If you think you are beaten, you are;*
> *If you think you dare not, you don't;*
> *If you'd like to win, but think you can't,*
> *It's almost certain you won't.*
> *Life's battles don't always go*
> *To the stronger or faster man*
> *But sooner or later the man who wins*
> *Is the one who thinks he can.*[457]

You do not have to fail. It is all in what happens when you fall down or make a mistake. You can either live in regret over that which has transpired, reliving it over and over in your mind, or you can get up, learn from your mistake, and go forward with winning in your mind.

When Peter was walking towards Jesus on the water and started to fall, he cried, "Lord, save me." "And immediately Jesus stretched forth his hand, and caught him, and said unto him, O thou of little faith, wherefore didst thou doubt?" (Matthew 14:31).

Jesus wants His children to trust in Him and believe that He will not let them sink or fail. He is there for them at all times. The main thing is to not doubt.

Again Jesus was telling His followers to not doubt in Mark 11:23: "For verily I say unto you, That whosoever shall say unto this mountain, Be thou removed, and be thou cast into the sea; and shall not doubt in his heart, but shall believe that those things which he saith shall come to pass; he shall have whatsoever he saith."

This is the day to not doubt, but to believe that all things are possible with God.

December 2

"That ye might walk . . . with joyfulness" (Colossians 1:10-11).

*I*t is essential that a Christian serve the Lord with joyfulness. There is a stern warning in Deuteronomy 28:47-48 to those who do not do this: "Because thou servedst not the LORD thy God with joyfulness, and with gladness of heart, for the abundance of all things; Therefore shalt thou serve thine enemies which the LORD shall send against thee, in hunger, and in thirst, and in nakedness, and in want of all things: and he shall put a yoke of iron upon thy neck, until he have destroyed thee."

This is astounding: we are destroyed simply by our lack of joyfulness, gladness and thankfulness to the Lord. We choose our destiny by our attitude towards God.

"The greatest saint in the world is not he who prays most or fasts most; it is not he who gives most alms, or is most eminent for temperance, chastity or justice. It is he who is most thankful to God, and who has a heart always ready to praise God. This is the perfection of all virtues. Joy in God and thankfulness to God is the highest perfection of a divine and holy life." —WILLIAM LAW[458]

To live a life of joyfulness unto the Lord requires a surrendered life unto Him. Self must be put under and the higher laws of God must rule.

"This is the only way to find fullness of joy—complete, unconditional surrender to God. 'Yield yourselves unto God.' There is no very great measure of joy in a half-hearted Christian life. Many so-called Christians have just 'enough religion to make them miserable.' They can no longer enjoy the world and they have not entered into the 'joy of the Lord.'" —R. A. TORREY[459]

Principal Rainy, of whom a child once remarked that she believed he went to heaven every night because he was so happy every day, once used a fine metaphor about a Christian's joy. "Joy," he said, "is the flag which is flown from the castle of the heart when the King is in residence there."[460]

To be truly joyful is to learn to share Christ with other people. This happened to William Gladstone. One morning when he was writing an important speech to deliver that day in Parliament, there came a knock at the door, and standing there was a boy whom he had won the confidence of by showing him kindness. He asked Mr. Gladstone if he would come to see his brother who was dying. He said, "Won't you please come and show him the way to heaven?" Leaving his work for the most important work of a Christian, he made his way to the bedside of the little boy where he shared the gospel of Jesus Christ. After returning home, Gladstone wrote at the bottom of the speech he was preparing, "I am the happiest man in London, England, today!"

December 3

"But thanks be to God, which giveth us the victory" (I Corinthians 15:57).

Victory for a Christian comes through Jesus Christ. I Corinthians 15:57 declares: "But thanks be to God, which giveth us the victory through our Lord Jesus Christ." John Burroughs, the naturalist, stated that when a hawk is attacked by crows or kingbirds, he does not make a counterattack, but soars higher and higher in ever widening circles until his tormentors leave him alone. God's children likewise overcome their enemies by living in a higher realm of fellowship with the Lord, and by prayerfully waiting before Him for daily renewal of strength.

Sometimes victory is slow in coming, but it comes if one will wait and hope. George Matheson wrote the following: "There are times when things look very dark to me—so dark that I have to wait even for hope. A long deferred fulfillment carries its own pain, but to wait for hope, to see no glimmer of a prospect and yet refuse to despair; to have nothing but night before the casement and yet to keep the casement open for possible stars; to have a vacant place in my heart and yet to allow that place to be filled by no inferior presence—that is the grandest patience in the universe. It is Job in the tempest; it is Abraham on the road to Moriah; and it is Moses in the desert of Midian."

No matter where you stand today, waiting for victory to come, follow the instructions of Psalm 42:5: "Why art thou cast down, O my soul? and why art thou disquieted in me? hope thou in God: for I shall yet praise him."

It is time to worship, praise, and pray to Him no matter what happens in life. A sign on a church bulletin board in Los Angeles once read: "When your knees knock, kneel on them."

When things come your way that are hard to bear, spend time

on your knees and let God put strength into them. The hard things and difficulties, the disappointments and hopes that are crushed, can all be lifted when we spend time in His presence.

As the hawk knows the way to defeat his enemy is to soar higher, likewise, we can defeat our enemies by waiting on the Lord as stated in Isaiah 40:31: "But they that wait on the LORD shall renew their strength; they shall mount up with wings as eagles."

This is the day to soar high through the strength of the Lord Jesus Christ!

December 4

"Go forward; slack not" (II Kings 4:24).

*T*his was the command of the Shunammmite woman after her boy had died. She was going to where she could get her victory: to the man of God who had the answer. Defeat lay behind her, but victory was in front of her. She chose victory over defeat.

Wherever you stand today, it does not matter if there is defeat or heartache, you must go forward to victory as the following poem says so well:

With every rising of the sun,
Think of your life as just begun,
The past has canceled and buried deep
All yesterdays: there let them sleep.
Concern yourself with but today;
Grasp it and teach it to obey
Your will and plan.
Since time began, today has been
The friend of man.
You and today: a soul sublime
And the great heritage of time.
With God himself to bid the twain,
"Go forth, brave heart: attain! Attain!"
—AUTHOR UNKNOWN

President Theodore Roosevelt once said, "It is only through labor and painful effort, by grim energy and resolute courage, that we move on to better things."

God is with you so move forward and be not afraid as Joshua 1:9 commands: "Be strong and of a good courage; be not afraid, neither be thou dismayed: for the LORD thy God is with thee whithersoever thou goest."

Once during a war in which Napoleon was engaged, many of his men were falling back in disorder and defeat. He cried to the drummer boy, "Beat a retreat!" Saluting smartly, the heroic drummer boy said, "Sir, you never taught me to beat a retreat. I can only beat a charge!" The lad's reply kindled new courage in Napoleon, who instantly gave the command, "Then beat a charge, drummer boy!" He did, and seeming defeat was turned into victory.

This is the day to keep moving toward victory. It is no time to retreat, for you shall win if you continue onward.

December 5

"Taught of God to love one another" (I Thessalonians 4:9).

Paul advised the Christians at Thessalonica that it was already known to them that God taught them to love. I Thessalonians 4:9 states: "But as touching brotherly love ye need not that I write unto you: for ye yourselves are taught of God to love one another."

It was emphasized by Jesus in His teachings while on earth and was a sign to unbelievers of the true disciples because of their love for one another. He gave the new commandment in John 13:34-35: "A new commandment I give unto you, That ye love one another; as I have loved you, that ye also love one another. By this shall all men know that ye are my disciples, if ye have love one another."

"One of the glories of Christianity is the place it gives to love. It sums up all religious duty in love to God, and all ethical duty in love to man. It has set before humanity as the fullest revelation of God and the highest expression of manhood the life of Jesus Christ, whose name is a synonym of love. It has made love the dominant characteristic in the nature of God himself, and therewith has written love across the whole universe." —WALTER RAUSCHENBUSCH[461]

To be able to love and share with others is the greatest way to live. It is opening up self as one would open a window and let the fresh breath of air into the room. Opening the window of self and giving to others love and encouragement are what life is all about as the following poem depicts:

> *Let me not shut myself within myself*
> *Nor dedicate my days to petty things,*
> *Let there be many windows in my life,*
> *The entrance to my heart a door that swings.*
>
> *Save me from self-preferment that would gain*
> *Its cloistered place, safe sheltered from the strife.*
> *But purposeful and calm and sweet and sane,*
> *Lord, keep me in the Living Room of life.*
> —AUTHOR UNKNOWN[462]

This is the day to stay in the Living Room of life and give of yourself to those who are in need of love, care, and advice. To be able to love others is the highest attainment on earth. Today, begin to let God teach you how to love His way.

December 6

"*David encouraged himself in the LORD his God*" (I Samuel 30:6).

David had lost everything. The enemy had invaded his city while he and his men were gone, took all the wives, children and treasures, and then burned the city. When David and his band arrived home and found that everything had been taken, they began to weep profusely. The men were greatly distressed and took up stones to kill David. That is when he encouraged himself in the Lord and began to pray. God of course answered his prayer and the end result was that they went to the enemy's camp and killed them. Afterwards they retrieved everything that had been stolen from them: their families, herds and flocks and jewels.

You may feel or have felt like David when everything seemed

to be slipping from your fingers or slowly drifting away from you. When the distress comes, that is the time to pray as David prayed.

Life can steal your dreams, but you have to fight for them. God's answer to David after he prayed is found in I Samuel 30:8: "Pursue: for thou shalt surely overtake them, and without fail recover all."

If your dreams have been stolen from you and instead of going forward you feel like you are on a treadmill, with no beckoning dream, that is the time to go after them. As long as there is God [and He will always be], there will always be opportunities and dreams. Get out of the pit of despair and live again and take advantage of every opportunity even if it comes dressed in overalls and hard work. It is there, look for it. Think not of what is lost, but look ahead to what can be gained and attained as the following poem illustrates:

DAUNTLESS
I will not think of treasures lost,
Of time that's past and gone;
As long as faith is in my heart
I shall go bravely on.
And other treasures I shall find
To keep me and sustain;
As long as faith is in my heart
Life cannot be in vain.

And though I know that I shall meet
Dark tempests on my way,
As long as hope is in my heart
I see a shining ray;
And flowers shall bloom along my path
And birds to me shall sing;
As long as hope is in my heart
My spirit high shall wing.
—MARY BLOCK[463]

This is the day to let your spirit wing high, to follow your dream and get it back. Look not behind you, but *pursue*, *overtake*, and *recover*!

December 7

"For God, said he, hath made me forget all my toil" (Genesis 41:51).

Joseph named his first-born son Manasseh, which signified that the pain and the toil of yesteryears were over and God had helped him to forget the rejection of his brothers and the long lonely road he had traveled to where he was then. "And Joseph called the name of the firstborn Manasseh: For God, said he, hath made me forget all my toil, and all my father's house" (Genesis 41:51).

Joseph was forgetting the pain of his father's house. He remembered his family, but he did not feel bad towards them. Just as God helped Joseph forget the past, He will do the same for you. The past is over, forget the bad and remember the good.

"*It's but little good you'll do, watering last year's crops* [words from George Eliot]. Yet that is exactly what I have seen hundreds of my patients doing in the past twenty-five years—watering with freely flowing tears things of the irrevocable past. Not the bittersweet memories of loved ones, which I could understand, but things done which should not have been done, and things left undone which should have been done." —Dr. Frederic Loomis[464]

To the wise, every day is a new day. Watering yesterday with tears today does no good. What's done is done. The only thing that can be done about it is to pray for God to soften the blows that still bring pain to your mind. Ask Him for mercy and help in the time of need to heal and help you forget just as He did for Joseph. Then go forward, stomping on the negative things of the past and carefully tread each moment of the new day.

"Today is a new day. You will get out of it just what you put into it. . . . If you have made mistakes, even serious mistakes, there is always another chance for you. And supposing you have tried and failed again and again, you may have a fresh start any moment you choose, for this thing that we call 'failure' is not the falling down, but the staying down." —Mary Pickford[465]

Joseph, whom God helped to forget the hurts of the past, walked each new day with hope and anticipation of better things. When his second son was born, his attitude was reflected in what

he named him as shown in Genesis 41:52: "And the name of the second called he Ephraim: For God hath caused me to be fruitful in the land of my affliction."

Joseph admitted that he had been hurt and afflicted, but he did not let it mar his today, but with God's help he became a better man for what he had experienced at the hands of those who did him wrong.

This is the day to put the past where it belongs: in the past, and do not let it stain the now with tears and regrets.

"God loveth a cheerful giver" (II Corinthians 9:7).

God loves those who give cheerfully and they will be blessed according to what they give as declared in II Corinthians 9:6: "But this I say, He which soweth sparingly shall reap also sparingly; and he which soweth bountifully shall reap also bountifully."

When someone gives with a cheerful heart, it brings a smile to God's face. He notices and it makes Him happy. II Corinthians 9:8-9 continues: "And God is able to make all grace abound toward you; that ye, always having all sufficiency in all things, may abound to every good work: As it is written, He hath dispersed abroad; he hath given to the poor: his righteousness remaineth for ever."

He promises that the giver will have sufficiency in all things. There will never be want to the giver. The more he gives, the more will come back to him. What is given is never lost; it is just an investment in the bank of heaven.

"Giving to the Lord is but transporting our goods to a higher floor."[466]

Everything God made gives back; it is an eternal law: to receive is to give.

God made the sun—it gives.
God made the moon—it gives.
God made the stars—they give.
God made the air—it gives.

God made the clouds—they give.
God made the earth—it gives.
God made the sea—it gives.
God made the trees—they give.[467]

God made you—the choice is up to you.

There are many things people can give. They can give of themselves to different charities, they can give money, they can give influence; the list is endless what can be given. To give of self is one of the greatest ways to find happiness.

"To me there is in happiness an element of self-forgetfulness. You lose yourself in something outside yourself when you are happy; just as when you are desperately miserable you are intensely conscious of yourself, are a solid little lump of ego weighing a ton." —J. B. PRIESTLEY[468]

This is the day to give, for it not only brings happiness to the one who gives, but it makes God happy. The glow that comes from being a cheerful giver cannot be bought. It is just the end result of an action ordained of God.

"Happiness is a perfume you cannot pour on others without getting a few drops on yourself." —RALPH WALDO EMERSON[469]

"But I give myself unto prayer" (Psalm 109:4).

The disciples did the same thing, as recorded in Acts 6:4: "But we will give ourselves continually to prayer, and to the ministry of the word."

This is a great thing when people give themselves to prayer. Prayer is the way to power and great things are accomplished. Abraham prayed and Isaac was born. Moses prayed and God opened the Red Sea for a miraculous crossing. Joshua prayed and he was visited by the captain of the host of the Lord. Hannah prayed and God opened her womb. Jehoshaphat prayed and God delivered him from the enemy. Elijah prayed and fire fell from heaven. Elisha prayed and a dead boy came to life. Daniel prayed and God sent an angel. Jonah prayed and God rescued him from

the belly of a fish. Paul and Silas prayed and God sent an earthquake to deliver them from prison. The church prayed for Peter and God sent an angel to deliver him.

Prayers are powerful for they bring humanity into the realm of divinity. The finite touches infinite; man touches God where miracles abound.

Not only is prayer powerful, but every prayer that is prayed will be rewarded, for God has commanded His children to pray. God rewards those who are obedient to the call of prayer, those who obey His commandments.

Revelation 22:12 depicts this: "And, behold, I come quickly; and my reward is with me, to give every man according as his work shall be."

When God told Jonah to go to Nineveh and preach to them that He was going to destroy it if they did not repent, Jonah ran from the call. But when God put him at the bottom of the sea in the belly of a fish, he repented and cried as recorded in Jonah 2:7: "When my soul fainted within me I remembered the LORD: and my prayer came in unto thee, into thine holy temple." As soon as Jonah was spit out of the fish's mouth, he went to Nineveh and preached the word of the Lord. This caused quite a stir in the city and the king sent word to be proclaimed in the streets for the people to fast and pray to God for mercy: "But let man and beast be covered with sackcloth, and cry mightily unto God: yea, let them turn every one from his evil way, and from the violence that is in their hands" (Jonah 3:8). God rewarded their works as shown in Jonah 3:10: "And God saw their works, that they turned from their evil way; and God repented of the evil, that he had said that he would do unto them; and he did it not."

This is the day to give yourself to prayer and experience the power that is transferred from God to you as you go into His throne room. It will change your life for the better!

"The kingdom of God is within you" (Luke 17:21).

When the Pharisees demanded of Jesus to tell them when the kingdom of God should come, he answered, "Neither shall they say, Lo here! or, lo there! for, behold, the kingdom of God is within you."

The world around you cannot touch or change what is on the inside of you if you do not allow it to do so. When a person is filled with the Holy Spirit, there comes a change within him as stated in II Corinthians 5:17: "Therefore if any man be in Christ, he is a new creature: old things are passed away; behold, all things are become new."

When a person becomes new in Christ, his carnal appetites change and his desires are turned more toward things with eternal value. Inside of him a light went on and darkness was evicted. Excitement and the glow of love took up residence. It was not anything that happened outside of himself, but it was an inner change.

Ephesians 3:16-17 speaks about this inner self: "That he would grant you, according to the riches of his glory, to be strengthened with might by his Spirit in the inner man; That Christ may dwell in your hearts by faith."

When God sets up His kingdom inside you, He takes up residence and sits on the throne of your heart. It is the kingdom of God within you; therefore, that is from where your happiness and joy spring.

"Real happiness is not dependent on external things. The pond is fed from within. The kind of happiness that stays with you is the happiness that springs from inward thoughts and emotions. You must cultivate your mind if you wish to achieve enduring happiness. You must furnish your mind with interesting thoughts and ideas. For an empty mind grows bored and cannot endure itself. An empty mind seeks pleasure as a substitute for happiness." —WILLIAM LYON PHELPS[470]

This is why it is so important after the kingdom is set up inside of you to continually feed the mind with the thoughts of the One who sits on the throne in your heart room. His thoughts are found in the Word of God and He whispers thoughts to you while you are in prayer. So this day take time to pray and read His Word. Let the King of the kingdom work for you by absorbing His Word as stated in Psalm 119:130: "The entrance of thy words giveth light; it giveth understanding unto the simple."

December 11

"Yet it is not finished" (Ezra 5:16).

God is interested in His people doing a good work and finishing what they start. God told Zerubbabel to build the Temple in Jerusalem, but their adversaries tried to stop them by sending a letter of intent to Darius the king. Their answer to the king concerning the matter is recorded in Ezra 5:16-17: "Then came the same Sheshbazzar, and laid the foundation of the house of God which is in Jerusalem: and since that time even until now hath it been in building, and yet it is not finished. Now therefore, if it seem good to the king, let there be search made in the king's treasure house, which is there at Babylon, whether it be so, that a decree was made of Cyrus the king to build this house of God at Jerusalem."

So a search was made and the scrolls were found which stated: "In the first year of Cyrus the king the same Cyrus the king made a decree concerning the house of God at Jerusalem, Let the house be builded" (Ezra 6:3). The result of all this is recorded in Ezra 6:15: "And this house was finished on the third day of the month Adar, which was in the sixth year of the reign of Darius the king."

Genesis 2:1 records: "Thus the heavens and the earth were finished, and all the host of them." Then God rested on the seventh day, and after resting went on to the next thing.

Ralph Waldo Emerson reminds us in the following paragraph to finish each day well, to not mull over the mistakes, but go on to the next day:

"Finish every day and be done with it. You have done what you could. Some blunders and some absurdities no doubt crept in; forget them as soon as you can. Tomorrow is a new day; begin it well and serenely with too high a spirit to be cumbered with your old nonsense. This day is all that is good and fair. It is too dear, with its hopes and invitations, to waste a moment on the yesterdays."[471]

When Jesus was on earth, He was sent with a purpose, and the main thing was that He finished what He was supposed to do as depicted in John 4:34: "Jesus saith unto them, My meat is to do the will of him that sent me, and to finish his work." As He hung on the cross, He uttered those pain-filled words, "It is finished,"

and bowed His head and died. But the finish was not yet; He was yet to be resurrected.

At the end of Paul's life he spoke those famous words: "I have fought a good fight, I have finished my course, I have kept the faith" (II Timothy 4:7).

This is the day to determine to finish this day well. Then put a period on it, rest during the night, and begin a new day in the morning. What will happen today is history tomorrow and cannot be resurrected, so do your best to live it with excellence!

December 12

"They . . . condemn the innocent" (Psalm 94:21).

The psalmist described those who criticize and condemn in Psalm 94:21-23: "They gather themselves together against the soul of the righteous, and condemn the innocent blood. But the LORD is my defence; and my God is the rock of my refuge. And he shall bring upon them their own iniquity, and shall cut them off in their own wickedness; yea, the LORD our God shall cut them off."

This is exactly what happens to those who are critical and condemn someone who is doing his best to do what is right. They are cut off from blessings, and the sin of their own tongue is visited upon them. The best thing to do when you are unjustly criticized is to keep on doing the thing that you know to be right.

Abraham Lincoln once said, *"If I tried to read, much less answer, all the criticisms made of me, and all the attacks leveled against me, this office would have to be closed for all other business. I do the best I know how, the very best I can. And I mean to keep on doing this, down to the very end. If the end brings me out all wrong, ten angels swearing I had been right would make no difference. If the end brings me out all right, then what is said against me now will not amount to anything."*[472]

The Lord has promised to intervene in behalf of those who are being condemned as declared in Isaiah 54:15-17: "Behold, they shall surely gather together, but not by me: whosoever shall gather together against thee shall fall for thy sake. Behold, I have created the smith that bloweth the coals in the fire, and that

bringeth forth an instrument for his work; and I have created the waster to destroy. No weapon that is formed against thee shall prosper; and every tongue that shall rise against thee in judgment thou shalt condemn. This is the heritage of the servants of the Lord, and their righteousness is of me, saith the Lord."

If you are criticized, know that you have a kinship with the Lord who was unjustly condemned and put to death. He bore it all without saying a word. "And the men that held Jesus mocked him, and smote him, And when they had blindfolded him, they struck him on the face, and asked him, saying, Prophesy, who is it that smote thee? And many other things blasphemously spake they against him" (Luke 22:63-65).

"Don't mind criticism. If it is untrue, disregard it. If it is unfair, keep from irritation. If it is ignorant, smile. If it is justified, learn from it."

> *You may go through the world,*
> *But 'twill be very slow,*
> *If you listen to all*
> *That is said as you go;*
> *You'll be worried and fretted,*
> *And kept in a stew,*
> *For critical tongues*
> *Must find something to do,*
> *For people will talk.*
> —Author Unknown[473]

If it is your turn to be criticized, bear it with grace and follow the example of the Lord. Work harder, and keep going forward and eventually God's weapons will silence those who accuse.

December 13

"*Ye have not passed this way heretofore*" (Joshua 3:4).

When Joshua was preparing the children of Israel to get ready to cross over the river of Jordan, he knew that they had

never been there before so he was giving them instructions what to do as recorded in Joshua 3:4: "Yet there shall be a space between you and it [the ark], about two thousand cubits by measure: come not near unto it, that ye may know the way by which ye must go: for ye have not passed this way heretofore." It was a new way, and it brought new possibilities for them. They were going to cross the Jordan River BEFORE there was a way to go. God had told Joshua: "And it shall come to pass, as soon as the soles of the feet of the priests that bear the ark of the LORD, the Lord of all the earth, shall rest in the waters of Jordan, that the waters of Jordan shall be cut off from the waters that come down from above; and they shall stand upon an heap. . . . And as they that bare the ark were come unto Jordan, and the feet of the priests that bare the ark were dipped in the brim of the water, (for Jordan overfloweth all his banks all the time of harvest,) That the waters which came down from above stood and rose up upon an heap. . . . And the priests that bare the ark of the covenant of the LORD stood firm on dry ground in the midst of Jordan, and all the Israelites passed over on dry ground" (Joshua 3:13, 15-17).

Today is a brand-new day ready to be lived. You have not passed this way before. There are new possibilities, opportunities, and incidents to experience. Resolve to live this day as the following reading encourages one to do:

Live each day to the fullest. Get the most from each hour, each day, and each age of your life. Then you can look forward with confidence, and back without regrets.

Be yourself—but be your best self. Dare to be different and to follow your own star.

And don't be afraid to be happy. Enjoy what is beautiful. Love with all your heart and soul. Believe that those you love, love you.

Forget what you have done for your friends, and remember what they have done for you. Disregard what the world owes you, and concentrate on what you owe the world.

When you are faced with a decision, make that decision as wisely as possible—then forget it. The moment of absolute certainty never arrives.

And above all, remember that God helps those who help themselves. Act as if everything depended upon you, and pray as if everything depended upon God.

—S. H. Payer[474]

You have never been this way before, but walk in it with hope in your heart and look for that God-made pathway in which you should go.

December 14

"Thou greatly enrichest it with the river of God" (Psalm 65:9).

There is a river of God described in Revelation 22:1: "And he shewed me a pure river of water of life, clear as crystal, proceeding out of the throne of God and of the Lamb."

The Lord is as a river to us as promised in Isaiah 33:21: "But there the glorious LORD will be unto us a place of broad rivers and streams."

That river today is a river of love. I John 4:8 states: "God is love." His love was demonstrated in John 3:16: "For God so loved the world, that he gave his only begotten Son, that whosoever believeth in him should not perish, but have everlasting life."

Love came, Love gave His life, and Love was resurrected. Because He lives we can face our tomorrows. Jesus was God according to John 1:1, 14: "In the beginning was the Word, and the Word was with God, and the Word was God. . . . And the Word was made flesh [Jesus], and dwelt among us, (and we beheld his glory, the glory as of the only begotten of the Father,) full of grace and truth."

Jesus said in John 10:10: "I am come that they might have life." That life is in the water Jesus spoke about in John 4:14: "But whosoever drinketh of the water that I shall give him shall never thirst; but the water that I shall give him shall be in him a well of water springing up into everlasting life." If Jesus is God and God is love then everything that emanates from Him is love. It is a river of love.

"Love is the river of life in this world. Think not that ye know it who stand at the little tinkling rill, the first small fountain. Not until you have gone through the rocky gorges, and not lost the stream; not until you have gone through the meadow, and the stream has widened and deepened until fleets could ride on its bosom; not until beyond the meadow you have come to the unfathomable ocean, and poured your

treasures into its depths—not until then can you know what love is." —HENRY WARD BEECHER[475]

His love cannot be measured as described in Ephesians 3:17-19: "That Christ may dwell in your hearts by faith; that ye, being rooted and grounded in love, May be able to comprehend with all saints what is the breadth, and length, and depth, and height; And to know the love of Christ, which passeth knowledge, that ye might be filled with all the fulness of God."

We are told what to do with this river of love that begins with Him and is put in our heart when we know Him. I John 4:7 commands: "Beloved, let us love one another: for love is of God; and every one that loveth is born of God, and knoweth God."

Let that river flow today!

December 15

"There be four things which are little upon the earth, but they are exceeding wise" (Proverbs 30:24).

Little things are important. Sometimes they make the difference between life and death physically and spiritually.

Billy Sunday's choir leader, Mr. Rodeheaver, told the following touching story about a boy who sang in his choir. He said, "*Joey was not quite bright. He would never leave the tabernacle at night till he could shake my hand. He would stand right next to me until the last man had gone, in order to say good-by. One evening a man came forward to speak to me. He said, 'I want to thank you for being so kind to Joey. He isn't quite bright, and has never had anything he enjoyed so much as coming here and singing in the choir. He has worked hard during the day in order to be ready in time to come, too, and it is through him that my wife and my five children have been led to the Lord. His grandfather, seventy-five years old and an infidel all his life, and his grandmother have come tonight, and now the whole family are converted.'" —SUNDAY SCHOOL BANNER[476]*

One never knows the great effect of a small effort made to help someone. The following poem depicts these results:

A little push when the road is steep
May take one up the hill;
A little prayer when the clouds hang low
May bring the soul a thrill.
A little lift when the load bears down
May help one to succeed;
A little pull when the will slows down
May help one gain his speed.

A little clasp from a hand that's kind
May lift from crushing care;
A little word from a voice that's sweet
May save one from despair;
A little smile when the heart is sad
May bring a sunbeam in;
A loving word when the spirit droops
May help one rise and win.

—AUTHOR UNKNOWN[477]

Little things are important. Benjamin Franklin once said, "For want of a nail the shoe was lost; for want of a shoe the horse was lost; and for want of a horse the rider was lost; being overtaken and slain by the enemy, all for the want of care about a horseshoe nail."

The question is asked in Zechariah 4:10, "Who hath despised the day of small things?" Whoever does despise small things is not wise. The old song says it well, "Little is much if God is in it." He makes a little go a long way.

December 16

"The just shall live by his faith" (Habakkuk 2:4).

To live by faith is to be guided by, inspired by, and lifted by faith. Faith comes from God as stated in Romans 12:3: "God hath dealt to every man the measure of faith." Each person will determine what he does with that faith. Some will let it die, others stifle it, while others will exercise it and it will grow.

Faith can be increased according to II Corinthians 10:15: "when your faith is increased, that we shall be enlarged by you according to our rule abundantly." In II Thessalonians 1:3 Paul wrote to the church at Thessalonica and commended them on their increase in faith: "We are bound to thank God always for you, brethren, as it is meet, because that your faith growth exceedingly, and the charity of every one of you all toward each other aboundeth." In Luke 17:5, the disciples asked Jesus to increase their faith: "And the apostles said unto the Lord, Increase our faith."

The Lord's answer to them is recorded in Luke 17:6: "And the Lord said, If ye had faith as a grain of mustard seed, ye might say unto this sycamine tree, Be thou plucked up by the root, and be thou planted in the sea; and it should obey you." Jesus was telling them to use what faith they had.

Faith is very crucial to living an abundant life. It is impossible to please God without it. There is no question whether one should have faith; it is set in stone. There must be faith!

"Faith bestows that sublime courage that rises superior to the troubles and disappointments of life, that acknowledges no defeat, except as a step to victory; that is strong to endure, patient to wait, and energetic to struggle. . . . Light up, then, the lamp of faith in your heart. . . . It will lead you safely through the mists of doubt and the black darkness of despair; along the narrow, thorny ways of sickness and sorrow, and over the treacherous places of temptation and uncertainty." —JAMES ALLEN[478]

This is the day to seek to live in faith, walk by faith and grow in faith. Let nothing jar or move your steadfastness, but be firm in the knowledge of God and His power. The following poem says it well:

Let nothing disturb thee,
Let nothing affright thee.
All things are passing.
God never changes.
Patience gains all things.
Who has God wants nothing.
God alone suffices.

—ST. THERESA OF AVILA[479]

December 17

"*Greater is he that is in you, than he that is in the world*" (I John 4:4).

You have the power to change things around you instead of surroundings changing you. When you are filled with God's Spirit, you have power that a normal person does not have. Wherever you are and whomever you are with cannot change what is inside of you, because you are steadfast in Christ and His doctrines. The Rock lives inside of you, and you are founded on the rock Christ Jesus. He will empower you and help you to walk through extenuating trials without them affecting you negatively.

"*Just as so many rivers, so many showers of rain from above, so many medicinal springs do not alter the taste of the sea, so the pressure of adversity does not affect the mind of the brave man. For it maintains its balance, and over all that happens it throws its own complexion, because it is more powerful than external circumstances.*" —SENECA[480]

This is exemplified in the story of Daniel and the three Hebrew young men. They were taken captive to a people who were idolaters and worshiped a heathen god, but it did not affect their worship of the one true God. When Nebuchadnezzar gave a command for all the people to come to the dedication of the image which he had set up, a herald cried aloud: "To you it is commanded, O people, nations, and languages, That at what time ye hear the sound of the cornet, flute, harp, sackbut, psaltery, dulcimer, and all kinds of musick, ye fall down and worship the golden image that Nebuchadnezzar the king hath set up: And whoso falleth not down and worshippeth shall the same hour be cast into the midst of a burning fiery furnace" (Daniel 3:4-6).

The rest of the story is that the three Hebrew boys refused to do this and the king had the furnace heated seven times hotter and they were thrown into the furnace. The threats of the king could not shake what was inside of them and they were willing to die for their faith and convictions.

They did not die, because God came to the rescue. Three men went into the furnace, but the king saw four walking around inside

the fire and said, "Did not we cast three men bound into the midst of the fire? They answered and said unto the king, True, O king. He answered and said, Lo, I see four men loose, walking in the midst of the fire, and they have no hurt; and the form of the fourth is like the Son of God" (Daniel 3:24-25).

Then the king went near and called into the furnace to the young men, "Come forth!" When they came out, the fire had no power to burn them, their hair was not singed, neither was the smell of fire upon them.

This is the day to walk in power, not man's power, but God's power and His Spirit, and He will bring you out victoriously!

December 18

"Nothing will be restrained from them, which they have imagined to do" (Genesis 11:6).

God made man and He knew the power of belief and of unified efforts, so when He saw that the people were building the tower of Babel, Genesis 11:6 records what He said: "And the LORD said, Behold, the people is one, and they have all one language; and this they begin to do: and now nothing will be restrained from them, which they have imagined to do."

He was saying, "Nothing can stop them!" The mind is a powerful thing and has direct influence over a person. An interesting scripture found in Ezekiel 8:12 says, "Then said he unto me, Son of man, hast thou seen what the ancients of the house of Israel do in the dark, EVERY MAN IN THE CHAMBERS OF HIS IMAGERY?"

The phrase that is emphasized is *every man in the chambers of his imagery.* This means that everyone has a chamber of imaginations and in that place is where thoughts live. They help regulate a person's actions and outlook on life. Everyone will decorate his chamber with what he chooses to think on and about. Pictures will line the hallways of the chamber: pictures of doubt or faith, pessimism or optimism, worry or trust, life or death. There are many pictures to choose from, but each will choose his destiny by his thoughts.

Proverbs 23:7 states: "For as he thinketh in his heart, so is he." This is the day to place a picture on the walls of your chamber that says: IT CAN BE DONE!

IT CAN BE DONE
The man who misses all the fun
Is he who says, "It can't be done."
In solemn pride he stands aloof
And greets each venture with reproof.
Had he the power he'd efface
The history of the human race;
We'd have no radio or motor cars,
No streets lit by electric stars;
No telegraph nor telephone,
We'd linger in the age of stone.
The world would sleep if things were run
By men who say "It can't be done."
—AUTHOR UNKNOWN[481]

Nothing can restrain you from doing what you imagine to do except yourself, and of course, God. The question is all about belief. God gets angry with people who will not believe. When Moses sent the twelve spies to Canaan to see what needed to be done to take the city that God had promised them, ten came back with an evil report that they could not take the city. Joshua and Caleb said, "We can!" and the ten said, "We can't!" God pronounced a blessing upon Joshua and Caleb and called the report of the ten *evil*.

Choose today to join those who say, "We can," and receive God's blessing.

December 19

"Give us help from trouble" (Psalm 60:11).

Sometimes, holidays can bring unwanted stress and tensions. More is expected out of you, gifts to buy for other people, and attendance at more activities is required. The budget is stretched as well as the nerves. Troubles seem to increase at times and you feel stretched in different directions.

This is the time to take time to call on the Lord. Tell Him exactly

how you feel and let your troublesome times remind you of others who feel worse pain than you. Then learn of Him and of the pain, and the river of healing that He gives you let it flow out to another in need. God will help those who call on Him as stated in Psalm 86:7: "In the day of my trouble I will call upon thee: for thou wilt answer me."

> *Oh, face to face with trouble,*
> *Friend, I have often stood,*
> *To learn that pain hath sweetness,*
> *To know that God is good.*
> *Arise and meet the daylight,*
> *Be strong and do your best,*
> *With an honest heart and a childlike trust*
> *That God will do the rest.*
> —Margaret E. Sangster[482]

So rise this day from your knees and know that God is good and He will help you handle all difficulties and problems. Do not try to do it yourself, but lean upon the Lord and He will show you the way. There is no need for fear and anxiety when He is taking care of things.

A little girl once said to her mother, "Mommy, you and Daddy acted awful worried and scared at the supper table last night. Was it because you thought that the bad men would blow up the world? Mommy, when I'm worried and scared, you comfort me. God will comfort you. I'm sure He will tell you He is looking after things, just like you tell me. He will take care of us!"

The mother was a faithful Christian and felt rebuked by her little girl's trust in God's faithful care and said, "I guess we did act worried and scared. I am sorry, dear."

It is easy to tell the children to not worry, God will work it all out when they need reassuring, but the heavenly Father is saying to His children today, "Fear not, for I am with you!"

December 20

"Which are the prayers of saints" (Revelation 5:8).

*P*rayers never die. They are bottled in golden vials as stated in Revelation 5:8: "And when he had taken the book, the four beasts and four and twenty elders fell down before the Lamb, having every one of them harps, and golden vials full of odours, which are the prayers of saints."

Revelation 8:4 also states: "And the smoke of the incense, which came with the prayers of the saints, ascended up before God out of the angel's hand."

This is the day to invest in that which is esteemed so precious by God that He orders the prayers to be bottled and kept in heaven. Take time in the busy season of the year to pray. Pray for the family. Pray for the lonely, the heartbroken, and those who do not know how to pray. Pray for the government and the leaders of this nation. Paul admonished the church to pray in I Timothy 2:1-3: "I exhort therefore, that, first of all, supplications, prayers, intercessions, and giving of thanks, be made for all men; For kings, and for all that are in authority; that we may lead a quiet and peaceable life in all godliness and honesty. For this is good and acceptable in the sight of God our Saviour."

To pray is good in the sight of God. If prayer is considered to be first on the list and is considered to be good, then by all means we must pray.

A PRAYER FOR EVERY DAY
God let me find the lonely ones
Among the throng today
And let me say the word to take
The loneliness away:
So many walk with aching hearts
Along the old highway.

So many walk with breaking hearts,
And no one understands;
They find the roadway rough and steep
Across the barren lands;
God help me lighten weary eyes,
And strengthen nerveless hands.

God help me brighten dreary eyes,
And let my own grief be

A sure reminder of the grief
Of those who walk with me.
When words fail—hands fail—let me go
In silent sympathy.
—GRACE NOLL CROWELL[483]

As the morning is fresh, take a fresh you into the presence of the King of kings and come boldly to His throne as stated in Hebrews 4:16: "Let us therefore come boldly unto the throne of grace, that we may obtain mercy, and find grace to help in time of need."

December 21

"For he hath broken the gates of brass, and cut the bars of iron in sunder" (Psalm 107:16).

*T*oday is the day to open the gates of love as never before. Misunderstandings encase people behind bars and gates. They suffer in misery and life loses its song. These gates and bars need to be broken and cast away. If someone has wronged you, it is time to make it right, for Romans 12:10 states: "Be kindly affectioned one to another with brotherly love; in honour preferring one another."

It is no secret that one cannot love God if he does not love his brother as illustrated in I John 4:20-21: "If a man say, I love God, and hateth his brother, he is a liar: for he that loveth not his brother whom he hath seen, how can he love God whom he hath not seen? And this commandment have we from him, That he who loveth God love his brother also."

Phillips Brooks knew of some of the misunderstandings in his congregation and the inward misery of those who were embroiled in private wars. The following excerpt is taken from the message he preached one Sunday morning so long ago:

You who are letting miserable misunderstandings run on from year to year, meaning to clear them up some day;

You who are keeping wretched quarrels alive because you cannot quite make up your mind that now is the day to sacrifice your pride and kill them;

You who are passing men sullenly upon the street, not speaking to them out of some silly spite, and yet knowing that it would fill you with shame and remorse if you heard that one of those men were dead tomorrow morning;

Or letting your friend's heart ache for a word of appreciation or sympathy, which you mean to give him someday;

If you only could know and see and feel, all of a sudden, that the time is short, how it would break the spell! How you would go instantly and do the thing which you might never have another chance to do?[484]

As the congregation streamed out of the church that day, people who had not spoken in years greeted each other and discovered it is what they wanted to do all along. Neighbors were speaking to one another and many who had held grudges resolved to be more generous in the future—when suddenly they all felt happier and at peace with themselves and the world.

This is what happens when we do it God's way: forgive and ye shall be forgiven.

December 22

"I wish above all things that thou mayest prosper" (III John 2).

God had a wish for His children recorded in III John 2: "Beloved, I wish above all things that thou mayest prosper and be in health, even as thy soul prospereth." He wished them to prosper and be in health in the natural as well as the spiritual.

God wants His children to be successful as stated in Joshua 1:8, but it has certain requirements that go with it: "This book of the law shall not depart out of thy mouth; but thou shalt meditate therein day and night, that thou mayest observe to do according to all that is written therein: for then thou shalt make thy way prosperous, and then thou shalt have good success." Here again He desires for them to have success and prosper, but this comes through reading, meditating, and abiding in the Word of God. Pictures from His Word should line the walls of our minds, so that we can have what He wants us to have.

May this Christmas season bring you special blessings of cheer and hope as you celebrate the birth of the Christ child, and may He give you the things that cannot be bought with money but are of eternal value as the following poem depicts:

MY CHRISTMAS WISH
I've wished a very special wish
For you this Christmas-tide;
It reaches far beyond today,
'Tis high and deep, and wide.

I wish for you the angels' song
That tells of hope and love;
I wish the radiance of the Star
To guide your thoughts above.

I wish for you the sturdy faith
That led the Wise Men three
Through cold of night, o'er desert drear,
The Holy Child to see.

I wish for you a humble heart,
With purpose strong and true—
The blessing of the Christ, our Lord—
This is my wish for you.
—EDWARD BOS[485]

May this day bring you a *song* of hope and love, *faith* to lead you forward, and a *humble heart* that follows God's leading!

December 23

"*Gave their own selves to the Lord*" (II Corinthians 8:5).

The example of Macedonia is a beautiful one. They gave not out of their abundance but out of their want as stated in II Corinthians 8:2-3: "How that in a great trial of affliction the abun-

dance of their joy and their deep poverty abounded unto the riches of their liberality. For to their power, I bear record, yea, and beyond their power they were willing of themselves." What a testimony! They first gave themselves to God and then out of their want they gave to the needs that were presented to them.

To be known as a giver is one of the greatest things that can be said of a person. May this season not be one of stress and unhappiness, but let it be ruled by Christ's attitude, that of being a giver. Everywhere He went He did good and lifted people by giving to them what they needed. He fed the multitude when they were hungry; He opened the blind man's eyes so that he could see; He made the cripple walk, and raised the dead. He gave a fallen woman hope when she was condemned; He spoke to a woman at the well and changed her life for the better; and He died on a cross for a world that was lost, so that they might be saved.

"*Christ is the Christmas giver. Many of the richest and sweetest joys human hearts can experience were born into the world when Christ was born. Let us name a few from among the many. One is the joy of knowing the nature of God. Christ is Immanuel, God with us; so near that we could see and understand and know him.*" —AUTHOR UNKNOWN[486]

As Christ was a giver, may we be a giver also. Let it rule our life and may we know the joy that comes from giving out of our want. Let us pray the following prayer today:

LET ME BE A GIVER

God, let me be a giver, and not one
Who only takes and takes unceasingly;
God, let me give, so that not just my own,
But others' lives as well, may richer be.
Let me give out whatever I may hold
Of what material things life may be heaping,
Let me give raiment, shelter, food, or gold
If these are, through Thy bounty, in my keeping.

But greater than such fleeting treasures, may
I give my faith and hope and cheerfulness,
Belief and dreams and joy and laughter gay
Some lonely soul to bless.

—MARY CAROLYN DAVIES[487]

December 24

"He . . . lifteth up the beggar" (I Samuel 2:8).

Hannah prayed a prayer in the Temple after God had opened her womb and Samuel was born. I Samuel 2:8 is part of her prayer: "He raiseth up the poor out of the dust, and lifteth up the beggar from the dunghill, to set them among princes, and to make them inherit the throne of glory: for the pillars of the earth are the LORD'S, and he hath set the world upon them."

When Jesus went into the synagogue on the Sabbath day, the words He read are recorded in Luke 4:18: "The Spirit of the Lord is upon me, because he hath anointed me to preach the gospel to the poor; he hath sent me to heal the brokenhearted, to preach deliverance to the captives, and recovering of sight to the blind, to set at liberty them that are bruised." This is why He came. Take special note of those He came to help and set free, for as we minister to them, we are actually ministering to Christ.

With trembling hand the lonely beggar knocks. Cautiously the door cracks narrowly ajar and fear peers out on ragged want. At once the door slams shut, and as the beggar turns to go, the winds of cold indifference buffet him anew. For one brief pause he looks upon the passing throng, then quietly he moves to lose himself therein. Where does he go? Beggars? The world is filled with those who starve—hungering, ever hungering for love. Hear them as they cry:

"Love me with your heart, not with your shallow self alone."

"Love me for what I am—my frailties—my differences—not by the measure of society."

"Love me for the sake of love—enough to help me feel a little more secure in my world of fear-filled adversity."

Time is autumn-old, and ere its chill becomes the frost and snow of winter's dress, compassion fires must burn with brighter glow. Jesus said, "Inasmuch as ye did it unto the least of these, my brethren, ye have done it unto me" (Matthew 25:40).

Even now a beggar knocks.

—LOUISE BARKER BARNHILL[488]

Let this be the season to open your heart and help those who really need helping. So many times we heap so much on top of so much in our own little circle, while the beggar knocks silently with his eyes and we rush madly on in our holiday dash forgetting the true reason of the season. Jesus is the reason for the season and we should help fulfill Matthew 25 especially at this time of the year.

December 25

"And she shall bring forth a son, and thou shalt call his name JESUS" (Matthew 1:21).

The story of Jesus' birth is special. He was not born in a palace but in a stable. "And she brought forth her firstborn son, and wrapped him in swaddling clothes, and laid him in a manger; because there was no room for them in the inn" (Luke 2:7).

"Over 2,000 years ago Jesus was born. He possessed neither wealth nor influence. In infancy He startled a king: in childhood He amazed the doctors!

"The names of the past proud statesmen, scientists, philosophers, and theologians have come and gone; but the name of this Man abounds more and more. Herod could not destroy Him, and the grave could not hold Him.

"He stands forth upon the highest pinnacle of heavenly glory, proclaimed of God, acknowledged by angels, adored by saints, feared by devils, as the living, personal Christ, our Lord and Savior." —AUTHOR UNKNOWN

ONE SOLITARY LIFE

Here is a man who was born in an obscure village, the child of a peasant woman. He grew up in another obscure village.

He worked in a carpenter shop until he was thirty, and then for three years he was an itinerant preacher.

He never owned a home. He never had a family. He never went to college. He never traveled two hundred miles from the place he was born.

He never did one of the things that usually accompany greatness. He had no credentials but himself. He had nothing to do with this world except the naked power of his divine manhood.

While still a young man, the tide of public opinion turned against him. His friends ran away. One of them denied him.

He was turned over to his enemies. He went through the mockery of a trial. He was nailed upon a cross between two thieves. His executioners gambled for the only piece of property he had on earth while he was dying, and that was his coat. When he was dead he was taken down and laid in a borrowed grave through the pity of a friend.

Nineteen wide centuries have come and gone, and today he is the centerpiece of the human race and the leader of the column of progress.

I am far within the mark when I say that all the armies that ever marched, and all the navies that ever were built, and all the parliaments that ever sat, and all the kings that ever reigned, put together, have not affected the life of man upon this earth as powerfully as has that one solitary life. —AUTHOR UNKNOWN[489]

December 26

"That we may be able to comfort them" (II Corinthians 1:4).

*P*aul in writing to the Corinthians stated that as God comforts us in our trials, so should we should comfort others in their time of trial as recorded in II Corinthians 1:2-4: "Grace be to you and peace from God our Father, and from the Lord Jesus Christ. Blessed be God, even the Father of our Lord Jesus Christ, the Father of mercies, and the God of all comfort; Who comforteth us in all our tribulation, that we may be able to comfort them which are in any trouble, by the comfort wherewith we ourselves are comforted of God."

How can a person know how someone else is feeling if he or she does not experience trouble or pain? Those who have suffered know better how to help another who is suffering than someone who has never been there. The following poem expresses it beautifully:

Till poverty knocked at her door,
She never knew how bare

The uneventful days of those
Who have but want and care.

Till sorrow lingered at her hearth,
She never knew the night
Through which troubled souls might fare
To gain the morning light.

Till suffering had sought her house,
She never knew what dread
Many wrestle with, or what grim fears
Of agony are bred.

And yet till those unbidden guests
Had taught her to possess
A clearer sight, she never knew
The height of happiness.
—Charlotte Becker[490]

So if this year has brought you pain, suffering and heartbreak, just know that God allowed it for good so that you might learn to have compassion for those who will walk the same road tomorrow. You will be there for them and walk them through it with God's grace.

"*A jewel is a bit of ordinary earth which has passed through some extra-ordinary experiences.*" Be that jewel for Jesus today, shine and help others find their way.

December 27

"*Have mercy upon me, O God, according to thy lovingkindness: according unto the multitude of thy tender mercies blot out my transgressions*" (Psalm 51:1).

Let this be a day of repentance and cleansing and pray this morning, "Whatever I have done to offend someone, or whatever I have said that has cast doubt, please Lord, forgive me is my prayer. Let me be a vessel of honor in Your house. Let me bring glory to Your name and help others to see You in me. Create in me a clean heart and renew a right spirit within me. Restore unto me Thy joy and let me walk in Your ways."

MY EVENING PRAYER
If I have wounded any soul today,
If I have caused one foot to go astray,
If I have walked in my own willful way—
Good Lord, forgive!

If I have uttered idle words or vain,
If I have turned aside from want or pain,
Lest I myself should suffer through the strain—
Good Lord, forgive!

If I have been perverse, or hard, or cold,
If I have longed for shelter in Thy fold,
When Thou hast given me some part to hold—
Good Lord, forgive!
Forgive the sins I have confessed to Thee,
Forgive the secret sins I do not see,
That which I know not, Father, teach Thou me—
Help me to live.
—CHARLES H. GABRIEL[491]

Let me live this day with the scales taken from my eyes, to be able to see my fellow man as You see them. May my heart be tender towards You and others and not hard and cold! Let me be as a hearth where a warm fire of love glows so that others can warm by my fire. Take the pettiness of spites and trifling hurts from my spirit and wash me and make me clean. This is my prayer today, Lord.

December 28

"These stones shall be for a memorial unto the children" (Joshua 4:7).

Joshua told the men to pick up twelve stones and place them in the Jordan River where the feet of the priest stood which

bare the ark of the covenant. He said in Joshua 4:21-24, "When your children shall ask their fathers in time to come, saying, What mean these stones? Then ye shall let your children know, saying, Israel came over this Jordan on dry land. For the LORD your God dried up the waters of Jordan from before you, until ye were passed over, as the LORD your God did to the Red sea, which he dried up from before us, until we were gone over: That all the people of the earth might know the hand of the LORD, that it is mighty: that ye might fear the LORD your God for ever."

Joshua was concerned about those who were following in the years to come. He wanted the influence of the years of God's manifestation in the midst to be preserved.

As you come to the end of this year and are approaching a new year, may you pause and think on the influence of your life and determine to live the coming year well not only for yourself, but for those who are following behind you as the following poem depicts:

THE BRIDGE-BUILDER

An old man going a lone highway
Came at the evening, cold and gray,
To a chasm vast and wide and steep,
With waters rolling cold and deep.
The old man crossed in the twilight dim,
The sullen stream had no fears for him;
But he turned when safe on the other side,
And built a bridge to span the tide.

"Old man," said a fellow pilgrim near,
"You are wasting your strength with building here.
Your journey will end with the ending day,
You never again will pass this way.
You've crossed the chasm, deep and wide,
Why build you this bridge at eventide?"

The builder lifted his old gray head.
"Good friend, in the path I have come," he said,
"There followeth after me today
A youth whose feet must pass this way.
The chasm that was as nought to me
To that fair-haired youth may a pitfall be;

He, too, must cross in the twilight dim—
Good friend, I am building this bridge for him."
—Will Allen Dromgoole[492]

This is the day to build memorials for times to come, to build bridges for the children and others to cross over, and to live well for those who walk in your shadow.

December 29

"We spend our years as a tale that is told" (Psalm 90:9).

Each of us writes every day a page in our book of life. The pages of this year make a chapter that is soon to close. Each chapter is a book in itself. Let it finish well by abiding in Christ and asking for mercy for all that has happened. Then as the old year fades away and the new year is ushered in, we will close the book on this particular year as the following poem illustrates:

THE OLD YEAR
What is the old year? 'Tis a book
On which we backward fondly look,
Not willing, quite, that it should close,
For leaves of violet and rose
Within its heart are thickly strewn,
Marking Love's dawn and golden noon;
And turned-down pages, noting days
Dimly recalled through Memory's haze;
And tear-stained pages, too, that tell
Of starless nights and mournful knell
Of bells that toll through troubled air
The De Profundis *of despair;*
The laugh, the tear, the shine, the shade,
All 'twixt the covers gently laid,
No leaves uncut, no page unscanned—
Close it and lay it in God's hand.
—Clarence Urmy[493]

This is the day to close the book of this year and lay it in God's hand. He is merciful. He has a big eraser for the things that were done in moments of anger, and because of a repentant attitude, they are no more. So let God have the whole year: the good things and the bad things.

He is the author and finisher of our faith as stated in Hebrews 12:1-2: "Let us run with patience the race that is set before us, Looking unto Jesus the author and finisher of our faith." What was not written correctly, He knows how to make it look good, for He is a good Editor!

So let your mind rest in the Lord and be at peace. This is promised in Isaiah 26:3: "Thou wilt keep him in perfect peace, whose mind is stayed on thee: because he trusteth in thee." Trust Him today!

December 30

"I will help thee" (Isaiah 41:13).

The end of the year is here and God's children need to know that He will help them make the transition successfully from this year to the next year. He said in Isaiah 41:10: "Fear thou not; for I am with thee: be not dismayed; for I am thy God: I will strengthen thee; yea, I will help thee; yea, I will uphold thee with the right hand of my righteousness." That is the promise for this time of changeover.

So do as the following poem describes and go into the next year without fear or anxiety over what has happened this year or what might happen next year, but realize that the Lord is there to help you:

MY BOOK OF LIFE
I closed another chapter
In my book of life today,
And paused for meditation
As I laid the book away.

I thought of smudgy pages
Where the record was not clear,

And dreary lines of trouble
Clouded o'er by doubt and fear.

It's now too late to alter
And script that's dried and set:
The story's far from perfect,
But it's vain to stew and fret.

I asked the Lord to pardon
The mistakes that mar the book,
And give me grace and courage
By a hopeful, Christ-ward look.

So, now, there lies before me
A new chapter clean and white.
And I hope to write its pages
So the plot will turn out right.

I trust the final chapters
Will the Master's plan reveal,
And weave the many fragments
To depict a life that's real.
—Author Unknown[494]

December 31

"The Lord bless thee, and keep thee" (Numbers 6:24).

The end of another year has come. It is over and a new one beckons to you. In your journey from one year to another year, may the blessing of the Lord be upon you! May you make right decisions, putting emphasis on things of value and deepening your experience with God!

The blessing is pronounced in Number 6:24-26: "The Lord bless thee, and keep thee: The Lord make his face shine upon thee, and be gracious unto thee: The Lord lift up his countenance upon thee, and give thee peace."

GOD BE WITH YOU
May His counsels sweet uphold you,
And His loving arms enfold you,
As you journey on your way.

May His sheltering wings protect you
And His light divine direct you,
Turning darkness into day.

May His potent peace surround you,
And His presence linger with you,
As your inner, golden ray.
—Author Unknown[495]

God has blessed you with a fresh beginning. Old things are passed away and a new year has dawned. What you do with this blessing is up to you. Let the thoughts of the King of kings abide in your mind, and may you find in Him everything that is good and fine. Let this year be untarnished and full of good things that will give you good memories.

Today is the day to begin again as the following poem says so well:

BEGIN AGAIN
Every day is a fresh beginning,
Every morn is the world made new.
You who are weary of sorrow and sinning,
Here is a beautiful hope for you—
A hope for me and a hope for you.

Every day is a fresh beginning;
Listen, my soul, to the glad refrain,
And, spite of old sorrow and older sinning,
And puzzles forecasted and possible pain,
Take heart with the day, and begin again.
—Susan Coolidge[496]

Notes

1. Alexander, A. L., compiler, *Poems that Touch the Heart*, (Doubleday, NY: 1941), pp. 132-133.
2. *Ibid.*, p. 188.
3. Johnson, Joseph S., Jr., *A Field of Diamonds*, (© 1999), p. 146.
4. *Ibid.*, p. 144.
5. Knight, Walter B., *Knight's Treasury of Illustrations*, (William B. Eerdmans, Grand Rapids: 1963), p. 61.
6. Watson, Lillian Eicher, editor, *Light from Many Lamps*, (Simon & Schuster, NY: 1951), p. 29.
7. Knight, p. 239.
8. Tan, Paul Lee, *Encyclopedia of 7700 Illustrations*, (Assurance Publishers, Rockville, MD: 1979), 3637.
9. *Ibid.*, 1170.
10. Knight, p. 112.
11. *Ibid.*, p. 113.
12. Tan, 1775.
13. Knight, p. 115.
14. Tan, 2034.
15. Johnson, p. 118.
16. Knight, p. 178.
17. *Ibid.*, p. 177.
18. Tan, 1997.
19. Knight, p. 170.
20. *Ibid.*, p. 171.
21. *Ibid.*, p. 170.
22. Alexander, p. 40.
23. *Ibid.*, p. 190.
24. Tan, 4096.
25. Knight, p. 83.
26. *Ibid.*, p. 84.
27. *Ibid.*, p. 121.
28. Tan, 3821.
29. *Ibid.*, 1968.
30. Knight, p. 425.
31. *Ibid.*
32. Tan, 1858.
33. *Ibid.*, 1861.
34. *Ibid.*, 1863.
35. Knight, p. 152.
36. Tan, 1928.
37. *Ibid.*, 86.
38. Cowman, Mrs. Charles A., *Streams in the Desert*, (Cowman Publications, Inc., Zondervan Publishing House, Grand Rapids: 1965), p. 39.
39. Tan, 3845.
40. *Ibid.*, 3808; author's paraphrase.
41. Knight, p. 117.
42. Tan, 2023; author's paraphrase.
43. *Ibid.*, 6283.
44. *Ibid.*, 6284.
45. Knight, p. 149.
46. Tan, 3822.
47. *Ibid.*, 2184.
48. Knight, p. 320.
49. *Ibid.*, p. 374.
50. *Ibid.*, p. 370.
51. Tan, 6838.
52. Knight, p. 383.
53. Tan, 4629.
54. *Ibid.*, 419.
55. *Ibid.*, 651.
56. *Ibid.*, 97.
57. *Ibid.*, 98.
58. *Ibid.*, 121.
59. *Ibid.*, 409.
60. *Ibid.*, 411.
61. *Ibid.*, 425.
62. *Ibid.*, 483.
63. *Ibid.*, 573.
64. *Ibid.*, 2258.
65. *Ibid.*, 572.
66. *Ibid.*, 577.
67. *Ibid.*, 392.
68. *Ibid.*, 391.
69. *Ibid.*
70. *Ibid.*, 3982.
71. *Ibid.*, 4124.

[72]*Ibid.*, 4110.
[73]*Ibid.*, 4111.
[74]*Ibid.*, 4112.
[75]*Ibid.*, 4117.
[76]*Ibid.*, 4125.
[77]*Ibid.*, 4134.
[78]*Ibid.*, 4148.
[79]*Ibid.*, 4151.
[80]*Ibid.*, 4162.
[81]*Ibid.*, 4166.
[82]*Ibid.*, 5836.
[83]*Ibid.*, 4278.
[84]*Ibid.*, 4281.
[85]*Ibid.*, 6578.
[86]*Ibid.*, 7354.
[87]Knight, p. 137.
[88]Tan, 3862.
[89]Knight, p. 295.
[90]Tan, 3520.
[91]*Ibid.*, 3521.
[92]*Ibid.*, 3081.
[93]Knight, p. 136.
[94]Tan, 2669.
[95]*Ibid.*, 4224.
[96]Knight, p. 44.
[97]*Ibid.*, p. 45.
[98]*Ibid.*
[99]*Ibid.*, p. 46.
[100]Tan, 4229.
[101]Knight, p. 325.
[102]Tan, 5200.
[103]*Ibid.*, 4350.
[104]*Ibid.*, 4776.
[105]Knight, p. 10.
[106]*Ibid.*
[107]Tan, 5851.
[108]*Ibid.*, 1986.
[109]*Ibid.*, 7125.
[110]*Ibid.*, 7143.
[111]*Ibid.*, 5848.
[112]Knight, p. 374.
[113]*Ibid.*
[114]Tan, 4092.
[115]*Ibid.*, 4152.
[116]*Ibid.*, 914.
[117]Knight, p. 184.
[118]Tan, 1157.
[119]Knight, p. 190.
[120]*Ibid.*, p. 430.
[121]*Ibid.*
[122]*Ibid.*, p. 433.
[123]*Ibid.*, p. 179.
[124]*Ibid.*, p. 178.
[125]*Ibid.*, pp. 152-153.
[126]*Ibid.*, p. 114.
[127]*Ibid.*
[128]*Ibid.*, p. 373.
[129]Johnson, p. 160.
[130]Knight, pp. 151-152.
[131]Howell, Clinton T., compiler, *Lines to Live By*, (Thomas Nelson, Nashville: 1972), p. 49.
[132]*Ibid.*, p. 71.
[133]Alexander, p. 289.
[134]Howell, p. 179.
[135]Tan, 6879; author's paraphrase.
[136]Ibid.
[137]Howell, p. 172.
[138]Johnson, p. 97.
[139]*Ibid.*, p. 114.
[140]*Ibid.*, p. 115.
[141]Tan, 3284.
[142]*Ibid.*, 3286.
[143]*Ibid.*, 3287.
[144]Johnson, p. 115.
[145]Howell, p. 32.
[146]Johnson, p. 116.
[147]Howell, p. 31.
[148]*Ibid.*, p. 33.
[149]*Ibid.*, p. 44.
[150]Watson, p. 152.
[151]Knight, p. 426.
[152]Tan, 1509.
[153]Felleman, Hazel, selector, *Best Loved Poems of the American People*, (Garden City Books, NY: 1936), pp. 100-101.
[154]Howell, p. 144.
[155]Tan, 1511.
[156]*Ibid.*, 6704.
[157]*Ibid.*, 2939.
[158]*Ibid.*, 6705.
[159]*Ibid.*, 6717.
[160]*Ibid.*, 6719.
[161]*Ibid.*, 6722.
[162]*Ibid.*, 831.
[163]*Ibid.*, 835.

[164]*Ibid.*, 3511.
[165]*Ibid.*, 3514.
[166]*Ibid.*, 3919.
[167]*Ibid.*, 3215.
[168]*Ibid.*, 3200.
[169]*Ibid.*, 3201.
[170]*Ibid.*, 3217.
[171]*Ibid.*, 3223.
[172]*Ibid.*, 3294.
[173]*Ibid.*, 3296.
[174]*Ibid.*, 2489.
[175]*Ibid.*, 3134.
[176]*Ibid.*, 4482.
[177]*Ibid.*, 2014; original told by C. Perrin; author's paraphrase.
[178]*Ibid.*, 2039.
[179]Howell, p. 187.
[180]Johnson, p. 153.
[181]Alexander, p. 379.
[182]Tan, 2046.
[183]*Ibid.*, 1895.
[184]*Ibid.*, 2137.
[185]*Ibid.*, 2545.
[186]*Ibid.*, 3142.
[187]*Ibid.*, 3156.
[188]*Ibid.*, 6908.
[189]*Ibid.*, 6912.
[190]*Ibid.*, 6911.
[191]*Ibid.*, 1839.
[192]*Ibid.*, 1840.
[193]*Ibid.*, 1835; author's paraphrase.
[194]*Ibid.*, 2936.
[195]*Ibid.*, 2940.
[196]*Ibid.*, 3788.
[197]Knight, p. 327.
[198]Watson, p. 18.
[199]*Ibid.*, pp. 66-67.
[200]Tan, 4550.
[201]*Ibid.*, 4569.
[202]Knight, p. 439.
[203]*Ibid.*, p. 204.
[204]*Ibid.*
[205]*Ibid.*, p. 427.
[206]*Ibid.*, p. 184.
[207]*Ibid.*, p. 304.
[208]*Ibid.*, p. 303.
[209]*Ibid.*
[210]Tan, 4517.
[211]*Ibid.*, 1887.
[212]*Ibid.*, 1889.
[213]*Ibid.*, 337.
[214]*Ibid.*, 339.
[215]*Ibid.*
[216]*Ibid.*
[217]*Ibid.*, 1499.
[218]*Ibid.*, 2841.
[219]*Ibid.*, 1840.
[220]*Ibid.*, 2855.
[221]*Ibid.*, 7682.
[222]*Ibid.*, 781.
[223]*Ibid.*, 779.
[224]*Ibid.*, 1939.
[225]*Ibid.*, 3212.
[226]*Ibid.*, 3794.
[227]*Ibid.*, 6925.
[228]*Ibid.*, 6648.
[229]*Ibid.*, 6654.
[230]*Ibid.*, 6633.
[231]*Ibid.*, 4656.
[232]*Ibid.*, 4384.
[233]*Ibid.*, 1376.
[234]*Ibid.*, 4251.
[235]*Ibid.*, 4255.
[236]*Ibid.*, 1231.
[237]*Ibid.*, 1232.
[238]*Ibid.*, 1299.
[239]*Ibid.*, 1298.
[240]*Ibid.*, 1300.
[241]*Ibid.*, 1348.
[242]*Ibid.*, 1351.
[243]*Ibid.*, 4147.
[244]*Ibid.*, 4149.
[245]*Ibid.*, 4646.
[246]*Ibid.*, 4649.
[247]*Ibid.*, 621.
[248]*Ibid.*, 3172.
[249]*Ibid.*, 3166.
[250]*Ibid.*, 4912.
[251]*Ibid.*, 4774.
[252]*Ibid.*, 1429.
[253]*Ibid.*, 3097.
[254]*Ibid.*, 3091.
[255]*Ibid.*, 3090.
[256]*Ibid.*, 3094.
[257]Knight, p. 265.
[258]*Ibid.*, p. 264.
[259]*Ibid.*, p. 265.

[260] *Ibid.*
[261] Tan, 6085.
[262] *Ibid.*, 3214.
[263] *Ibid.*, 3208.
[264] *Ibid.*, 5609.
[265] *Ibid.*, 3534.
[266] *Ibid.*, 5166.
[267] *Ibid.*, 4648.
[268] Alexander, p. 174.
[269] Tan, 1850; author's paraphrase.
[270] Alexander, p. 50.
[271] Tan, 2821.
[272] *Ibid.*, 6295.
[273] *Ibid.*, 6289; author's paraphrase.
[274] *Ibid.*, 6193.
[275] *Ibid.*, 7070.
[276] Alexander, p. 284.
[277] *Ibid.*, p. 285.
[278] Tan, 5965.
[279] *Ibid.*, 5961.
[280] *Ibid.*, 5854.
[281] Alexander, p. 272.
[282] *Ibid.*, p. 194.
[283] *Ibid.*, p. 168.
[284] Tan, 6213.
[285] *Ibid.*, 2026.
[286] Knight, p. 16.
[287] Tan, 6462.
[288] Knight, p. 407.
[289] *Ibid.*
[290] *Ibid.*, p. 140.
[291] *Ibid.*, p. 141.
[292] Tan, 4756.
[293] *Ibid.*, 2024.
[294] Knight, pp. 447-448.
[295] *Ibid.*, p. 21.
[296] Tan, 6887.
[297] *Ibid.*, 6888.
[298] Knight, p. 305.
[299] Tan, 4524.
[300] *Ibid.*, 4529.
[301] *Ibid.*, 4165; author's paraphrase.
[302] *Ibid.*, 5838.
[303] *Ibid.*, 5839; author's paraphrase.
[304] Knight, p. 297.
[305] *Ibid.*, p. 134.
[306] *Ibid.*
[307] Alexander, p. 252.
[308] Knight, p. 48.
[309] *Ibid.*, p. 49.
[310] *Ibid.*, p. 2.
[311] Tan, 413.
[312] *Ibid.*, 414.
[313] Knight, p. 84.
[314] Tan, 2008.
[315] *Ibid.*, 4159; author's paraphrase.
[316] *Ibid.*, 2010.
[317] *Ibid.*, 2009.
[318] *Ibid.*, 1493; author's paraphrase.
[319] *Ibid.*, 2027.
[320] *Ibid.*, 2029.
[321] *Ibid.*, 4571.
[322] Johnson, p. 78.
[323] Tan, 2030.
[324] *Ibid.*, 2051.
[325] *Ibid.*, 1890.
[326] *Ibid.*, 1893.
[327] *Ibid.*, 1891.
[328] *Ibid.*, 1922.
[329] *Ibid.*, 1918.
[330] Johnson, p. 152.
[331] Tan, 4095.
[332] *Ibid.*, 4098.
[333] *Ibid.*, 4101.
[334] *Ibid.*, 4123.
[335] Howell, p. 63.
[336] Tan, 4157.
[337] Alexander, pp. 19-20.
[338] Tan, 6653.
[339] Felleman, p. 89.
[340] Knight, p. 3.
[341] *Ibid.*, p. 150.
[342] *Ibid.*, p. 215.
[343] *Ibid.*, p. 218.
[344] *Ibid.*, p. 250.
[345] *Ibid.*, p. 266.
[346] *Ibid.*, p. 267.
[347] *Ibid.*, p. 275.
[348] *Ibid.*, p. 445.
[349] *Ibid.*
[350] Alexander, p. 80.
[351] Tan, 4336.

352 Felleman, pp. 113-114.
353 Alexander, p. 35.
354 Knight, p. 18.
355 *Ibid.*, p. 10.
356 Tan, 419.
357 *Ibid.*
358 *Ibid.*, 6891.
359 Watson, p. 99.
360 *Ibid.*, p. 222.
361 Tan, 2028.
362 Alexander, p. 235.
363 Knight, p. 105.
364 *Ibid.*, p. 266.
365 *Ibid.*, p. 267.
366 *Ibid.*, p. 114.
367 Tan, 2164.
368 *Ibid.*
369 *Ibid.*, 2150.
370 Knight, p. 133.
371 *Ibid.*, p. 154.
372 *Ibid.*, p. 161.
373 *Ibid.*, p. 143.
374 *Ibid.*
375 *Ibid.*, pp. 198-199.
376 Tan, 7270.
377 *Ibid.*, 3290.
378 *Ibid.*, 4137.
379 Howell, p. 43.
380 Tan, 4140.
381 *Ibid.*, 1259.
382 Knight, p. 223.
383 *Ibid.*, p. 179.
384 Tan, 3218.
385 Knight, p. 60.
386 *Ibid.*, p. 297.
387 Cowman, Mrs. Charles E., *Streams in the Desert, Volume Two*, (Cowman Publishing Company, Zondervan Publishing House, Grand Rapids: 1966), January 26.
388 Tan, 857.
389 *Ibid.*, 4628.
390 Felleman, p. 79.
391 Tan, 6882.
392 Johnson, p. 24.
393 Tan, 410.
394 Johnson, p. 52.
395 Knight, p. 151; author's paraphrase.
396 Johnson, p. 108.
397 Knight, p. 70.
398 *Ibid.*, p. 72.
399 Johnson, p. 125.
400 Knight, p. 70.
401 Tan, 3105.
402 Johnson, p. 140.
403 Knight, p. 202.
404 Felleman, p. 350.
405 Johnson, p. 175.
406 Knight, p. 404.
407 Tan, 5261.
408 *Ibid.*, 1856.
409 Knight, p. 12.
410 *Ibid.*, p. 57.
411 *Ibid.*, p. 58.
412 Tan, 5703.
413 Knight, p. 135.
414 Johnson, p. 10.
415 *Ibid.*, p. 149.
416 Alexander, p. 239.
417 Johnson, p. 14.
418 Tan, 1875.
419 *Ibid.*, 1874.
420 Johnson, p. 158.
421 Tan, 1870.
422 *Ibid.*, 1868.
423 Alexander, p. 216.
424 Knight, pp. 17-18.
425 Tan, 1906.
426 Knight, p. 54.
427 Howell, p. 116.
428 Alexander, pp. 316-317.
429 Tan, 1494; author's paraphrase.
430 Alexander, pp. 320-321.
431 Howell, p. 115.
432 *Ibid.*, p. 134.
433 Tan, 2068.
434 Knight, p. 114.
435 *Ibid.*, p. 115.
436 Johnson, p. 21.
437 Alexander, p. 332.
438 *Ibid.*, p. 165.
439 Johnson, p. 148.
440 *Ibid.*
441 *Ibid.*, p. 89.
442 *Ibid.*, p. 28.

[443] *Ibid.*, p. 26.
[444] *Ibid.*, p. 176.
[445] Tan, 6593.
[446] *Ibid.*, 6606.
[447] *Ibid.*
[448] *Ibid.*, 6592.
[449] *Ibid.*, 6585.
[450] Alexander, pp. 329-330.
[451] Tan, 6588.
[452] *Ibid.*, 6578.
[453] Alexander, pp. 217-218.
[454] Tan, 2739.
[455] *Ibid.*, 4548.
[456] *Ibid.*, 4660.
[457] Howell, p. 28.
[458] *Ibid.*, p. 113.
[459] Johnson, p. 71.
[460] Tan, 2824.
[461] Johnson, p. 128.
[462] Howell, p. 103.
[463] *Ibid.*, p. 64.
[464] Watson, p. 223.
[465] *Ibid.*, p. 158.
[466] Tan, 1842.
[467] *Ibid.*, 1841.
[468] Watson, p. 14.
[469] *Ibid.*, p. 15.
[470] *Ibid.*, p. 20.
[471] Howell, p. 157.
[472] Tan, 937.
[473] Knight, p. 91.
[474] Howell, p. 133.
[475] *Ibid.*, p. 112.
[476] Tan, 5820.
[477] Knight, p. 110.
[478] Watson, p. 38.
[479] *Ibid.*, p. 43.
[480] *Ibid.*, p. 87.
[481] Alexander, p. 274.
[482] *Ibid.*, p. 251.
[483] *Ibid.*, p. 293; Felleman, p. 298.
[484] Watson, p. 199.
[485] Tan, 2736.
[486] Johnson, p. 41.
[487] Alexander, pp. 71-72.
[488] Johnson, p. 167.
[489] *Ibid.*, p. 120.
[490] Howell, p. 57.
[491] Felleman, pp. 297-298.
[492] Alexander, pp. 273-274.
[493] *Ibid.*, p. 189.
[494] Knight, p. 239.
[495] Alexander, pp. 235-236.
[496] Howell, p. 158.